D1800194

# ATLANTIC STUDIES ON SOCIETY IN CHANGE

# NO. 86

Editor in Chief, Béla K. Király

Associate Editor in Chief, Peter Pastor

# Budapest
# A History from Its Beginnings to 1998

András Gerő and János Poór, Editors

Translated by Judit Zinner and

Professors Cecil D. Eby and Nóra Arató

Social Science Monographs, Boulder, Colorado
Atlantic Research and Publications, Inc.
Highland Lakes, New Jersey

Distributed by Columbia University Press, New York
1997

EAST EUROPEAN MONOGRAPHS, NO. CDLXII

The publication of this volume was made possible by grants from
*Postabank és Takarékpénztár* (Postal and Savings Bank),
the Municipality of Budapest, and
the Cultural Committee of the City Assembly of Budapest.

Copyright © 1997
by Atlantic Research and Publications, Inc.

All rights reserved, including the right to reproduce this book or
portions thereof in any form whatsoever, without the written
permission of the publisher.

Library of Congress Catalog Card Number 97-60826
ISBN 0-88033-359-6

Printed in the United States of America

# Contents

# Preface to the Series and Acknowledgments

The present volume is a component of a series that, when completed, will constitute a comprehensive survey of the many aspects of East Central European society.

The books in the series deal with peoples whose homelands lie between the Germans to the west, the Russians, Ukranians, and Belorussians to the east and north, and the Mediterranean and Adriatic seas to the south. They constitute a particular civilization, one that is at once an integral part of Europe, yet substantially different from the West. The area is characterized by a rich diversity of language, religion, and government. The study of this complex area demands a multidisciplinary approach, and, accordingly, our contributors to the series represent several academic disciplines. They have been drawn from the universities and other scholarly institutions in the United States and Western Europe, as well as East and Central Europe. The contributors of the present volume are prominent Hungarian experts of the field.

The editors, of course, take full responsibility for ensuring the comprehensiveness, cohesion, internal balance, and scholarly quality of the series we have launched. We cheerfully accept this responsibility and intend this work to be neither justification nor condemnation of the policies, attitudes, and activities of any persons involved. At the same time, because the contributors represent so many different disciplines, interpretations, and schools of thought, our policy in this, as in the past and future volumes, is to present their contributions without major modifications.

Special thanks are due to Mr. Zsolt Sebestyén for the set designand to Professors Cecil D. Eby and Nóra Arató for copy-editing the text.

Budapest, March 15, 1997.

Béla K. Király
Editor in Chief

*Miklós Lackó*

# An Overview

Research in recent urban history points in two directions. The first is to relate the problems of urbanization to the macro-economic, social, and cultural development of different countries and regions. The second is to highlight the many-faceted micro-problems of urbanization by applying the research tools of history and related disciplines, even those of medicine and modern psychology. The latter approach often questions long-standing preconceptions such as family disintegration caused by urbanization, a concept not always borne out by historical data. In a novel way research on urban history also introduces cities as scenes of communication and information exchange. Consequently, by resorting to comparative methods of historical research, the unique peculiarities of city development are highlighted.[1]

"European cities were born with Europe and Europe was created through them," writes Gábor Gyáni.[2] European evolution has always stood on two pillars—progress and preservation. As Leonardo Benevolo puts it, cities have retained this duality by "being both engines that move us towards the future and anchors that connect us to the past."[3] This duality allows for progress while preserving the cityscape. A city is an "ossified memory" that sets its eyes on the future.

After the decline of the Roman Empire and the devastation caused by the great migrations, towns in Western and Central Europe experienced a renaissance between the tenth and eleventh centuries. After the last waves of migrations many ancient town settlements revived because of technological advance and periods of relative peace in Christian Europe. The ancient model was buried and gave way to innovation in architecture, town-planning and management, and the status of the town. Benevolo describes medieval cities: "They do not strive for a uniform, regular or perfect shape but accept, instead the imperfect, irregular, and the unfinished... Hence the variety and originality of the cities formed between the eleventh and fourteenth century." European towns in the expanse between the Mediterranean and Northern Europe bore no resemblance to an oriental me-

1

tropolis which had to absorb a huge population. "These towns were small but accomodating, foci of diverging and contrasting commercial and cultural traditions."[4] A population of merchants, artisans, and the poor settled within or around these flexible towns where the town-walls had to be frequently rebuilt to include the suburbs. By the end of the 15th century the network of towns of Western and Central Europe had evolved in those areas where the feudal system was most advanced. The Hanse towns spread this development to backward Northern and Northeastern Europe. The modern age expanded the influence of these independent, rigorously regulated cities. In the fifteenth and sixteenth centuries the city network became stabilized to offer a home to increasing numbers of people and professions. Plans were initiated to regulate and correct the once perfectly functioning imperfections. Self-sufficient peasant settlements became connected to the network of cities. After periods of stagnation and decline cities finally seized the reins of leadership and an increasing area of the countryside reflected their hegemony.

Soon certain cities broke away from this network for political reasons, such as a city becoming the seat of a monarch and his court, or because it became the center of a nation-state. By way of example, the population of Amsterdam was 50,000 in the late Middle Ages, growing to 125,000 by the early seventeenth century, and to 200,000 by the end of the century. The population of Paris was 200,000 at the end of the 16th century, but within forty years it was more than 400,000, and in the middle of the nineteenth century the population was 1,200,000, due to the impact of the Industrial Revolution. After the 16th century London housed 11–12 per cent of the population of England. Its population was 1,000,000 by the end of the eighteenth century, increasing to 2,400,000 within fifty years.[5]

In predominantly rural areas East-Central Europe urban development languished. Except for the Northern Hanse towns, only Prague stood out with a population of 50,000 in the mid-fifteenth century. The Prague city center of the Middle Ages and early modern times was preserved intact. Hungarian urban development shared the backward features typical of regions east of the River Elbe. Indeed, its geographic isolation and historical turbulence made the proun of urbanization difficult and halting.

* * *

The history of Budapest is a good example of troubled development. Although in the third century Aquincum, a Roman military and residential town, had a population of 40–50,000, there was no continuity between the ancient and medieval towns. Several waves of migration in the fourth and fifth centrury annihilated the ancient city, the ruins of which were revealed only recently through excavations. The remains of Aquincum were probably used as building materials in Óbuda.

The growth of Hungarian medieval cities fell one and a half centuries behind Western Europe. It began in the twelfth and the first decades of the thirteenth century, but the early towns, including older Pest and Buda, were almost totally destroyed by the Mongol invasion of 1241–42. A comparatively peaceful era of Westernization followed until the Turkish occupation of Hungary.[6] Roughly estimated, in the fourteenth century Buda had a population of 12–15,000 and Pest (including surrounding smaller settlements) had 10,000, whereas Óbuda remained a small rural town. Contemporary accounts described the 145 years of Turkish occupation as destructive of the earlier Western beginnings because of alien concepts imposed by the invaders. The decline is demonstrated by the fact that around 1700, after theTurks had been driven out of the country, the population of Buda was the same as it had been in the fifteenth century and that of Pest did not even reach half of the fifteenth century figure. Moreover, Pest had fewer inhabitants than the "large" towns of Győr, Pozsony, Kolozsvár, and Debrecen, all with less than 10,000 people, whereas there were a number of cities with over 100,000 inhabitants in Europe. Vienna was among these cities, although only in the sixteenth century it did become a permanent seat of the Habsburgs, while Buda had been a royal city since the fifteenth century, and Buda and Pest were the geographical and economic centers of the country.

The eighteenth century was a turning point. The historian, Gyula Szekfű was justified in calling it the century of denationalization but also the first major takeoff for Pest-Buda (the original name of the capital). At the beginning of the nineteenth century the population of the country had grown from four to ten million within one hundred years. At the beginning of national renewal, the Reform Period in the 1820s, Pest with its 50,000 inhabitants was the largest town of the country, topping Buda with its 30,000. Óbuda, the borough north of Buda, had 10,000 residents. From the 1860s on, the pace of development took place. In the middle of the century Pest had 100,000 souls, the more conservative Buda surpassed 50,000, whereas the population of Óbuda stood at 12,000. At the unification in 1873 the total for the three towns was 300,000. Within the preceding forty years the modern metropolis known as Budapest evolved. Its popu-

lation reached 900,000 before World War I, with another 100,000 in the
suburbs. It became the fifth or sixth largest city of Europe and first in rate
of growth. The city-scape, shaped during these forty years, did not change
much in the significantly diminished "Trianon country" between the two
wars, although the modernization of the town continued in spite of deteriorating political conditions.

The forty years of peace between 1873 and 1914 yielded rapid quantitative and qualitative progress, although there were losses also, as a
number of downtown buildings in the Hungarian empire or classicist style
(the most outstanding early nineteenth century Budapest architecture) disappeared. Nearly everything required by a European capital was accom-
plished during this period: the regulation of a several kilometer long section
of the Danube by diverting its flow into a structured water-bed, the construction of the main bridges across the 300–500 meter wide river and of
the main avenues and boulevards modelled on Viennese and Paris patterns,
and the erection of railway stations, turning Budapest into the .... of the
network of railroads (a concentration now considered excessively centralized). Anyone travelling from the north-eastern areas to south or west or
south-west, had to cross the capital. The national, metropolitan status and
what this implied in terms of institutions, public buildings, and city planning, were important stimulants of the rapid development.[7] The hospital
network and health service came into existence during these forty years,
and kept pace even in the years of extremely rapid development.[8] The
mortality rate per thousand was 43 in 1873—an extremely high figure—but
within ten years it dropped to 29, to 20.6 by the turn of the century, to
18.5 by 1910, and after the temporary increase of the war years, by 1930
the rate dropped to 15.3, and under 15 by the end of the 1930s.[9] (Recent
statistics do not show further improvement.) Almost all the museums, except for the National Museum built earlier, theaters, most of the school
and university buildings were built during those forty years. From the
1880s the writer Sándor Bródy, paid close attention to the construction of
the new metropolis and, sometime in the 1890s, he had good reason, to
exclaim both literally and figuratively, "Behold! here is a town that is
building its churches."[10]

There was another decline in 1944–45 the population decreased because more than 100,000 Budapest inhabitants—Jews, soldiers, and civilians—perished in the War. The 1945 "liberation", inherited a town in ruins,
resembling German cities. During the few years of freedom after the War
many signs of destruction were quickly removed. Ruined appartments were

restored, some bridges were reconstructed or replaced by temporary ones, railroad service and public transport resumed. Yet the reconstruction of the Castle is still in progress. In 1949 an Act extending the municipal administration to include the suburbs. Its territory became one and a half times larger and the number of inhabitants increased to 1.64 million. During the forty years after 1948, under the conditions of "existing socialism", when the pursuit of quantity in every field became the rule, the population continued to increase and, at its peak, in spite of large-scale emigration following the defeat of the 1956 revolution, it exceeded 2,000,000. This artificial increase, closely connected to the extensive industrial development, was followed by a gradual decrease from the 1980s that continues today. The fall in the birthrate, and above all the forced mass migration which caused a radical change in traditional lifestyles and a consequent deterioration in living standards account for much of the decrease. The country and its capital were "nationalized." Apartment construction tried to follow the population increase until the mid-1970s. Low quality housing projects, with a 25–30 year life span, were erected in the neglected outskirts and suburbs of Budapest. Today, the one-hundred-year-old public buildings, the majority of the 80–100 year old residential buildings in the downtown areas, and most of the "new" housing developments are in need of complete reconstruction.

* * *

A city can be examined from several viewpoints, that of the tourist, of the city historian, or an ordinary resident. The tourist looks mostly for the exotic, the peculiar, the historian seeks out the historical layers of a city, and the resident is focussed on the present, the period since childhood. The inhabitant looks for intimacy and not for the beauty of the town, just like a peasant who rarely admires the beauty of the landscape. Intimacy is difficult to achieve for the tens and hundreds of thousands who move into a new or expanding city. Walter Benjamin, the passionate researcher of modern urban life says, "The outskirsts are parts of a town where an exceptional state prevails, the battle between the city and the countryside is uninterrupted and is a matter of life or death."[11] This struggle accompanies Budapest life from its metropolitan beginnings till the 1970s, both on the outskirts and in some of the downtown districts. "Your own lot with a small house" movement started at the beginning of the century and it was tolerated even during the more progressive period of the Kádár-regime. The movement mixes the traditions of an agrarian society with the modern urban longing for nature.

Integrating people of different languages and ethnic backgrounds is even more complicated. The capital, along with the smaller towns of the country, played special roles in this process. The settlements on the site of present Budapest have been inhabited by people of many languages and ethnic groups: Germans, Slovaks, Italians, Muslims, Serbians, Jews and countless other nationalities. There were periods in the Middle Ages and the eighteenth century when the Hungarian ethnic group was in a minority. Political trends often viewed this particularity as negative and considered the excessive German and Jewish participation in urban development a phenomenon of "denationalization" and emphasized the "inorganic" route of Hungarian urbanization, while the extraordinary assimilating force of the towns should rather be admired. There are several reasons why the Hungarian-speaking population predominated in Hungary before 1918. One is the voluntary, automatic assimilation stimulated by the liberalism which prevailed for almost the entire nineteenth century. Another reason was the monarchy with its accomodating philosophy and religious tolerance that characterized the ruling circles of old Hungary, promoting rapid assimilation to the Hungarian language, to the Hungarians, and to their culture. The development of Budapest certainly owes a lot to this process. In the eighteenth century more than half of the population of Pest was German while the percentage of Hungarians was around 20 per cent. In the middle of the nineteenth century the ratio of the German inhabitants was still 56 per cent and that of the Hungarians was 37 per cent. The ratios turned around within thirty years. In 1880 57 per cent of the population was Hungarian and 37 per cent was German. At the turn of the century the ratio was 80 per cent versus 14 per cent and in 1930 the ratio of Germans was only 3.8 per cent. In the meantime, the originally 5–6 per cent Slovaks diminished to half of their original size and then to 1 per cent.[12]

The religious distribution of the population was closely related to assimilation, since religion is today a language and ethnic issue as it was in the days of old. It had particular relevance to the Jewish population that had been present in both Buda and Pest for centuries. Although they were temporarily expelled, they moved out to surrounding areas, mainly to Óbuda. They were relatively numerous among the new-comers to the capital from the 1830s and 1840s. Probably there was no other metropolis in the world in the twentieth century (until the 1944 holocaust) where the population comprised Jews or people of Jewish background in such a large proportion: an estimated 200,000 or 20 per cent of the total population. They played a prominent role in transforming Budapest into a metropolis. (In the same period Vienna, described as "Jewish", had only 8 per cent). Contrary to overt or hidden, extreme or moderate anti-Semitic views, the high ratio did not benefit special Jewish interests nor was it part of a "world conspiracy".[13]

* * *

It was primarily writers and poets, not historians who described the intimacy and familiarity of Budapest. Each of them spoke about a different feature and locale of the city. The essayist and writer of fiction, Antal Szerb, the author of the most lively Hungarian and world literary histories and who perished in the holocaust, wrote a lyric account of his Budapest in 1935 called "Budapest Guide for Martians."[14] In his book he claims, "If one day I had to leave the town for good, I would grow old the same day..."

Antal Szerb's *Guide* is remarkable because he visualizes the past and the present of the town as one entity. He does not strive for objectivity, instead he focuses on what he admires whether it be historical site or a stretch of a street evoking memories. "I want you to be acquainted with the town." And all that is expressed by "the eroticism of streets leaning towards each other... the climatic conditions of squares and statues, the literary associations of bus numbers or something like that..." Observing the Chain Bridge (Lánchíd) and its sequel, the Tunnel (Alagút), he concludes "Pest has two layers, one is the baroque layer that is fundamentally Catholic and is the soul of the German citizenry and the other is the Empire layer that evokes the memory of a great Hungarian moment, the Reform Period, a moment that disappeared since." The Hungarian, German, Jewish eclecticism of the modern capital is not alien to him either. (The Dohány Street Synagogue built in Moorish style is still the largest synagogue in Europe.) Besides the Chain Bridge he also points out the Danube embankment, the overwhelming effect of the great river that Jules Romains, the famous French writer, describes as follows:[15] "The view of Budapest with the Danube is one of the most beautiful river-city views, most probably the most beautiful in Europe along with the Thames of London and the

Seine of Paris." The Danube embankment has not so much mellowed with age, but is more monumental while retaining a human scale.

The 1989–1990 change of regime may have designated Budapest the center of a new market economy. It is to be hoped that the unpleasant aspects of the transition will diminish and Budapest will become a modern, dynamic European metropolis with more unique and original features of the divided yet unified city, where the mountainous region and the great plains meet and where the natural environment organically and harmoniously blend into the view of the man-made landscape.

# Notes

1. Gábor Gyáni, *A modern város történeti dilemmái* [The Historical Dilemmas of the Modern City], (Debrecen, 1995) 9.
2. Leonardo Benevolo, *A város Európa történetében* [The City in the History of Europe], (Budapest, 1994) 9.
3. Ibid., 9.
4. Ibid., 41.
5. Anthony Sutcliffe, "A környezet ellenőrzése és tervezése az európai fővárosokban 1850–1914 között" [Environmental control and design in London, Paris, and Berlin between 1850 and 1914] in *A modern város történeti dilemmái* [The Historical Dilemas of Modern City], 109–123.
6. Jenő Szücs, *Az utolsó Árpádok* [The last Árpáds], (Budapest, 1993) 27–32, 53–57, 266–278. This monograph surveys the evolution of the Hungarian town.
7. Sutcliffe, *A modern város történeti dilemmái*, 110–224.
8. Gerard Kearns, W. Robert Lee, and John Rogers, "Politikai és gazdasági tényezők kölcsönhatása a városi közegészségügy fejlődésében" in Gábor Gyáni, *A modern város történeti problémái*, 127–153.
9. *Fővárosunk* [Our Capital], II. (Budapest, 1940) 77.
10. Sándor Bródy, "Budapest reggel" [Budapest In the Morning], *Fehér könyv* [White Book], (Budapest, 1900), 77–79.
11. Walter Benjamin, "Városképek" [City impressions] in *Kommentár és profécia* [Comments and Prophecy], (Budapest, 1969) 73.
12. *Fővárosunk* [Our Capital], I. (Budapest, 1939) 108–112.
13. The numerical proportion of people of Jewish religion was 23 per cent both in 1910 and 1920, 20 per cent in 1930, and not quite 16 per cent in 1941. This rate decreased to 11 per cent in 1945 and to 9 per cent in 1949. The data are from, *Hét évtized a hazai zsidóság életében* [Seven Decades in the Lives of the Hungarian Jewry], vol. I. Gyula Zeke, *Statisztikai táblák* [Statistical Tables], 187–188. About the history of the Budapest Jewry see also,

*A zsidó Budapest* [The Jewish Budapest], vols I–II., ed. Géza Komoróczy, Budapest, 1995.

14. The quotations are from, Antal Szerb, *Budapesti kalauz marslakók számára* [A Budapest Guide for Martians], (Budapest, 1945) 2nd ed.

15. In Pál Granasztói, *Budapest arculatai* [Aspects of Budapest], (Budapest, 1980) 55.

*Gábor Ágoston*

# History of Budapest from Its Beginnings to 1703

## Roman Heritage: Aquincum

The area of present-day Budapest was sporadically inhabited already in the first millennium B. C. Archaeological finds indicate that the *Eravisci* of Celtic origin lived in present-day *Tabán* and also on Gellért Hill. The first town in the area of the future Hungarian capital was built by the Romans. It was made up of three settlements in the first and second centuries A.D., namely the settlements of the *Eravisci*, the military camp set up at the center of today's *Óbuda* together with the military town (*canabae*) around it; and a civilian town (*municipium*) north of the military one.

In A. D. 106 Aquincum became the provincial capital of the smaller part of Province Pannonia called Lower Pannonia (*Pannonia inferior*) when it was divided into two by Emperor Trajan (98–117). Its first proconsul was Hadrian, later himself an emperor. The town developed ever faster around the turn of the first and second centuries. When Emperor Hadrian (117–138) visited Pannonia in A. D. 124, he raised the civilian town to the rank of *municipium*. In 194 the town's development gathered fresh momentum when Emperor Septimius Severus (193–211), elevated to the throne by the legions stationed in Pannonia, made the capitals of Lower and Upper Pannonia, Aquincum and Carnuntum (Deutsch-Altenburg)[1] *coloniae,* as a gesture of gratitude. In the early part of the third century Emperor Caracalla (211–217) annnexed legionary camp Brigetio (Szőny) to Lower Pannonia and, as a result, the number of the Roman legions stationed this province equalled those in Upper Pannonia, enhancing the importance of the capital Aquincum. The visit of Emperor Caracalla in 214 stimulated the architectural features of the town.[2]

After the middle of the third century barbarians invaded the province several times. These invasions and the policies and administrative reforms of the emperors from Illyria contributed to the decline of Aquincum's political and cultural importance, even though the transformations were followed by a short-lived economic boom. In the fourth century Aquincum once again was fortified to enable it to resist barbarian attacks. From the middle of the century, however, the population tended to move from this border town toward the center of the province. In the early fifth century the Romans evacuated the civilian town.[3]

The settlement of the *Eravisci* on the slopes of rocky Gellért Hill owed its importance to the fact that it overlooked one of the most important spots for crossing the Danube. Important commercial roads converged there, since the river was the narrowest at that point. At the foot of the hill, near the ferry, artisans and merchants settled in future *Tabán* protected by the fortified settlement (*oppidum*) on top of the hill. The cemetery of the *Eravisci* was at the foot of the hill, on the *Lágymányos* side. The Romans occupied the *oppidum* on Gellért Hill around the beginning of our era. The native population first retreated to the area of present-day *Tabán*, then in the first century they were settled next to the Roman fortresses by the Danube creating the so-called *civitas Eraviscorum*. Thus the Romans could keep the natives under their control, and ensure the supply of their military camps. Although during the reign of the Flavius dynasty (69–96) direct control over the *Eravisci* ceased, they remained subordinated to the Roman civilian town. The fine pottery they produced first combined Celtic forms with Roman taste, but later adjusted to Roman demands and lost its original character.[4]

The first legionary camp (*castrum*) within the confines of future Budapest was built in 89 A. D. with palisades. It was in this camp that the future proconsul and emperor Hadrian served as deputy commander. In the days of Trajan and Hadrian the palisade was replaced by a stone fortification. When the *Marcomanni* raided the region between 166 and 180, a new camp was built west of the old one measuring 570 by 476 meters with walls 1.4 meters wide. This second camp was rebuilt several times. The most important modifications took place in the 330s when the camp was strengthened: the length of walls became 720 by 300 meters, and the thickness of the walls doubled. Six thousand troops were garrisoned in the legionnaire camp surrounded by walls and a moat. The total number of residents together with the technicians amounted to some ten thousand persons. There were workshops where armour was produced and repaired, a large military bath, a hospital, barracks, shops, granaries, and store-houses in the camp. The camp was gradually abandoned by its inhabitants in the late fourth century.[5]

Northeast of the legionnaire camp, on present-day *Hajógyári sziget* (Shipyards Island in District III) stood the palace of Hadrian, first proconsul in the years 106–108. It was he who ordered the palace built, but later it was rebuilt several times. The luxurious palace had nearly one hundred rooms, corner turrets, a portico, a large hall in the middle, and was decorated with mosaics and frescos all over. With its 8,000–10,000 square meters of floor-space it was one of the largest palaces of proconsuls in the empire.[6]

As with other camps along the Danube and the Rhine, there were two civilian settlements around the legionary camp of Aquincum. The military town called *canabae* looked like a town but was not invested with the rights of a town. It was located directly around the military camp. Its inhabitants were the soldiers' families, as well as artisans and dealers serving the military. They used the same cemetery as the soldiers. The military town occupied 140 hectares in an area surrounded by present-day *Bogdáni, Hévíz, Bécsi,* and *Nagyszombat* Streets. Its southwestern section was occupied by industrial plants, workshops of brickmakers, potters, blacksmiths, glass-blowers, bakers, etc. The eastern part was occupied by a port and storehouses. At the turn of the second and third centuries the military town was further urbanized, presumably partly due to the visit of Emperor Caracalla in 214. The former wood and mud construction had been replaced by stone by the first decades of the third century. The density of population increased. Public utilities were built, and heating with hot air was spreading. Watermains were laid to conduct water from *Árpád-forrás* (Árpád Spring) to the dwelling-houses through lead-pipes. The two- or more storied palaces along the Danube in the northeastern part of the settlement were even more ostentatious than the ones in the civilian town bearing the rank of *colonia*. Along the roads leading out of the military town there were industrial plants, relay stations, and inns.[7]

Around the middle of the second century the largest amphitheater of the Danubian region was built on the territory surrounded by present-day *Nagyszombat, Pacsirta, Viador,* and *Bécsi* Streets. The military amphitheater (132 by 108 meters) seated an audience of ten to thirteen thousand and offered gladiatorial fights. It was smaller than the *Coliseum* in Rome, but its arena was larger (90 by 66 meters as opposed to the 85 by 54 meters of the latter). The reason might have been that the amphitheater was designed for military drills and parades.[8]

It was also typical of legionary camps along the Danube that the civilian town was separated from the military one by open space. In 124 it was

raised to the rank of *municipium*, and in 194 it became a *colonia*. The
civilian settlement covered a trapezoidal area of about 30 hectares with an
aqueduct resting on pillars across the middle taking the lukewarm medicinal water of the springs of the present-day *Rómaifürdő* [Roman Bath] to
the legionary camp. Like the military towns, the civilian town was crossed
by two main roads along a north-south and an east-west axes, intersecting
at right angles. Parallel to these avenues there were narrower streets de-
limiting the residential areas. They were three to eleven meters wide, with
covered drain-pipes. The center of town life was the *forum* with the town
hall and the courthouse. There were also shops around the square, as well
as a marketplace, and an extensive public bath. Southeast of the marketplace were large dwelling-houses with inner courtyards, while to the north
there were smaller ones. The houses consisted of three to four rooms heated
by a system of hypocausts, and were connected to the watermains. Ar-
chaeologists have found remains of glass-blowers' workshops and metal
foundries, as well as oil- and wine-presses. The town flourished in the first
half of the third century. Its inhabitants must have numbered between ten
to twelve thousand. Outside the town there were relay stations and inns,
and also a potters' district of 160,000 square meters—the most significant
industrial establishment of Pannonia. When the legal differences between
the military and the civilian towns faded away in the third century, the
two towns slowly amalgamated into a single city. Including the neighboring suburbs of villas and the adjoining villages, its population may have
reached forty to fifty thousand.[9]

When the Huns occupied Pannonia in 433, Aquincum lost its urban
character. Its buildings were later used by Longobards, Avars, as well as
conquering Hungarians. Although the Roman type of urban administration
did not survive in Hungary, the Roman heritage is indisputable. The conquering Hungarians made use of the remains of the late Roman *castrum*
when they settled down in the Aquincum area. The later settlement of
Óbuda followed the street network of Aquincum and its boundaries were
also determined by Roman edifices. The Roman strongpoint called *Contra
Aquincum* on the left bank of the Danube (on present-day *Március 15. tér*
[March 15 Square]) in the early fourth century to defend the Roman settlements against the attacks of the barbarians was the predecessor of the
future town of Pest.[10]

## *Medium Regni*: the City from the Hungarian Conquest to 1541

At the time of the Hungarian conquest the area of future Budapest became the seat of the princes. Óbuda to the north was referred to in documents as *medium regni*, i.e., the center of the country, as early as 1241. In 1250 the same attribute was applied to *Budavára*, the castle of Buda built by King Béla IV (1235–70) after the Mongol invasion of 1241–42. The former centers of the country, Fehérvár where coronations and royal burials took place, and Esztergom, the ecclesiastical center of the country did not, however, lose their significance. In the early fourteenth century Buda is called "the center of the country and the largest of the towns". From that time on Buda was considered the country's capital, though the royal court and offices were still at Visegrád. As in several other European countries, the capital and the royal seat were separated. In the early fifteenth century the court moved to Buda, so the two functions were united in the same city. The significance of Buda was further enhanced by ever more frequent sessions of the national diets held mostly in Buda on the east bank of the Danube, or sometimes on a meadow along a brook called *Rákos* on the Pest side. Members of the royal council, church dignitaries and magnates bought houses in Buda and the noblemen attending the diets also stayed there. The network of trade routes also met under Buda and the most important fairs were held there. This central role of Buda lasted until the Turks occupied the town 1541.[11]

The conquering Hungarian tribes took over the Carpathian Basin between 895 and 900. The area of present-day Budapest became the domain of the two highest-ranking chieftains. *Kurszán* was the paramount religious chief called *kende* or *kündü*. He occupied the Roman remains of Aquincum in what became Óbuda. He spent the winter there, while his summer quarters were in *Csallóköz*. Árpád, the *gyula* or the chieftain exercizing actual power, spent the summers on Csepel Island, and the winters around the present-day town of Pécs.[12]

Óbuda seemed to be a most suitable princely seat. The Roman military amphitheater was still almost intact and became known as *Kurszán's* castle. Its walls offered protection for the prince and his people.[13] The favorable geographic position of the territory west of the Danube also contributed to its safety against Pechenegs attacking from the east. The nearest

ford on the Danube was between the two settlements called *Megyer* north
of *Kurszán's* castle. The current was slow at this place and the shallows
enabled the nomadic horsemen to ford the river. The road coming from
the ford at Megyer on the right bank of the river narrowed at Óbuda in
the vicinity of the hills, making control easier for the Hungarians. The
place could be easily defended also against Franks attacking from the west,
since the winter quarters of the chieftains could be approached only by the
narrow roads along the Danube. Following *Kurszán's* death in 904 Árpád
assumed the powers of the paramount religious chief and absorbed the
settlement. He was buried on the slopes of the Óbuda hills where the royal
chapel of *Fehéregyháza* was erected to honour the founder of the dynasty.[14]

Árpád and his people found suitable summer quarters on the nearly
fifty kilometer long and five to six kilometer wide Csepel Island, for there
was plenty of room for the princely stud-farm. The kings of the House of
Árpád kept their horses and hunted there in the centuries to come. There
was a ford on the Danube in operation just below the island, at *Szigetfő*
(Rácalmás).

Present-day Pest was also a preferred location for the chieftains. After
the Hungarians' defeat at Augsburg in 955 the reigning prince Taksony
moved to the left bank of the Danube for fear of an attack from the west.
His winter quarters might have been east of the Danube and south of Árpád's quarters around Pécs. The summers he spent along the Csepel branch
of the Danube, around the future Taksony village. He settled Muslim merchants and Bulgarian and Slav ferrymen around *Contra Aquincum* in the
area what was to become today's Inner City. The remains of the Roman
fortress offered protection, while the ferry contributed to the development
of commerce.[15]

As both Prince Géza (972–997) and King St Stephen (1000–38) held
their residence at Esztergom, Óbuda, called Buda until the mid-thirteenth
century, and its vicinity lost much of their importance. Óbuda retained a
royal manor serving as the economic center of the surrounding royal estates. The collegiate church founded there by King Peter (1038–41,
1044–46) in honor of apostle St Peter and finished during the reign of King
St. László (1077–95) was to play an important role in the development of
the town and, in fact, in the cultural life of the whole country. It was around
this chapel in the northern part of the town (around today's *Főtér* [Main
Square] that the *civitas*, the ecclesiastical center of the town, developed.
A church, a palace for the provost, houses for clergymen and servants, and

annexes were built there. The chapel was the private church of the king and was not under the jurisdiction of the bishop of Veszprém, but rather under the archbishop of Esztergom. In 1148 it was given the right to collect tolls in the neighborhood and to fish the Danube from the *Megyer* ferry to the Csepel Island, giving rise to endless law suits between the chapter and the burghers of Buda. The chaplain of the chapel was the provost, who belonged among the highest dignitaries of the country already in the twelfth century, immediately after the bishops in rank. In 1186 Provost Adorján, a graduate of the University of Paris, was the leader of the king's chancellery. His successors were vice-chancellors. Even the Anonymous Notary of King *Béla* III (1172–96), author of *Gesta Hungarorum*, a chronicle of ancient Hungarian history, is supposed to have been the provost of the chapter at Buda.[16] The royal manor house used from the late twelfth century for receiving monarchs from abroad must have stood somewhere near the chapel. In 1189 King *Béla* III and his wife Margaret Capet, sister of the French king Philip *August* II, received one of the leaders of the third crusade, Holy Roman Emperor Frederick *Barbarossa* in this palace after his visit at Esztergom. The other center of the town southeast of the chapel, called *villa*, evolved around the ferry and the marketplace and was inhabited by artisans and merchants.

In the early thirteenth century the growth of the town gathered momentum. King *Imre* (Emeric) (1196–1204) awarded the former royal residence at Esztergom to the archbishopric in 1198 and moved his seat to the recently built royal palace in the southwestern corner of the *civitas* of Buda (present-day nos. 2–4, *Kálvin köz*). King Béla IV commenced his reign from there. From 1238 on he spent Lent mostly at the Buda court, where he administered justice during the spring. At that time Buda, that is, Óbuda was practically the administrative center of the country. Its development was halted by the Mongol invasion of 1241–42.[17]

We know less about the town on the left bank, the future Pest. Componding the problem is the fact that the settlement at the Buda end of the Pest ferry at the foot of Gellért Hill was also called Pest. Since it is also mentioned as *Kisebb Pest* (Smaller Pest), it is believed that it was founded later than the one on the left bank of the river.

The Pest on the left bank centered around the Roman fortress held by Muslim merchants called *böszörmények*. This area was also a royal demesne, where the Hungarian kings stayed from time to time. The meadow along the Rákos brook was the place where the royal army assembled before a campaign. This fact is first mentioned in 1074. The Church of

Our Lady (*Nagyboldogasszony-templom*) founded by the king and mentioned as a chapel as early as 1046 was subordinated directly to the archbishop of Esztergom rather than to the bishop of the diocese. This earliest church of Pest must have been built next to the Roman *Contra Aquincum*, using its stones. This was where Bishop Gellért (*Gerardus* in Latin), an important figure in organizing the early Hungarian Church, was buried. As bishop of Csanád he was the author of the first theological work written in Hungary entitled *Deliberatio*. He was killed in the autumn of 1046 by anti-Christian rebels aiming to restore paganism. They threw him down from the rocks of *Kelenföldi* (present-day Gellért) Hill.[18] The three-naved and twin-steepled church built on top of this church in Romanesque style in the late twelfth century was destroyed during the Mongol invasion.[19]

Next to the village of merchants and ferrymen around the Roman fortress there was another settlement of Hungarian and Slav peasants, for their eleventh and twelfth century cemetery was unearthed in the garden of the nearby Károlyi palace.

Sporadic data on the tolls collected by the town and the taxes paid by Muslim merchants provide evidence of remarkable economic development in the early thirteenth century. The settlement of German artisans and merchants between 1218 and 1225 gave further impetus to this process. The new settlers, referred to in the sources as *Theutonici* or Germans to distinguish them from the Saxons of *Kisebb Pest*, may have come from Austria. Indirect evidence of this is the fact that one of the most distinguished burghers in Pest was a man called Werner, who was among the *Ritter-Bürger* or patricians of Vienna and had estates in Lower Austria. It was probably these German settlers who demolished the castle of Pest on the site of the Roman fortress to build their own homes of these stones to the east of the castle. This area became the new center of the town, with its main square in the same place where the Faculty of Arts of the Eötvös Loránd University lies today. During this period the Muslim merchants who had played an important role in the commercial and financial life of the town moved to an area called *Újbécs*. In spite of the efforts of the Pope and the leaders of the Hungarian Church the Muslim merchants of Pest could not be eliminated from economic life. What is more, they were granted the same rights as the German settlers. This made the differences between the two districts less marked to the point where they gradually merged.[20]

The Mongol invasion put a halt to this steady development. The army of Batu Khan defeated that of King Béla IV at Muhi near the Sajó River

on April 11, 1241, and ravaged the settlements on the left bank of the
Danube. The townwalls of Pest and the palisade hastily erected along today's Bajcsy-Zsilinszky Road were not strong enough to protect the town
from the Mongols. Pest was a plundered heap of ruins reduced to ashes
when they left. The warriors of Batu Khan crossed the frozen river in early
1242 and also destroyed unwalled Óbuda.

Although the conquering Mongols withdrew from Hungary when their
grand khan died back home in Mongolia, their return was feared. Seeing
that only castles and towns protected by strong walls were able to resist
the nomads, King Béla IV launched a massive program of castle-building.
Towns, too, had to be defended, for weapons and armor were produced
there. Furthermore, the rural population could find shelter within their
walls. Beyond their role in defence, the towns played an important part in
the commercial and economic life of the country. The king tried, therefore,
to reorganize the economy, establish new economic centers and grant them
privileges as part of his program of reconstruction. As a part of this concept,
he founded Buda opposite Pest, on the right bank of the Danube, on today's
Castle Hill, called in those days "the hill of Pest". The choice of the site
was ideal from every aspect. It was the most suitable hill for the purposes
of fortification, and the waterway, as well as the trade of the ferries could
be controlled easily from there. The privileged burghers of Pest on the
other side of the river supplied the inhabitants for the new town. In 1247
the king ordered the German citizens of Pest who survived the Tartar on-
slaught to move to the hill and combine their forces with Hungarians living
on the northern slopes of the hill and those coming from Óbuda, to build
a town surrounded by walls. The ethnic and topographical origin of the
town's inhabitants was reflected in its names. It was called *Budavár* (Buda
Castle) or *Budaújhely* (Buda New Place) after the original home of the
Hungarians coming from Óbuda, but it was also called *Pestújhely* (Pest
New Place) or *Ofen* after the German settlers from Pest. Eventually *Ofen*
became the final German name for Buda, although earlier it had been the
German name for Pest.[21] The privileges granted to the Germans of Pest
prior to the Mongol invasion and confirmed in 1244 were extended to the
inhabitants of the newly built castle, especially since originally these privileges applied also to the burghers of *Kisebb Pest* on the Buda side.[22]

The different origins of the settlers caused a particular dualism regarding both church and settlement affairs. Hungarians lived around *Szombathely tér* (today's *Bécsikapu tér* or Vienna Gate Square). That is where
they built their single-nave small church dedicated to St Mary Magdalene

in the northern part of the castle hill. The church hardly differed from the
village churches of the day. The Germans coming from Pest settled in the
central part of the hill and built the main church of the town, the triple-
naved Church of Our Lady between 1248 and 1269. Until its reconstruction
between 1874 and 1896 it retained much of its medieval character. The
size of the two churches reflect the differences in the financial and social
positions of the two communities. The dualism of the settlement was also
reflected in the existence of two marketplaces: the Hungarians held their
weekly fairs at *Szombathely* Square whereas the Germans held their national fairs at the square today called *Dísz tér* (Parade Square). Although
there were no legal differences between the two ethnic groups, the German
burghers played the leading role in the administration of the town up to
the fifteenth century.[23] South of the German district, around present-day
*Szent György tér* (St George Square), Hungarians and Jews lived together,
the former in the eastern part of the district, in St John Street around the
Franciscan cloister dedicated to St John, and the Jews in the then Jewish
Street (present-day *Szent György* or St George Street) somewhat to the
west of where their synagogue might have stood.[24]

There were three gates along the townwall: the *Szombat* (Saturday)
Gate in the north, the Jewish Gate in the east, and the St. John Gate facing
the Danube. The *Kammerhof* or mint stood presumably near *Szombat* Gate.
The street network and the uniformity of the plots suggest that the new
town had been planned. The differences between the narrow but long plots
suggest the contrasting financial standing of their owners. The houses of
the wealthier persons must have been several stories high and were built
directly fronting the street. The vaults opening onto the streets might have
been used as shops or workshops. Behind them came dwelling-rooms, then
outbuilding in the courtyards where implements for viticulture and other
agricultural activities were kept. There were several levels of cellars be-
neath the houses.

Below the Castle Hill were settlements that belonged to the town, under
the jurisdiction of the elected judge of Buda (from 1264 a *rector* appointed
by the king himself). Such were *Új Buda* (New Buda) to the northeast,
adjoining the Hungarian district on Castle Hill, later called *Szentpéter* (St.
Peter), inhabited by Hungarians. The settlement called *Kisebb Pest* before
the Mongol invasion, later *Kelenföld* (or *Kreinfeld* in German), between
the *Tabán* and the Gellért Hill to the south, was the other precinct belonging to the castle.

The foundation of Buda represented a new, hitherto unknown type of settlement in Hungary in that it was a castle (*castrum*) in itself. It differed from earlier types in which castles built on hills constituted the center around which the town was built. *Budavár* (the Castle of Buda) was practically a fortified civilian town, to become the center of the country or *medium regni* in 1250. In 1255 it was granted the right of holding national fairs for two weeks in September. Only Fehérvár had been granted this privilege before. So Budavár became the center of the country not because it was a royal seat, but because of its role in its economic and commercial life. It was the first planned town of Hungary founded by the king.[25]

On present-day *Margitsziget* (Margaret Island) called the Island of Rabbits in those days construction was in accordance with the fortification plans of the city. A fort for the Knights of St John was erected at its southern end and one for the archbishop of Esztergom in the north. The former was built on the ruins of a Roman fortress. A Franciscan cloister, and one of the most important convents of medieval Hungary, first Augustan later Dominican, was also built on the island where Margaret, the eventually canonized daughter of King Béla IV lived as a nun.[26]

After the construction of Budavár, Óbuda and Pest lost much of their importance. It was in 1261 that the former Buda was first called Óbuda (*Vetus Buda*), though the usage of this placename was not firmly established. When the royal court moved from there, the town lost many of its artisans and dealers. The place of Germans moving from Pest to the Castle Hill was taken by Hungarians, but some of the artisans and the ferrymen were still German. The marketplace was behind the parish church, near the ferry. Although Pest did not grow as conspicuously as Buda, it was soon reconstructed as an important ferry-landing and market. The Franciscan cloister was erected before 1288 at *Ferenciek tere* [Franciscans' Square]. East of the cloister there was a large open area, the future livestock market of the 16th century.[27]

* * *

In 1301, at the extinction of the House of Árpád, almost all the major dynasties of Central Europe entered into competition for the Hungarian throne. It was first won by the Angevins of Naples (1301–82), then by the House of Luxembourg (1387–1437). The century and a half when the House of Anjou and Sigismund of Luxembourg (King of Hungary 1387–1437) ruled the country witnessed a successful attempt at integration into Europe. The towns played a decisive role in this process by their participation in European commerce. It was under the reign of Sigismund that the towns were granted the status of estate; this meant that from that time on their representatives took part in legislation at the national diet together with the prelates, the magnates and the nobles of the counties.

The Habsburgs appeared on the Hungarian throne for the first time in 1437–39, and from 1458 to 1490. Matthias (*Corvinus*) Hunyadi made an attempt at founding a new dynasty in Central Europe. This was the time when the expansionist Ottoman Empire began to threaten the southern borderlands of the country, having already conquered the Balkans. The Turkish threat contributed to various attempts at combining forces in the region—once under the Habsburgs, once under the Jagiellos—in the form of personal union. These attempts were only partially successful. At the Battle of Mohács in 1526 the ill-prepared Hungarian forces suffered a major defeat at the hands of the Ottoman army, one of the best of the day. Hungary still managed to stop the invasion along a line dividing the country in halves. Buda fell into Turkish hands in 1541 and became the seat of the northernmost province of the Ottoman Empire for a century and a half. The year 1541 marked the end of an important period in the history of the town, that of medieval rise and decline.

During the struggle for the throne after the extinction of the House of Árpád the burghers of Buda supported pretenders who were to lose the struggle; they turned against Charles Robert of Anjou, the future monarch, who was supported by the Pope. As a consequence, the papal legate excommunicated the town. The burghers of Buda and their priests excommunicated the head of the Catholic Church and all the bishops of Hungary in return. Consequently, King Charles Robert established his royal seat first at Temesvár, and from 1323 at Visegrád. The latter town flourished as a royal residence in the days of the Angevin kings.[28]

During the reign of the House of Anjou, Buda was a royal seat only for a short period (1347–55). Only after 1405 did Sigismund of Luxembourg move to the town for good. The economic policies of the Angevins and Sigismund initiated favorable developments there. Both kings confirmed the staple right of the town, which meant that all foreign and Hungarian merchants were to sell their goods at Buda, and they were not allowed to choose a different route. Should they try to circumvent this rule, the burghers had the right to confiscate their goods. The meeting of the kings and princes of the region at Visegrád in 1335 was also favorable for Buda. The participants (Charles Robert, King of Hungary, John, King of

Bohemia, and Casimir, King of Poland, as well as several princes) met to explore ways to evade the staple right of Vienna which had the effect of considerably increasing the price of commodities imported from the West. A new trade route was devised connecting southern Germany direclty with Buda, by-passing Vienna. Hungarian gold also played a great part in the commercial boom of the day. Due to the economic policy of the Anjou rulers the mining of precious metals received an impetus. Hungary produced nearly one third of the western world's output of gold in those years. The Hungarian *florin* introduced in 1325 on the model of the gold coin of Florence called *fiorino d'oro* became the favorite currency of Europe, so western merchants were eager to bring their goods to Buda. The self-government of the town was strengthened, as indicated by the fact that from 1346 on the highest dignitary of the town was once again an elected judge.

In 1402 King Sigismund granted staple right to five towns along the border and exempted their burghers from that of Buda to avoid "doing harm to the whole community of our country for the sake of the growth of a single town."[29] However, this measure did not involve any disadvantage to Buda, since the king moved the royal court there. Buda became a royal seat again, which brought along an unprecendented boom in construction both as regards the royal palace and the houses of the burghers. The nobles holding office at the royal court bought houses or palaces in the town the style of which influenced the taste of the burghers. When Sigismund became increasingly involved in international affairs first as King of the Romans from 1410, then as Holy Roman Emperor from 1433, he spent less and less time at Buda, turning his attention more toward Pozsony (today's Bratislava). Buda nonetheless flourished economically and culturally. It was the site of important international meetings and political decisions. The Byzantine Emperor John VIII spent eight weeks there during his tour of Europe in search of allies against the Ottomans.[30] In 1436 Sigismund ordered an inventory of homes in Buda, because he entertained plans for moving the Council of Basel to the Hungarian capital. The king wished to make the castle and the royal palace of Buda worthy of the town's growing international role by large-scale construction projects in the late Gothic style of Western Europe. The royal palace reached its greatest dimensions during his reign.

The so-called *Ofner Stadtrecht* or Buda Book of Statutes compiled between 1405 and 1421 is a rich source for economic and social life in those days.[31] Based primarily on the Magdeburg law, the unwritten law of contemporary towns, and on royal patents, the book dealt with the method of electing the body of magistrates, the tasks and rights of the judge and the main officeholders of the town, the rights of merchants and artisans, and the relationship of foreign merchants and the town. This codification was necessary because economic growth attracted foreign merchants to Buda in large numbers, the most important of whom were cloth merchants from south German provinces, Italian financiers, and merchants dealing in spices and silk. The Italian colony was so significant that one of the main streets, the present-day *Országház* (Parliament) Street, was named *Olasz* (Italian) Street. The Jewish community also played an important role in the life of the town. Ousted in 1360 by King Louis the Great, they returned in 1364 and settled around the *Kammerhof* at the lower end of today's *Táncsics Mihály* Street which became the core of the ghetto, since the houses of Jews on the northern side of the castle district had been given to Hungarian nobles.[32]

The reign of the Anjou rulers had an impact on Óbuda. In 1343 King Louis the Great donated the royal fort of Óbuda to his mother, Elizabeth. From that time on the fort and the royal demesne belonging to it were the property of the queens of Hungary. The widowed Queen Elizabeth had the second church of the provostship built, together with the convent of the Clare-nuns. The Humanist Pietro Ransano noted in the late fifteenth century that "there are only few convents in the whole Christian world more beautiful than this one."[33] During the reign of King Sigismund Óbuda played a key role in the cultural life of the country. In 1389 the king founded an institution of higher learning there which functioned as a university from 1395 with the authorization of the Pope. It was granted a second patent in 1410. From then on it was a full-fledged university with four faculties, the chancellor of which was to be the current provost of the Óbuda chapter. The university did not survive its founder. It presumably no longer existed when King Sigismund died.[34]

The cultural center of Hungary shifted to the royal palace in the age of King *Corvinus*. Buda became an acropolis of early Renaissance culture and Humanism. Surprisingly enough Renaissance appeared in Hungary earlier than in other countries north of Italy and it received fresh vigor directly from the great cultural centers of that country, mainly from Florence. Besides the king's personal interest this was due to his marriage to the Italian princess Beatrice of Aragon in 1476, strengthening the king's relations with Italian Renaissance artists and humanist thinkers.[35] One of King Mátyás's greatest achievements was his famous library called *Bibliotheca Corviniana* housed in a building next to the royal palace, overlooking the Danube. Its core buildings was the personal library of the king. When the books in the royal chapel and the queen's library were added to it, its holdings must have amounted to 3,000–3,500 volumes. In those days only the Vatican library equalled its stock. The Medicis owned approximately 1,000, and the Prince of Urbino 1,100 volumes. Besides bibles and various theological writings, the *Bibliotheca Corviniana* had several books by ancient, medieval and contemporary authors on history, geography, philosophy, astronomy, the natural sciences, and medicine. Contemporary writings on architecture and warfare were also present in that magnificent library. The Greek codices were a specially valuable part of the collection. It was probably King Mátyás, who owned the largest collection in Europe. Such codices were rarities even in Italian libraries. Although most of them were Italian copies of originals to be found in Italy, the king had workshops for copying, illuminating, and binding books in Buda. Several Italian, mainly Florentine, artists of the miniature-painters' workshop worked not only for the king, but also for prelates and nobles. The famous leather bindings of the *Corvinas* were produced in the palace workshops. Well-known humanists of the day, mainly Italian, like Galeotto Marzio and his son, Taddeo Ugoleto, as well as Antonio Bonfini, Felix Ransanus, and the German Joannes Regiomontanus were among the librarians of the *Bibliotheca Corviniana*.[36]

## Demography

It is not easy to determine the size of the population of Óbuda, Buda, and Pest during this epoch, because sources refer only to certain groups of inhabitants. By the late 15th century, besides the native townspeople of Buda, the high dignitaries of the royal court and their large retinue and great numbers of servants spent most of the year in Buda. Similarly, the nobles coming from the provinces to attend the sessions of the diet or the law-court (the so-called *octavas*) stayed in town for a period each year. On the other hand, work in the fields reduced the number of the inhabitants each summer. Taking all this into account, the number of inhabitants in Buda (Logod and Felhéviz included) must have been around twelve to fifteen thousand, in Pest (with the outskirts) around ten thousand during the years of the Jagiellos. There are no reliable data on Óbuda from that period.[37]

In contrast with earlier periods when a family of burghers may have remained in the town for over a hundred years, from the second half of the fifteenth century native citizens were replaced in two or three generations, like in Vienna and other big cities of Europe. This was mainly due to the rules of inheritance within the guilds, the law of inheritance in general, and the customs of marriage derived from them. The widows of Buda enjoyed the same rights in this respect as the offspring, so they often inherited large fortunes. The rich widows of craftsmen were often married by young journeymen. Since these elderly women rarely had children by their new husbands, the families died out in two or three generations. The survival of the family names of the late guildsmen was ensured by the curious Buda custom according to which men marrying widows assumed the names of their first husbands or the surnames of the fathers-in-law.

As in other large cities of Europe, the population of Buda did not grow through natural increase, but through immigration. Those who moved to Buda and Pest between 1440 and 1529 came mostly from other Hungarian towns and boroughs, mainly from Vác, Pozsony, Kassa, and Pécs, while those moving to Óbuda came mostly from villages and certain boroughs. The place of origin of the newcomers indicates the hierarchy of the three towns: Buda and Pest offered better prospects for townspeople, while Óbuda attracted villagers.

In those days the majority of the residents of Buda were Hungarians, but there was a considerable German and Jewish minority. Other nationalities, such as Slovaks, Croats, and Serbs were also represented, and long-distance trade brought Italians, Austrians, and Poles. Due to the personal union of Hungary and Bohemia there were also Czechs and Silesians in Buda.

The citizens both of Buda and Pest were clearly divided into three strata: patricians, middle class, and plebeians. Patricians from the 1430s were increasingly honored by diplomas and other documents, bearing the title *circumspecti*. The stratum of patricians consisted mainly of jurors, wealthy and respected merchants, butchers, tailors, furriers, gold and silversmiths, bakers, and glaziers, as well as a few noblemen.

Documents relating to judges and the surviving lists of council members reveal that the leading stratum of the town was more limited than before and Buda was practically led by merchants. For seventy-five years between 1440 and 1529 thirty judges held the highest office in the town. Fifteen of them were merchants and held the post for fifty-two years, ten persons of unknown occupation for seventeen years, three office employees for four years, and two artisans for two years. Taking only the twenty with known occupations into account we find that 75 per cent of the judges had been merchants and held the office for 90 per cent of the period under discussion. The vocations of members of the town council were similar. Forty-three of the one hundred and twenty aldermen had been merchants (35 per cent), the occupations of another forty-three persons is unknown, nineteen had been artisans (15.8 per cent), and fifteen were intellectuals (12.6 per cent). Leaving the unknown category out of consideration again, the proportion of merchants among the aldermen was 59 per cent. Those artisans who became members of the ruling body of the town belonged to guilds and were considered *circumspecti*, i.e., patricians; they were, by virtue of their occupations, in close relationship with merchants.[38] The change in Pest was similar but still more conspicuous. The body of aldermen, composed of six members prior to 1469, was expanded to twelve to equal those of Pest and Buda.

## The City under Ottoman Rule[39]

Although Sultan Suleiman marched into Buda both in 1526 and 1529, he did not occupy it at once. It was not because he was aware of the military and financial burdens of conquering a territory so far away from the logistic center of the Ottoman empire and falling outside the radius of action of his army. It happened because of the loyalty of János Szapolyai, elected King of Hungary in 1526, and because the Turkish garrisons in the occupied forts of the *Szerémség* ensured adequate control over Hungary. When Szapolyai died and Ferdinand I of Habsburg (1526–1564) (also elected King of Hungary by a portion of the Hungarian nobility in 1526) became sole ruler of Hungary, the Sultan thought that the time had come to conquer Buda and those parts of Hungary that had been held by Szapolyai before. Suleiman took Buda by ruse on August 29, 1541, on the fifteenth anniversary of the Battle of Mohács. Thereafter the country was divided into three parts. The Hungarian Kingdom under Habsburg rule dwindled to one third of its former dimensions (about 100,000–120,000 square kilometers) in the western and northern parts of the country. The central territories of equal size were attached to the Ottoman Empire. The somewhat smaller eastern portion of the country became the Principality of Transylvania in Turkish dependency. Buda, capital of the medieval Hungarian Kingdom, became the center of the northernmost province of the Ottoman Empire, the *Vilayet* of Buda, for the next 145 years. After the unsuccessful Turkish siege of Vienna in 1683 the Christian states of Europe, uniting their forces under the Holy League, considered that the time had come to expel the Turks from Hungary. The liberation of Buda on September 2, 1686, was a key episode of this process.

In 1541 the Ottoman leadership deployed 2,653 soldiers to Buda and 914 to Pest to defend the newly conquered territories. To strengthen defence another 4,196 soldiers were transferred from Ottoman fortresses in Southern Hungary. Most of these men were not Turks but Orthodox Southern Slavs. There were many Bosnians, Croats, and Serbs among the Muslims, also. In the streets of Buda one could meet Hungarians, Latins (from Ragusa), Jews, and Gypsies of Orthodox Christian faith, called *kiptis* in the registers, besides the conquering Turks and Southern Slavs.

The soldiers lived in barracks, or were quartered in private homes around the forts, and mingled with the civilian population. Those belonging to the garrison of Buda lived around the royal palace, along the walls, and around the gates. The barracks of the janissaries were in present-day *Fortuna* and *Országház* Streets, as well as around the Vienna Gate. The cavalry was billeted outside the walls, in a suburb. The Pasha of Buda first moved into Martinuzzi's house, then into another one on the banks of the Danube. Prior to the siege of 1598 he, too, moved to the castle and established his office somewhere around the present-day *Várszínház* (Castle Theater). The Aga of the janissaries settled near Vienna Gate. The remaining Hungarians lived in streets north of today's *Dísz tér* and in *Víziváros* (Watertown), i.e., in the area between present-day *Széna tér* (Straw Square) and the Buda end of the *Lánchíd* (Chain Bridge). The Italians lived in *Olasz* (Italian) Street, the Jews in *Zsidó* (Jewish, present-day *Táncsics Mihály*) Street. A large number of Gypsies also lived in *Víziváros*, separate from the Christian Hungarians and the Jews.

Ottoman tax registers are excellent sources for the identification of the population of Buda. The inhabitants were registered by street, as was common in case of larger towns, or by districts (*mahalle*). These administrative units were generally named after a significant building of the Muslim faith in traditionally Muslim towns, but in Buda they were named after streets. So there was an *Olasz ucca* [Italian Street] *mahalle*, a *Szentgyörgy ucca mahalle, a Mindszent ucca mahalle, a Szombathely ucca mahalle, a Szent Pál ucca mahalle, an Ötvös ucca mahalle, a Zsidó ucca mahalle, a Szent Péter mártír ucca mahalle*, and a *Kopt mahalle*. The Ottoman authorities kept records of the inhabitants of the town by their religion. In the first six units Christians, in the seventh Jews, and in the last Orthodox Gypsies bearing South Slav names lived.

## Non-Muslim Inhabitants of Buda in the Second Half of the 16th Century[40]

| Date | Registered Christians | Christian taxpayers | Registered Jews | Jewish taxpayers | Registered Kipti | Kipti taxpayers | Total of registered | Total of taxpayers |
|------|------|------|------|------|------|------|------|------|
| 1546 | 366 | 136 | 101 | 50 | 56 | 30 | 523 | 216 |
| 1547 | 238 | 123 | 100 | 33 | 60 | ? | 398 | 156 |
| 1559 | 329 | 160 | 58 | 40 | 63 | 34 | 450 | 234 |
| 1562 | 240 | 175 | 122 | 49 | ? | ? | 362 | 224 |
| 1580 | 223 | 190 | 86 | 64 | 90 | 82 | 399 | 336 |
| 1590 | 228 | 140 | 120 | 103 | ? | ? | 348 | 243 |

The largest group was that of Christians. Those who prepared the tax rolls of 1559 remarked that 209 out of the 366 Christians registered in 1546 had died, three heads of families disappeared, and seven moved elsewhere. By 1559 forty-five young people had become taxable, ninety-five heads of families and forty-two unmarried young men had moved into town. During the thirteen years since the first assessment the number of Christians in Buda decreased by only ten per cent.

The second largest denomination in Buda was Jewish. In 1547, 73 Jewish families were registered with 33 persons paying tax (*cizye*). From among the 101 Jewish persons registered in 1546, 12 had died and 70 had moved from Buda by 1559. In the meantime, 35 heads of families and 3 unmarried men moved to the town, and one young man became taxable. The tax assessment in 1547 also recorded the place of origin of the newcomers: 25 families returned or moved to Buda from Istanbul, Kavala, Salonika, and Monastir. The number of those who left Buda exceeded that of the newcomers. In 1559 the number of registered Jews was only 58 per cent of their number in 1546. However, by the end of the century the tendency reversed, and the increase became remarkable. While in 1546, 72 heads of families were registered, their number was already 104 in 1590—an increase of 44 per cent.

The most conspicuous growth of population was recorded among the Orthodox Gypsies. The number of the registered heads of families rose by 12 per cent between 1546 and 1559, and by 75 per cent between 1546 and 1580. This increase is significant, since it was this ethnic group that most likely adopted the faith of the conquerors. This considerable increase of the *Kipti* population of Buda was primarily due to immigration.

The population of Pest was somewhat more uniform. There are no Jews and Orthodox Gypsies to be found in the registers. All the 121 families on the registers were Hungarians. Sixty-six per cent of the inhabitants registered in 1546 had died or moved from the town by 1559. The newcomers, however, made up for these losses, so the population of the town did not decrease in that period. The situation was similar in Óbuda. Although 34 per cent of those registered in 1546 had died or moved from the settlement by 1559, the number of residents remained unchanged due to immigration.

The conquerors gradually shaped the towns according to their own traditions. Those who approached the towns first caught sight of the high towers of the *djamis*, the *minarets*. Most *djamis* were converted Christian churches. Christian symbols and pieces of furnitures were removed and the stone floor was covered with carpets. *Mihrabs* denoting the direction of Mecca were built with a pulpit (*minber*) for the Friday prayer.

The characteristic districts of Muslim towns, the *mahalles*, soon evolved around the *djamis*. Elementary schools (*mekteb*) and secondary schools (*medrese*) were built, as well as baths and public kitchens (*imaret*) for the poor. There were artisans' workshops and retail stores everywhere. In larger towns they were grouped by trade. In Buda, for example, boot-makers, potters, and coppersmiths had separate streets for themselves. The covered market-hall stood on the square in front of present-day *Mátyás templom* (Matthias Church) with stands and stores for local craftsmen.

This extension of the Eastern world seemed alien to western travellers who had visited the same places decades earlier. The Turks had built booths or stands in the streets, and bricked up the windows of all churches and dwelling-houses. Both Turkish and Western sources speak of slow but overall decay. "Houses collapse one after the other. Nothing new is built, except for shelters against rain and snow. Larger hall or rooms are subdivided into cells with walls improvised of stone, clay, and wood, to resemble stables. They filled up the cellars with rubbish, since they do not need them. No one is owner and master in his own house."[41]

One must remember, however, that the former capital of the medieval Hungarian Kingdom became only one of the provincial capitals of the Ottoman Empire and lay almost 1,500 kilometers from its cultural center. The greater the distance from Istanbul, the smaller and simpler the buildings because of lack of funds to maintain them. Constant warfare did not favor building projects, either. "Why should we build at all? Christians might come at any moment and ruin everything with their bombs. It is much more important to have money that you can take along when needed." This was how the Turks of Buda explained their situation to a German servant living among them in 1605.[42] This was, however, poor comfort to the original inhabitants of Buda who were forced to witness the slow decay of their city during the 145 years of Ottoman rule.

# Notes

1. E. Swoboda, *Carnuntum. Seine Geschichte und seine Denkmäler* (Graz-Köln, 1964).

2. Árpád Dobó, *Die Verwaltung der römischen Provinz Pannonien von Augustus bis Diocletianus* (Budapest, 1968).

3. Tibor Nagy, "Római kor" [Roman times], in László Gerevich, ed., *Budapest története az őskortól az Árpád-kor végéig* [History of Budapest from prehistoric times to the end of the Árpád dynasty], in László Gerevich, ed., *Budapest története* [History of Budapest], (Budapest, 1975), vol. 1, 112.

4. Éva B. Bónis, *Die spätkeltische Siedlung Gellérthegy–Tabán in Budapest* (Budapest, 1969), 223–237.

5. László Kocsis, "Aquincum castra," *Archeológiai Értesítő*, no. 110 (1983).

6. János Szilágyi, "Az aquincumi helytartói palota" [The procuratorial palace of Aquincum], in *Budapest Régiségei*, 18 (1958), 53–70. Summary in German, ibid., 71–77.

7. Klára Póczy, "Aquincum-castra, canabae, colonia (Az 1976–1980 közötti ásatási eredmények összefoglalása)" [*Aquincum-castra, canabae, colonia.* Summary of archaeological excavations between 1976 and 1980], in *Budapest Régiségei*, 25 (1984), 15–25. Summary in German, 26–29; Anna Kaiser and Klára Póczy, *Budapest római öröksége* [The Roman heritage of Budapest] (Budapest, 1984).

8. János Szilágyi, *Aquincumi amfiteatrumok* [Amphitheaters in Aquincum] (Budapest, 1956).

9. András Mócsy, *Pannonia and Upper Moesia: History of the Middle Danube provinces of the Roman Empire* (Boston, 1974); András Mócsy, *Pannónia a korai császárság idején* [Pannonia in the early period of the Roman Empire] (Budapest, 1975), 136, 158–167; Klára Póczy, *Aquincum polgárvárosa* [The civilian town of Aquincum]. Materials of an exhibition at the *Budapest Történeti Múzeum* (Budapest, 1983).

10. The term "Roman heritage" comes from Erik Fügedi. See Erik Fügedi, "Topográfiai és városi fejlődés a középkori Óbudán" [Topographic and urban development in medieval Óbuda], in *Tanulmányok Budapest múltjából* (Budapest, 1959), vol. 13, 9–10. Cf. also idem., "Városok kialakulása Magyarországon" [Town development in Hungary], in idem., *Kolduló barátok, polgárok, nemesek. Tanulmányok a magyar középkorból* [Mendicant friars, burghers, nobles. Aspects of the Hungarian Middle Ages] (Budapest, 1981), 311–314.

11. Jenő Szűcs, *Az utólsó Árpádok* [The last members of the Árpád dynasty] (Budapest, 1993), 56–57; Julianna Altmann, et al., *Medium Regni* (Budapest, 1996), 5–8.

12. György Györffy, *King Saint Stephen of Hungary* [New York, 1994), 22–23.
13. György Györffy, "Kurszán és Kurszán vára. A magyar fejedelemség kialakulása és Óbuda honfoglaláskori története" [Kurszán and Kurszán's castle. The formation of the Hungarian principality and the history of Óbuda around the Hungarian conquest], in *Budapest Régiségei*, 16 (1953), 9–34. Summary in German, 35–40.
14. György Györffy, "Budapest története az Árpád-korban" [History of Budapest during the Árpád dynasty], in László Gerevich, ed., *Budapest története* [History of Budapest], vol. 1, 251–258.
15. Ibid, 258–262.
16. György Györffy, *Anonymus. Rejtély vagy történeti forrás* [The Anonymous chronicler: A riddle or a historical source] (Budapest, 1988), 45.
17. Györffy, "Budapest története az Árpád-korban," 268–281.
18. For the organization of the Catholic Church in Hungary and the activities of Bishop Gellért see Györffy, *King Saint Stephen*, 151–155. The bishop's body was finally buried at Csanád, the seat of his bishopric.
19. László Gerő, *A pesti belvárosi templom* [The Inner City parish church of Pest] (Budapest, 1956).
20. Györffy, "Budapest története az Árpád-korban," 281–288.
21. Szűcs, op. cit., 54–55.
22. Erik Fügedi, "Középkori magyar városprivilégiumok" [Privileges of medieval Hungarian towns], op. cit., 306.
23. Szűcs, op. cit., 55.
24. Géza Komoróczy, ed., *A zsidó Budapest. Emlékek, szertartások, történelem* [The Jewish Budapest. Memories, rituals, history] (Budapest, 1995), 13.
25. Szűcs, op. cit., 56; Györffy, "Budapest története az Árpád-korban," 307–308.
26. Gerd Biegel, *Budapest im Mittelalter* (Braunschweig, 1991).
27. Györffy, "Budapest története az Árpád-korban," 308–309, 312–313.
28. József Laszlovszky, ed., *Medieval Visegrád. Royal Castle, Palace, Town and Franciscan Friary* (Budapest, 1995); Gergely Buzás, "The Royal Palace at Visegrád," *The Hungarian Quarterly*, 35 (1994), 98–109.
29. András Kubinyi, "Budapest története a későbbi középkorban Buda elestéig" [The history of Budapest in the late Middle Ages until the fall of Buda to the Turks], in László Gerevich, ed., *Budapest története* [History of Budapest] (Budapest, 1975), vol. 2, 49.
30. Gyula Moravcsik, "Bizánci császárok és követeik Budán" [Byzantine emperors and their envoys in Buda], *Századok*, 95 (1961), 832–847.
31. Károly Mollay, *Das Ofner Stadtrecht* (Budapest, 1958).
32. Komoróczy, op. cit., 16–20.
33. Biegel, op. cit.
34. Elemér Mályusz, *Zsigmond király uralma Magyarországon 1387–1437* [The reign of King Sigismund in Hungary, 1387–1437] (Budapest, 1984), 223–225.

35. For King Matthias as a supporter of culture and on Hungarian Renaissance culture in general see Jolán Balog, *Die Anfänge der Renaissance in Ungarn—Matthias Corvinus und die Kunst* (Graz, 1975); idem, *Mátyás király és a művészet* [King Matthias and art] (Budapest, 1985); *Matthias Corvinus und die Renaissance in Ungarn* (Schallaburg, 1982), *Katalog der Ausstellung* (Wien, 1982).

36. Csaba Csapodi, *The Corvinian Library. History and Stock* (Budapest, 1973).

37. Kubinyi, op. cit., 134.

38. Kubinyi, op. cit., 139.

39. See Géza Perjés, *The Fall of the Medieval Kingdom of Hungary: Mohács, 1526, Buda, 1541* (New York, 1989). For the Mohács debate and opposing opinions see Pál Fodor, "Ottoman Policy towards Hungary, 1520–1541," *Acta Orientalia Academiae Scientiarum Hungaricae* 45 (1991), 271–345; Gábor Ágoston, "The Boundaries of an Empire: the Action Radius Theory and the Ottoman Conquest of Hungary" (Paper presented at the Turkish Studies Association of North America mini-conference May 10, 1996, at McMaster University, Hamilton, Ontario, Canada. To be published in *Turkish Studies Association Bulletin*.

40. Gyula Káldy-Nagy, *A budai szandzsák 1546–1590. évi összeírásai. Demográfiai és gazdaságtörténeti adatok* [Registers of the Buda Sanjak from 1546–90. Demographic and economic data] (Budapest, 1985), 150–153.

41. Hans Dernschwamm, *Erdély, Besztercebánya, Törökországi útinapló* [Travelogue from Transylvania, Besztercebánya, and Turkey] (Budapest, 1984), 498.

42. Gábor Ágoston, *A hódolt Magyarország* [Conquered Hungary] (Budapest, 1992), 134.

*János Poór*

# Buda, Pest, and Óbuda Between 1703 and 1815

## Demography and Society

Travelling through Hungary in 1717, the English writer Mary Wortley was shocked by the sad plight of a once-flourishing country. Her surprise was not unexpected, since the population was smaller after the expulsion of the Turks than in the early 16th century and did not even reach four million. Because of the Rákóczi War of Independence between 1703 and 1711 along with a serious plague epidemic Hungary had suffered further population losses. In 1720 the population can be estimated at about 4.3 million. With less than fourteen people living on each square kilometer, the population density was far below that of the developed regions of Europe.[1]

Even the privileged free royal towns had few inhabitants.[2] Around 1700 there were already a dozen towns with over 100,000 inhabitants in Europe, the imperial capital Vienna among them.[3] Two hundred and fifty kilometers from Vienna, Buda could boast of only 13,000–16,000 inhabitants in the first decades of the 18th century. Urbanization in Hungary was slow to develop. The former royal seat on the right bank of the Danube was only the second largest city of historical Hungary after Brassó (Brashov) in Transylvania. At the same time, the size of the population of Pest on the left bank of the river lagged behind that of Kolozsvár (Cluj-Napoca), Nagyszeben (Sibiu), Komárom, Debrecen, Pozsony (Bratislava) and Győr, all with less than 10,000 inhabitants. Pest had 3,900 residents in 1700, 1,700 in 1708, 3,400 in 1716, and 6,000 in 1726.[4] Pest was afflicted more seriously than Buda, both by the episodes of Rákóczi's war of independence and the plague in the later years of the war.

During the following decades of the 18th century Hungary experienced a population boom. Though the accuracy of the first modern census of Emperor Joseph II in the years 1784–1787 is still questionable, it appears certain that the population of the country had grown by over one hundred per cent during the 18th century, and exceeded ten million by the beginning

35

of the 19th century. Buda did not develop as fast as the national average,
but Pest exceeded it by far and became economically more important. With
its more than 50,000 inhabitants Pest became the largest city of Hungary
in the 1820s exceeding Debrecen, Pozsony, Szabadka, Kecskemét, Szeged,
and Buda with its estimated 30,000 inhabitants.

In both cities the population was divided: on the one hand there were
the burghers* who enjoyed political rights and, on the other, the commoners who did not. The former represented an insignificant minority throughout the period both in Buda and Pest, perhaps no more than a mere 3 per
cent of the inhabitants. In Buda there were 180 of them in 1691 and 380
in 1723. In Pest the overall number of burghers up to the early 18th century
was no more than a hundred. At the end of the century the size of the
populations in Buda and Pest tended to eqaulize. The number of burghers
in each was about 600.

Although statistics on burghers are never precise, the number of those
newly admitted to this exalted status was as follows:

|            | Buda | Pest |
|------------|------|------|
| 1686–1705  | 565  | 483  |
| 1706–1710  | 105  | 28   |
| 1711–1720  | 553  | 185  |
| 1721–1730  | 403  | 221  |
| 1731–1740  | 386  | 262  |
| 1741–1750  | 417  | 265  |
| 1751–1760  | 356  | 305  |
| 1761–1770  | 413  | 405  |
| 1771–1780  | 519  | 487  |
| 1781–1790  | 659  | 692[5] |

Considering the small proportion of citizens with full political rights,
it becomes obvious that the mobility of the citizens of Buda and Pest was
high in those years. If all those admitted among the burgher class had
remained in the cities, the ratio of burghers would have increased substantially regardless of mortality rates.

---

*    Full-term "burghers" of the towns and mining cities.

The ranks of the population with full political rights were filled mainly from the outside. Between 1686 and 1790, 44 per cent of the citizens of Pest whose origin could be traced came from abroad (mainly from the territory of the Holy Roman Empire, and primarily from the hereditary Habsburg provinces), 26.5 per cent came from other parts of Hungary, and only 29.5 per cent were natives of Pest. The rate of the native-born was, however, growing throughout the century, whereas the rate of those coming from outside was diminishing, even though the relative predominance of the latter remained unchanged.[6] Prior to 1750 foreign settlers represented an absolute majority among the newly accepted burghers. No parallel data are available for Buda, but the usual assumption is that Buda attracted people from roughly the same regions as Pest.

In Pest artisans predominated among the new burgher class, others being landlords, landowners and persons living on private capital. In the period between 1751 and 1790, 942 craftsmen became burghers. Out of that total 600 persons received the privileges of burghers between 1771 and 1790. Furthermore, over 200 persons whose professions are not known became burghers in the 1780s.[7]

The number of noblemen and aristocrats was gradually growing among the burghers. They arrived and resided in the city mostly as civil servants or landowners in the vicinity. In contrast, the rate of farmers was diminishing to an especially low level in the second half of the century, indicating that the agricultural character of the city was disappearing. The same tendency applied to military men who became burghers.

Artisans also predominated in Buda throughout the 18th century among the newly accepted burghers. Nevertheless, Buda had fewer artisans, their ratio dropping from over 60 percent to below 50 per cent in the second half of the century. The rate and number of those with "unknown" calling were, however, rising with well-to-do vine-growers among them.

While only burghers possessed full political rights and dominated public affairs by their financial and social prestige, their predominance was gradually challenged by the commoners.

Several tax assessments of Buda offer a picture of urban society different from that reflected in the lists of newly admitted burghers. Since these lists do not enumerate the non-taxable part of the population and do not make it possible to judge the rate of persons with or without political rights among the taxpayers, they are unsuitable for the formulation of an accurate picture.

Seemingly valid censi were taken in Pest between 1772 and 1781 by order of the Administrative Council (*Helytartótanács*).[8] The population figures of the city were broken down for each year (with the exception of 1778).[9] Unfortunately, this use is dubious because temporary inhabitants were sometimes not registered.[10]

Comparing the data coming from tax assessments and other censi with the total number of the population one can estimate that nearly half of Pest's society consisted of cotters and day-laborers as early as the first half of the 18th century. Their high proportion indicates not only that agriculture was still an important factor in the life of the city, but also that the urban character was getting ever stronger, as many of these cotters and day-laborers worked in building construction trades.

The census ordered by Emperor Joseph II was more scientifically planned for assessing an urban society and tabulated the male population of Pest and Buda capable of earning their livelihood, i.e., not just the burghers and taxpayers, consisting of the following categories in 1787:

| Male population | Pest | Buda |
|---|---|---|
| Priests | 477 | 120 |
| Noblemen | 697 | 744 |
| Officials, *honoratiores* (educated non-nobles) | 124 | 343 |
| Burghers (artisans) | 975 | 1,098 |
| Peasants | 180 | 1 |
| Heirs of burghers or peasants | 794 | 1,161 |
| Cotters | 3,958 | 4,279 |
| Discharged soldiers | 28 | 26 |
| Other | 1,017 | 1,198 |
| Those under 18 years | 2,975 | 3,111 |
| Total | 11,225 | 12,081[11] |

It becomes obvious from this that the overwhelming majority of the population of both towns consisted of cotters. (At that time Buda had 26,532 and Pest 24,297 inhabitants.)[12] Artisans and merchants were also heavily represented in both cities. The ratio of cotters was quite high even in comparison with other royal free towns; the ratio of noblemen was also remarkable, while the number of priests in Pest was also above the national average.

$$* * *$$

The overwhelming majority of the population of Buda and Pest consisted of Germans, Hungarians, and Slavs (mostly Serbs). In Buda the Germans constituted a majority throughout the whole period. According to the census of 1714 their rate was 52 per cent, that of the Serbs living predominatly in the *Tabán* district was 41 per cent, and that of the Hungarians was a mere 5 per cent. The relative proportion of these ethnic groups did not change significantly in the given period. The ethnic distribution in Pest was totally different at the beginning of the period. According to contemporary registries, out of the 1,090 known permanent residents 409 were Hungarians, 352 Germans, 137 Serbs, and 192 of other national origin between 1686 and 1696. Thus the relative majority (nearly 40 per cent) was made up of Hungarians.[13] The national distribution of city-dwellers changed totally after Rákóczi's War of Independence. The ratio of Hungarians fell to 24 per cent in 1720, to 18 per cent in 1735, and to 15.9 per cent in 1746. The rate of Serbs also decreased, and later stagnated. It was 18 per cent in 1715, 18.5 per cent in 1735, and 16.9 in 1746. At the same time the percentage of the German ethnic group grew significantly, to 51, 58.5, and 67.2 per cent in the respective years. The ratio of Hungarians kept decreasing, amounting to a mere 10 per cent in the 1770s.[14]

There were hardly any Jews in Buda in the 18th century. They appeared there after the liberation of the city from the Turks and settled in the *Víziváros* (Watertown) district, but there were only about thirty Jewish families in the 1720s and 1730s. Their activity was limited by the city council throughout the period, they were not allowed to own real estate or to build a synagogue, and were even expelled from the city by a royal order (1746). Neither did Jews live in Pest during most of the 18th century. Their settlement there was made possible by Joseph II's Edict of Toleration in 1783. Subsequently they reappeared also in Buda. The census of 1787 still found very few of them (114 persons in Pest, and 26 in Buda). In 1793 there were 126 Jewish families in Pest with 515 members. They lived mostly in the districts *Terézváros* (Theresatown) and *Újváros* (Newtown) or

*Lipótváros* (Leopoldtown). Their large-scale immigration was to take place in the 19th century, mostly from the 1840s onward.[15]

*Óbuda* (Old Buda), adjacent to Buda on the north was under the jurisdiction of a landlord. From 1766 it became a crown property. It was basically an agrarian town (not a free royal city), so its character differed from Buda and Pest. The census of Emperor Joseph II counted 5,804 inhabitants there in 1785.[16] The overwhelming majority of these were serfs. In the second half of the century the number of cotters grew rapidly and they outstripped the serfs.by the 1770s. The ratio of artisans among taxpayers was also growing but remained below 20 per cent. The number of the gainfully employed male population (Jews excluded) amounted to 1062 in 1789, 20.5 per cent of whom were land-holding serfs, 34.1 per cent cotters owning a house, and 18.4 per cent cotters without ownership of a house. 18.9 per cent were artisans, 5.2 per cent were servants, and 2.9 per cent were merchants.[17] The Jews were becoming an increasingly decisive factor in the life of Óbuda in the 18th century. From the initial settlement in the 1710s their number grew to 300 in the 1740s, and to about 1600 in the late 1780s. The anti-Semitism of Pest and Buda must have played an important role in their growing numbers in the more tolerant Óbuda.

## City Government

1703 was a decisive year in the modern history of Buda and Pest. The two cities received a patent and regained the status of royal free city from King Leopold I against a redemption. The patent stipulated that both cities be given back their right to send voting delegates to the diet. The constituents were entitled to elect a mayor (in Pest a judge) through a body of electors, but the election was to be attended by a royal commissioner. The city-council (Inner Council or Senate) was entitled to determine weights and measures, to exercise control over the market, to admit new burghers, to administer orphans' affairs, to exercise the right of presentation (*kegyúri jog*: privileges of ecclesiastical institution's patrons), to adopt local ordinances, to organize public work, to levy local taxes, and to resolve certain disputes. The council had the right to act as court of justice in cases of civil law. It elected its own new members, administered the city's funds, controlled the activity of the officials, and filled the vacancies in the municipal offices. The royal free city was free from any intervention on the part of military and county authorities, as well as from those of the Chamber.[18]

The year 1703 was a significant milestone in the status of the two cities, since in the previous decades they had fallen under the jurisdiction of the Buda Directorate of the Court Chamber (*Hofkammer*). After their liberation from Turkish rule the mayor of Buda, the judge of Pest, and the magistrates of both were nominated by the inspector of the Chamber. The unrestricted power of the Directorate over the cities was only seemingly softened by the fact that the mayor of Buda and the judge of Pest were elected by the burghers from among the three nominees of the directorate from 1688 and from 1692 on, respectively. The jurisdiction of the city-council was also limited. In civil cases one was supposed to lodge an appeal against the decision of the city-council with the directorate, while in criminal cases the council conducted the proceedings, but was entitled only to recommend the directorate a sentence. The two cities resolutely fought for self-government and were partly successful in the end. In 1696 the Court Chamber investigated the complaints and moderated the excessive power of the Directorate to a certain extent. The directorate lost its right to confirm the new leaders of the two cities and transferred this right to the Court Chamber. The accounts were to be examined by the city-council and the burghers, though under the supervision of the directorate. The directorate had the right to decide only in appeal cases. Later the city-council was allowed to elect it own members. Despite these concessions there was no self-government before 1703.

After receiving the royal patents, a decisive majority of Buda and Pest only changed masters. The era of self-government brought the rule of a minority: a limited group of people with civic rights.

Buda was governed by the council possessing full powers, chaired by the mayor. The council was enpowered to elect its own members. In 1705 a so-called outer council of twelve was set up to supervise administrative and financial matters. The outer council, however, was subordinated to the city council that appointed its members. It was headed by a so-called speaker nominated in most cases by the city council. The meetings of this new body were held with the speaker in the chair but there were attempts to involve the representatives of all the burghers also.

Although in theory all burghers of Buda were allowed to take part in the election of officials during those years, it was otherwise in practice. In 1707, for example, the mayor was elected with only sixty-six votes. Elitism ruled since only the mayor and the judge of Buda held elective posts, while vacancies on the city council were filled by the council itself without the participation of the outer council or of the citizens.

After the exceptional power of the city-council gave rise to repeated complaints, the Hungarian Court Chancellery and the Hungarian Chamber ordered an inquiry in 1722 to examine charges of abuses of authority. The royal commissioners thereafter introduced important reforms in municipal administration. Besides the city council and the outer council a so-called "council of one hundred" was set up from the ranks of the constituents. Actually, it had seventy-eight members. Together with the outer council having thirty members at that time it constituted the body of electors. Its most important task was to discuss the grievances of the inhabitants and submit them to the city council. It also played a part in levying taxes and supervising accounts. The council of one hundred and the outer council together were also called "council of one hundred" or *communitas*. Both bodies were headed by the speaker nominated by the outer council from among its own members or from those of the council of one hundred, and elected by the *communitas*. All the other vacancies were filled according to valid regulations. New members of the council of one hundred were nominated by the outer council and elected by the *communitas*. Vacancies on the outer council were filled in the same way, but the list of nominees was to be presented to the *communitas*, and especially to the city council that could interjest its veto.[19]

However, the council argued that it not only had the right of veto but also the right to nominate the speaker and all members of the two bodies in question. A royal decree of May 5, 1727, provided that should the council be able to prove its lawful exercise of the disputed rights, it would be free to exercise those in the future, as well. It soon turned out, however, that the disputed rights were not in their sphere.

The royal decree not only aimed to straighten out spheres of authority but also to introduce an important modification: it dissolved the council of one hundred and replaced it by a so-called *electa communitas* besides the outer council, the members of which were the suburban judges[20], two suburban jurors from each suburb, the guild-masters of all guilds and the two oldest masters of each guild.[21] The new body was permanent. The *electa communitas* and the outer council together were called *communitas, Bürgerschaft* or *electa communitas*.

After 1727 the most important duty of the *electa communitas* was to elect or reelect the leaders of the city on Saint George's Day. The outer council nominated three persons for the post of spokesman, their nomination was confirmed by the city council, and finally the *communitas* elected one of them. Later the speaker was nominated by the city council. Then the mayor and the judge were elected. These two officials could be elected from among the members of the city council, at first on nomination by the council, and later without it. All members of the city council were eligible, and it was the right of the *communitas* to vote.

New members for the city council, the outer council and the *electa communitas* were elected only when a vacancy occurred. Procedures for appointing members to the outer council and the electoral board were regulated by the directive of 1722, although in 1730 and in 1772 the city council appointed new members to the outer council. The procedures for filling vacancies on the city council were even more ambiguous. Until 1727 the council itself filled the vacancies, and the royal decree of 1727 did not regulate the election of the members of the city council, either. In 1730 the council appointed a new member, while in 1736 it was the *communitas* that elected a new alderman.[22]

In his directive of 1737 to the city magistrates the royal commissioner brought the election of city officials under regulation. The mayor and the judge were to be elected by the outer council and the body of electors from among the members of the city council. The same applied to new senators (city aldermen) with the exception that they were to be elected from among the three nominees of the city council or the royal commissioner.[23] After 1736 senators were usually nominated by the city council.

Significant changes occurred in the activity of the council and the *communitas* in 1763 and 1774. From 1763 onward two persons were elected as speakers, a German and a Hungarian. In 1774 the king ordered that the guild-like *electa communitas* be reorganized, since its large membership proved unwieldy. It was replaced in April, 1775, by a "council of sixty" attached to the outer council and its members were nominated by the city council. In 1776 the city-council filled the vacancies on the outer council and the council of sixty, but both the speaker and the outer council protested and the practice was abandoned.[24] During the reign of Emperor Joseph II the outer council and the council of sixty, closely cooperating thus far, were formally united.

Compared with the stipulations of the patent of 1703 and the practice of the following years the sphere of authority of the city-council became somewhat more limited. Since the council had the right to nominate new members—and these senators were elected for life—the leadership of Buda was dominated by a narrow stratum of patricians throughout the period.

Their excessive power was further enhanced by the fact that with the exception of the mayor, the judge, and the speaker, all leaders and officials of the city were appointed by the city council without the participation of the electors.

The administration of Pest was somewhat different from that of Buda, but similarly complicated. In 1705 the board of burghers filled four vacancies on the city council and the twenty-four members of the outer council were elected by the representatives of the burghers. They also elected the speaker (until 1769 Pest had two of them), the judge and the captain of the city. The city council supervised the outer council as well as the electorate. It filled the vacancies among the senators itself, while the outer council, which played a part in levying and assessing taxes, was subordinated to it.

The Council of one Hundred was organized in Pest in 1725, but its organization was not made permanent before 1731. A directive of the royal commissioner from 1731 stipulated that the city council had the right to fill vacancies both on the outer council and the council of hundred. It is difficult to interpret the clause that "men of merit" should be consulted first. The speaker were to be elected by the electorate. The election of new senators was not regulated by the directive. It rather called upon the council to refrain from filling the vacancies until a royal order provided for the manner of doing it. At the same time, as usual in other documents of the day, it requested that the electorate should pay due tribute to the council.[25]

As the election of officials in 1733 shows, vacancies on the senate were filled by the city council electing one of the three nominees of the outer council. In 1735 the new senator was elected by the council from among the three candidates of the outer council and the council of hundred.[26] The right to nominate new members being more important than the right to elect them, the burghers had a greater say in the composition of the leading body of the city in Pest than in Buda where senators were nominated by the city council. This, however, did not last very long. In 1751 the Administrative Council changed the practice in Pest, too, and henceforth senators were to be nominated by the city council and elected by the outer council and the council of one hundred. The burghers even lost the authority to nominate the speaker—a right conferred upon the city council.

The primary leader of the city, the judge, could be elected in Pest from among the members of the city council. After 1751 only three members of the council nominated by the council itself remained eligible.[27] After 1773 Pest, like Buda, had a mayor. The city council had the right to appoint all specialized officials and the suburban courts set up after the 1730s were kept subordinated to it.

\* \* \*

Since Óbuda was not a free royal town, it lacked self-government similar to that of Buda and Pest. In the 18th century it was the private property of the Zichy family and all attempts to restore the old privileges of the village dating from the earlier decades of the century were doomed to failure. On instructions issued by Miklós Zichy in 1746 the settlement was administered by a council consisting of eight German and four Hungarian jurors, a market inspector, a notary, and a Hungarian and a German village drummer. Vacancies among the jurors were filled by the village community from among three nominees of the landlord. The village mayor or judge was elected from among the twelve jurors, a German in two successive years, giving way to a Hungarian in the third. After 1761 Óbuda also had an outer council of twenty-four, but the number of its members fluctuated.

In 1766 Óbuda changed hands. Miklós Zichy's widow turned it over to the Hungarian Chamber, and the settlement became a royal estate managed by a bailiff of the Chamber. The community feared loss of its privileges, but no significant changes occurred. The judge was elected by the community from among the three nominees of the landlord, while the other officials could be elected without restriction. There were no more rules to determine the rate of Germans and Hungarians, either. The idea of uniting Óbuda with Buda was rejected by Maria Theresa in 1776.[28]

The rapidly growing Jewish community of Óbuda had a separate body of self-government, with a similarly restricted scope resembling the Christian community.[29]

## Evolution of the City

The cities of Buda and Pest, liberated from Turkish rule and from the patronage of the Directorate of the Court Chamber, regenerated demographically as well as physically. The framework of urban life was expanded, although the historical city centers—the castle district in Buda and the inner city surrounded by walls in Pest—certainly did not lose their predominance and harbored the most important municipal, county, and national institutions, cultural and educational centers. Moreover, the aristocrats moving to Buda or Pest chose these districts as their places of residence. However, the suburbs began to assume even greater importance, especially from the economic point of view.

The shift of the center of gravity in Pest was evident in the demolition of the city gates: the Watergate opening to the Danube, the *Váci* Gate at the northern end of *Lipót* (today Váci) Street, the *Kecskeméti* Gate at the end of *Uri* (today Kecskeméti) Street, and the *Hatvani* Gate at the end of the *Hatvani* (today Kossuth Lajos) Street leading toward the towns Vác, Kecskemét, and Hatvan respectively. Downtown Pest became a commercial, political, and cultural center. It became crowded by the middle of the 18th century. New residents settled primarily in the suburbs. In the 18th century Pest had two large suburbs, the Lower and the Upper Suburb. The Lower Suburb called *Terézváros* (Theresatown) from the 1770s, became the most populous district by the 19th century with artisans as the most decisive stratum of its population. Also the burgeoning Jewish population preferred this part of the city. South of *Terézváros* lay the Upper Suburb, later called *Józsefváros* (Josephtown). It preserved its agricultural character longer than *Terézváros*, and its built-up area did not reach as close to the Inner City as the *Terézváros*. South of *Józsefváros* lay *Ferencváros* (Francistown), separated from the former but very similar to it in its character. A new district of 18th-century Pest called *Újváros* (Newtown), after 1790 *Lipótváros* (Leopoldtown) founded by Emperor Joseph II was built according to a regular plan and became the most distinctive district of Pest in the first decades of the 19th century.

The Castle District of Buda, ruined during the siege, was surrounded by similarly ruined suburbs in the early 18th century. *Tabán* to the south had been totally depopulated, but due to a massive Serb immigration in the late 17th century it became the most populous district of Buda by the early 18th century. *Víziváros* (Watertown), north of the Castle District and spreading as far as the Danube, also lay in ruins. However, it was an important commercial district including also *Horvátváros* (Croatiantown) and *Halászváros* (Fishertown) and become even larger than *Tabán*. The adjacent and sparsely populated district called *Országút* (Highway) was named after the highway (today Margit Boulevard) running through it. The northernmost part of Buda was called *Újlak* (New Lodge) along the highway leading toward Vienna (*Bécsi* Road) and the *Óbudai* (today *Lajos*) Street. It spread as far as today's *Nagyszombat* Street at the southern end of Óbuda. At the beginning of the century this district was more populous than the one called *Országút*, but it lagged behind it once again by the early 19th century. *Krisztinaváros* (Christinatown), to the west of the Castle, was in ruins and totally depopulated after the reconquest of Buda and it was populated again only in the second half of the 18th century. It received its name after Archduchess Maria Christine, daughter of Maria Theresa.

The landscape was characterized by ruined, mostly single-story buildings and empty lots both in Buda and Pest even as late as the early 18th century. Great changes occured, however, in the course of the century, partly due to the activities of monastic orders in shaping the outward appearance of the cities, supported both by the state and private funds.

The generous donations of György Szécsényi, Archbishop of Esztergom, made it possible for the Jesuits to begin large-scale works in the castle of Buda. They took possession of the Church of Virgin Mary (*Nagyboldogasszony*, later Matthias church) and its neighborhood, and by 1687 were teaching at their grammar school.[30] By 1702 they had constructed their monastery and school dormitory, adjacent to the northern aisle of the church (on the site of the present-day Hilton Hotel). Between 1702 and 1715 the Jesuits erected a building south of the church for a seminary and a secular boarding-school. Opposite the monastery and the dormitory on *Szentháromság* (Holy Trinity) Square, where they already had a single-story building, they erected a two-story academy by 1747. (They had carried on academic training since 1713.)[31] The Jesuit institutions in the middle of the castle district dominated Buda in the 18th century.

After the dissolution of the Jesuit order in 1773, and especially during the reign of Joseph II, the three institutions served various educational purposes and housed important national institutions.

Partly for their services during the War of Liberation from the Turks, in 1690 the Franciscans received a large site in the northern side of the castle district, at the end of *Úri* (Noblemen's) and *Sütő* (Baker) Streets (today *Országház*, i.e., Parliament Street) with the ruined parish church of St Mary Magdalene dating from the Middle Ages. In 1701 they bought an additional site for a monastery. The construction of the monastery and the renovation of the parish church took a long time.[32] The monastery had a complicated history from the 1780s, and housed several important government offices.

The Clare-nuns or *klarisszák** established their nunnery in the neighborhood of the Franciscan friars. They bought their first building site from the Carmelites in 1706 in *Uri* Street on the side toward the castle wall. The first pieces of their ever-expanding lot next to the Franciscans on the other side was bought in 1718, and their nunnery was built, though not quite completed, in the 1720s. The city council of Buda failed to curb their expansionist tendency, for the nuns had patrons of high standing, most notably Maria Theresa, who commissioned the Lord Chief Treasurer (*tárnokmester*) and the President of the Hungarian Chamber to mediate between the city and the order, supervising the nuns' interests. The nuns finally collected for themselves a huge bloc.[33] After the dissolution of the order in 1782 the still unfinished buildings of the Clare-nuns, together with the adjacent Franciscan monastery, housed important state offices or government institutions like the diet.

The ruined mosque near the royal palace at the other end of the castle (today's *Színház*—Theater—Street) was given to the Carmelites in 1693. They built their first church there in 1725-1736. In 1784 this order also fell victim to the ecclasiastical reforms of Joseph II. In 1787 the church was converted into a theater.[34] The first theatrical performace in Hungarian was staged within its walls in 1790 by the troupe of László Kelemen, and Beethoven gave a concert in it in 1800. Today it is once again a theater under the name *Várszínház* (Castle Theater).

Church construction was not confined to the castle itself. The magistrate bought a building by the upper marketplace of *Víziváros* (today Batthyány Square) for the purposes of a new church in 1724. The tabernacle was consecrated in 1746 and the construction of the parish church dedicated to Saint Anne was completed in 1762. However, it was consecrated only much later, in 1805.

In the vicinity of the marketplace, on present-day *Fő* (Main) Street a Capuchin church and convent were built on the site of the mosque and the nearby salt stores. The new church was consecrated in 1716. The monastery was finished by 1777, when the church was enlarged also.

The other church on *Fő* Street was also built on the site of a former mosque and its annexes. The Franciscans started to build their monastery there in 1703. The cornerstone of the church was laid in 1731, the taber-

---

* Klarisszák or Clare-nuns: female branch of the Franciscan order founded in 1212 mostly to educate girls. In the thirteenth century the order was brought to Hungary, in 1782 Joseph II abolished the order.

nacle was finished in 1735, and the church was consacrated in 1757. In 1785–87 the monastery, handed over to the Viennese St Elizabeth nuns, was converted into a hospital. The Saint Catherine parish church was built in *Tabán*, on present-day *Attila* Street. The mosque standing on the site was in perfect state and was converted into a chapel by the Greek Catholics of the district in 1689. The new church was finished in 1776, but the fire of 1810 left it in ruins. It was renovated in 1812 and 1818.

The Greek Orthodox denomination also had a church in *Tabán*. It was built by the Serbian Church in 1697 on present-day *Hadnagy* (Lieutenant) Street. A new church was erected between 1742 and 1751. In 1810 it also fell into ruins and was demolished in 1949.

The Augustinians built their small church in the *Országút* district on present-day *Margit* Boulevard in 1707, as well as a monastery from 1724 on. The cornerstone was laid in 1754, and the church consecrated in 1770. In 1785 the whole complex was turned over to the Franciscans of *Víziváros*, who had been forced to transfer their monastery and church in that district to the St Elizabeth nuns. Later they enlarged their new monastery.

In *Krisztinaváros*, on present-day *Krisztina* Square there stood a chapel already in the early 18th century, but it was damaged during the fire and explosion in the castle in 1723. In 1725–26 a new chapel was built, to be enlarged in 1752. The new church, however, dates from between 1795 and 1797.

These new or renovated churches and monasteries contributed greatly to the urban outlook of Buda after the destruction resulting from the Turkish occupation and the liberation campaigns. The most spectacular changes, however, were due to the renovation and enlargement of the royal palace, the symbol of Buda even today. Its reconstruction was financed primarily by the royal court.[35]

Like most of Buda, the royal palace had to be rebuilt from its ruins. The first phase of its reconstruction took place between 1715 and 1723. This was the time when the Baroque palace of King Charles III was built on top of the ruins of the former palace.[36] The southeastern part of the present-day palace was rebuilt in those years, and another wing toward the north was also added to the western wing, which was not attached to the central building. The palace of Charles III remained, however, unfinished. It was his successor, Maria Theresa who completed it between 1749 and 1770.[37] The detached wing was demolished, and the palace was significantly externded towards the north. The three wings were open toward the west and surrounded the present-day Courtyard of Lions.

The palace was designed as a residence for the king, and the Hungarians kept repeating at the diet that they wished to see their monarch in Buda. Neither Maria Theresa, nor her successors transferred their seat to Buda. Nevertheless, the castle had high-born occupants: between 1766 and 1777 Prince Albrecht of Saxony and Teschen, *Locumtenens* of Hungary and his wife, Archduchess Maria Christine, and later Archdukes Alexander Leopold and Joseph, Palatines of Hungary. During her visit to Hungary, Maria Theresa herself stayed there for a short time in 1764. The palace was a temporary home also for Mary Ward's nuns. After 1777 it housed part of the *Nagyszombat* (today's Trnava) university transferred to Buda, but later served primarily as the residence of the palatine.

At the time when Maria Theresa's palace was built, the southern side of present-day *Szent György* (Saint George) Square was occupied by an armory built between 1686 and 1696 on the site of the former Turkish arsenal. It burnt down during the fire of 1723, when the explosion also caused severe damage to Charles III's palace still under construction, but was rebuilt by the early 1730s. This building no longer exists.

To the north from there, at the beginning of present-day *Színház* (Theater) Street there were two barracks in those days. Count Sándor Vince built his palace on this site in 1805–6, which became the Prime Minister's office later.[38]

Between 1763 and 1786 stables were built on the western side of the square, on the site of former stores and barracks. The most representative building of the western side, the palace of the Teleki family next to the stables, dates from between 1787 and 1794.[39]

As regards function, the most important building of Buda was the townhall on *Szentháromság* (Holy Trinity) Street opposite the *Nagyboldogasszony* (Virgin Mary) church. It housed the city council until 1873. It was built on ruins from 1702 on, and the first council-meeting was held there in June, 1710. The fire of 1723 caused great damage to it. Between 1770 and 1774 it was extended by a wing facing *Uri* Street.

The reconstruction of Óbuda was also in process in the 18th century. Three of the most important constructions deserve mention. The Zichy family, the landlords of Óbuda had a manor-house built in *Fő* (Main) Street. Its construction began in the early years of the century, and was completed only in 1752 by retaining elements of the old building. The manor house was built by Miklós Zichy who inherited the estate in 1745.

Even Maria Theresa visited it in 1764. After the Chamber purchased Óbuda from the widow of Count Miklós Zichy the manor-house served economic purposes.

The monastery of the Trinitarian order near the village of Kiscell was built thanks to a donation from the widow of Count Péter Zichy in 1738 (today a museum). The countess also gave the Trinitarians the chapel built at Kiscell in 1724. The construction of the monastery began in 1744; in 1748 the friars moved in , although the monastery was completed only in the 1760s. The cornerstone of the church was laid in 1747, and it was completed around 1758.

Another church was built with the financial support of Countess Zichy between 1744 and 1749 in present-day *Lajos* (Louis) Street, dedicated to Saint Peter and Saint Paul.

Pest was destroyed and depopulated during the Turkish rule by the liberation campaigns and by the plague, becoming almost totally desolate after Rákóczi's War of Independence. One third of the Inner City was uninhabited in the early 18th century.[40] The church and monastery constructions played an important role in reshaping the city here as well.

The Inner City Parish Church (next to present-day *Erzsébet*—Elisabeth Bridge) was originally given to the Jesuits. Its reconstruction took place between 1725 and 1740.[41] The Pauline friars inherited the *djami* and the adjacent buildings in *Kecskeméti* (today's *Papnevelde*—Seminary) Street in 1686. Their monastery was built between 1715 and 1744, and their church (later the church of the university) between the 1720s and 1742. The Servite and the Franciscan friars also received their plots with the buildings on them prior to the turn of the century. The Servites built their church and monastery between 1725 and 1732 on present-day *Szervita* (Servite) Square. The Franciscan church was built on the emplacement of a *djami* (on present-day *Ferenciek*—Franciscans' Square) between 1727 and 1738. The Piarists were invited by the city council of Pest to open their school there in 1717, so their building was bought for them by the city. It was a semi-finished house between *Galamb* (Pigeon) Street and *Régiposta* (Old Post Office) Street, facing the Danube, originally owned by the Jesuits. In 1718 the Piarists moved in.[42] In 1762 they moved into another building, namely, the former Esterházy palace next to the parish church. They sold their old home in 1789, on the site of which a church was built.

The most important public building of Pest was the old city hall by the Elisabeth Bridge, owned by the city since the end of the 17th century. It was rebuilt several times. One of the largest buildings of the city in the 18th century was the Palace of the Invalid in *Irgalmasok* (Brothers of Mercy) Street, the present-day *Városház* (City Hall) Street. Its construction was financed by Archbishop György Szécsényi, who donated the income from some of his estates for the purposes of the hospital. The building site was marked off in 1716. Eugene of Savoy, head of the imperial war council, wanted to turn it into a hospital for veterans from all parts of the empire, but the Austrian and Czech chancellors blocked his plans.[43] The construction was stopped in 1741. Emperor Joseph II removed the veterans and used the building as barracks. Today it houses among others the offices of the Mayor of Budapest.

The second largest building of Pest—the so-called New Building or *Neugebäude* was erected on present-day *Szabadság* (Liberty) Square in the district later called *Lipótváros* in 1786-1787, but it was not really finished owing to financial difficulties. The huge building served as barracks and ordnance stores.[44] The building no longer exists.

Palaces of the aristocracy multiplied when the leading families of the country moved into the city. The one in *Uri* (today's Károlyi) Street built in 1696 was one of the finest. In 1744 it was owned by the archbishop of Kalocsa, in 1747 by Ferenc Barkóczy, bishop of Eger, and in 1768 by Antal Károlyi, Lord Lieutenant of Szatmár county. The palace was rebuilt several times. Among its distinguished guests were Maria Theresa and Francis of Lorraine in 1751, Palatine Joseph in 1803, and Archduke Charles in 1803 and 1804.[45]

The dynamically developing city of Pest, which overtook Buda as an economic center in the 18th century and as a population center in the 19th, found an influential patron in the person of the Palatine of Hungary, Archduke Joseph. In 1801 the palatine suggested to his elder brother, King Francis I, that townplanning in Pest should be entrusted to an independent body. This was the origin of the Town Embellishment Commission brought about in 1808. This commission worked on the basis of the palatine's plans from 1805 on, which, in turn, were based on the concept of architect János Hild.[46]

## Palatine Archduke Joseph's Plans to Develop and Beautify the City

The Palatine came up with an elaborate assessment of the measures necessary to beautify the city. He contended that the inner city had been deteriorating ever since the eighties of the 18th century. Up to that time it had been inhabited by noblemen and merchants, but these had moved to *Lipótváros*, partly in search of greater comfort and partly because of the high rents and the danger of floods in the inner city. The inner city was improved only where it was adjacent to *Lipótváros*, but it basically remained in its former desolate state. The construction of a sewer system was one of the most immediate needs, the palatine emphasized. The strong wind often covered the streets with sand, and after rainfalls it turned into mud blocking traffic. In order to improve hygiene and for the sake of beautification blacksmiths' workshops were to be removed, and stairs leading directly to the streets should be prohibited. Those already built were to be demolished together with other similar road-blocks.

The bank of the Danube was badly in need of planning. Its section along the inner city was neglected and, with the exception of a short stretch around the pontoon-bridge,[47] it was unsuitable or at least inconvenient for loading and unloading goods. Sewage dumped here from the houses and streets in the vicinity made the whole neighborhood an unhealthy place for working or living. The street along the bank of the river had to be filled up and paved, and railings placed along the bank to avoid accidents. The cemetery and the slaughter-house needed to be removed from the inner city for sanitary reasons, and the botanic gardens for reasons of townplanning. The shipping office and the round bastion were also to be removed or demolished.[48] The plots should be sold as building sites, the palatine remarked.

A separate chapter with the same points of view dealt with *Lipótváros*. Construction should be allowed only within the framework of a general plan for the improvement of the city. The stretch of the Danube bank was to be paved, the district was to be supplied with a drainage system, and the gutters emanating unpleasant odors, especially in summer, were to be covered. The plans included the construction of a new promenade, and the removal of the customs office, the salt-office, and the Office for the Purchase of Tobacco from the streets near the Danube.[49] The weighing-house (on present-day Roosevelt Square) was to be pulled down and its site, together with that of the adjacent promenade, to be sold as building sites. The plan spoke also of building new churches, schools, theaters, and cóncert halls.

As regards the outskirts, the plan emphasized the binding of the sandy soil there, regulating the market-places, the construction of a workhouse and new barracks, and digging a fish-pond and a miller's pond. Finally it spoke of filling up and paving the highways, specifically those leading toward Hatvan, Soroksár, Vác, and Üllő, in order of importance. The palatine believed ten years would be needed to accomplish these improvements.

The king's reply arrived three years later and the committee was set up. However, its activity was unsatisfactory, for in the ten years suggested by the Palatine the committee achieved less than half the plan.[50] Archduke Joseph's ideas were praiseworthy despite the flawed execution. He also gained distinction as a patron and sometimes owner of cultural institutions.

## The Twin Cities as Political and Cultural Centers of the Country

Until the 1780s Pozsony (today's Bratislava) was the political and administrative center of Hungary. This was the city where the Hungarian Diet met though, unfortunately for the Hungarian estates, it was rarely convened by the monarch. It met only three times (1712–15, 1722–23, 1728–29) during the reign of Charles III (1711–40), three times (1741, 1751, 1764–65) under Maria Theresa (1740–80), and never under Joseph II. The most important Hungarian government institutions functioned in Pozsony. These were the *Helytartótanács* (Administrative Council), and the Hungarian Chamber (*Camera hungarica*). The center of higher education, the university was in Nagyszombat (Trnava). The only central institution located in Pest was the Royal Supreme Court (*Curia regis*).[51]

The 1770s and 1780s were decisive decades in the history of the two cities. Population was rapidly growing. Buda and Pest became economic centers due to their advantageous location. They were soon to become the cultural and political center of the country as well.

The university founded in 1635 at Nagyszombat moved to Buda in 1777. This had a considerable impact on cultural life at Buda and its environs.

The Faculty of Law and the Faculty of Arts occupied part of the royal castle, along with the higher grades of the secondary school and the Theresa Academy.[52] The Museums of Physics, Natural History, and Mechanics, the coin collection and the university library were also located in the castle. The faculty of theology occupied part of the former Academy of the Jesuit order along with the lower grades of the secondary school, with the municipal elementary school attached to them, transferred from the neighboring Corvin House. The Central Seminary moved into the former Jesuit dormitory. The university was given several sites for the purposes of a botanic garden in *Krisztinaváros*. The internship of the future doctors took place at the St John Hospital. The university also got the Corvin House for the purposes of a printing press.[53] The convocation ceremony of the first school-year in Buda took place in the Royal Palace on November 3, 1777.

No sooner had the university taken up its quarters in Buda than Joseph II ordered it in 1784 to leave the city with the exception of the observatory, the printing press, and the secondary school. The faculty of law and the faculty of arts moved to Pest, to present-day *Curia* Street. The faculty of arts functioned temporarily in the building of the Piarist order.[54] The faculty of medicine got the building of the Directorate of Legal Affairs at the corner of Hatvani and *Újvilág* (New World—today Semmelweis) Streets, but actual education began in the Pauline monastery.

The fate of the theological faculty was also very complicated. It was temporarily transferred to Pozsony and worked in cooperation with the General Seminary there.[55] Between 1790 and 1805, however, its activities were suspended.[56] The theological faculty was reopened in Pest in 1805,[57] coupled with a substantial move once again.[58]

The ups and downs in the life of the university accompanied the Josephinian administrative reforms representing a watershed in the history of the two cities, especially Buda. For example, the transfer of the university was due mainly to these reforms, since its buildings were needed by the arriving central offices, the Administrative Council among them, to be transferred there in 1784, when Joseph II made Buda the political capital of Hungary. A law promulgated in 1723 established the *Helytartótanács* (Administrative Council) expected to function in the Hungarian capital.

Besides the buildings of the former Jesuit monastery and the university, the convents of the Franciscans and the Clare-nuns were also to house central governmental offices.

The headquarters of the Supreme Military Command were relocated into the Royal Palace, while the Hungarian Chamber took up its quarters in the former Jesuit Seminary, and the Administrative Council in the former Jesuit Academy. The Supreme Court transferred from Pest moved into the convent of the Clare-nuns, where the diet was supposed to meet. Actually, the diet met in this building but rarely—once during the sessions of 1790–91, then in 1792, and again in 1807. The building was better known for the fancy balls of Buda from 1786 on.

The Franciscan friary and church were also converted into offices, when the order was dissolved by the ruler in 1786. This Franciscan church soon saw an exceptionally ceremonious occasion: Francis I was crowned King of Hungary within its walls in 1792. In the same year the Supreme Command was removed from the royal palace owing to the arrival of Palatine Alexander Leopold, and took up its quarters in the Franciscan friary.

The death of Joseph II was a turning point in the history of the Administrative Council and the Hungarian Chamber. The two government institutions were once again separated after the emperor's death. The Administrative Council did not receive immediately all the offices assigned to it e.g. the Franciscan's closter because it served as a jail in the period of 1794–95. At that time a group of the Martinovics conspiracy was kept there.[59]

The university and the national institutions set up in Buda and Pest added to the splendor of the two cities. Their activities forced the highest dignitaries of the country to move to Buda and Pest including archdukes as palatines, the Lord Chief Justice, the Chief Justice, aristocrats, noblemen and commoners as employees. Count J. C. Hoffmannsegg, a traveller from Saxony, visited Pest and Buda in the 1790's and described the Buda mansions of Károly Zichy and József Haller as centers of social entertainment. He expressed his appreciation for the erudition of the Hungarian aristocracy, and spoke of the civilian population of the two cities with a certain haughtiness, albeit no ill-will.[60]

The aristocracy and officials and, above all, university professors and students had a stimulating effect on the cultural life of the two cities. The appearance of these new consumers of culture profoundly influenced the development of theaters, printing presses, bookshops and, above all, libraries.

With the transfer of the university to Buda in 1777, the university library became housed in the Palace and, in 1784, the library followed the university to Pest where it was placed in a wing of the Franciscan monastery. In the 1770s and 1780s its holdings grew rapidly and was enriched first by the libraries of the Jesuits, and later by those of the monastic orders dissolved by Joseph II. Its holdings can be estimated at 20,000–22,000 volumes around 1790.[61] Outstanding scholars of the day like György Lakits, György Pray, István Schönwiesner, and György Márton Schwartner were among its directors. The collection was open to the public from 1779, and in 1780 it was the first to get the rights of a government deposit library in Hungary. The library still had many problems. Its funding was inadequate and the delivery of deposit copies was not always regular.

The National Széchenyi Library, created on private initiative and generously supported by its founder, was in a more favorable position. In 1802 a former student of the Theresianum in Vienna and a former Josephinian official, Count Ferenc Széchényi offered his library of several thousand volumes, his archive, and his collections of maps, engravings, heraldic figures, and coins to the nation. The king was pleased to hear of the offer. The deed of foundation was prepared at the end of the same year, and the library opened its gates on August 20, 1803. The formal opening ceremony took place on December 10 with the participation of the Palatine. The founder had the right to enrich the collection and to appoint the head librarian. The document stipulated that the collection should never be mixed with that of the University Library. The Széchényi Library also received the right to acquire deposit copies.

The diet of 1807 in Buda commemorated the endowment of Ferenc Széchényi, "by which he laid the foundations of a future national museum with commendable zeal." The National Museum was established by the Diet in 1808. A considerable sum had already been collected for its purposes through public contributions on the initiative of the Palatine. As in the case of the library, the most valuable pieces in the collection came from a Széchényi donation. The Diet entrusted Palatine Joseph with the administration of the museum's affairs, the control of its finances, and the arrangements for the construction of its building. The National Széchényi

Library became practically part of the National Museum established in 1808, though their relationship was not quite clear from the start. Széchényi's rights were certainly impaired, for the warden of the library was to be appointed by the Palatine.[62]

The library was originally opened in the Pauline monastery that also housed the Supreme Court in those days. In 1807 it was moved to the neighboring Greater Seminary where the National Museum collection was to be stored. Hence the facilities were far from satisfactory.

Wishing to resolve the proper placement of the collections, Antal Grassalkovich offered a site for a new building fit for a museum in 1808. The new building as we can see it today was built as late as 1846.

Theatrical life in Buda and Pest had advanced greatly by the early 19th century since 1774. Performances had been held in Pest in the round bastion (*Rondella*) on the bank of the Danube at the end of today's *Régiposta* (Old Post) Street with a seating capacity of five hundred,[63] but this building was small, dark and unsuitable for the purpose, as Count Hoffmannsegg justly remarked. It was demolished in 1815.

In Buda the Reischl house, built of wood, served as a theater presumably since 1783.[64] The Castle Theater, established in 1787 and converted from a Carmelite church, was finally a worthy home for drama. It could hold 1,200 people and even Hofmannsegg found it "beautiful enough", reminding him of the theater in Dresden.

Plans for erecting a new theater to replace the Round Bastion in Pest emerged as early as the 1790s, but they were realized only in 1812 when the German Theater of Pest, capable of holding an audience of 3,500, was opened in *Lipótváros*, on present-day *Vörösmarty* Square. The prologue and the epilogue written by August Kotzebue and performed at the première were set to music by Beethoven.[65]

The theater of Pest mentioned so many times by travellers was the one for animal-fights located in a new building near the present-day Basilica in 1787. Its "peformances" were banned in the early 19th century.

## The Jacobin Conspiracy

Pest and Buda, the political and intellectual centers of Hungary were hotbeds of the short-lived Hungarian Jacobin movement, which evolved in the wake of the French Revolution. The leader of the movement was Ignác Martinovics, a man of high erudition but dubious political past, who established two secret societies in 1794 called *Magyarországi Reformátorok Titkos Társasága* (Secret Society of Hungarian Reformers) and *Szabadság és Egyenlőség Társasága* (Society of Liberty and Equality). The societies were headed by four directors: József Hajnóczy, Ferenc Szentmarjay, János Laczkovics, and Jakab Sigray.

The Society of Reformers attempted to win over the nobility. As laid down in a manifesto, its moderate program refrained from attacking the prerogatives of the nobility. The program of the Society of Liberty and Equality was, however, more radical as it addressed three major foes of humanity: the monarchy, the nobility, and the Church. As these three enemies of the people oppressed the "nation of mankind", it called for people to revolt against them.

Nearly 300 persons were to join the organization, but the movement was quashed by the authorities before it could accomplish anything. Martinovics was arrested in Vienna in July, and his testimony turned the attention of the authorities toward Pest. Palatine Archduke Alexander Leopold had József Hajnóczy, Ferenc Szentmarjay, János Laczkovics, and Jakab, Count Sigray arrested. These leaders and some of their followers were taken to Vienna for interrogation.

The arrest shocked the country, and Pest county protested against the Jacobins' interrogation in Vienna, which skipped the Hungarian court of competent jurisdiction, the *Királyi Tábla* (Royal Court of Appeal) located in Pest. This protest was soon joined by other counties, so the defendants were finally brought to Buda in November, 1794. Some of them were kept in custody in the former Franciscan monastery, and some in the barracks of the Guards nearby. So Buda became the scene of the first show trial in Hungary. The trial took place at the Royal Court of Appeal in 1795. The Jacobin leaders, who had circulated their manifestos, but had actually done nothing to realize their aims were found guilty of high treason. Eighteen of them were sentenced to death, and seven sentences were carried out in the spring of 1795. Martinovics and four other leaders were beheaded on today's *Vérmező* (Bloody Meadow) on May 20, 1795.

The measures used to stifle the movement and reassert the power of the royal court, the subsequent atmosphere of distrust, and the investigations to follow imposed inhibitions on the political and intellectual life of

Buda and Pest for a long time. Several political leaders of the two cities were put out of the way for a certain period, among them some whose houses and erudition had been highly complimented by Count Hoffmansegg. Certain university professors met the same fate. The political rigor of the court was relieved only around the turn of the century, mostly due to the conciliatory attitude of a Habsburg archduke, Palatine Joseph, who had the embellishment of the Hungarian capital at heart.

\* \* \*

It can be justly stated that the twin cities of Buda and Pest regaining self-government in 1703 underwent an enormous development in the following hundred years. The 18th century witnessed rapid demographic growth as well as economic and infrastructural development in the whole country. The expulsion of the Turks brought, however, special advantages for these two cities by the Danube. Their geographical location predestined them to become commercial and economic centers, as well as destinations for immigration. Pest, formerly an insignificant village, had become the largest city of the country by the early 19th century. The rural suburbs soon merged with the original inner city of Pest and the castle district of Buda as the economy and population grew.

The political decisions of the monarchs in the 1770s and 1780s emphasized the exceptional position of Pest and Buda among the sixty-one royal free cities to be found in the lands of the Hungarian crown at the time of the census taken during the reign of Joseph II. The transfer of the university and of the most important government offices, then the palatine's (archdukes of the House of Habsburg) transfer to Buda shifted the foci of political and cultural life to Pest and Buda.

The local political structures changed only to the smallest degree. When the patronizing control of the Directorate was over, the leadership and administration of the cities moved into the hands of an insignificant minority imposing their control. The possession of political rights by a minority, and their participation in the governing bodies of the cities sharply divided the urban society from a legal point of view; feudal privileges, however, tended to lose their significance as regards a person's economic and social standing.

The year 1703 was a political landmark in the history of the two cities, and the early 18th century was a starting point for reconstruction and demographic growth. The early 19th century represented only another stage in the ever more dynamic development of the two cities.

## Notes

1. Imre Wellman, "Magyarország népességének fejlődése a 18. században" [The population of Hungary in the 18th century], in Pál Zsigmond Pach, ed., *Magyarország története* [History of Hungary], vol. 4, *Magyarország története 1686-1790* [History of Hungary, 1686–1790], ed. Győző Ember and Gusztáv Heckenast (Budapest, 1989), pt. 1, 40–41.
2. The royal free cities were privileged settlements with self-government. They were free to send deputies to the lower house of the diet. At the time of Emperor Joseph II there were sixty-one of them in royal Hungary, Transylvania, and Croatia. However, they represented only a small portion of the population.
3. Pierre Chaunu, *A klasszikus Európa* [Classic Europe] (Budapest, 1971), 195.
4. Lajos Nagy and György Bónis, *Budapest története a török kiűzésétől a márciusi forradalomig* [History of Budapest from the expulsion of the Turks to the March Revolution], ed. Domokos Kosáry, in László Gerevich, ed., *Budapest története* [History of Budapest] (Budapest, 1975), vol. 3, 127.
5. Kosáry, ed., op. cit., 132.
6. Immigrants played a decisive role also in the growth of the whole population of the country, especially in Pest. As Zoltán Fallenbüchl maintains, the annual 5 per cent growth of the population of Pest between 1700 and 1770 was not at all due to natural population growth, but rather to immigration. The majority of the new settlers came from abroad, the rate of the Hungarians being 31 per cent in the late 17th century, 30 per cent in the 1740s, 39 per cent in the 1750s, and 45 per cent in the 1760s. Between 1687 and 1770 32.2 per cent of all immigrants came from the lands of the Hungarian crown. See Zoltán Fallenbüchl, "Pest város népességének származáshelyei a statisztika és a kartográfia tükrében (1687–1770)" [Places of origin of the inhabitants of Pest as reflected in statistics and cartography, 1687–1770], in *Tanulmányok Budapest múltjából* [Studies of Budapest's past](hereafter TBM) (Budapest, 1963), vol. 15, 240, 268, 278, and 284.
7. Occupational distribution of newly accepted citizens in the course of the 18th century:

| Pest | 1687–1750 | 1751–1790 | Total |
|------|-----------|-----------|-------|
| Farming | 68 | 84 | 152 |
| Handicraft industry | 674 | 942 | 1,616 |
| Catering | 56 | 53 | 109 |
| Commerce | 109 | 190 | 299 |
| Transport | 60 | 34 | 94 |
| Civil service | 62 | 127 | 189 |
| Military forces | 24 | 12 | 36 |
| Other | 20 | 328 | 348 |
| Unknown | 350 | 118 | 468 |

| Buda | 1687–1750 | 1751–1790 | Total |
|------|-----------|-----------|-------|
| Farming | 102 | 24 | 126 |
| Handicraft industry | 1,179 | 764 | 1,943 |
| Catering | 106 | 14 | 120 |
| Commerce | 155 | 107 | 262 |
| Transport | 83 | 22 | 105 |
| Civil service | 89 | 58 | 147 |
| Military forces | 11 | 2 | 13 |
| Other | — | 3 | 3 |
| Unknown | 600 | 800 | 1,400 |

(See Kosáry, ed., op. cit., 139–140.)

8. The Administrative Council [*Consilium regium locumtenentiale hungaricum*] was the most important administrative body in Hungary. From 1724 it worked at Pozsony, then in 1784 Emperor Joseph II transferred it to Buda and amalgamated it with the Hungarian Chamber [*Camera regia hungarica* or *Helytartótanács*] transferred to Buda from Pozsony (Pressburg) at the same time. When the emperor died, the two administrative organs were separated again.

9. Gusztáv Thirring, "Pest város népessége az 1771–1781. években" [The population of Pest in the years 1771–1781], *Magyar Statisztikai Szemle* 12, no. 2 (1934), 156.

10. Mihály Pásztor, "A hatvanesztendős 1879. évi XXVIII. törvénycikk" [The sixty-year-old Article 28 of 1879), *Városi Szemle* 25, no. 4 (1939), 516.

11. Gusztáv Thirring, *Magyarország népessége II. József korában* [The population of Hungary during the reign of Joseph II] (Budapest, 1938), 132–133. The heirs of burghers and peasants were those heirs of burghers, artisans, merchants and peasants who followed the trade of their fathers. The category

"cotters" covers here day laborers, servants, minor clerks in the service of private persons, physically handicapped people, widowers with children, non-noble officials, and adult sons of *honoratiores*. The category "other" covers adult sons of burghers and peasants, who are not direct heirs of their fathers.

12. Thirring, op. cit., 117. The actual number of the population contains also the aliens staying in the city and does not include those city-dwellers who are temporarily absent.

13. Dezső Dümmerth, *Pest város társadalma 1686–1696* [The society of Pest, 1686–1696] (Budapest, 1968), 73.

14. Kosáry, op. cit., 151–152.

15. Thirring, op. cit., 138, 387.

16. Thirring, op. cit., 112.

17. Kosáry, ed., op. cit., 148.

18. The royal patents of Buda and Pest were basically identical. For the patent of Pest from October 21, 1703, see Vera Bácskai, ed., *Források Buda, Pest és Óbuda történetéhez 1686–1873* [Sources to the History of Buda, Pest, and Old Buda, 1686–1873] (Budapest, 1971), 29–33.

19. See the directive issued to the body of electors after November 23, 1722 in György Bónis, ed., *Pest-Budai hivatali utasítások a XVIII. 'században* [Official directives of Pest-Buda in the 18th century] (Budapest, 1974), 54–58.

20. Some suburbs of Buda like *Víziváros* [Watertown], *Újlak* [New Lodge], and Tabán were headed by sub-courts. (In the Tabán there were two of them.) The city council wished to appoint all suburban judges, mayor's counsellors, and other officials, but its efforts were frustrated in Tabán and in Újlak. However, it sent commissioners to the suburban elections, who presumably had the right to nominate candidates. See István Nagy, "A választó polgárság testülete Budán a XVIII. században" [The body of electors in Buda in the 18th century), in *TBM* (Budapest, 1959), vol. 13, 155 and Kosáry, ed., op. cit., 438. Later there were sub-courts also in the district *Országút* [Highway], in 1790 there were five of them.

21. István Nagy, op. cit., 149.

22. op. cit., 153.

23. Kosáry, ed., op. cit., 167. The chapter on city administration was written by György Bónis.

24. Nagy, op. cit., 160–161.

25. Ferdinand Laffert to the city council on August 7, 1731. Points 2, 3, and 24. See Bónis, op. cit., 101.

26. Albert Gárdonyi, "Pest hatósági szervezetének kialakulása a Szlávy-féle statutumig" [The development of the administrative organs in Pest up to Szlávy's statute), *Városi Szemle* 32, no. 7 (1946).

27. Kosáry, ed., op. cit., 173.

28. Ibolya Felhő, "Mária Terézia úrbérrendezése a Buda és Pest környéki helységekben" [Maria Theresa's urbarial reform in the environs of Buda and Pest], in *TBM* (Budapest, 1971), vol. 18, 138.

29. Kosáry, ed., op. cit., 178–180, 447.

30. István Mészáros, *Az iskolaügy története Magyarországon 966–1777* [History of education in Hungary, 966–1777] (Budapest, 1981), 447.

31. Gyula Szalay, *A királyi egyetemi katolikus gimnázium története 1687–1937* [History of the Royal Catholic Grammar School of the University, 1687–1937] (Budapest, 1937), 31. The buildings of the seminary and the academy were demolished early in this century.

32. Oszkár Paulinyi, "A M. Kir. Belügyminisztérium budai várbeli székházának története" [History of the building of the Royal Hungarian Ministry of the Interior in the Buda Castle], in *TBM* (Budapest, 1938), vol. 6, 24.

33. Paulinyi, op. cit., 33.

34. Margit Vladár Claudemé, "A Várszínház története" [History of the Castle Theater], in *TBM* (Budapest, 1943), vol. 10, 172.

35. Alajos Hauszmann, *A magyar királyi vár építésének története* [History of the construction of the Hungarian Royal Castle] (Budapest, 1900), 19.

36. György Bánrévy, "A budai királyi palota újjáépítése III. Károly alatt" [The renovation of the Royal Castle of Buda under Charles III], in *TBM* (Budapest, 1932), vol. 1, 7. Contrary to other historians, the author puts the completion of the palace, or rather the cessation of the work, to 1723 (see p. 42).

37. István Czagány, *A budavári palota és a Szent György téri épületek* [The castle of Buda and the buildings on Saint George Square] (Budapest, 1966), 25–27.

38. In 1803 Vince Sándor might have bought not these two barracks but a large building replacing them on the same site (Czagány, op. cit., 157).

39. The site of the Teleki palace had been empty since the middle of the century. The artillery barracks and the gun-emplacement standing there earlier had long been demolished. Neither the stables, nor the palace are in existence now.

40. Flóris Rómer, *A régi Pest* [Old Pest] (Budapest, 1873), 97.

41. Kálmán Lux, "A budapesti belvárosi plébániatemplom" [The parish church in the inner city of Budapest], in *TBM* (Budapest, 1933), vol. 2, 16–18.

42. Sándor Takács, *A főváros alapította budapesti piarista kollégium története* [History of the Piarist College founded by the city of Pest] (Budapest, 1895), 38–40.

43. Arnold Schoen, *A budapesti központi városháza* [The central City Hall of Budapest] (Budapest, 1930), 23.

44. Franz Schams, *Vollständige Beschreibung der königlichen Freystadt Pest in Ungern* (Pest, 1821), 89.

45. Elemér (Réh) Révhelyi, "Az Egyetem-utcai volt Károlyi palota építésének története" [History of the construction of the former Károlyi Palace in Egyetem Street], in *TBM* (Budapest, 1933), vol. 2, 89, 96.

46. "József nádor fölterjesztése Pest város szépítése tárgyában, 1805. június 1." [Memorandum of Palatine Joseph relative to the improvement of the city of Pest], in Sándor Domanovszky, ed., *József nádor iratai* [Papers of Palatine Joseph] (Budapest, 1929), vol. 2, 63–110.

47. The pontoon-bridge that was taken to pieces every winter stood at the end of *Kishíd utca* [Small Bridge Street]. In 1787 it was removed in the level of *Nagyhíd utca* [Great Bridge Street]. See Gábor Preisich, *Budapest város-építésének története Buda visszavételétől a kiegyezésig* [History of the construction of Budapest from the recapture of Buda to the Compromise] (Budapest, 1960), 30.

48. Schams confirms that these removals and demolitions actually took place (Schams, op. cit., 449).

49. The new Customs Office building (today's University of Economics) was built only after the Compromise. The Salt-office and the Office for the Purchase of Tobacco were soon removed. See Kosáry, ed., op. cit., 259.

50. Schams identified thirty-five projects to be done, fourteen of which were mentioned as completed, ten were under way, and eleven were still waiting to be realized. The following projects were among the latter: building of a parish church in *Lipótváros* (Leopoldtown) and in *Ferencváros* (Francistown), resettlement of the Piarists into the Servite monastery, demolition of the scale house, removal of the city council to the former Piarist building, building of a workhouse, removal of the shooting range from the center of the city, etc., (see Schams, op. cit., 449–450).

51. The term Royal Supreme Court included the supreme courts of Hungary, i.e., the *Hétszemélyes Tábla* [Seven-member Court of Appeal] and the *Királyi Tábla* [Royal Court of Appeal]. Its seat was in Pest, but Joseph II transferred it to Buda. After his death it was relocated to Pest.

52. This grammar school was the former school of the Jesuits that had merged with the university. The Theresa Academy was a new institution brought about in Buda. Its students were recruited from those of the academy of the nobility at Nagyszombat and of the former boarding school of the Jesuits. (See Szalay, op. cit., 57–59.)

53. István Sinkovics, ed., *Az Eötvös Loránd Tudományegyetem története* [History of the Eötvös Loránd University of Arts and Sciences] (Budapest, 1985), 85.

54. Imre Szentpétery, "A bölcsészettudományi kar 1635–1935" [History of the Faculty of Arts, 1635–1935], in *A Királyi Magyar Pázmány Péter-Tudományegyetem története* [History of the Royal Hungarian Pázmány Péter University of Arts and Sciences] (Budapest, 1935), vol. 4, 246.

55. The establishment of general seminaries was ordered by Joseph II on November 1, 1783 but they started to function only from May 1, 1784. Seminaries were originally planned to function in Buda, Kassa (Košice), Pécs, and Kalocsa, but they were finally set up in Pozsony (Bratislava), Eger, and Zágráb (Zagreb). The emperor ordered the teaching staff of the general seminary at Pozsony to be accepted as member of the *universitas*. See Egyed Hermann and Edgár Artner, "A hittudományi kar története 1635–1935" [History of the Faculty of Theology], in *A Királyi Magyar Pázmány Péter-Tudományegyetem története* [History of the Royal Hungarian Pázmány Péter University of Arts and Sciences] (Budapest, 1938), vol. 1, 182.

56. In 1786 Emperor Joseph II ordered the general seminaries at Zágráb and Eger, brought about simulataneously with that in Pozsony, to be merged and transferred to Pest to a building on the site of the present-day central building of Eötvös Loránd University. It is difficult to interpret the relationship of the theological institutions of Pozsony and Pest. Joseph II found it natural to see the Faculty of Theology at the same place where the other faculties of the university were to be found. Examinations could be passed at the faculty at Pozsony, but graduation took place exclusively in Pest. The problem was resolved in 1790 when all general seminaries were abolished and the activities of the faculty of theology were suspended.

57. In 1802 the Administrative Council suggested that the university should occupy the Pauline monastery, and the Supreme Court residing there should regain its former building in *Kúria utca* (Curia Street) used by the faculty of law and the faculty of arts. However, the monastery proved to be too small for the three faculties and the seminary, especially when the Széchényi Library was set up there in 1803. So the Administrative Council suggested the university to occupy the building of the Great Seminary, which was accepted also by the Chancellery (see Pauler, op. cit., 317.)

58. It was King Francis I who decided to set up a seminary by the university on January 11, 1802 (see Hermann and Artner, op. cit., 286).
The number of the university students around the turn of the century fluctuated as follows:

| Academic years | Students |
|----------------|----------|
| 1780–1781 | 500 |
| 1785–1786 | 970 |
| 1789–1790 | 644 |
| 1794–1795 | 301 |
| 1800–1801 | 440 |
| 1807–1808 | 648 |

(See Sinkovics, ed., op. cit., 385.)

59. For the troubled history of the Franciscans and the Poor Clares see Paulinyi, op. cit., 35–42.

60. *Reise des Grafen Hofmannsegg in einige Gegenden von Ungarn bis an die türkische Gränze* (Görlitz, 1800), 108–110.

61. Csaba Csapodi, András Tóth, and Miklós Vértesy, *Magyar könyvtártörténet* [History of libraries in Hungary] (Budapest, 1987), 160.

62. Jenő Berlász, *Az Országos Széchényi Könyvtár története 1802–1867* [History of the National Széchényi Library, 1802–1867] (Budapest, 1981), 109–111.

63. Jolán Kádár, *A budai és pesti német szinészet története 1812-ig* [History of German performing arts in Buda and Pest to 1812) (Budapest, 1914), 11–13.

64. Ibid., 23.

65. Jolán Kádár, *A pesti és a budai német szinészet története 1812–1847* [History of German performing arts in Pest and Buda, 1812–47] (Budapest, 1923), 7–8. The building has been demolished since.

*László Csorba*

# Transition from Pest-Buda to Budapest, 1815–1873

## Demography and Society

The most important dividing lines between periods in world history are not necessarily viable starting points for new eras in the history of a city. Incessant wars came to an end, with the battle of Waterloo on June 18, 1815. After Napoleon's defeat and exile not even the most powerful conservative rulers were able to restore the Europe that existed prior to 1789. The situation was, however, different in the countries under Habsburg rule. While people in other parts of Europe, from Madrid to St Petersburg and from London to Vienna, were struggling to restore world order, the city of Pest was preoccupied with defending itself against cholera attacking from the direction of the Transdanubian region of the country.

Chancellor Klemens Lothar von Metternich once remarked, "Asia begins at the end of *Landstraße*". Was he exaggerating? In hardly more than half a century the rich and populous twin cities of Buda and Pest were on the threshold of union, thus becoming a metropolis, and were ambitious rivals of the "big ones", primarily of Vienna. Their rapid development was fed by the same energy that gave impetus to the period of bourgeois development in general, beginning in Hungary with the Reform Era (1825–48). The unbroken development of Pest, Buda, and Óbuda (Old Buda) was a glorious chapter in demolishing feudal conditions and building a free society, based on equality of its citizens, and market economy.

As shown in the preceding chapters, the remarkable developments of the 18th century, especially the economic ones, created conditions that made the region of the three cities comparable to other European towns in the last phase of the Napoleonic wars. Development was continuous in the 19th century as well, as manifested primarily in population growth. There were several national, local, and ecclesiastical censi in this period that enable us to reconstruct the pace and dimensions of this development, even if not with hundred per cent accuracy.[1]

### Population Growth of Pest, Buda, and Óbuda
### between 1809 and 1869

|      | Pest    | Buda   | Óbuda  | Total   |
|------|---------|--------|--------|---------|
| 1809 | 32,980  |        |        |         |
| 1812 |         | 22,272 |        | 62,458  |
| 1817 |         |        | 7,206  |         |
| 1819 | 45,472  |        |        |         |
| 1821 |         | 27,471 |        | 80,272  |
| 1822 |         |        | 7,329  |         |
| 1827 | 56,577  | 30,001 | 7,535  | 94,113  |
| 1838 | 64,374  | 31,245 | 7,712  | 103,331 |
| 1846 | 100,000 | 40,500 | 7,690  | 148,190 |
| 1851 | 119,391 | 53,614 | 12,174 | 185,179 |
| 1857 | 136,566 | 55,230 |        | 191,796 |
| 1869 | 202,293 | 67,000 | 16,002 | 285,295 |

The chart reveals exceptional population growth in Pest. At the beginning of the period its population surpassed that of Buda by only one third, two decades later by half, but just prior to the union of the three cities there were three times as many inhabitants on the left bank of the Danube as on the right bank of the former historical capital of the country. Naturally, the pace of the population growth in Pest differed from district to district. Between 1806 and 1848 the population increase in the inner city, limited as it was the medieval town walls, resulted in merely a twofold increased in territory. The population of *Józsefváros* (Josephtown), the most slowly developing suburb, was only two and a half times as large at the end of the period as it was at the beginning. At the same time, population increase in *Terézváros* (Theresatown) and in *Ferencváros* (Francistown) was much more dynamic—three and a half and four times as many inhabitants, respectively. The largest growth of population occurred at *Lipótváros* (Leopoldtown) in the north, called not a district but "Newtown" and built according to a definite plan, with a sixfold increase. The apparent growth of the new districts is measured by the rate of population increase: 14 per cent of the total population of Pest lived in *Lipótváros*, 9.18 per cent in *Ferencváros*, while 38.1 per cent lived in *Terézváros* on the eve of the March Revolution of 1848.

The population of the castle district of Buda stagnated in the first half of the century and rising above 4,000 only in the 1840s. In the district called *Országút* the population grew only slowly, while in *Újlak* and *Tabán* it fluctuated. *Krisztinaváros* (Christinatown) increased relatively dynamically, while *Víziváros* (Watertown), the most populous district of all, increased by 500–1,000 people each year, exceeding 11,000 on the eve of the revolution of 1848. In the first half of the century *Óbuda*'s (Old Buda's) population did not grow significantly, but in the 1850s it nearly doubled within a few years.[2]

The chart above also shows that the steady development in the pre-1848 era continued even during the first years of neo-absolutism (the 1850s), and that there was a sudden spurt of population growth from the second half of the 1850s. By the late 1860s every third inhabitant was a newcomer arriving in this last phase of the city's development. The most decisive factor throughout the period was the capitalist development in the wake of the revolution of 1848, attracting large masses to the city. This large-scale economic development of the second half of the century gathered momentum in the early 1860s, accelerated but not caused by the Austro-Hungarian Compromise of 1867.[3]

While in the late 18th century only the combined population of Pest, Buda and Óbuda surpassed that of Debrecen or Pozsony, in 1846 the population of Pest alone was double that of Debrecen, and by the late 1860s *Terézváros* alone was more populous than Szeged, the second largest Hungarian city of the day with its 70,000 inhabitants.[4] At the beginning of the century the three cities were much smaller than Vienna with its 230,000 inhabitants. However, by the middle of the century the population of the imperial capital only doubled, while that of Pest had grown four times, and by the early 1870s already six times, when it became the second largest city in the Monarchy and the sixteenth largest in Europe, leaving urban centers like Milan, Rome or Brussels behind.[5]

The exceptional growth of Pest was therefore a result of massive im-migration motivated by various economic and social factors, shown in the following chart:

| | Pest | | Buda | | Rate of aliens (%) |
|---|---|---|---|---|---|
| | native | alien | native | alien | |
| 1851 | 96,398 | 22,993 | 45,957 | 7,657 | 17.7 |
| 1857 | 81,483 | 55,083 | 42,685 | 12,545 | 35.2 |
| 1869 | 157,312 | 44,981 | 54,415 | 12,585 | 21.3 |

The weight of immigration in the demographic processes is shown by the fact that in the years 1868–70, when there were no epidemics in the country, the average number of births surpassed deaths by only 216. The newcomers arrived primarily from neighboring Pest and Fejér counties, then down the Danube from Nyitra and Komárom, and finally from Bács county in the south. In these decades the twin cities were a magnet for people living in the overpopulated and poorer counties, especially in Northern Hungary. As regards the other lands of the Monarchy, many immigrants came from Bohemia and Moravia, Lower and Upper Austria, Galicia, Bukovina, and Silesia, while Germany became the primary source of immigrants among the foreign countries.[6]

The demographical situation of the three cities was modified also by the villages that later became part of Greater Budapest. In the first half of our period, i.e., between 1810 and 1846 the villages on the Buda side (Békásmegyer, Pesthidegkút, Promontor, Tétény, Kistétény, and Albert-falva founded in 1819) and Csepel on the island of the same name in-creased their population by 55 per cent altogether (from 5,341 to 8,278 inhabitants), but the main cause of this development was not so much the catalyzing effect of the vicinity of a developing metropolis but the possi-bility of employment on the Ráckeve estate, the vinyards owned by citizens of Buda and Pest, and the newly opened stone-quarries. Since similar op-portunities were much less frequent on the other side of the Danube the rate of the population growth at Palota, Káposztásmegyer, Cinkota, Ker-esztúr, Csaba, Soroksár, Szentlőrinc, Gubacs, and Szentmihály and Újpest just in the process of formation was only 43 per cent (from 7,437 to 10,672 inhabitants altogether). The changes that took place after the War of Independence (1848–49) invariably show the influence of the neighboring big city on the increase of the population, even if it varied from village to village. Taking the data of the whole suburban belt together, the population growth was 57.3 per cent (from 19.940 to 31.374 inhabitants), i.e., not significantly different from that during the Reform Era. But while the Buda side practically stagnated with 12 per cent (from 9.095 to 10.227), the villages on the Pest side grew by nearly 95 per cent (from 10,845 to 21,147). The most rapidly growing villages were Rákospalota, Keresztúr, Soroksár, and Újpest, the latter becoming the absolute record-holder with more than 1,100 per cent in the period. In the case of Újpest it was handicraft industry, and from the 1860s also manufacturing that attracted people; in the case of the three other villages it was the growing demands of the metropolis on agricultural produce that could support more and more people. The stagnating or even declining villages must have attracted fewer people from outside than they gave to the spreading metropolis nearby.[7]

## City Government

The political and military consequences of the Napoleonic era did not alter the administrative order in Buda and Pest. In both cities actual power remained in the hands of the so-called inner council led by the mayor. This body consisted of the city captain, the town-clerk, and eleven life-long city-councillors. They exercised the right of presentation (*kegyúri jog*—the privileges of the patron of ecclesiastical institutions), maintained law and order, exercised the right of market inspection, of exacting tolls, certifications, and of industrial control. They levied local taxes, elected deputies to the diet, and were authorized to decide all administrative or legal cases, issues of orphanage, guardianship, and management of property. They organized local elections, framed local ordinances, elevated persons to the status of burghers as well as granted honorary citizenship.

The outer council with its twenty-four members originally dealt with taxes, supervision, certifications or the standardization of measures, and various other economic issues. By the beginning of our period, however, this body had amalgamated with the *centumviratus* in Pest and the *sexaginta viratus* in Buda. Accordingly, a hundred burghers from Pest and sixty from Buda joined the outer councils and merged with them. The members of these bodies constituted the electorate at the time of reelection of the city council. At the same time, they were the members of the city council, called "elected burghers." The system of reelection still rested on the royal decree of 1755 providing that the right of nomination was preserved for a royal commissioner not only in the case of the highest municipal officials like the mayor, the justice, the captain, the councilors, the speaker, the accountants, and the treasurer, but also in the case of the "elected burghers."[8]

This system which consolidated the rule of a closed body of privileged burghers was much criticized during the pre-1848 era, the founding stage of bourgeois development. The criticism was sharp in the long-drawn debate about cities in the diet. The most outstanding figures of the Liberal opposition were naturally ready to remedy this practice the roots of which went back to unwritten feudal laws, according to which the vote of all free royal cities together equalled that of a single county. But even the reformers did not wish to grant the suffrage to each one of them until they represented the interests of all citizens rather than just the privileged. On February 18, 1848, Lajos Kossuth, the leading spokesman of the reform opposition, said in a debate on the direct election of municipal authorities by the population the following: "I have principles that I shall never give up, even if the cause of the royal cities will come to naught, and I know that the royal cities also entertain such principles. I tell you frankly that should the case of the cities be settled without direct election applying to both deputies and municipal officials in the future, I will have none of it. I rather see it remain unsolved than let it happen without direct election."[9]

It was, therefore, as a natural outcome of this debate that Article XXIII of the April Laws of 1848 codified bourgeois transformation for the free royal cities. Mór Szentkirályi, Kossuth's colleague and fellow-deputy from Pest county at the diet was the leader of the parliamentary committee that drafted the original motion. This well-known reformer politician was to play an important role in the life of Pest in later years. The law stipulated that the free royal cities were independent municipal authorities, the officials of which were to be elected from among the whole population of the cities by burghers meeting the following property qualifications: a) those who had owned a plot or a house within the boundaries of the city for at least a year, the limit of value varying according to the size of the city (the lowest limit was 200 silver florins in smaller cities, 700–1,000 florins in bigger ones, and 2,000 florins in Pest); b) those who had lived in the city for at least a year as artisans with at least one journeyman, or as registered merchants or manufacturers with workshops, premises or factories of their own; c) those who had lived in the city for at least a year as doctors, surgeons, lawyers, engineers, artists, teachers, or members of the Hungarian Academy of Sciences paying a minimum of 40–100 silver florin rent,commensurate with the size of the city; d) those who had settled in the city for at least two years and had an income of at least 200–600 silver florins either as salaries or as return on investment (in Pest 800 florins). In the spirit of legal continuity characteristic of the 1848 legislation, the law also provided that those who had had suffrage before would not lose it even if they did not comply with the above enlisted preconditions.

Strict regulations were promulgated how to conduct the general meetings for the reelection of the mayor, the chief justice, the chief captain of the city, the vice-captains, the aldermen, the notaries, the municipal attorneys, the archivists, the land registrar, the accountant, the chief medical officer, the chief surgeon, and the chief engineer. Any resident of the city could be member of the newly elected body of representatives irrespective of religious affiliation (within the limits of "legally recognized" denominations). These people and the members of the council exercising operational control constituted the general assembly, chaired by the mayor or the senior alderman. The meetings were public at all levels, but the elections were held by secret ballot.[10]

The size of the representative body corresponded to the size of the settlement, so it had 278 members in Pest and 168 members in Buda. In Pest the administrative reform took place between June 13 and 24, 1848, and the well-known Liberal, Lipót Rottenbiller, became mayor. However, the only other member of the reform opposition in the leadership of the city was Ignác Lángh, the new chief captain of the city. The transformation took place in Buda from May 27, but the new leaders were neither real supporters nor opponents of bourgeois reforms.[11]

Although it had no immediate consequences, it may be worth noting that Prime Minister Bertalan Szemere, (head of the government of Hungary after the declaration of independence in Debrecen on April 14, 1849) issued a decree on June 24 providing that "the municipal authorities of Buda, Pest and Óbuda are to be united and the twin capitals are to be considered one under the name Budapest."[12] By the time this regulation could have been executed, counter-revolutionary Habsburg-Austrian troops were marching in the streets of these cities. On their heels, the imperial officials repealed not only the decrees issued by the Szemere cabinet (considered rebellious) but also those of the preceding Batthyány cabinet, although it had been appointed by King Ferdinand V and was fully "legitimate." By virtue of a provisional decree issued on October 17, 1849, by Habsburg authorities all free royal cities were to be governed by the territorially competent district commanders or the civil district high commissioners. Nominations for the post of mayor were from among the loyal followers of the new era. The appointments were signed by General Julius Jacob Baron Haynau, Commander-in-chief of the imperial troops in Hungary, and by imperial commissioner Baron Karl Geringer. On September 18, 1851, another decree was issued providing that the city councils of Pest and Buda were to be elected for three years with 42 and 30 members, respectively. Their members were to be appointed by the imperial governor. In the 1860s the residents were allowed to elect the members of the city councils, but these were to be confirmed by the reestablished central administrative council (*Consilium Locumtenentiale Hungaricum* or *Helytartótanács*).[13]

Because of defeats suffered in the campaign for Italian unification the young Emperor Francis Joseph I was forced to make significant concessions in home politics. The so-called October Diploma, issued in the autumn of 1860, contained both federal and constitutional elements and made possible the reorganization of the municipal authorities of the royal free cities. Adherence to the achievements of 1848 was shown by the fact that in early 1861 Lipót Rottenbiller, the mayor of the revolutionary era, was reelected. The constitutional spring was, however, followed by an absolutistic autumn. The demands of the Diet meeting in the same year concerning the restoration of the laws of 1848 were rejected by the monarch, so the activities of the new municipal authorities were suspended again. Faithful supporters of Habsburg absolutism returned to Pest once again, although they no longer had unrestricted power. Their mandate was only for the period of the new absolutistic arrangement, considered provisional even by the Court.

The last significant administrative change in the twin cities took place in 1867, at the time of the conclusion of a Compromise between the Habsburgs and Hungary. There were signs of restoration of parliamentary conditions already from 1865, when the central authorities finally permitted the 1848 veteran, Lipót Rottenbiller, to resume his seat as mayor. He was followed by Mór Szentkirályi, head of the newly elected three hundred strong representative body, when the Minister of the Interior of the newly appointed Hungarian government restored the rights of the royal free cities. An outstanding member of the new administration was Chief of Police Elek Thaisz who was to play a significant role in the history of the city.

The general meeting for the reelection of officials held on May 6, 1867, elected six new administrative officials, six deputy clerks, ten junior clerks of the court, six deputy prosecutors, and two archivists, one for the court and one for the council.[14]

The administrative history of Óbuda was much less complicated. In the first half of the period discussed in this chapter the settlement was a royal estate and was led by an inner council headed by the chief justice and controlled by an outer council. In 1840 its superior authority, Pest county, made it a corporate country town. As a result of Act XXIII of 1848 the outer council was replaced by a representative body of seventy-five members. Following the suppression. of the War of Independence the authorities of neo-absolutism took a legally detrimental, but economically and socially timely measure by incorporating Óbuda into the city of Buda as a suburb with a council and a justice of its own. The former estate of the Zichy family had two representatives on the inner council of Buda, the town clerk and the superintendent of the tax office of the Chamber (*Camera Hungarica* or Hungarian Court Chamber, the highest authority on taxes). In 1861, however, it was more important to remedy the grievances than to prepare for the administration of the future metropolis, so the country town of Óbuda regained its independence. The legal status of the settlements changed for the last time two years prior to the unification of the cities. Act XVIII of 1871 made it a corporate town with a mayor at its head.[15]

## Town Planning and Townscape

As we proceed with the history of Budapest and approach modern times, the factors influencing the outward appearance of the city change and conscious townplanning supersedes the spontaneous development of earlier times. The historical heritage of Buda and the economic growth of Pest were supported by the program of Emperor Joseph II (1780–90) for developing provincial capitals and by the efforts of Archduke Joseph (1796–1847) to develop a worthy seat for himself as a palatine. The so-called Project for the "Embellishment of Town" was just as epoch-making as the idea of establishing the "Town Embellishment Committee" independent from the city council of Pest. The funds of the latter having been wasted by the 1810s, only a small part of the project could be realized.[16] The greatest merit of the Committee was that it was able to supervise the

large-scale construction works of these decades, so that Pest became one
of the most beautiful and harmonious neo-classical townscapes in the Reform Era. This came to an end when the cannons of the Habsburg general
Heinrich Hentzi—who, in retaliation against the Hungarian troops besieg-
ing the fort he defended—launched a heavy artillery bombardment of the
city of Pest in May, 1849, causing immense damage to the civilian population and the buildings.

The inner city, just like the city centers of other large cities of the
continent, could not meet the requirements of the day any longer in the
first half of the 19th century. It remained an important administrative,
ecclesiastical, and educational center, but the economic life of the city
shifted to *Lipótváros*. "An endless row of palaces, and what a bustling city,
what a traffic!" These were the words of the Danish author of fairy-tales,
Hans Christian Andersen, when he walked along the Danube on the Pest
side. The rapid increase of the population described in the chapter on
demographic changes was coupled with large-scale construction resulting
inchess-board pattern of streets. "Pest seems to have lined up her palaces
along the Danube just to welcome foreigners in a proper manner," remarked Tullio Dandolo in his guide-book published in Turin.[17] This part
of the city was in fact never called a suburb but an extension of the inner
city. The first towngate to be pulled down was the one at the end of Váci
Street leading to this district. After 1810, palaces of magnates were erected
along *Nádor* (Palatine) Street one after the other, and some of the most
magnificent ones are still standing. Wealthy Greek (Albanian and Macedo-
Wallachian) merchants settled around *Színház* (Theater) Square (today's
Vörösmarty Square), *József nádor* (Palatine Joseph) Square, and the New
Marketplace (today's Elisabeth Square), as well as along *Bálvány* (Idol)
Street (today's October 6 Street), and *Két sas* (Two Eagles) Street (today's
*Sas* [Eagle] Street). The harmony of function and form culminated in the
so-called Tradesmen's Palace at the end of what was probably the most
impressive group of buildings of the district along the *Rakpiac* or Loading
Quay (today's Roosevelt Square). The most significant architectural masterpiece was József Hild's neo-classical hall of Commercial Citizens' Association of Pest (*Pesti Polgári Kereskedelmi Testület*), which played an
important economic role in those days. Later the building became known
as the Lloyd Palace, since it was taken over in the 1850s by the Pester
Lloyd Company, a firm that played an important role in the evolution of
commerce as well as in the consolidation of business ethics.[18]

The other palaces of *Rakpiac* also owed their harmonious façades to the inspiration of József Hild. The Diana Bath and the palaces of the Libaschinszky-Koburg, the Nákó, and the Ullmann families were major contributions to the unique view of the Upper Danube embankment. For the time being, *Lipótváros* could not spread further north, as the New Building (the ill-famed barracks called *Neugebäude* built in 1814) blocked the way. Behind it there were lumberyards up to the line of the present-day *Nagykörút* (Great Boulevard). Beyond *Nagykörút* there were huge tobacco storage facilities owned by the Ullmann family. Then came farmsteads and simple houses with yards connecting *Lipótváros* with the more densely populated *Terézváros*, the population of which consisted mostly of artisans and tradesmen who associated with the inner city more than with the farmers and mostly Slovak day-laborers of *Józsefváros*, employed in the vinyards of *Kőbánya*. The garden-suburb east of today's *Múzeum* Boulevard was built over very slowly, the advantage of which was that there remained plenty of room for the Botanic Gardens of the university, the National Theater, the National Museum, and the National Riding-hall. The situation of the sparsely populated garden-suburb of *Ferencváros* was similar during the first half of the 19th century, though some important changes were just on the brink of realization, namely, parcelling out plots in this area created the future network of streets on both sides of the *Nagykörút* (Great Boulevard).

Although Pest was expanding rapidly, it occupied only one tenth of its officially determined territory bounded by an 18th-century ditch dug for this purpose. The creation of the City Park in 1799, originally called *Stadtwäldchen* or City Grove was meant to bind the quicksand as well as serve as a park and promenade. Large-scale townplanning in this area took place only after 1818. Planting trees beyond the lake and parcelling out the garden-suburb of Hermina Meadow, named after the late daughter of Palatine Joseph, lasted till the 1830s. At the same time, in the vinyards of the area, planted to bind the sand (around doctor Sebestyén Rumbach's medicinal bath called Iron Baths in today's Mihály Munkácsy Street) splendid villas with gardens were built so quickly that by the eve of the revolution the territory had become a fashinable residential area of the well-to-do middle class and of high-ranking officials.[19]

The highway to Vác was straightened and rows of trees were planted along it, so it started to attract settlers, especially among workshop and factory owners. The rapid construction of the highway leading to Soroksár in the south was primarily due to the adjacent military establishments:

depots, hospital, bakery, and silo. All cemeteries were moved beyond the ditch marking the city boundary. The marshes along Üllői Street were drained, and the hog-farms were banished beyond the boundaries of the suburbs. The territory of vinyards at *Kőbánya* (Quarry) and *Újhegy* (New Hill) remained unchanged, but the growing number of winecellars and garden houses were places of recreation for ordinary citizens.[20] Across the fields meandered the *Rákos-patak* (Crab Creek) with the *Paskál*, *Rákos*, and *Ördög* mills operating at times of high water.

Although Buda, the ancient seat of the kings of Hungary, was not wholly dormant during the Reform Era, it developed at a much slower pace than Pest, largely because the economic, social, and intellectual energies of the bourgeois transformation found a wider outlet on the other side of the Danube. In fact, the hilly terrain limited development on the Buda side. What is more, the inhabitants of Buda insisted on preserving their agricultural land, especially their vinyards.[21]

The outline of the Castle District, developed in the 18th century, and also that of *Víziváros* (Watertown) proved to be final. In contrast with the aristocratic character of the hill, the latter district was primarily the home of merchants. During the famous national fairs of Buda crowds in *Fő* (Main) Street covered every square foot of space, and residents turned their houses into stores and shops. Most new houses were built in *Krisztinaváros* (Christinatown), though three large parks or gardens became obstacles in creating continuous settlement in the area.[22] The Horváth Garden was surrounded by high stone walls and was built in the styles of French and sometimes of English gardens of the day. The Buda city council failed to obtain the *Tábornokrét* (General's Meadow, today's *Vérmező* or Bloody Meadow), but they planted a row of trees around it and covered the *Ördögárok* (Devil's Ditch). The War Council was not willing to divest itself of the drill-ground for the time being. A row of villas was built in present-day *Városmajor* (City Manor) Street not only for wealthy families but also for members of the well-to-do middle class like the painter Miklós Barabás.[23]

Visitors from Pest on their way to *Városmajor* often walked through the streets of the village-like *Országút* coming from the pontoon-bridge located near *Deák* Street (then *Nagyhíd* Street). The slowly growing City Park on the Pest side was too far for them. Exotic figures of the East wearing turbans and kaftans were not uncommon in this busy commercial district, as Muslim pilgrims came to visit the northernmost holy place of the Islam faith, the tomb of Gül Baba, dervish of the *Baktashi* Order.

Construction of the city hospital and the hospital of the Sisters of Charity was completed in 1817 as a donation of Royal Councillor István Marczibányi. The order also received the income of the *Császár* (Emperor's) Bath from Marczibányi, so it could treat poor patients free of charge. *Újlak* (New Lodge) remained a small village, and *Tabán*, the largest settlement of vinyard day-laborers, also remained a district of adobes with shingle-roofs. "Just like a Rumelian village on the slopes of the Balkans", a contemporary traveller described the view, indicating that the settlement on the slopes of Gellért Hill and *Naphegy* (Sun Hill) was very different from the future metropolis by the Danube.[24]

The vinyards and cool forests of Buda soon became the favorite places of resort and recreation for citizens from both Buda and Pest. The first real summer residence in neo-classical style was built in 1820 and is marked "*Laszlovszky tusculanuma*" (Laszlovszky's villa) on contemporary maps. Two years later there was also the villa of the Kalmárffy family and a votive chapel dedicated to the Virgin Mary next door. By the 1830s and 1840s rows of villas appeared in *Zugliget* (Hidden Grove), in the grove called *Szépjuhászné* (Beautiful Shepard's Wife), around the restaurant of the same name, and on the slopes of *Svábhegy* (Swabian Hill). In several cases there were also farmsteads around the villas. They, however, did not resemble market-oriented farms but rather archaic imitations of gentry manors. The fashion of that day preferred the lifestyle of noble landowners, which burghers tried to imitate in the valleys of the Buda hills. Small summer restaurants sprang up to cater for holiday-makers. The restaurant called *Isten Szeme* (God's Eye) became renowned because there occured the arrest of Lajos Kossuth on May 5, 1837. (His bronze bust prepared by sculptor István Tóth can still be seen in the place of the one-time restaurant.)

The beauty spots of the Buda Hills have been bearing their present names only since 1847. Royal Councillor Gábor Döbrentei, the famous organizer of literary life, sponsored the idea of replacing German placenames with Hungarian ones already in 1844, and three years later the city council of Buda decided to put the idea into practice. Some new placenames lacked historical authenticity, yet others came from diplomas and deeds of old times (*Kelenföld, Sasad*) or, if invented by Döbrentei himself, were at least inspired by events in the recapture of Buda from the Turks in 1686 and other historical events taking place in the area (*Hunyad-orom, Vérhalom*). Some were metaphrases of German names (*reiche Ried—Gazdagrét* meaning rich meadow). A jolly christening ceremony was held on

June 16 on *Tündérhegy* (Fairy Hill). Wanting to adopt Hungarian ways, even the German residents of the region accepted the new names propagated on printed sheets: *Csatárka, Csillebérc, Kőérberek, Kurucles, Pasarét, Szemlőhegy, Törökvész, Vérhalom, Virányos, Zöldmál,* and *Zugliget* are among the most beautiful names.[25]

Óbuda, a country town of the Chamber (state property), was a quiet place along the Danube till the middle of the 1830s. The last significant event affecting its social life was the large-scale settlement of Jews at the time of the Napoleonic wars giving rise to the construction of a wonderful neo-classic synagogue in 1820–21. The six-story building of the former silk filatory was in ruins and served as a quarry for the neighborhood. The former Trinitarian monastery of Kiscell housed a military depot and barracks. Life began to change in Óbuda when the first docks and workshops of the new shipyard were built on the Little Island (*Kis-sziget*) in 1836. From that time, the flourishing factory played a decisive role in the transformation of the agricultural settlement into an industrial suburb.[26]

The River Danube had always been an important factor in the lives of the settlements on its banks, but now the side-wheelers brought the world and its treasures much nearer to the ford at Aquincum and the slopes of the Gellért Hill. Thus the regulation of the river and the construction of dams and embankments would have been put on the agenda anyway, even without the recurring floods. The floods by themselves did not motivate people to do something about them, not even the one in 1830 which caused immense damage. So another catastrophe occurred in March 1838. The severe winter made the Danube freeze down to the bottom and the ice still blocked the waterway at the northern end of the Csepel Island when the sudden thaw sent a flood down the river. *Víziváros* was the first to be inundated, then the dikes on the Pest side broke in three different places on March 13. *Terézváros*, the inner city, and *Ferencváros* were flooded quickly. The greatest danger was not the water itself but drift-ice which destroyed more than three thousand houses in the three cities and in the neighboring smaller settlements. Barely a quarter of the houses remained intact in Pest, and a mere 12 per cent in Óbuda. The human loss was relatively low, some 151 people died. Brave men did their best to rescue others, Baron Miklós Wesselényi the most famous among them. He saved the most lives and property. In Pest the flood lasted for six days, in Buda a fortnight (though it was restricted to a smaller area there), destroying buildings and assets worth twenty million and two million silver florins, respectively.[27]

The improvement of dams and the regulation of waterways became top priorities thereafter. River control alone was able to forestall such calamities. On the orders of Palatine Joseph a project was prepared by the government for regulation of the river, but the necessary funds were not available in the following decade. From the mid-1840s Count István Széchenyi himself tried to solve the problem as president of the transportation section of the government. However, he proved more successful in promoting the cause of a permanent bridge. This was at first resisted because many believed the piers would block the way of drift-ice and increase the danger of floods.

The idea of a permanent bridge had long been debated. It had been on the agenda of the government ever since the days of Joseph II, and data had been collected regularly on the nature and movement of the river. The project could, however, be put to practice only by a man with vision. Count István Széchenyi explained to members of the Budapest Bridge Association established in 1832 that the bridge would be a remarkable feature of the city, an achievement of modern technology that could not have been built ten years earlier anywhere in the world. At the same time, it would connect the eastern and the western halves of the country providing Buda and Pest with an opportunity for becoming the commercial and administrative center as well as a national capital of Hungary. Moreover, there were egalitarian implication because the nobility would no longer be exempt from paying taxes, since everybody would have to pay bridge-toll. The general sharing in taxation would, in turn, contribute to the creation of a unified bourgeois society. In this way Széchenyi made the bridge the symbol of progress away from a feudal past.[28]

Széchenyi's knowledge of England was invaluable. In George Sina, a Viennese banker of Greek extraction, he found his financier; in William Tierney Clark his designer and in Adam Clark his engineer. Construction started three years after the diet adopted Act XXVI of 1836. The foundation-stone was laid on the Pest side on August 24, 1842 by the Austrian marshal of the Napoleonic wars, Archduke Charles. The chains were installed in the summer of 1848; thus, at the time of the revolution the provisional drive-way was in place for both friends and foes. Seeing the victory of the *Honvéd* army, General Hentzi, who defended the Buda castle against the Hungarians, ordered his soldiers to blow up the bridge on May 21, 1849, but—due to the wisdom of Adam Clark—the demolition expert failed to reach the chain-well. The explosion killed the officer charged with blowing up the bridge, but the bridge itself remained intact.[29] It was ironical that the bridge was inaugurated on November 20, 1849, by General Julius Haynau, the Austrian commander-in-chief, who had participated in the suppression of the Hungarian War of Independence.

Regulations put into force in October, 1838, played an invaluable role in coordinating construction works throughout the city. They were drafted because of the theory that most houses had been damaged in the flood due to poor construction. Some people thought that the city center of Pest should be rebuilt farther away from the river, but this did not occur. It was only at Csepel that the leaders of the village and the estate insisted on moving the settlement to a higher place, giving rise to a regular network of streets around the present-day main square.

The campaigns of the War of Independence were an ordeal for the twin cities. Despite the warnings of Artúr Görgey, Commander-in-chief of the Hungarian army, General Hentzi started bombarding civilian dwellings in the last days of the siege of Buda. He bombarded Pest even though no shot fired at the Castle originated from there. The reconstruction of Pest took place under the supervision of the Habsburg neo-absolutist authorities. In Buda the new imperial administration reconstructed the royal palace in its Baroque splendor in order to symbolize unrestricted royal power (though Emperor Francis Joseph I rarely stayed in it, and it was inhabited mainly by his uncle, Archduke Albrecht, the governor). The Citadel built on Gellért Hill symbolized oppression. This fort, called by Nándor Borostyáni the Hungarian Bastille, was finished in 1854 and was designed to check possible Pest rebellions. Since it was not a modern fortress in a truely military sense, its masters relied on it for psychological effect.[30]

Political oppression could, however, not change the fact that the city and its region became the center of the national economy as a result of economic and political developments in the Reform Era. The leaders of the Bach regime had to accept the liberation of the serfs promulgated by the laws of 1848. So it became evident to everyone after the first dark years of fear that Pest-Buda was to remain the heart of the country. The City Embellishment Committee ceased to exist and was not replaced by an operative body that could have dealt with urban planning and exercize control as required by the developing metropolis. Such a body was set up only after the Compromise: in March, 1870 the Municipal Board of Public Labor was established and headed by Prime Minister Gyula Andrássy himself to organize and control the development of the Hungarian capital from the highest post of executive power. In his younger years Andrássy had learnt municipal politics from the great István Széchenyi. He brought about this promising institution three years before the unification of the three parts of the capital in the hope of overcoming particularism and contributing to the rise of this rival of Vienna.[31]

From September 1855 on traffic was greatly accelerated by the tunnel under Castle Hill. The carts and carriages crossing the Chain Bridge did not have to go around the Castle Hill any longer but could drive directly to the highway leading to Székesfehérvár through the tunnel made in the previous year and widened into a public road. The other significant construction work of the decade was the completion of the paved embankments of the Danube. Experts had suggested that the threat of silting could be minimized by increasing the flow of water, so the river-bed was narrowed by the new embankments. This produced a relatively wide strip of land along the river filled up with the surplus stone resulting from tunnel drilling. The new plots on this strip of land became the most expensive ones in the city and the money paid by the new owners to the city covered not only the expenses of paving the embankments but produced high benefits for the city council. The sums were so high that they muted the criticism of a public opposed to the settlement of wealthy foreigners. The plots were finally won by Hungarian institutions enjoying the confidence of the public: the Exchange, the First Hungarian General Insurance Company (*Első Magyar Általános Biztosító*), Hotel Hungária, and the Thonet family. (The lot bought by the latter had been reserved for the new National Theater. The price the family paid for it was used for building the Opera in *Sugárút* [Avenue, presently Andrássy Avenue]).[32]

The new row of houses along the embankment on the Pest side built in eclectic styles gradually displaced the neo-classical look of the city created by Palatine Joseph, though the fatal blow was dealt to the remnants of the Hild era only by the Second World War and subsequent "Socialist" architecture. There was only a short Romantic period between the eclectic and neo-classical periods as a consequence partly of the belated arrival of British Gothic revival in Central Europe, and partly due to the fact that neo-classic interiors were accepted by the public of Pest and Gothic elements manifested themselves mostly in exterior motifs and window-frames. The buildings that deserve to be mentioned are the Pekáry House built by the architect Ferenc Brein, the Unger House designed by Miklós Ybl on *Múzeum* Boulevard, the Pichler House designed by Ferenc Wieser on St Stephen Square, the Hermina Chapel of Joseph Hild in the City Park, and the castle-like building of the one-time Buda High School (today's Ferenc Toldy Grammar School) designed by art teacher Johann Petschnig, in the courtyard of which a small mortar signalled noon every day until 1942. These remarkable masterpieces are today surrounded by eclectic buildings. The peak of Hungarian Romantic architecture is the Concert Hall (*Vigadó*) designed by Frigyes Feszl, combining Eastern and ancient Hungarian motifs.

The remains of neo-Gothic architecture are railings in dark staircases and one along the Danube on the Pest side also designed by Feszl. Eclectic architecture imitating Parisian and Viennese patterns increased the number of houses in Pest by 29 per cent between 1853 and 1872. Modern technology could be detected in railway stations, stores, warehouses, and factories where formerly unthinkably large expanses were spanned and strange shapes appeared due to the use of concrete. The eclectic style of Ybl also applied Renaissance elements as manifested, for example, in the palaces of the Esterházy and the Károlyi families in present-day Pushkin Street, in a great number of blocks of flats, and in his masterpiece, the Main Customs Office (*Fővámház*) today housing the University of Economics.[33]

The construction of public utilities was also a touchstone in the course of the creation of a unified metropolis, and the outcome was promising. The authorities of Pest, Buda, and Óbuda signed the first contracts with a company of investors from Vienna and Trieste in 1855 and subsequently built gas-works producing 4.5 million cubic meters of gas for nearly 50,000 lamps in the streets and households in the three cities a year before unification. Watermains were constructed first in Buda. The filtrated water of the Danube was pumped up to the eight common wells of the Castle from the Chain Bridge first by a treadmill and, from 1856 onward, by Adam Clark's steam engine. The first provisional waterworks of Pest were wells bored near the site of the present parliament building. The mains supplied 127 streets and squares with water by the end of 1868. Until the unification of the city several new wells and large storage ponds at Kőbánya were added to the system. The modernization of drainage , however, was still in the planning stage and the issue remained unresolved until several cholera epidemics persuaded the city fathers in the period following its unification to build collecting mains parallel to the Danube and a pumping station to transfer their contents to the river south of Budapest.

Other technical achievements caused fast improvements. Between 1868 and 1872 Pest alone spent 2.5 million *forints* on paving the streets or covering them with asphalt. This made traffic easier for horse-drawn omnibuses, but laying tracks finally proved indispensable. The first regular horse-car was launched on August 1, 1866 from the present-day *Kálvin* (Calvin) Square toward Újpest via *Kiskörút* (Little Boulevard) and the *Váci* Street. The significant income made it possible to build new lines on the right bank of the Danube as well. As early as 1869 one could take a horse-car to Óbuda. In 1870 an extraordinary vehicle was built to take passengers up to the Castle. On the initiative of István Széchenyi's younger son, Ödön, a funicular railway was built connecting the Buda abutment of the Chain Bridge with the royal palace.[34]

Moreover, Count Széchenyi was forward-looking in promoting the establishment of fire departments in Pest. In the 1850s the company had only three old water-engines, so the bigger workshops and factories had to arrange for their own fire protection. Based on his English experiences, in 1862 the Count suggested that a voluntary fire department be organized. The authorities of Habsburg neo-absolutism were, however, afraid of creating a para-military organization and gave their consent only on the eve of the Compromise. In the new situation created by the Compromise a professional staff could be authorized (also suggested by Széchenyi). In January, 1870, the voluntary fire brigade started its work at the fire department in the inner city. One month later professional firemen set up their department on the premises of the inner city Parish Church. They had to intervene on fifty-five occasions in the first year and one hundred and three times the following year.

Public health was probably the most backward aspect of city life in Pest-Buda. The housing shortage was acute owing to massive immigration into the city. Many were forced to live in overcrowded tenements, most of which were erected in neighborhoods poorly provided with sewer mains and in generally unsanitary conditions. There were no more than 20,000 beds in public hospitals on the eve of the unification. Although there were a few national institutions (for example the mental hospital on *Lipótmező* or Leopold Meadow), the extension of the out-patient departments was the physicians' primary contribution to the improvement of public health. Not only money was lacking, but also a healthy outlook was badly needed. Instead of enacting the protective measures ordered by the administration but found too expensive, even Mayor Lipót Rottenbiller preferred visiting cholera patients in the *Rókus* hospital, to demonstrate the non-infectious nature of the disease, rather than admit the need for isolation wards. A royal commissioner was needed to set up the wards and take the necessary measures.

The belt of villages around the city became organic parts of the metropolis. Demands of the city for manpower, food, and raw materials affected the economic and social character of these settlements. Since their livelihood depended increasingly on the city, they became suburbs with a quasi-metropolitan appearance. Their most important function was to supply the city with food through self-regulating market mechanisms. City authorities could be sure that their marketplaces would attract farmers and guarantee an adequate food supply. Most private slaughter-houses of Pest were closed down in 1863 and only thirty-two were allowed to receive animals after that. Even this measure was meant to be provisional and a central slaughter-house was planned, mainly on the German model, along *Soroksári* Street in the southern sector of the city. The opening ceremony was held on July 27, 1872, and city aldermen were pleased with the modern cold-storage, paved roads, and the conspicuous water tower, which became the symbol of the institution.[35]

In six decades three discrete provincial towns fused into a modern metropolis which became the capital city of Hungary. This development was partly random, partly planned. The godfather of the new city was István Széchenyi who recorded his relationship to the evolving city in the last chapter of his book *Világ* (Light), the second volume of his trilogy. Quoting from a letter by an "Englishman" he wrote: "The name of your capital should be changed to Budapest, and the new name will sound just as familiar in a few years, or even months, as Bucharest. This way two cities, not always on good terms today, would become united. What an advantage this would be for them, what a flourishing capital they would make in no time. Especially if the diet would meet not in Pozsony on the western border and so far away from Transylvania, but in the heart of the country."[36] His advice was accepted by the nation and the city. Paragraph 1 of Act XXXVI of 1872 states: "Buda and Pest, royal free capital cities, as well as the borough of Buda and the *Margit sziget* (Margaret Island) having been carved out of the county of Pest—will be united into a single municipality under the name of Buda-Pest, the capital city."[37]

## Society in Change

Besides demographical changes, the changes in administration, and the evolution of infrastructure it behooves us to characterize the urban society behind the inert statistics and archival materials. No sources, however, are

available from the first part of the century to cover the financial and occupational stratification of the population. All we know about Buda is that
the ratio of aristocrats, senior officials, army officers, and members of the
professions increased significantly between the late 18th century and the
1820s. At the same time, the ratio of vinyard owners and artisans had
diminished. Among the artisans, members of guilds were outnumbered by
skilled workers without certificates and not belonging to any guild. Also
the number of day-laborers increased greatly in Buda in the Reform Era.

More reliable taxpayer data are available about Pest. According to a
record of 1840, the ratio of tradesmen increased from 10 per cent at the
beginning of the century to 17 per cent, while that of artisans decreased
from 33.3 per cent to 25.5 per cent in the same period. This piece of
information seems to contradict what has been said of the development of
handicraft industry in the city, but journeymen, most of whom were skilled
workers without certification, have to be taken into consideration. They
were identical in numbers with the guildsmen in 1840 (so their number
had doubled in the first four decades of the century), and their numbers
taken together showed a five per cent increase. Some indirect data reveal
that the officials and the intelligentsia constituted six per cent of the male
population of the city on the eve of the revolution compared to the one
per cent at the beginning of the century. On the basis of similarly indirect
calculations one can establish that nearly five per cent of the inhabitants
of Pest belonged to the nobility during the Reform Era.

The religious character of Budapest underwent significant changes during this period. Municipal statistics reveal that although the rate of Catholics had been decreasing slightly in the first part of the century, they still
constituted 70 per cent of churchgoers in 1847. The rate of Orthodox be-
lievers decreased from 2.4 per cent at the beginning of the century to 1
per cent by the mid-century, the causes of which will be discussed later.
The rate of Lutherans increased greatly, from 0.65 per cent to 3.37 per
cent, and that of Calvinists from 0.42 to 1.56 per cent. The increase of the
Jewish population is more significant. In 1806 they made up 5.23 per cent
of the inhabitants in Pest, but already in 1847 reached 12.96 per cent. Their
rate was the highest in Óbuda (41.4 per cent in 1813, and 37 per cent in
1847). The drop among Catholics continued in Pest between 1857 and
1869 (from 72.5 per cent in 1857 to 68.28 per cent in 1869), the ratio of
Lutherans stagnated around 6 per cent, but the Orthodox fell to a mere 0.5
per cent. The ratio of Calvinists grew from 3.18 to 5.2 per cent in the
period, and of Jews from 17.41 to 19.64 per cent, though their increase

was as remarkable as earlier. Many of them must have moved over from Óbuda, since the Jewish population there decreased significantly in this decade, from 31.5 to 18.4 per cent.[38]

Owing to the significance of the Jewish population in the economic and social history of the twin cities it is essential to describe the development of their community in our period. While there were only 14 Jewish families in Pest in 1787, their numbers rose to 549 by 1820. The heads of 354 families dealt with commerce. In 1833 the number of Jewish families was already 1,111 and that of the heads of families dealing with commerce was 716. Their settlement in the twin cities accelerated in the 1840s, as Act XXIX of 1840 made it easier for them to move into cities in general. The increase of their number in the country was most dynamic between 1825 and 1869 (two and a half times higher than at the beginning—190,000 and 542,000, respectively). 8.3 per cent of all Jews in the country (44,890 persons) lived in Budapest in those days.[39]

The role of the Jewish inhabitants of Pest-Buda is relatively well-known. Originally restricted to the very tiresome and poorly paid trade of agricultural produce and by-products like leather, wool, feathers, the Jewish population was aided by the growing demands of industry for raw material. Their trade became a major source of the accumulation of commercial capital. The prosperity of their similarly traditional financial activity was also due to bourgeois development and the growing demand for credit. Jewish tradesmen and financiers concentrated in cities and became members of the leading circles of the evolving upper middle-class in Hungary. Experts emphasize[40] that it was their bourgeois aspect rather than their Jewishness that played the decisive role in this development. The old bourgeoisie insisted on its traditional and privileged forms of commerce and industry based on guilds. They were unable to fulfill the requirements of modern industrial methods as Hungary forged ahead on the road toward capitalism. Further, the process of embourgeoisement and the steps toward an equality of rights in economic, political, and religious life alike widened the range of Jews' possibilities of self-assertion and their adoption of bourgeois manners. So by the mid-19th century, i.e., within a single generation, the economic and social weight of the Jewry grew immensely in Hungary, especially in Pest-Buda, the hub of the developing national market.

The Jewish community of Pest arrived from three directions. Some came from state-owned or private large estates and were likely to continue in the business as wholesalers of cash-crops. Assisted by their business connections, they arrived from the Bohemian and Moravian provinces,

Austria, and Eastern Prussia. The third group arrived from the direction of Poland and Ukraine. Their culture and life-style differed greatly from the other two groups.[41]

The highly stratified Jewish community of Pest first settled mainly in the southern part of the northern suburb called *Terézváros*. In 1882 this part of the district became independent and was named after Queen Elizabeth (wife of Francis Joseph I). Tolerated by the suburban authorities or bearing a temporary residence permit, the Jews of Pest and other Jews visiting the fairs established their synagogue first in a modest room of the so-called Hauszlir House of *Király* (King) Street, then in an apartment rented in the huge apartment building of the Barons Orczy. This building on the corner of *Király* Street and *Károly* (Charles) Boulevard represents an interesting facet of Budapest's history. It had 48 apartments with 142 rooms and kitchens, and 37 vaulted cellars and was the home of 284 tenants. It housed also two synagogues, a "Russian" bath, three restaurants, a dance hall, a café, a slaughter-house, and shops selling groceries, clothing, and tomb-stones. According to rumors of the day, this building, popularly known as *Judenhof* because of the great number of Jewish tenants, brought one gold coin for the owner every hour. In a relatively large room on the first floor of the left wing the Jewish community furnished their new synagogue in 1820. As the number of the faithful grew rapidly, they were forced to open a new one with 585 chairs on two floors. This larger synagogue served the community for more than forty years, until a new house of God was built on Rumbach Sebestyén Street.[42]

Religious reforms intending to modernize rituals and meet the demands of linguistic assimilation were present also among the Pest Jewry. This was the attitude of the congregation belonging to the so-called "Temple of Cult" in the Orczy Building. It introduced the choir, the sermon, the separate service for women, and the shortened ritual. With its economic and social weight as a background, it was this congregation that built one of the main ornaments of Budapest and the largest and most beautiful synagogue of Central Europe in *Dohány* Street, on a plot owned by the Baldácsy family, between 1854 and 1859.[43]

Another ethnic group in old Pest were the Greeks. The term was broadly used to include all those of Greek Orthodox faith. They came from the Ottoman Empire to the Habsburg countries attracted by opportunities in commerce. With their wealth, they played an important role in the economic and social life of the city. However, when the Greek freedom fight was successful and Ottoman control of the Balkans declined, substantial numbers returned to their homeland. Those who remained assimilated with the Hungarians. In our days only their church facing the Danube on the Pest side, the largest Greek Orthodox church in Hungary, reminds us of this element of society.[44]

The decrease in the ratio of the Orthodox denomination was, therefore, not merely a religious fact, but indicated also the decrease of a separate ethnic group and the assimilation of Macedo-Wallachians, and of the Hungarian Serbs called *rác*—living in Pest mostly in the inner city and in the *Tabán*. In the six decades discussed in this chapter, the Hungarian character of Pest-Buda gradually accelerated. In the middle of the century the Hungarians and the Germans dominated, and it is interesting to note that the Hungarians were in a minority only in Buda. The society of Pest was virtually evenly balanced. Social stratification largely coincided with ethnic distribution. The aristocracy, high-ranking officials and significant members of the intelligentsia were Hungarian, while the artisans were generally German, though there was a poor but powerful layer of Hungarian artisans as well. The same taxonomy applies to commerce, where there were several other elements besides the German, for example, the Jews also speaking German in those years. Vegetable gardens around Pest were mainly in the hands of Germans and Slovaks, while the vinyards of Buda were owned mostly by Germans and Serbs. Three quarters of the industrial population were German, and the rest was Hungarian and Slovak. Slovaks comprised the largest segment of women servants and day-laborers.

The large-scale settlement of newcomers in the city in the 1850s altered the ratios. At first sight, the data are surprising, since only the Calvinists can be considered definitely Hungarian among the newcomers. As compared to 1851, the ratio of Hungarians within the population seems to decrease slightly on the eve of unification. At the same time, contemporaries maintained that the city was irrevocably on the road to becoming a Hungarian city. The explanation is that the traditional German population of Pest-Buda and the Slovaks arriving in several waves assimilated rapidly, involving serious political consequences.[45]

Let us project the above described social structure to the map of the city. The wealthiest people lived in the inner city and in *Lipótváros*. They were mostly landlords, wholesale dealers, members of the greater bourgeoisie and the middle class. The streets north of the *Neugebäude* (*Újépület*) were inhabited also by workers and those in the southern part of the Inner City by members of the petty bourgeoisie. In the inner part of *Terézváros* the middle class mixed with the petty bourgeoisie, while the latter shared their blocks of apartments with workers in the outer section of the district, and also in *Józsefváros* and *Ferencváros*. This territorial segregation, aggravated by the fact that the public buildings and institutions representing state life were also situated in *Lipótváros*, became symbolic also in the social and political life of the city. The mass demonstrations at the end of the century aimed at taking over the bourgeois districts and to defend the workers' districts in case of a counterattack. The castle district of Buda was the home of officials and owners of vinyards. Those who had no room left in the overcrowded district occupied mostly *Krisztinaváros*. The *Tabán* was occupied by less wealthy vine-growers and also by a great number of derelicts. In *Víziváros* and *Országút* (Highway) there were tradesmen, artisans, and vine-growers. This latter group could be found also in Óbuda in ever decreasing numbers, but the district was characterized more by the growing number of industrial workers who tended to become members of the petty bourgeoisie.[46] This district was also called "the Hungarian Lyon" owing to the great number of textile mills there.

## Pest-Buda as the Cultural and Political Center of the Country

Even though the most significant factor in the development of Pest as capital of Hungary was its location as a major national market, its political and cultural institutions served as magnets attracting population. University professors represented a stratum of highly qualified intellectuals since the end of the previous century, and the two secondary schools (that of the Piarist fathers in Pest and that of the Jesuits in Buda, also turning Piarist in 1828) included outstanding teachers. There were several primary schools to supply the secondary schools with students. The third secondary school was opened by the Lutherans in Pest, in 1823. It accepted pupils belonging to other denominations as well, even Orthodox and Jewish children. The versatile development of the system of education was an indication of how well the city fulfilled this important function. A so-called *Ipartanoda* (Higher Technical School) named after Palatine Joseph opened its gates in 1846. From 1856 it functioned as a polytechnic college, and from 1871 as an independent university. The first teachers' college and a college for kindergarten teachers were established in 1844. Music was taught in both the singing schools and the school of music at the Pest-Buda Association for Musicians (*Pest-budai Hangászegyesület*), and the first academy of art called the First Hungarian Academy of Painting (*Első Magyar Festészeti Akadémia*) was opened by Jacob Marastoni in 1846. The military academy named *Ludovicum* after the wife of King Francis was built by Mihály Pollack in 1836, but instruction within its walls did not begin until 1872.[47]

An intellectual center requires outstanding libraries and collections. In the period discussed in this chapter the University Library, the National Library, and the National Museum fulfilled this requirement. In 1832 the Jankovich library, and in 1846 the Horvát collection containing together nearly 60,000 books, manuscripts, objects, and diplomas were added to the national collections. Third in importance was the collection of the Learned Society (*Tudós Társaság*) founded by József Teleki, taken over by the Academy in 1837. The library of the Greek Orthodox community of Pest called *Bibliotheca Graeco Vlachicae Pestiensis Communitatis* was opened in 1824, and two years later the *Matica Srpska* opened its library thanks to Száva Tököli. The first picture gallery of Pest was based on paintings donated by László Pyrker, Archbishop of Eger, in 1846 and exhibited in the National Museum. The collection was exceptionally rich in Italian paintings purchased by the archbishop when he was Patriarch of Venice. The National Picture Gallery (*Nemzeti Képcsarnok*) was launched in the building of the National Museum in the same year and aimed to collect the best of contemporary art. The famous *Vándorló oláh család* (A Migrant Wallachian Family) by Miklós Barabás was, for example, donated by the Home Guard of Pest (*polgárőrség*). The Pest Art Association (*Pesti Műegylet*) was founded to organize exhibitions, and its greatest concern was how to harmonize its members' demand for popular art from abroad to satisfy daily demands and their wish to support quality national historical art.[48]

Pest had been the national center of literary life since the end of the 18th century even though all writings were subjected to censorship. The burghers of the city, the *honoratiores* or non-noble intellectuals, or at least those who supported the assimilation of non-Hungarians and the spread of liberal ideals constituted a public wide enough to support writers. The most outstanding writers could support themselves by writing alone. The printing press of János Tamás Trattner published several works by outstanding Hungarian writers like Gábor Dayka, Ferenc Kazinczy, or Miklós Zrínyi from 1813 onward for a public supplied formerly mainly with books in German. The writers of Pest fought alongside Kazinczy for creating a standard literary language, and the leading role of the city in Hungarian

literary life was gradually acknowledged. When István Marczibányi provided in his will for a prize to reward works serving the development of
linguistics and the cultivation of the Hungarian language, outstanding representatives of the Hungarian aristocracy, led by Palatine Joseph, appeared
at the ceremony to pay their respect to scholars and poets like György
Fejér and Sándor Kisfaludy.

The year 1817 was a milestone in the literary life of Pest. A literary
magazin edited by György Fejér and entitled *Tudományos Gyüjtemény*
(Scholarly Collection) was launched, and Károly Kisfaludy, the leader of
the new Hungarian literature, settled in the city. When, at a carnival meeting held by the printer Trattner in 1821, the enthusiastic writers of Pest
pooled their resources for a new almanach dedicated purely to fiction, they
entrusted the editorship of the *Aurora* literary journal (1821–37) to Kisfaludy, a former army officer, now famous for his successes on stage. His
periodical published the works of the generation of young romantic writers
like Mihály Vörösmarty, József Bajza, Ferenc Schedel (later Toldy), and
Gergely Czuczor. On June 10, 1826, Pál Szemere and Ferenc Kölcsey
joined Kisfaludy and his circle in Szemere's home in Pest, uniting all
outstanding figures of Hungarian romanticism in one camp. In the beginning they had literature foremost on their minds, but they soon moved to
promote the cause of liberal political reform. The members of the Aurora
Circle played a significant role in preparing the public for the idea of a
learned society, so when Count István Széchenyi put it into practice, it
was welcomed by the audience of Pest.

The Society, called the Academy of Sciences from the early 1840s,
was led, among others, by Bajza, Vörösmarty, and Toldy, similar to the
one founded in 1831 in memory of Károly Kisfaludy, who met an untimely
death. The Kisfaludy Society became the leading institution of literary life
and supported *Athenaeum*, the new periodical of Bajza and his friends.
The role of the periodical in spreading the idea of reform diminished with
time and was succeeded by Lajos Kossuth's political daily *Pesti Hírlap*
from 1841 on.[49]

The theater was the other form of art to propagate the causes of national
culture and of bourgeois development. The period between 1812 and 1847
was the golden age of the German Theater of Pest, with its affiliate, the
Castle Theater of Buda. It was damaged first by the flood, then by a fire
in 1847, and finally by the bombs of General Hentzi. If the public had
been more supportive, the theater might have survived these calamities,
but the Hungarian Theater of Pest, established in 1837 in the former

Beleznay Gardens at the corner of today's Rákóczi Street and *Múzeum* Boulevard in 1837, had greater appeal for the middle-class public eager to assimilate. The Round Bastion (*Rondella*) having been pulled down in 1815, Hungarian-language performances were held in Pest and Buda only by· occasional visiting companies throughout the period. In 1833 part of the Hungarian troupe of Kassa (today's Kosice) came to play permanently in the Castle Theater and formed the Theatrical Company of Buda (*Budai Színjátszó Társaság*) led by János Simontsits, Chief Constable of Óbuda. Four years later, actors of this company became leading artists of the Hungarian Theater of Pest, nationalized under Act XLIV of 1840 and renamed the National Theater.[50]

That Pest became the real political center of modern Hungary was undoubtedly the work of Count István Széchenyi. His was the first comprehensive program to lead the country out of feudalism toward modern bourgeois economy and society, and he assigned an important role to the twin cities in this process. He maintained that the country needed a center where all forces of change could converge, where exchange of views would encourage a critical public opinion focused upon the future. Among his targets were: horse-races to promote horse-breeding but, beyond its economic and military significance to attract the aristocracy and the wealthy, and to create increasing opportunities for the "exchange of ideas". A casino was needed, i.e., a club as an ideal setting for gathering political information and of forming opinion in political matters. The Danube was to be regulated at the Iron Gates and make it suitable to connect the West with Eastern Europe and the Balkans via Pest, that could thus become a grandiose "distributor" of material and spiritual goods. A bridge was also necessary to break the medieval isolation of the cities and turn them into a unified city, the capital of Hungary. A ship-yard was needed in Óbuda, a cylinder mill, a National Pantheon on Gellért Hill, a National Theater by the Danube, and so on. An endless flow of visions, some of which were realized by the Count himself, some by others later, while only few of them failed to materialize.[51]

Széchenyi considered the creation of real public opinion one of the most important prerequisites for making Pest-Buda a legitimate capital city. Paradoxically, when this public opinion manifested itself as a true political force, it turned against him and took sides with Lajos Kossuth and his followers in their controversy with "the greatest Hungarian". It became, however, obvious in those years that Pest, in spite of the Diet still hanging on in Pozsony, had become the real political center of the country.

# Notes

1. Lajos Nagy, "Budapest története 1790–1848" [The history of Budapest, 1790–1848], in László Gerevich, ed., *Budapest története* [History of Budapest], vol. 3, *Budapest története a török kiűzésétől a márciusi forradalomig* [History of Budapest from the expulsion of the Turks to the March Revolution], ed. Domokos Kosáry (Budapest, 1975), 264, 275, 287, 298, and 373–374; Károly Vörös, "Pest-Budától Budapestig 1849–1873" [From Pest-Buda to Budapest, 1849–1873], in László Gerevich, ed., *Budapest története*, vol. 4, *Budapest története a márciusi forradalomtól az őszirózsás forradalomig* [History of Budapest from the March Revolution to the October Revolution], ed. Károly Vörös (Budapest, 1978), 185, 187. The uncertainty of the data referring to this period is reflected in the discrepancy between pages 264 and 374 in Nagy and the numerical error on page 185 in Vörös. In making the chart I made use also of Anton Jankovich, *Pesth und Ofen mit ihren Einwohnern* (Ofen, 1838), 94–111; Josef Vincent Haeufler, *Buda-Pest (Historisch-topografische Skizzen von Ofen und Pest und deren Umgebungen)* (Pest, 1854), 52–66; Franz Schams, *Vollständige Beschreibung der königlichen Freystadt Pest in Ungern* (Pest, 1821), 104-106; Jos[ef] And[reas] von Dorffinger, *Wegweiser für fremde und Einheimische durch die königl[iche] Freystadt Pesth* ([Pest], 1827), 25–27; and "Pest és Buda népességszáma különböző források alapján" [The population of Pest and Buda in various sources], Appendix, in Gábor Preisich, *Budapest város-építésének története Buda visszavételétől a kiegyezésig* [History of town-planning in Budapest from the recapture of Buda to the Compromise] (Budapest, 1960).

2. Kosáry, ed., op. cit., 374.

3. György Kövér, *Iparosodás agrárországban* [Industrialization in an agrarian country] (Budapest, 1982), 15, 18; György Szabad, "Az önkényuralom kora (1849–1867)" [The age of neo-absolutism, 1849–1867], in *Magyarország története 1848-1890* [History of Hungary, 1848–1867], ed. Endre Kovács (Budapest, 1979), vol. 1, 555–557.

4. Dorffinger, op. cit., 563–564; Vörös, ed., op. cit., 186.

5. Emile Levasseur, *Les populations urbaines en France comparées ŕ celles de l'etranger* (Paris, 1887), quoted by Domokos Kosáry in his introduction to Kosáry, ed., op. cit., 9.

6. For the chart and further data on immigration see Vörös, op. cit., 185–186.

7. Kosáry, ed., op. cit., 300, 303; Vörös, ed., op. cit., 188-189; Ernő Lakatos, *Budapestkörnyék 1848-ban* [Budapest's vicinity in 1848], in: *Tanulmányok Budapest múltjából* [Studies from Budapest's past] (Budapest, 1957), vol. 12, 316-323.

8. József Flaxmayer, *Budapest közigazgatási szervezete és alkalmazottai 1686-től 1872-ig* [The administrative structure of Budapest and its employees from 1686 to 1872] (Budapest, 1936), 35–42, 47–48; Lajos Schmall, *Adalékok Budapest székes főváros történetéhez* [Data on the history of the capital city of Budapest] (Budapest, 1899), vol. 1, 1–140.

9. *Kossuth Lajos az utolsó rendi országgyűlésen 1847/48* [Lajos Kossuth at the last feudal Diet in 1847–48], ed. István Barta (Budapest, 1951), 546-547.

10. Dezső Márkus, ed., *Magyar törvénytár, 1836–1868. évi törvényczikkek* [Hungarian law code, articles from the years 1836–1868] (Budapest, 1896), 246–248.

11. Spira György, "A forradalmi ország szíve" [The heart of the revolutionary country], in Vörös, ed., op. cit., 48–51.

12. Ibid., 101.

13. Vörös, ed., op. cit., 128–133.

14. Ibid., 251–253.

15. Flaxmayer, op. cit., 139–160.

16. Kosáry, ed., op. cit., 263.

17. Both authors quoted in Gyula Antalffy, *Reformkori magyar városrajzok* [Sketches of Hungarian towns in the Age of Reform] (Budapest, 1982), 196–197.

18. Mihály Pásztor, *A százötvenéves Lipótváros* [The hundred and fifty-year-old Leopoldtown] (Budapest, 1940), 66–68, 117–121, 142–151; for neoclassical town planning in general see Anna Zádor, *Klasszicista Pest* [The neoclassical Pest] (Budapest, 1993).

19. Kosáry, ed., op. cit., 266–271.

20. For the cemeteries see Jolán Fejér, *Budapest székesfőváros temetőinek története* [History of cemeteries in capital city of Budapest] (Budapest, 1933), 83–90; for Kőbánya see Schams, op. cit., 100–103, and György Szalai, *Kőbánya története* [The history of Kőbánya] (Budapest, 1970), 35–36.

21. Kosáry, ed., op. cit., 274–277.

22. Éva L. Gál, "A Krisztinaváros topográfiája (1770–1872)" [Topography of Christinatown, 1770–1872], in *Tanulmányok Budapest múltjából* [Studies from Budapest's past] (Budapest, 1972), vol. 19, 196–207.

23. Zoltán Banner, ed., *Barabás Miklós önéletrajza* [Autobiography of Miklós Barabás] (Cluj-Napoca, 1985), 140.

24. Kosáry, ed., op. cit., 281–282; Dezső Schuler, *Adatok a Tabán történetéhez és rendezéséhez* [Data on the history and town planning of Tabán) (Budapest, 1934), 10–23.

25. For the villas see Albert Gárdonyi, "A budai hegyvidék első nyaralótelepei" [The first summer resorts of the Buda Hills], in *Tanulmányok Budapest múltjából* (Budapest, 1933), vol. 2, 162–180; for the christening ceremony see *A budai hegyek és dűlők elnevezése az 1847. évi Június 17-én tartott közgyűlés határozata szerint* [The names of Buda hills and fields according

to the decision of the general meeting of the city council on June 17, 1847] (Buda, 1847); László Siklóssy, *Svábhegy* [Swabian Hill] (Budapest, 1929), 10–11, 54–60.

26. Kosáry, ed., op. cit., 287–288.

27. Károly Németh, ed., *A pest-budai árvíz 1838-ban* [The flood in Pest-Buda in 1838] (Budapest, 1938), 15–71, 105, and 194–216.

28. László Csorba, *Széchenyi István* [István Széchenyi] (Budapest, 1991), 86–87, 90–93, 105–107, and 121–124.

29. Spira, op. cit., 94.

30. Lóránt Radnai, *A Citadella* [The Citadel] (Budapest, 1963), 14–22.

31. László Siklóssy, *A Fővárosi Közmunkák Tanácsa története. Hogyan épült fel Budapest? 1870–1930* [The history of the Municipal Board of Public Works. How Budapest was built, 1870–1930] (Budapest, 1931), 80–95.

32. Haeufler, op. cit., 266; Siklóssy, op. cit., 59–62.

33. Vörös, ed., op. cit., 192–203; László Gerő, *Pest-Buda építészete az egyesítéskor* [Architecture in Pest-Buda around the unification of the city] (Budapest, 1973), 117–196.

34. Mihály Pásztor, *A közvilágítás alakulása Budapesten* [Street-lighting in Budapest] (Budapest, 1930), 83–109; Gyula Gerlóczy and Géza Dulácska, eds., *Budapest és környéke természetrajzi, orvosi és közművelődési leírása* [Budapest and its environment from the aspects of natural history, health, and culture] (Budapest, 1879), vol. 3, 34–87.

35. Vörös, ed., op. cit., 207–217.

36. István Széchenyi, *Világ, vagyis felvilágosító töredékek némi hiba és előítéletek eligazítására* [Light, or informative fragments about the correction of some mistakes and prejudices] (Pest, 1831), 509.

37. Quoted in Károly Vörös, *Egy világváros születése* [The birth of a metropolis] (Budapest, 1973), 96.

38. Kosáry, ed., op. cit., 378–381; Vörös, ed., op. cit., 240.

39. László Berza, et al., *Budapest lexikon* [Budapest encyclopedia] (Budapest, 1993), vol. 2, 666; Péter Újvári, ed., *Magyar zsidó lexikon* [Hungarian Jewish Lexicon] (Budapest, 1929), 153; Vera Bácskai, *A vállalkozók előfutárai* [The forerunners of enterpreneurs] (Budapest, 1989), 18; Walter Pietsch, "A zsidók bevándorlása Galíciából és a magyar zsidóság" [Jewish immigration from Galicia and the Hungarian Jewry], Valóság 21, no. 11 (1988).

40. György Szabad, "A polgári jogegyenlőség elleni támadás és kudarca a század végi Magyarországon" [Attack against civic rights and its failure at the end of the nineteenth century in Hungary], *Társadalmi Szemle* 37, nos. 8–9 (1982), 70–71.

41. Anikó Gazda, "A magyarországi zsinagógák ismertetése megyék szerint és a budapesti zsinagógák" [The synagogues of Hungary according to counties and the synagogues of Budapest], in László Gerő, ed., *Magyarországi zsinagógák* [Synagogues of Hungary] (Budapest, 1989), 223.

42. For the Viennese models see Hugo Gold, *Geschichte der Juden in Wien* (Wien, 1966), 27–29; see also Tamás Raj, *Budapest—A Dohány utcai zsinagóga* [Budapest—The synagogue of Dohány Street) (Budapest, 1984).

43. Péter Buza, *Pest-budai történetek* [Stories from Pest-Buda] (Budapest, n.d.), 99; Zsigmond Grossmann, *A pesti zsinagóga* [The synagogue of Pest] (Budapest, 1905), 3.

44. Feriz Berki, ed., *Az orthodox kereszténység* [Orthodox Christianity] (Budapest, 1975), 127–140; Pásztor, op. cit., 59–68.

45. For assimilation in general see János Kósa, *Pest és Buda elmagyarosodása 1848-ig* [The Magyarization of Pest and Buda before 1848] (Budapest, 1937).

46. Vörös, ed., op. cit, 239–243; Gábor Gyáni, "Nyilvános tér és használói Budapesten a századfordulón" [Public squares and their users in Budapest at the turn of the century], *Századok* 128, no. 6 (1994).

47. Kosáry, ed., op. cit., 473–480; György Balanyi, Zoltán Lantos, eds., *Emlékkönyv a magyar piarista rendtartomány háromszáz éves jubileumára* [Essays published in commemoration of the tercentenary of the Hungarian Diocese of the Piarist Order] (Budapest, 1943), 165–176; Ödön Hittrich, *A budapesti ágostai hitvallású evangélikus gimnázium első száz esztendejének története* [The first hundred years of the grammar school of Lutherans of the Augustinian Confession in Budapest] (Budapest, 1923), 19–52; Kornél Zelovich, *A m. kir. József műegyetem és a hazai technikai felsőoktatás története* [History of the Royal Hungarian Joseph Technical University and of technical higher education in Hungary) (Budapest, 1922), 64–68, 75–148.

48. Kosáry, ed., op. cit., 484–486; Ferenc Kollányi, *A Magyar Nemzeti Múzeum Széchényi Országos Könyvtára 1802–1902* [The National Széchényi Library of the Hungarian National Museum, 1802–1902] (Budapest, 1905), 311–462; Máté Kovács, ed., *Könyv és könyvtár a magyar társadalom életében az államalapítástól 1849-ig* [The role of books and libraries in the life of the Hungarian society from the foundation of the state to 1849] (Budapest, 1963), 543–564, 579–590; Géza Entz, *A magyar műgyűjtés történetének vázlata 1850-ig* [A short history of the collection of art in Hungary till 1850] (Budapest, 1937), 72–87; Gabriella Szvoboda-Dománszky, "A Pesti Műegylet története 1838–1867" [History of the Pest Art Association, 1838–1867] (Diss. for the candidate's degree, Budapest, 1995).

49. Kosáry, ed., op. cit., 492–503; József Waldapfel, *Ötven év Buda és Pest irodalmi életéből 1780–1830* [Fifty years of literary life in Buda and Pest, 1780–1830] (Budapest, 1935), 222–348; Anna Fábri, *Az irodalom magánélete. Irodalmi szalonok és társaskörök Pesten 1774–1848* [The private life of literature; literary saloons and circles in Pest, 1774–1848] (Budapest, 1987), 371–607; Pál Pándi, ed., *A magyar irodalom története 1772-től 1849-ig* [History of the Hungarian literature from 1772 to 1849] (Budapest, 1965), 189–205, 287–294, 363–366, and 376–381; István Sőtér, A sas és a serleg.

*Akadémiai arcképek* [The eagle and the goblet. Academic portraits] (Budapest, 1975), 9–25.

50. Kosáry, ed., op. cit., 506–509; Tivadar Rédey, *A Nemzeti Színház története. Az első fél évszázad* [History of the National Theater. The first half century] (Budapest, 1937), 63–223; György Székely, ed., *Magyar színháztörténet 1790–1873* [History of the Hungarian theater, 1790–1873] (Budapest, 1990), 170–189, 221–233, and 264–324.

51. Vera Bácskai, "Széchenyi tervei Pest-Buda felemelésére és szépítésére" [Széchenyi's plans to develop and beautify Pest-Buda), *Budapesti Negyed* 1, no. 2 (1993), 5–13; idem., *Széchenyi pesti tervei* [Széchenyi's plans for Pest] (Budapest, 1985); László Csorba, "Budapest-gondolat és városegyesítés" [The Budapest idea and the unification of the city], *Budapesti Negyed* 1, no. 2 (1993), 18–25.

*Károly Vörös*

# Birth of Budapest
# Building a Metropolis, 1873–1918

Between 1849 and 1873, the capital of a country defeated in its war of independence and democratic revolution became once again the economic, political and cultural center of Hungary, in spite of a period of counter-revolutionary oppression. In 1873 Pest, Buda and Óbuda were permanently unified, after a temporary unification in 1849, and modern Budapest was born.[1]

In the following quarter of a century the city fulfilled all the economic, political and cultural tasks anticipated by the 1873 unification. Budapest became a metropolis. In 1896 the country celebrated the millennium[2] of the Hungarian conquest by a glamorous city revealing for visitors and residents the results of capitalist development in the previous decades. As the fastest growing city on the continent, Budapest became an economic center as a commodity market, a labor market, a city of finances, industry and culture.

1896–1918 was a period of vigorous if controversial capitalist development. The controversies, already manifest in the glitter of the millennial celebrations, loomed large. There was sharp conflict between old solutions and new demands in several areas. Public utilities and housing conditions proved inadequate for the burgeoning population. The political and municipal administrations, along with the traditional educational institutions could not satisfy needs. It became evident that feudal vestiges had to be buried in favor of bourgeois democratic transformation. The phases in the development of Budapest were not unique or isolated, but rather integral to the process of capitalist transformation in the country over the previous seven decades. The manifestations of bourgeois capitalist transformation were more clearly visible in this town with less feudal residue. Although the more obvious the development, the sharper the contradictions as witnessed by Budapest.

This was the era of emerging cities and metropolises in Europe. Industry, commerce, transportation, the financial networks of Europe and the world, the specialized central institutions of a bourgeois state all favored this development. During the seven decades Budapest became one of the largest cities in Europe in terms of population, accompained by concomitant urban problems. The metropolis of various entwining factors and contradictions catered for modern thoughts and trends and also became exposed to opposing backwardness, which was antagonism also present in other European cities. Budapest was admired, despised, loved and hated.

## Population Growth, Internal Migration, Social Stratification and Living Standards

The total population of Budapest doubled during the quarter of a century between 1869 and 1896. It grew from 280,349 to 617,856. 717,681 people lived in Budapest in 1900 and 930,666 in 1913. With a population of 880,371 Budapest was the eighth largest city of Europe, following Hamburg, Moscow, St. Petersburg, Vienna, Berlin, Paris, and London in 1910. 4.2 per cent of the total population of Hungary (including Croatia-Slavonia) lived in Budapest. This vast increase was mainly the result of immigration. During World War I the city population increased because of an influx of refugees, many of whom became permanent residents. Immigration replaced the population lost in the war, estimated at 42,000, a figure which includes the decrease in birthrate and war casualties. The number of residents killed in war was about 28,000 (30–35,000 according to other estimates). The population of the Hungarian capital reached 1,010,000 by 1918.

After 1873 the age distribution of the Budapest population differed significantly from the rest of the country. 50.63 per cent of the 15–40 age group lived in the city while the national rate was 37.52 per cent, both in 1869 and 1890. The ratio of women, after a temporary decrease in 1869, surpassed that of men, especially in the 20–25 age group. In 1880 there were 1,068 women per 1,000 men while in 1900 this ratio increased to 1,071 per 1,000. The increase in women was caused by the demand for female domestic help, who came from rural areas.

Growth in Budapest was unevenly dispersed. The significance of the Buda side decreased in this period: in 1869 the Buda population was still 25 per cent of the total population, but by 1890 the rate decreased to 18,8 per cent and to 16.4 per cent by 1900. The Pest side increased in population along the outskirts and in the vicinity of industrial regions. Within the city the VIth, VIIth, and VIIIth districts grew in population, although the Xth increased the most. In 1900 the downtown population was hardly one seventh of that of Erzsébetváros, but the total population of the VIth, VIIth and VIIIth contained over half of the population of the capital. After 1870 the unique Budapest suburbs started to develop. Consequently, by 1890 the center of population growth shifted to the suburban areas. The first part of the twentieth century witnessed an even larger population growth in those areas.[3]

At the time of unification Budapest possessed the most advanced middle-class population in the country and this disparity became pronounced more with time. The following trends characterized this quarter century: an increase in the number of industrial workers and the intelligentsia (mostly civil servants), a decrease in the number of unskilled laborers, an increase of entrepreneurs and a strong polarization of income within the different strata. From the 1890s on the internal conflicts became more obvious. The most conspicuous of these was the stagnating number of industrial and commercial entrepreneurs compared to the previous period, the spectacular increase in civil servants, the growth of the female workforce (especially in industry and commerce), and a large increase in manual workers. The slowing rate of increase of small entrepreneurs, the accelerating increase and strength of the industrial labor force (with the continuous decrease in the ratio of unskilled laborers), the middle class becoming involved in the job market, the increase of the average income, coupled with the growing financial polarization of society were the main features of the transformation. World War I further widened the gap between the poles of society: the rich became richer, the poor became poorer. However, it also had a levelling effect on the lower-middle class and the expanding upper working class. Moreover the misery caused by the war resulted in further social tensions.

At the end of the nineteenth century a few occupations earned significant wealth for the upper-middle class: 94 mercantile, 94 real estate related, and 48 intellectual professions. The stability of the intellectual professions, however, was secured by inherited or previously acquired real estates. This period produced a new category within the upper middle class, the corporate executives who were major tax contributors.[4]

A small yet powerful stratum, the Budapest Jewish bourgeoisie rewarded with titles of the nobility for their economic importance, was of special significance in this period. 120 people from this stratum gained titles between 1850 and 1899, and sixty-seven of them were residents of

Budapest. The tendency was clear: this layer, most sensitive to economic trends and least bound by traditional social categories gravitated towards share-holding industrial and financial businesses, while their sons tended to occupy positions in government.

By 1890 the old Pest-Buda middle-class acquired special positions among the city leaders. Since their wealth, based on real estate, had been divided over generations, they became detached from the main tendencies of economic development. Yet because of the size and the stability of their wealth, they were able to qualify for corporate positions. Not being replaced by the younger generation and being deprived of continuity, they evolved into a closed, immobile stratum of patricians.

Another significant social trend was the withdrawal of the vital liberal aristocracy of the 1860s from municipal government by the end of the nineteenth century. Their alienation was done in part to the way capitialism evolved in Hungary. The rapid rise of a plutocracy and an accompanying middle-class with claims to financial and social leadership doubtless alarmed the aristocracy and the gentry.

The ruling bourgeoisie of millennial Budapest, although united by their fundamental interests, remained fragmented into easily identifiable social groups. Between the millennium and World War I a group of about five hundred people gained distinction in terms of both wealth and political influence. This layer of professionals, mostly lawyers, emerging from the native plutocracy while representing its political and public needs, were interrelated by kinship and property interests. Occupying important positions, they influenced the municipal and domestic economies and profited from them by their presence in the forefront of economic development.

War contracts and the ensuing windfall profits from the second half of 1916 increased the number of the wealthy in Budapest. According to tax returns from 1913 only one person paid an annual tax of 30–40,000 *korona*, but by 1917 the number had risen to twelve; whereas there were 104 people in 1913 and 200 in 1917 who paid an annual tax over 9,000 *korona*.

The objective criteria for a definition of the bourgeoisie, the biggest taxpayers in the city, might be parliamentary franchise.[5] In the capital city there were 16,000 registered voters in 1872, 20,348 in 1881, 39,337 in 1899, 58,522 in 1904, 75,044 in 1910, and 81,788 in 1912. The increase signified that the ratio of registered voters in Budapest grew to 8.63 per cent of the total population, that is one third of the male population above age 24. In Budapest a significant proportion of the middle class population became increasingly dependent on the state and on the big capital by the end of the nineteenth century. Among the redefined meaning of bourgeoisie financial situation, the size of wealth superseded values defined by type of employment. The burgher would be defined by income, not by his or her independence. The income and affluence that used used to be within reach to the self-employed now became available to employee as well. This manifestation of capitalist development, not limited to Hungary or Budapest, cast light upon the typical social distortions of the period: the absence of a strong, independent bourgeoisie. The real bourgeoisie was missing to a large extent from the civil society which evolved by the end of the century. The increasing number of civil servants and professionals of electoral power were poorly paid on the municipal income scale. The term bourgeoisie in its wider sense also included the petty bourgeoisie that constituted a significant layer of Budapest society. They were eligible to vote, although often they were identified only as skilled workers. The post office and the railroad employees, as well as the most highly paid industrial workers—mechanics, foremen, overseers, machinists, and printers—were among them. Yet at the end of the nineteenth century the majority of the working class and even the petty bourgeoisie were not franchised.

By time of World War I, the progressive age period of the Budapest bourgeoisie had come to an end. The expansion of the middle strata tapered off, the bourgeoisie lost its mobility and became a closed stratum. The petty bourgeoisie comprising the employed, the lower ranks of the civic servants, and the working class elite were the candidates for enfranchisement. The increase of the petty bourgeoisie was so overwhelming that the real middle class was unable to incorporate or assimilate them. The immobility of the middle class shed light on the weaknesses of the city development, which were already visible around the millennium. Although the capitalist development of the city was quick, a wide middle class from the pre-1848 period was missing and the great capitalists were in excess. Employees constituted the middle bourgeoisie while the classical petty bourgeoisie was replaced by the upper strata of the working class. By the beginning of the century there was a growing income gap between the bourgeoisie and the petty bourgeoisie, giving rise to fresh conflicts.

The urban working class contributed to the full development of the social structure of the city. By the end of the nineteenth century one third of the Budapest population consisted of the working class, a ratio identical to that of 1870. This ratio increased to 40 per cent during the economic boom beginning around 1890. The number of industrial workers increased from 192,000 in 1890 to 337,000 in 1910. Besides the quantitative increase, the working class was also restructured internally. Between 1873 and 1896 the agricultural proletariat declined as agriculture was driven out of the city. The number of domestic servants grew rather slowly because of the income decrease affecting a substantial part of the middle class. Day-workers underwent significant changes, since their number first grew and then in 1896 it started to decrease. Their integration into the working class was hindered by their rudeness and illiteracy which offended the educated industrial and transportation workers. Althought the city grew rapidly and its modern industry absorbed great amount of manpower, it was nevertheless less able to employ those without basic education. The recognition of this tendency might have prevented the most uneducated from moving to Budapest. Parallel with the growth of factory workers among the Budapest working class the ratio of skilled laborers increased also. In 1880 there were 50,000 industrial workers and the number grew to 125,000 by 1900. Along with the diminishing number of day laborers the number of skilled workers grew also a new category of workers evolved, the foremen. This period included the aggressive emergence of another characteristic stratum, the transportation workers: the railwaymen, sailors and road construction workers. Since Budapest played a major role in national transportation, this stratum gained special significance there. Their number was only 3,000 in 1870, reached 10,000 by 1890, and further increased to 15,000 by the turn of the century.

The number of the working class in Budapest increased during the period from the Hungarian millennium to World War I, within it industrial employees became the majority. The proliferation of mammoth industrial plants gave rise to specialization and division of labor within an increasingly young working class. After 1905 the evolving manufacturing industry mobilized further masses of young men in the countryside. There was an unparalleled need for skilled workers. The female workforce also increased within industry. Statistics indicate an overall rise in wages between 1900–1910 and significantly higher wages in Budapest. Yet there was an unexpectedly heavy fluctuation of workers among workplaces related to the cyclical changes in industry and the inflexibility among employers who hired and fired workers according to the demands of the moment. The world-wide phenomenon of workers using an economic boom to gain better wages allowed them to pursue the illusion of independence by changing jobs. Yet the gap in the 1890s between the working class, civil servants, and professionals widened further by the early twentieth century. After the 1904 municipal readjustment of salaries, a clerk at the bottom level of the office hierarchy would earn 1,000 *korona* annually. Industrial workers averaged about the same. Only 17 per cent of the Budapest workers earned above this level, while the clerical employees never went below the 1,000 *korona* level.[6]

'The social map of millennial Budapest showed Pest a center of economic life within an area surrounded by *Vámház* Boulevard, *Múzeum* Boulevard, *Károly* Boulevard, *Váci* Boulevard (today *Bajcsy-Zsilinszky* Street) and the *Újépület* (New Building), while in Buda the central government agencies occupied the area surrounded by *Margit* Boulevard, *Attila* Street and the Danube, the Castle, *Víziváros* (Watertown), *Krisztinaváros* (Krisztinatown) and the *Tabán*. Convenient housing conditions with comfortable, spacious apartments characterized these areas, populated by bourgeois families who relied on live-in servants. Similar conditions characterized the segments of Pest bordering downtown and extending as far as the *Nagykörút* (Grand Boulevard with today's section names: *Szent István, Teréz, Erzsébet, József,* and *Ferenc* Boulevards), north of *Andrássy* Street and from *Kerepesi* Street (*Rákóczi* Street) as far as *Üllői* Street. This area began developing after the unification of the city. Wealthy bourgeois with economic ties lived in the former area, and aristocrats and members of the grand bourgeoisie in the latter. Scattered among these blocks there were also smaller apartments occupied by families who rarely had domestic servants. These segments, became the residential area for the petty bourgeoisie, office clerks, and a rising number of the upper strata of the industrial working class. This characterized the Pest area, beyond *Nagykörút* (Grand Boulevard) to *Aréna* Street (today *Dózsa György* Street), south of *Keleti* (Eastern) Railway Station towards *Kerepesi* Cemetery and the *Ferencváros* reservoir (Haller Street). The surrounding areas of *Keleti* (Eastern) and *Nyugati* (Western) Railway Stations, *Józsefváros* and *Ferencváros*, as well as Buda with *Tabán, Újlak,* and *Óbuda* acquired increasingly proletarian overtones. The apartments were small, overcrowded, with sublets and night-lodgers, very few domestic servants. Factory workers, day-laborers, poor artisans without apprentices, grocers, clerks, office hands, railwaymen lived there. There were also living quarters for the hopeless, aimless lumpenproletariat.

The social-geographical configuration based on the 1890 and 1900 censi did not change considerably until World War I. New townships and suburbs beyond this area would eventually alter the larger townscape.[7]

While the changing life-styles reinforced centrifugal social tendencies, certain integrating processes evolved also. Ethnic assimilation was a process typical of bourgeois development turning Budapest, a multi-ethnic city at the time of unification, into a city with Hungarian majority population by the millenium. It was primarily migration into the city that altered the ethnic composition since the immigrants came from ethnically Hungarian areas. The city filled up with a Hungarian-speaking population, where the authorities and most of the press were Hungarian. Everyday communication necessitated a knowledge of the Hungarian language. Opportunities for exclusive use of German or Slovak diminished. Information was conveyed in Hungarian and the supremacy of the language was ensured by public education. From the 1860s Hungarian was the only language of public education. By the turn of the century Budapest became irreversibly Hungarian, at least linguisticallly.[8]

The centripetal and centrifugal social developmental processes had other impacts. Whether the important urban class, the Jews, or social movements, or struggles with hunger and old age, or new forms of crime, conflicts become apparent. The Jewish population became integrated into the social structure of the city, but conflicts between the orthodox and reform Jews remained. Antagonisms between the petty and grand bourgeoisie became distinct within denominational lines. Associations, formed to keep the newly forged bourgeoisie together eventually became divisive, cliques separating those whom they were supposed to integrate. Charity by itself proved unable to cope with poverty and the misery. Problems needed institutional intervention. Municipal crime which posed an insurmountable problem for the police forces of the three cities, was conquered when the forces were consolidated and enlarged.

Between 1896 and 1914 social mobility gave rise to further differentiating and integrating processes. The national and social assimilation of the Jewry, the expansion of the masonic movement, the formation of athletic and other associations, the interpretation of poverty as a social problem, and urban crime all affected social interaction. The assimilation of Jews was resisted because of envy and emerging anti-Semitism within the non-Jewish petty-bourgeoisie. As a result many middle-class Jews became disillusioned and lost respect for the social and national ideas encouraged by the previous generation. The free masonry movement broke up into traditionally liberal cosmopolitan main branch and the radical nationalist branche. Athletic associations consisted of clubs for athletes and clubs for fans, and these groups further divided into professional and amateur associations. These processes also had an impact upon the periphery of bourgeois society. New urban challenges elicited technologically and psychologically prepared modern criminals and modern "social workers" who applied scientific methods for alleviating destitution.

During World War I rising costs, food and housing shortages became endemic. Eight war bonds were issued threatening the savings and financial security of the middle class. Because of the absence of a strong middle class which could produce national wealth, living standards began to level off. Ironically these circumstances brought together masses of skilled workers, the petty bourgeoisie, and clerical workers within the same financial stratum due to uneven rates of salary raises, difficulties in public services, and the decreasing living standard. These social strata developed common political interests.

## Birth of Budapest and Municipal Policy

The House of Deputies discussed the unification bill from November 26 to December 9, 1872, and approved the bill unanimously. After the bill passed the Upper House in a single session on December 17, Francis Joseph signed it on December 22. By Act XXXVI of 1872 Budapest was born.

A few days after the enactment, the Minister of the Interior called on all three cities to elect a 34-member organizing committee within ten days as stipulated by section 134 of the Act. The committee set out to submit the detailed plans to the Municipal Assembly from March 20, 1873 on. During the ensuing nine months all the details of unification were hammered out. The administrative districts of the capital were outlined. *Erzsébetváros* (Elizabethtown), originally part of the VIth district, became independent as the VIIth district and *Kőbánya* as the Xth district. The election procedures of the municipal assembly were outlined as were its organs. Municipal statutes and administration were established and a coat of arms derived for the city.

The proposed regulations were quickly approved by the Minister of the Interior. The first elections for the first assembly were held on September 25–26, 1873. 16,000 enfranchised citizens elected two hundred deputies while two hundred more were selected from among the 1,200 most prominent taxpayers. In certain districts the ballots were cast after preliminary negotiations with local and national political cliques.

On October 25, 1873, the new deputies gathered for the first meeting of the assembly in the *Vigadó* building in Pest. On November 4, Károly

Ráth was elected chief mayor and Károly Kamermayer mayor, followed
by the election of the two deputy mayors on the next day. On November
17, 1873, the municipal council officially replaced the disparate city councils terminated the day before. Henceforth the united city was responsible
for the budget and all financial matters. That was the actual birthday of
Budapest.[9]

The Budapest assembly had a narrow social basis. Until the turn of the
century the electorate showed surprising apathy to filling its four hundred
seats (50 per cent of which were up for reelection every third year). Suffrage was subject to the same conditions as the national suffrage with
additional requirements for Budapest, such as: evidence of ability to read
and write, and two years of established residency. The indifference was
understandable as regard the two hundred deputies who did not depend on
the electorate. These deputies represented their own interests and convic-
tions, significantly affecting the effectiveness of the elected deputies.

The privileges enjoyed by the big taxpayers were not wholly ill-advised
for that period. Involving modern commercial, industrial, and financial
capital in public affairs was crucial for bourgeois transformation and city
development. In the 1870s it would have been hard to involve them without
granting them preference. The electorate consisted primarily of petty and
middle-bourgeois citizens who still tended to resist modernization. Extending a political role to progressive elements was undemocratic, but necessary under the circumstances. By the early-1890s economic progress was
noticeable. Involving the modern capitalists in the development of the city
proved to be beneficial both for the capitalists and the petty and middle-
bourgeoisie. Simultaneously, the greatest industrialists, and bankers, having gained substantial economic influence, started withdrawing from direct
participation in exercising authority over to the most unproductive capitalists, the real estate owners and the lawyers. This development did not
preserve the benefits of granting privileges to great taxpayers and proved
to be disadvantageous in municipal politics.

The indifference to self-government was due to the fact that membership and the election procedures of the assembly were controlled by a few
well-organized political groups who succeeded in placing their own people
into the assembly. The party politics and party system that had developed
and functioned in every major city by the end of the nineteenth century,
tightened the power lines in the assembly just as it did in parliament. The
antagonisms pertained to national parties but did not reflect specifically
on Budapest. The political campaigns started with parliamentary elections

and the same bodies organized municipal elections. Connections and cred-
its gained in the national campaign could become most useful in municipal
elections and, vice-versa, the municipal positions strengthened the organ-
izers' position in national politics by corrupting voters and candidates on
two fronts. In certain districts of Budapest omnipotent "bosses" appeared
with canvassers corrupting the electoral process and sealing the fate of the
districts. Social circles in the districts served as their institutional support.
These units usually supported the ruling Liberal Party.[10]

In the years before the millennium new parties responding to specific
municipal needs emerged and unsettled entrenched political interest
groups. They relied on the increasing numbers of petty bourgeoisie who
demanded that municipal policy conform to their professional and social
interests, without regard to the traditionally national and great bourgeois
interests. The petty-bourgeois citizens of *Terézváros* (Theresa-town)
formed the Communal Democratic Party headed by the young, yet politically experienced lawyer, Vilmos Vázsonyi. A similar organization was
established in the I. district by the "free citizens". Both parties were active
in the post-1896 period.

The unification Act XXXVI of 1872 determined the basis, framework
and scope of activity of municipal policy till World War I. It determined
the way Budapest was managed and financed. Its role in national policy
was defined. The legal status of the capital, its management, and its administration were all determined by the Act.

Self-government was implemented at the regularly and frequently held
assembly meetings. On behalf of the people of the capital the assembly
exercised the following rights and obligations: adopting ordinances; establishing the agenda of the assembly; establishing electoral and administrative districts; sponsoring city improvement projects; road, street, and public
utility maintenance; construction and public works; raising loans; establishing, canceling, or modifying communal taxes; basic property aquisition
and their sale; stating budget guidelines; accounting; electing officials,
boards, and committees; supervising civil servants, excusing them from
obligations, or suspending them; initiating disciplinary procedures; regulating salaries for office clerks, office-messengers, and janitorial workers;
establishing or canceling offices and jobs; managing, supervising and re-
porting on accounts run by the city; deciding appeals, and resolving mo-
tions. As a political organization the assembly had the right to debate national political issues; maintain their position and report on their position

to legislative authorities and branches of government, or directly to parliament.

Budapest also possessed constitutional guarantees. For instance, if the state government or a cabinet minister attempted to collect illegal taxes (taxation not passed by parliament) or to recruit additional soldiers, the municipal authorities had the right to veto the governmental measures. This constitutional guarantee, however, had its limitations. If a minister sustained a measure over the protest of the city or issued it under unusual circumstances, the minister would have the right to be in direct command of the municipal authorities and the city representatives could only place a *post facto* appeal to the parliament. This was a carefully elaborated state policy to balance local and state interests.

Although not appointed by the King the mayor was elected by the Assembly from among three nominees of the monarch. During his six years of office he could be relieved only upon his own request. The police force of Budapest, contrary to other town police forces, was a state entity but was substantially funded by the city. Finally, to the disadvantage of the municipal assembly, construction authority and street names were in the hands of the Municipal Council for Public Work, established in 1870. Its tasks consisted of preparation of ordinances bearing upon the whole city or individual districts, accomplishment of work, establishing directions and levels of streets, naming and systematic numbering of streets and public squares, and preparation of a plan concerning construction regulations.

The Budapest city administration was functioning according to the organizational by-laws and regulations prepared by Committee No 34 in the first half of 1873. Ordinances were issued to define the tasks of municipal officials: the mayor, deputy mayors, city aldermen, the town clerk, clerks to the municipality, district clerks, the municipal attorney, attorneys, the chief engineer, the chief medical officer, district medical officers, the chief auditor, and the chief archivist. The assembly voted on these positions and the officials were elected for seven years terms, except for the chief archivist who was elected for life. The mayor's sphere of activity was also defined. He was the president of the Council, a collective body which headed the executive branch whose members were the heads of different administrative branches. There were ten such branches: I. legislative and personnel, II. public construction, III. private construction, assessment and regulation, IV. orphanage and wardship, V. taxes and fees, VI. health, VII. financial and economic, VIII. educational, IX. industrial, police and poor law administration, and X. military departments. An alderman headed each department and there was a town-clerk supervising the secretariat of the mayor.

The municipal council administered the individual districts by its own borough magistracies placed into each districts. Each of these magistracies were headed by a district magistrate assisted by four to eight counselors and alternate counselors. The notary in each district did the routine administrative work assisted by one or two clerks, a delivery-man and an attendant.[11] The District Act enacted in 1893 authorized the borough magistrates to assume jurisdiction characteristic of villages, thus turning them into regular, highly differentiated offices.

The managerial work of the above authorities was supported by registration information, and archival offices, the office of the attorney and that of statistics. The different managerial branches were regulated by law, especially the controller's office which included tax accounting, tax collection, and financial affairs. The departmental operations of municipal auditing, engineering, finances, deposits, ward management, market management were meticulously regulated. The Chief Health Officer managed the health department. There were altogether 13 district physicians, 14 coroners, 26 midwives, and seven veterinarians on the staff of the city health institutes as well as a city pharmacist. The numerous educational staff, the fire department, and other special departments were also run, regulated and supervised by the city. 1,682 people were employed by the city in 1872, 523 of them were on its administrative staff. By 1897 the number had almost tripled to 4,932. Considering the extension of spheres and tasks, this expansion was not excessive.

Besides organizing the city residents and fulfilling some of their needs, the municipal government also managed city properties and incomes. A substantial part of city properties was comprised of real estate. The grand total value of all properties increased from 107.5 million *korona* to 305 million between 1875 and 1895. Equipment, raw materials, liquid funds, liquor license fees paid by the state in the amount of 11.5 million *korona* from 1890 on, and the estimated value of rent also formed part of city property. Actual revenues strengthened the city economy. The income of the city funds increased from 16,557,000 *korona* to 54,604,000 *korona* between 1874 and 1895. The main source of income between 1874 and 1895 was taxes and revenues from city property and public services; from 1880 the city increasingly relied on loans.

The total expenditures increased from 13,606,000 *korona* in 1874 to 53,464,000 in 1894. Among the main items the salaries and pensions of the administrative staff increased from 12.56 per cent to 15 per cent while the expenses of school construction grew from 13 per cent to 16 per cent. Almost 50 per cent of the city expenses went for infrastructural investments and maintenance. These investments were significant for city development, although the profit was small and the amortization rate slow. This type of addition to city property did not benefit the budget much since returns on investments were slow. Thus the city was compelled to raise loans very soon.[12]

The millennial years signaled an end to a period that started with the unification of the city. By 1892 Budapest was one of two capital cities of the monarchy, completely equal to Vienna in conformity with the logics of the dualist state arrangement.[13]

In the post-millennial period the institutional framework of municipal politics failed to keep pace with new political realities. The privileges extended to major tax-payers remained and the assembly and its sphere of activity were unchanged.

Certain new developments, however, could be detected in connection with the election of parliamentary deputies. Even though the regulations regarding suffrage stayed the same until World War I, inflation of wages encouraged upward social mobility which enfranchised large masses of people, especially after 1896. The growing dissatisfaction of the petty bourgeoisie was demonstrated by the national election victory of the opposition in 1906,[14] when the districts of the capital voted for the opposition candidates, except for *Lipótváros*, the stronghold of the grand bourgeoisie. By 1910 there were five Party of Work, one independent, and three opposition mandates. Two of the latter went to Vázsonyi's Democratic Party and one to the representative elected in the I. district by the "free citizens". Vázsonyi demanded the cancellation of the privileges of major tax-payers, the introduction of an independent, progressive city tax-structure, the nationalization of gas, electricity, railroad services, a social policy that provides fair labor conditions in all businesses and plants, free public education, and generally the protection for the petty bourgeois and the worker. By the first years of the century the local problems of Budapest had a profound impact on the results of the parliamentary elections. The beginnings of new political organizations which broke away from the national political forms and reflected urban social problems, appeared in Budapest first. The enfranchised middle-class citizens became somewhat less indifferent when they acquired a real voice in their affairs.

The 1905–06 political crisis and the years of the coalition government mobilized the political groups and the different political fronts became well-defined. Since the capital city vehemently opposed the Géza Fejérváry government, on February 19, 1906, the city's autonomy was suspended and a royal commissioner was appointed to administer Budapest. The commissioner's authority continued until April 8, when constitutional rights were re-established by appointing a government of the opposition. The new regime however, was not satisfied with the half-hearted opposition Budapest had demonstrated during the months of crisis and the fact that the majority of its assembly still favored the former regime. The district recognized that the old pro-government politics could not be pursued in the assembly but, resenting the new regime, they chose a third road policy, trying to transform their groups into unique urban parties. Their only partners in this venture might have been the democrats with a real urban program; but the latter were opposed to the district chiefs. Finally Vázsonyi tried to join forces with the Vth, VIth, VIIth, and VIIIth district chiefs by drawing them into his own urban democratic party and run City Hall. The first test of strength was the election of his own candidate István Bárczy for mayor. The urban coalition disintegrated before long but their one year long existence enabled the district chiefs to survive. Vázsonyi's position became firm enough not to be disregarded, and his influence grew. With the disintegration of this mayor municipal party, the balance of power in the assembly shifted once again into the old constellation. This process was hastened by the victory of the Party of Work over the coalition in the Spring of 1910.

The balance of power in the city politics did not seem to have changed a lot; it remained pro-government, was connected to the plutocracy, and relied on the prevailing district power groups. Yet three distinct differences were noticeable. Real urban problems and the corresponding programs of urban parties were reflected by the 1913 assembly policies. The party programs discarded the privileges extended to great tax-payers, and agreed on universal and secret suffrage. The balance of power among the parties became unstable increasing the weight of the city's executive body since they were in control of a vast administrative establishment. After 1905 distinctly liberal policies prevailed thanks to the influence of István Bárczy who set his stamp on the period which ended with the bourgeois democratic revolution of 1918.

A complete reform of the administration of the capital that was in perfect harmony with the new requirements took place in 1911. In June Bárczy submitted a proposal about the reorganization of the executive branch. The reform, accepted unanimously, relieved the mayor from managing a host of pending matters for the sake of more efficient leadership. The number of deputy mayors was increased to three and all the managerial and supervisory tasks formerly under the mayor were delegated to the deputy mayors, or the department heads. The assembly as a whole was no longer overburdened. A quorum was required at council meetings. The number of departments increased. At the end of the nineteenth century the tax department had been terminated while a supply and transportation department was set up. Social policy, educational, industrial (water supply and electrical), city economy, and economic departments were newly established. The old public construction department was spilt into roads and sewers and construction departments (the latter dealing with urban buildings) to be managed by engineering staffs. The engineering department was terminated and incorporated into the council, increasing efficiency and decreasing bureaucracy. Only the water service directorate, transformed into an independent office, remained outside of the council department system. The mayor's presidential department also became a council department. The departments were grouped into three clusters for more efficient administration each under the direction of a deputy mayor. The reform also affected the assembly that originally possessed a confusing system of departments. The area corresponding to each council department was supervised by a specialized committee, with the exception of the comptroller's office whose sphere of authority remained intact. The new structure of the municipal administration, the last major change before the war, reflected the shift in the managerial needs of the growing city. Technical and economic problems became the priority issues, unlike the sace of the year of 1873 when legal and administrative issues were dominant.

Municipalization, a significant aspect of the new policy, took place when industrial units supplying community services became municipal property. In 1910 the city expropriated the gas works and advertising companies. Directly or indirectly the city itself established profitable businesses. In 1909 a municipal bakery, in 1912 a municipal vegetable garden, and in 1913 a plant producing medical instruments and bandage materials were established. Other units were taken over by the city as corporations by purchasing majority of their shares. Apartment construction became an important venture of the new urban policy: 4,816 apartments were built between 1909 and 1913. A social and cultural center and public hostel was built on the boundary line between *Angyalföld* (today XIIIth district) and the Vth district to ease the miserable overcrowded houses. Investment in education, first of all construction of public elementary schools, also became a central issue in urban affairs. Between 1909 and 1912, 55 schools with 976 classrooms were built in the neglected suburbs. To provide and finance a higher quality of education was also a municipal task. The Pedagogical Institute was established for teacher training. The transformation of the Municipal Library into a network of public libraries (today *Ervin Szabó* Municipal Library) was part of the program to enhance general public education. All these projects met with widespread public satisfaction. Implementation of these policies required new personnel. There were many changes in City Hall as high ranking municipal officials who started their careers in the 1880s, gave way to young and talented professionals.[15]

Further increase in city property marked a new economic era. The 305 million *korona* property value of 1895 increased to 837 million by 1913. The periodical and incidental revenues of the municipal treasury greatly increased. The 54,604,000 *korona* of 1895 increased to 330 million by 1913, partially through the income from city-owned real estate and in particular from incomes of municipal plants. The ratio of expenditures changed. Public health expenses (not including hospital budgets) decreased from 15 per cent to 10.7 per cent as major hygiene related investments—water and a sewer system—had been completed. Investments, however, grew substantially from 16 per cent to 24 per cent related to the school system.

Since loans had to be raised several times, by the end of the first year of World War I Budapest's depts amounted to was 430,500,000 *korona*.[16] These debts were the result of a rational policy to cope with the demands of a European metropolis. The investment plans followed careful cost effectiveness calculations and most certainly, had it not been for the war, the investments would have been recovered.

The war completely disrupted the city management by modifying or canceling municipal plans in favor of increasing military expenditures. Three tasks had to be executed: military; public supply; and care for victims of war. In the first group the male population had to be enlisted. Secondly Budapest as a junction point had to accommodate large number of transient military units. The city had to build or refurbish a number of military hospitals in school buildings or in temporary barracks. For fulfillment of the second task: supplying the public with food the city organized the Public Supply Department with three subordinated offices: the flour office organized and operated a rationing system, while the milk office managed dairy issues and a third office arranged for produce transportation licenses and fodder distribution. Welfare and war relief activities expanded during the conflict. The Municipal Public Aid Office set up in the first days of the war offered counseling and orientation for the victims of war. A short time later mayor Bárczy organized the Central Aid Committee to coordinate social assistance. Direct aid to recruits was provided from state financial resources, which were transferred to the district governments. At the end of 1916 the Municipal Welfare Center took over the coordination of intermittent aid.[17]

The immense financial burden caused by the War was manifest in the municipal debt which grew to 617 million *korona* by mid-1918.

Questions of national policy became the focus of interest during the war overshadowing the issues of municipal politics. The social evolution of the turn of the century required even more forcefully the extension of the suffrage. Upon István Tisza's fall in 1917 the Suffrage Committee of the Municipal Citizens and Workers was founded as a result of an agreement among several political organizations, including Mihály Károlyi's opposition party[18] and the growing Social Democratic Party.[19] Vázsonyi played an important role in the Committee. The assembly passed a resolution seeking universal and secret suffrage and an end to the privileges of major tax-payers, which was submitted to Charles IV (the last king of Hungary, crowned in Budapest on December 30, 1916). The presence of major tax-payers in the assembly, however, subverted the efforts for reform. In the politically volatile years of the war City Hall lost its capacity to cope with political conflicts of such magnitude.

## Economy, Industry, Transportation and Communication

Railroads running to Budapest had been built by 1873. Between 1896 and 1914 the railroad network did not expand yet railroad traffic increased tremendously. Moreover, by 1896 water traffic on the Danube had also increased. By the eve of World War I Budapest was the largest port on the River Danube, measured by the volume of goods transported.

Between 1873 and 1896 telegraph and telephone lines reached the most remote points of the country. The telephone system first connected Budapest with Vienna in 1890 and by 1893–94 it became a country-wide intercity system. Between the millennium and the war the development of the telephone system superseded all other means of communication. In the first months of the war a powerful military radio telegraph relay station was constructed at Csepel to establish communication between Constantinople and the Central powers and it operated faultlessly.

Four major items formed the bulk of trade aimed to fulfill the needs of Budapest between 1873 and 1896: fuel (firewood and coal, the latter growing in proportion); grain; construction materials (bricks and lumber); as well as iron and steel goods. Transportation of handicraft articles, mostly textiles out of the city were also substantial in value. Besides textiles, iron and steel goods were exported in major quantities. Grain was exported in lesser quantities and mostly to the West. The exported grain left the city in the form of flour, beer or alcohol; similarly, the export of machinery surpassed that of iron or steel. Kőbánya's pig export had increased but was halted by the 1895 swine pestilence. Fuel and building materials were imported into town but were almost completely consumed. Between 1896 and 1914 the main items of transportation into the city were identical with the previous period: grain, raw materials, food, iron, steel and manufactured items (machinery included), construction materials and fuel.

From 1873 on the Budapest Commodity and Stock Exchange centralized the wholesale trade of the country. Its growth is manifest in the sales of grain: 3,838 thousand metric centners in 1873 and 9,888 thousand metric centners in 1896. Between 1896 and 1914 when the produce trade was decentralized the Budapest Commodity Exchange lost its former significance as intermediary and price regulator. The Stock Exchange remained the major market of the security business because the Commodity Exchanges in the provinces never traded securities. In spite of the vast increase in quantity and quality trade in Budapest did not offer as many economic opportunities between 1873 and 1896 as it had prior to 1873. Not only was commerce unable to influence the European markets but also the direction of the domestic market began to slip away by the early 1900s. Grain fairs as well as animal fairs started to transform into local market events.

By the beginning of the century a new technique for selling goods wholesale was established: the department store.

After 1914 the war economy restricted the use of increasing numbers of raw materials and produce by the civilian population. A complicated system of rules and regulations were introduced. Peace time free market was replaced by a thriving economic bureaucracy, with layers of official war agencies. However, merchants could not be completely ignored. The demands of war economy exposed the disintegrating commerical functions and network of the capital to a greater role than it had before. Giant monopolies evolved which effectively increased accumulated commercial capital, and functioned under the cooperative direction of Budapest wholesale merchants, military and civilian bureaucracy. The real profits were drawn by the large Budapest banks. At the outbreak of the war their produce departments were suddenly expanded and the banks readily participated in the war contracts and in the activities of different central agencies, both as financiers and beneficiaries.

Between 1873 and 1896 banks importing financial capital replaced the dominance of commercial banks which used to supply accumulate capital. After the cautious policies of the 1880s when development remained within the frameworks of traditional enterprises that resulted in slowly accumulating bank reserve funds, more radical policies marked the 1890s as banks and savings and loan associations were founded. In 1890 there were 17 banks, 10 savings and loan associations and 37 credit unions in Budapest (against 11 banks, 5 savings and loans associations, and 20 credit unions in 1880). Between 1896 and 1914 lending banks expanded activities to the national credit market and national industry. Taking over the stock exchange operations was the last significant move financial institutions made in Budapest. The credit institutions became so centralized that they became significant factors in the city's development. Banks paid substantial taxes to the city, extended tens of millions in loans, provided mortgage loans to real estate owners, and helped develop factories. In return their presence became more prominent in city politics.

Manufacturing gained great significance between 1873 and 1896, almost competing with commerce by the late 1880s. Milling and distilling industry, beer, brick-making, printing shops formed the industrial profile of the city. Iron and metallurgical industry, machine and vehicle industries proved to be the most adaptable branches. In 1896 the largest plants of Budapest—iron, metallurgical and machine industry—clustered around five specific areas: 1) foundries, tools, machine tools, engines; 2) agricultural machinery; 3) pumps, injectors, fire-engines; 4) railway carriages, freightcars, railway engines, boats and ships; 5) upcoming electrical industry, first of all the Ganz Electrical Plant with 1,200 employees and some smaller plants. The war materiel industry and the chemical industry were also developing, but the textile industry was not part of the industrial boom of the 1890s. By the millennium Budapest became the largest industrial center of Hungary.

Factors shaping industry in Budapest between the millennium and World War I remained the same as in the previous period. They included: the advantages of Budapest being a national administrative, economic and transportation center; growing urbanization; the developing public utility services; a concentrated labor force; growing co-operation among factories and several other factors prevailed during the economic boom between the 1890s and World War I. The manufacturing industry gained strength with respect to the number of workers and factories and underwent structural transformation in terms of modernization and growth, with the emergence of new plants in Budapest. As a result the city retained its supremacy, remaining the largest, most modern, and most complex industrial area of the country. The manufacturing industry developed dynamically in the suburbs adding to the territorial and organic expansion of industry as a whole.

The most important industrial branches remained the same in this period (iron, metallurgy, machine-tools, food processing, printing, construction and construction materials), but with modified ratios and significance by 1914. Compared with the milling, distilling or brick-making industries which developed only quantitatively, the leading industrial branches developed also qualitatively, motivated by the technological progress and increased demand. Because of the opportunities and increased demand the iron, metallurgical and machine-tool industries excelled both in terms of the number of workers and number of plants. The tool, electrical and war materiel industries dominated within this category. The chemical industry also showed remarkable progress in those years.

By late 1914 the war economy placed increased demands upon industrial branches which were concentrated in Budapest and its suburbs. There was a tremendous surge in the iron, metallurgical, machine-tool, and chemical industries and in factories producing war equipment. Contracts for weapons and military equipment were increasing. Even though the competition with Austrian industry was fierce, yet huge profits were made in the second year of the war. Military transportation became a profitable business both for large concerns and subcontractors. Investment, technological modernization and expansion added to their competitive edge which helped them meet the expectations of military production. A huge increase in production, the growing significance of large concerns, centralization, and the growth and influence of the Budapest financial world characterized the war-time industry.

Between 1873 and 1896 the main areas of small-scale production in Budapest consisted of cloth production iron, metallurgical and machine-tools, lumber and food-processing. Handicraft industry, also centered in Budapest, went through a period of fierce competition and differentiation of specific products. Its dependence on the commerce that utilized piece workers led to instability and shortage of credit. Simultaneously, however, certain workshops expanded into larger plants. After 1890 the garment industry was concentrated in large factories but retained the old technology. In the iron, metallurgical and machine-tool industries small entrepreneurs established small factories. The food-processing strengthened between 1890 and 1896 but stagnated afterwards.

The scattered, disunited manufacturing was mobilized during the war. There were heavy demands for manufactured articles, raw materials, uniforms and processed food. Military requirements could not rely on such scattered units and needed entrepreneurs to organize networks. A stratum of military transporters evolved who synchronized the production of small units and who were financially responsible for he timely delivery of quality goods to the military, thus promoting monopoly.

Because of the rise in population by 1881 the number of grocers and peddlers, who provided masses of people with basic products increased along with the number of haberdashers, hardware dealers, and larger grocery store owners. Between 1881 and 1890 fashion shops emerged and merchants, shops and store-clerks doubled in number. Population growth and urbanization continued to stimulate development between 1896 and 1914. The number of shops selling fancy goods, fashion articles, and grocery items to satisfy urban tastes grew very fast.

Among the different units of catering trade—taverns, pubs, restaurants, coffeeshops, and cafés—increased the most. With the expansion of urban habits bourgeois consumerism mushroomed. As the clerical and intellectual strata of society grew, the need for socialization beyond the family expanded. The quantitative increase of other catering units, compared with similar data from the millennial years, was proportionate with the population increase and reflected growing bourgeois demands. Cafés became the scene of petty bourgeois, bourgeois, and intellectual life and were clearly distinct from restaurants and taverns, frequented by the petty-bourgeoisie and the proletariat.

Between 1873 and 1896 agriculture in greater Budapest failed to meet the city's needs. The railroads and suburban railways expanded to rural areas and competition was strong. The fast growing Budapest population and the high cost of land led to subdivisions an edging out plots for non-agricultural use, even though Budapest was agrotechnically the most advanced area of Hungary at the beginning of the twentieth century.[20]

## Budapest as Capital and Its Development

After 1873 the unified Budapest became the capital in all respects of the Hungarian state within the Austro-Hungarian Dual Monarchy, with the status came all state, political, and administrative functions and the institutions that necessarily pertained to the capital of a bourgeois state. With the presence of the royal palace, even if it was rarely occupied, the Parliament, ministries, higher courts, expanding national agencies, Budapest acquired increasing significance and urbanization proceeded proportionately. City planning played a primary role in transforming needs and demands into the structures of urbanization.

In 1872 the Board of Public Works prepared the city-planning program of Pest, that of Buda in 1876, and that of Óbuda in 1883. The basic demand in Buda's plan called for adequate communication with Pest. Only the downtown districts of Buda and Óbuda were included in the first phase of the development program.

The Pest development plan was substantially changed when the *Központi Pályaudvar* (Central Railway Station, today *Keleti* or Eastern Railway Station) was completed by 1884. During construction *Baross* Square emerged, surrounding streets were widened, and the roads originally designed to cross the site of the station were eliminated. The second version of the plan was modified when the warehouses on the Danube embankment were completed. The third version launched the transformation of the northern section of *Lipótváros* because of the construction of the parliament building (enacted by Article LXVIII of 1880). In 1896 the parliament was half-completed when the impressive row of apartment buildings on *Alkotmány* Street and the Eastern side of *Tömő* (today *Kossuth Lajos*) Square with the building of the higher court emerged in the center of a rapidly developing district. The fourth of the city-plan was necessitated by the construction of two Danube bridges. After 1896 the transformation of the bridgehead around *Erzsébet* (Elizabeth) Bridge (built between 1897–1903) became of crucial importance. Between 1894 and 1896 *Ferenc József* (today *Szabadság*) Bridge was completed and via this bridge a substantial segment of *Átlós* Avenue (Diagonal, today *Béla Bartók*) connected downtown with *Kelenföld*. *Villányi* Avenue and *Alkotás* Street connected the outskirts with the city centers. The townplanners' intention was to direct traffic from *Nyugati* (Western) Railway Station (designed by the firm Eiffel and Co.,) and from the North-Pest industrial zone to *Margit* Bridge to relieve the overburdened *Lánchíd* (Chain Bridge). A road was also needed in Buda. By 1892 the stretch between *Széna* and *Szarvas* Squares was constructed and the *Margit* Bolevard was further developed. This connection opened up areas for expansion between *Déli* (Southern) Railway Station and *Városmajor*. A prominent part of the plan was the extension of the Western wing of the castle area launched by Miklós Ybl. It involved the development of *Palota* Street, a communication artery between the royal palace and the Western section of the castle, which was built between 1890 and 1895, and the reconstruction of a cluster of buildings between *Dísz* and *Szent György* Squares to suit the functions of the Ministry of Defense and the Headquarters of the Army High Command.

The city expanded farther after the government had purchased *Margitsziget* (Margaret Island), under Article XLVIII of 1908, from Archduke Joseph for eleven million *korona*. The Board of Public Works took it over in 1909 intending to transform it into a public park. The financial burdens, having been too heavy it had to be leased to a company. The outbreak of the war froze all city-planning activities and postponed half-completed construction projects for years.

The results of construction activities between 1873 and 1896 were monumental. The number of buildings grew from 9,351 to 16,233 many of them multi-story apartment buildings. By 1920 there were 20,020 buildings in Budapest, but between 1896 and 1914 town development and population growth began losing momentum.

After 1873, the construction of two main arteries in Pest and of large, impressive buildings and building clusters were the most significant changes. The Board of Public Works inaugurated *Sugár* (today *Andrássy*) Avenue in 1884, thus providing a modern, attractive, metropolitan boulevard for the city. The *Nagykörút* (Grand Boulevard) was by and large completed by the millennium with additional segments continuing till 1906. Its construction served several purposes: connecting outgoing avenues in an outer arc, housing the main sewer lines of the Pest side. Other major sites, as the row of palaces along the Danube esplanade, built by the turn of the century, and the impressive public buildings containing executive, legislative, cultural, or artistic institutions (Opera, new ministerial, judicial, university buildings, museums, churches) awed the people arriving from rural areas.

Eclecticism, the architectural style of the time, played an essential part in transforming the city-scape. At the time of the unification Italian neo-renaissance prevailed, its most typical examples being the rows of buildings of *Sugárút* and *Nagykörút*. Later French classicism, and neo-baroque took over. By way of illustration, Ybl was forced to build the *Krisztina*-town wing of the royal palace in neo-Baroque style at the special request of Franz Joseph. In the meantime neo-Gothic, Romanesque, and Moorish styles (although deprived from the typical dynamism of the brief period of Romanticism) returned, especially in the case of church buildings. From the end of the 1880s the separate styles gave way to composites. The parliament blends French Renaissance, Gothic, and Baroque, the latter in its ground-plan. Eclecticism responded to the eventual monotony of the monumental, massive buildings, playfulness of lights and shadows on the facades and interesting spatial arrangements. Then, during the first years of the twentieth century Eclecticism, after producing fundamentally new and effective values for decades, gave way to a new architectural approach, combining architecture and technology.

The rapid progress of modern architectural technology making use of concrete and steel offered tempting solutions for new departures in construction. The growing antagonism between historical and modern styles clearly indicated that the historical styles had become obsolete and that architecture needed to harmonize function, ground-plan and style by creating an innovative style. The Budapest town-scape became the center and proving ground for architectural endeavors reflecting the results of new innovative solutions. Ödön Lechner was a pathfinder in creating an imaginative Budapest town-scape. By the early 1890s he took meticulous care to harmonize ground-plans with the real functions and the frontal appearance of buildings. The new types of facades opened vistas for new ornamentation techniques. Eventually a certain variation of *Art Nouveau* (Secession style) emerged. By creating special Hungarian ornamentation Lechner pioneered aspirations that consciously broke away from Eclecticism and introduced Secession into the town-scape. New buildings began to reflect the new style, although by 1914 Secession was abandoned for buildings with minimal ornamentations.[21]

Public utilities, expanded as the city developed. The construction of the Budapest sewage system began in the 1870s and by the millennium the level of canalization downtown had reached European standards. All work started before 1896 was completed by 1914. In the years following unification, construction of new waterworks tried to keep pace with demand. By the time of the millennium water supply problem seemed solved, but in the post-1896 period a new crisis occurred. The public was dissatisfied with the quality and quantity of water coming from either the *Káposztásmegyer* or the *Újlak* (completed by 1897) waterworks. Although the quality gradually improved, by 1914 the supply of water still could not keep up with the growth in population.

Gas, played an important and exclusive role in public and private illumination between 1873 and 1896. Gas consumption steadily increased in the capital. In this period the first gas ovens appeared in private households and gas illumination retained its monopoly until the war. By the early years of the century the city was spectacularly illuminated, thus fulfilling the expectations of metropolitan night life.

Although electrical power arrived early, its use was limited for a long time. The first plants for industrial current were founded in 1893 to produce light and industrial energy. Between 1896 and 1914 electrical energy consumption became more conspicuous. In 1911 the *Nagykörút* (Grand Boulevard) and *Vámház körút* (Tollhouse Boulevard) with *Múzeum, Károly, Váci,* (today *Bajcsy-Zsilinszky*) Avenues were lit by electricity.

The period between unification and the millennium had brought along a major turn in mass transportation also. Although the horse-tramways, first introduced before unification, carried the bulk of transportation for a long time, the first experimental electric streetcar was installed along *Nagykörút* in 1887. From then on the gradual expansion of streetcars service was the main feature of mass transportation. From 1889 only electrified railroad lines were built. In 1895–96 the first subway line of the continent was constructed under the road bed of *Andrássy* Ave, starting from *Gizella* (today *Vörösmarty*) Square extending to the *Városliget* (City Park). Its stops were marked above ground by ornamental pyro-granite shelters. They subway train covered the 3.5 kilometer distance in ten minutes.

Rail-lines with clanging horse-tramways, huge double-decker omnibuses accompanied by the clicking sounds of the hoofs on well paved roads, the subway, he increasingly popular cog-wheel railway,[22] and the *Budavár* (Castle) funicular provided mass transportation in Budapest by the end of the millennial year.

In the period between the millennium and the war a network of electric streetcars displaced the horse-car tramways. The streetcar tram lines wove through the narrow streets of downtown and reached the still unpopulated but expanding suburbs. By then the omnibuses had lost importance in mass transportation. Private cars also appeared in the streets of the capital by the first years of the century in increasing numbers. There were 159 private cars in 1905, 568 in 1910, and 1,233 in 1912. The post office also operated over one hundred small cars to collect mail. Quite early in the period the need for rented cars and taxis emerged, although establishing a taxi service was hindered by the outbreak of the war.

Due to war regulations and unusual circumstances the condition of the buildings and the technical equipment of the city deteriorated quickly. The electric railway faced a crisis caused by shortage of staff, austerity measures which reduced the number of cars, and failures of maintenance. Overcrowded vehicles were the norm. As conditions deteriorated during the war years ordinances regulating heating and illumination further plagued urban existence.

The organization of a public health bureaucracy was of paramount importance after 1873. In 1881 anti-epidemic measures were adopted. Health administration and institutions expanded significantly by 1896. Patient care became more and more emphasized. The number of health workers grew accordingly. *Rókus* Hospital, *Szent János* Hospital, *Szent István* Hospital (1886), and *Szent László* hospital (1893) were managed by the city and they increased in size. The numbers of clinics also grew between 1896 and 1914, *Szent Gellért* Hospital in 1899 being a prime example. Although there were 11,000 hospital beds in Budapest in 1913, this large number proved to be insufficient for the increasingly numerous sick of the city and its vicinity.

The Budapest Volunteer Ambulance Association was founded in 1887 and it took over free rescue and first aid from the police. By the eve of the war the Budapest Ambulance Service was a well-run organization was drafted into the war health service.

The Sanitation Authorities, founded in 1894, took responsibility for hygiene in downtown Buda and Kőbánya center by 1902, and the suburbs of Pest by 1912–14, with an elaborate set of staff an up-to-date equipment.

Volunteer Fire Service, whose members were on duty together with professional fire fighters at the Central Fire Station, diminished. Volunteer units were maintained and were usually organized and run by one or two paid professional fire fighters at the major plants. In this period the fire service modernized its equipment and systematized its locations. In 1914 there were 451 professional fire fighters in Budapest.[23]

## Education, Arts, Sciences and the Press

The foundation of national cultural institutes were the most significant cultural development in Budapest between 1873 and 1896. The meaning of what is central in culture is more difficult to determine than in economy or administration. For descriptive purposes institutions designed to represent what is assumed to be the highest level of a profession or institutions which are able permanently or temporarily to shape the general taste or to influence the scale of cultural values, are considered central.

The two universities of Budapest assumed great importance during these years: the University of Arts and Sciences, founded in 1635 by Péter Pázmány in Nagyszombat and moved to Budapest in 1777, and the *József Nádor* Polytechnical University, established in the academic year of 1871–72. Both universities developed fast between 1873 and 1896 along with fast specializing research. The first female student was admitted in 1895–96 by the faculties of medicine and arts. With the large scale expansion of university libraries, Budapest stabilized its privileged position in national higher education. Other professions also centered their institutions of higher education in Budapest (e.g. national art college).

Separate research institutes were established in Budapest for certain areas of science and art that needed a staff larger than what was available at universities or public collections. Even network of agricultural research institutes, vitally important for an agricultural country, began developing in Budapest.

The post-unification era imparted a new vigor to the development of public collections in Budapest. First of all the National Museum grew enormously. The holdings of its library, the Széchényi National Library, which was a depository library for all Hungarian publications from the reform era, (1825–48) contained more than 530,000 volumes by 1896. Codices of great value were available in its manuscript section. The Museum of Fine Arts opened in 1906. The State Archives, restructured in 1874 to incorporate the material from executive offices, ministries, the archives of Transylvanian governor-generals, and those from government offices in Vienna, became the most important source for modern Hungarian historical research and maintained its reputation in subsequent years. In 1896 there were 111 public libraries in Budapest, most of them recently established. Thirty of these predated 1867. The combined libraries contained altogether 1,600,000 volumes. Three libraries, the Széchényi Library, the University Library, and the Library of the Hungarian Academy of Sciences, contained altogether 800,000 volumes in 1896 and 3,200,000 by the end of 1912.

After 1873 scientific associations, united by the Hungarian Academy of Sciences and located at Budapest, became increasingly influential in coordinating and directing the intellectual potential in the country. In 1896 there were already 13 scientific associations housed in Budapest, such as the Hungarian Society of Lawyers (1879), the National Ethnographic Society (1885), and the Society for Mathematics and Physics (1892). Membership reached 15,000 by the millennium. The societies of natural scientists, engineers, and historians had the largest membership. The National Philosophical Society (1900), the Society for the Social Sciences (1901), and the Soceity of Literary Historians (1911) added to the number of significant associations. In the scientific life of the turn of the century Budapest was the standard and the point of reference since its university departments, research institutes, laboratories, teaching hospitals, public collections, and libraries were of the highest scientific level.

The years between unification and the millennium confirmed the leading role of the city in newspaper and book publishing. The press became more specialized and the number of published items increased. Data from 1896 are available to testify to the key position Budapest played. 384 of the 999 nationally circulated papers were published in Budapest, close to 79,250,000 copies were delivered by mail, 68,250,000 in Budapest alone. In 1912, from among the 1,913 national periodicals 775 were published in Budapest. 40 per cent (124 million copies of the total number of 182 million) of the periodicals were mailed from Budapest. It was also after the turn of the century that the typical products of the penny press first appeared. The daily *Est* (Evening), with a circulation exceeding two hundred thousand was launched in 1910 and became the most widely read daily. The national press would publicize events in Budapest, whether political intrigues, crimes, or culture, because Budapest represented the norm of Hungarian society. In the 1880s this role was enhanced by new ways of book publishing through the support of powerful publishing houses with their own printing offices in the city. Dailies and periodicals also fostered a specifically Budapest oriented outlook.

Writers and journalists converged in Budapest around the publishers and Hungarian literature itself reflected this orientation. It gained a modern urban bourgeois flavor through its expanding literary groups, sensitizing writers towards social issues, and centralizing institutions capable of transmitting literature to the readers.

The period between 1873 and 1896 gave rise to some specialization in the theater. In 1875 the *Népszínház* (People's Theater) was created with the intent of relieving the *Nemzeti Színház* (National Theater) from producing popular plays and musicals. This was a major step toward specialization in the Hungarian language theater. These two theaters attracted the best actors, and playwrights of the country. All the worthwhile Hungarian or foreign plays of the time had their premiere in one or the other. If the reviews were favorable, they were carried to the provinces as well.

After the millennium theater life in Budapest became especially lively. New theaters were built: The *Vígszínház* (Comic Theater) in 1896, where most of Ferenc Molnár's plays were shown and the *Magyar Színház* (Hungarian Theater) which in 1897 presented operettas. The *Magyar Színház* was superseded by the *Király Színház* (King Theater) (1903) as an operetta theater. It became a modern art theater for the educated urban middle-class. Accommodating these processes that created a stratum of impatient, dissatisfied, radical intellectuals and employees, the number of experimental theater companies multiplied. They were mostly small companies, sometimes without a permanent place, striving for the adequate expression of new artistic and political trends in drama. The *Thália* Society (1904–1909), the most radical of these maverick groups, emerged from this movement. The structural changes of the city's theatrical institutes drove the *Népszínház* into bankruptcy, neverthelesss theatrical life flourished.

Motion pictures did not diminish the influence of the theater for a long time, on the contrary it complemented it.

After 1873 the role of the city in fine arts gathered momentum. Budapest was attractive because of its art market. Numerous galleries attracted artists since reviews of exhibtions publicized their work around the country. The need of public and private construction for ornamentation and more frequent orders from the bourgeoisie also attracted artists. As a result, a fine arts center was formed by significant artists of the period.

In the post-millennial epoch fine arts became specialized and was marked by a conflict of styles and trends. Modernism, which opposed the tenets of academism, was centered in Budapest a belated conflict compared with developments in Western European art. During the six years following József Rippl-Rónai's return from Paris in 1900, the climate became much more favorable, although the reception of the expressionist Group of Eight[24] (around 1909) and the groups forming around Lajos Kassák's *Ma*[25] remained cool. Still it was the highly cosmopolitan society of the city that was able to appreciate the new styles.

Between 1873 and 1896 a certain duality prevailed in the musical culture of the capital. Higher institutes of music education and institutes of performing arts had been government financed. Society required institutions to reflect local taste, for that purpose private, sometimes amateur, yet high quality orchestras were founded.

The Academy of Music was founded in 1875 and its first president was Franz Liszt. The Opera house was built by 1884 and the *Népopera* (Peoples Opera, today's *Erkel* Theater) opened in 1911. From the beginning of the twentieth century the City provided regular instrumental music education in its middle and high schools for gifted students. Concert played in concert halls improved, relying on a broader base of supporters. It was music among all the areas of culture in which field Budapest best fulfilled its leading role.

In city planning provisions were made for the education of the lower and middle levels of society. The network of institutions grew quantitatively but also new types of educational institutions were established due to the increase and differentiation of the population.

In the academic year 1873–74 there were 67 elementary schools for 30,463 students in the capital. By 1896–97 this number stood at 151 elementary schools catering to 51,192 children, and by 1912 the number increased to 218 for 61,507 students.

From 1884 industrial and trade schools were established. A qualified journeyman had to complete a three-year course within these new types of schools. Between 1897 and 1902 the city, reflecting the needs of manufacturing, introduced specialized training for apprentices. Middle and high school education were the stepping stones for economic and social mobility and these types of schools were in greatest demand. In the academic year of 1873–74 there were only 9 middle schools for 1,085 students in the capital, but by 1896–97 this number had grown to 27 for 7,440 students, and by 1914 to 54 for 20,000 students. Students graduating from these schools had access to a wide array of further educational opportunities.

In 1876 there were three eight-year *gimnazia* (classical) high schools and four *real-gimnazia* (modern) high schools, by 1896 there were twelve *gimnazia* and five *real-gimnazia*, in other words high schools of eight year curriculum, and by 1912 this number had increased to nineteen. The students of *real-gimnazia* type of high schools did not prepare for university studies requiring Latin as a pre-requisite. That is the reason why the number of these schools did not increase.

From 1875 the six-year high schools for girls were established at the demand of parents who wanted better education for their daughters. The curriculum paralleled that of the regular high schools, which had been restricted to boys. The first eight-year school for girls opened in 1896.

The crisis of the World War was best reflected in literature. Writers clustering around the periodical *Nyugat*[26] expressed their feelings about the war in various ways. The forms varied from open resistance, or complete rejection to meticulous detail and pleas for peace. The war was a spur to realism with its new forms of expression in literature, fine arts, and music. The war had an impact on modern music. In the 1917–18 season the Opera produced Béla Bartók's The "Wooden Prince" and "Bluebeards's Castle," and both Bartók and Kodály were surprised by the public acceptance of their compositions.[27]

In the Fall of 1918, after seven decades of stability and gradual change, a revolution loomed large in Hungary. The revolution was the response of Budapest above all to the military and political collapse of the Central Powers and its impact on society and economy.

## Notes

1. Material comprising this chapter was compiled by Boldizsár Vörös from the various essays of Károly Vörös, in László Gerevich, ed., *Budapest története* [History of Budapest], vol. 4, *Budapest története a márciusi forradalomtól az őszirózsás forradalomig* [The history of Budapest from the March Revolution to the October Revolution], ed. Károly Vörös (Budapest, 1978) 7–8, 311, 775. The notes of the compiler are identified with [B. V.]. Due to space restrictions several details were left out from this essay, for example the description of the suburban situation. These suburbs are outside the administrative boundaries of the city have close economic ties and good public transportation with Budapest [B. V.].

2. Hungarians migrating from east to west settled at the Carpathian Basin in the ninth century. "The time of their arrival was between 888 and 900 A.D. as stated by late nineteenth century historians. Consequently, the Hungarian government in preparation for the celebration of the Conquest, declared 1896 the year of the millennium." Budapest became the scene of major celebrations of the anniversary. Károly Vörös, "A millennium kora" [The age of the millennium] in *Budapest enciklopédia* [The Budapest encyclopedia], ed. Endréné Tóth (Budapest, 1982), 220–222. Ferenc Végh's interview with

Károly Vörös, "Március idusától az őszirózsás forradalomig" [From the Ides of March to the October Revolution], *Tudományos Magazin* 9, no. 3 (1976), 48–49. [B. V.].

3. For population trends see also Gusztáv Thirring, Budapest székesfőváros a millennium idejében [Budapest, capital city in the year of the millennium] (Budapest, 1898) corresponding chapters; Budapest félszázados fejlődése 1873–1923 [Development of Budapest in half a century 1873–1923] (Budapest, 1925), 9–64; Gyula Pikler, "A népesség" [The population], in *A negyvenéves Budapest* [The forty-year-old Budapest] (Budapest, 1913), 33–44.

4. The Acts of 1870. XLII and 1871. XVIII enacted the registration of major taxpayers (who paid state taxes) of municipalities and villages. Based on the register, the governing bodies included major taxpayers among their representatives, fifty percent of whom came from among the major taxpayers who were automatically included because of their financial status. See also Károly Vörös, *Budapest legnagyobb adófizetői* [The major taxpayers of Budapest] (Budapest, 1979), 7–8 [B. V.].

5. Until the unification only the Jewish emancipation expanded the circle of citizens with suffrage rights as defined by Act V of 1848. Act XXXIII of 1874 redefined voting rights and based it on tax categories. Vörös, ed., op. cit., 429.

6. For occupational trends see József Kőrösi, *Budapest fővárosa az 1881-ik évben. A népleírás és népszámlálás eredményei* [Budapest, capital city in 1881. Census data and census returns] (Budapest, 1881–1883), vols. 1–3; József Kőrösi and Gusztáv Thirring, *Budapest fővárosa az 1891-ik évben. A népleírás és népszámlálás eredményei* [Budapest, capital city in 1891. Census data and census returns] (Budapest, 1894–1898), vols. 1–3; idem, *Budapest fővárosa az 1901-ik évben. A népleírás és népszámlálás eredményei* [Budapest, capital city in 1901. Census data and census returns] (Budapest, 1903–1905), vols. 1–2; *Budapest félszázados fejlődése 1873–1923*, op. cit.

7. Corresponding chapters of Budapest in Kőrösi and Thirring, *Budapest fővárosa az 1891-ik évben*; Jenő Rákosi, "Budapest városrészei" [Boroughs of Budapest], in *Az Osztrák-Magyar Monarchia írásban és képben* [The Austro-Hungarian Monarchy in literature and pictures], ed. Rudolf, Crown Prince of Austria (Budapest, 1893), vol. 9, 169–192.

8. Gusztáv Thirring, *Budapest főváros demográfiai és társadalmi tagozódásának fejlődése az utolsó 50 évben* [Development of demographic and social structures of Budapest in the past 50 years] (Budapest), vol. 1, 302–328.

9. For organizational matters of the unification see Albert Gárdonyi, ed., *A főváros egyesítésére vonatkozó okmányok gyűjteménye* [Collection of documents about the unification] (Budapest, 1913); for a detailed description of the unification Károly Vörös, *Egy világváros születése* [Birth of a metropolis] (Budapest, 1973).

10. The Liberal Party was founded in 1875 and remained governmental party until 1905. The government crisis of 1905–1906 led to the defeat of the party and to its dissolution [B. V.].

11. The Act of Unification, the delineation of authority, and the first city ordinances in Aladár Márher "A szervezet" [The organization] in *A negyvenéves Budapest*, op. cit., 146–158; Gárdonyi, ed., op. cit.

12. About the economy see the relevant sections in Gyula Rácz, "A pénzügyek" [Finances] in A negyvenéves Budapest, op. cit.

13. The distinction between "capital" and "capital city" (equivalent of "főváros" and "székesfőváros") was terminated by a decree of the mayor in 1949, after the communist takeover. "Capital" became the only terminology [B. V.].

14. Following the Liberal Party Prime Minister István Tisza's violation of law 1904, the opposition parties formed a coalition and won the January 1905 parliamentary elections and the Liberal Party was defeated. However, Francis Joseph was not willing to nominate a prime minister from the parliamentary majority. Completely ignoring parliamentary procedures he appointed Géza Fejérváry, captain of the royal guards to form a government. The opposition did not vote for the minority government and "national resistance" was declared. Finally the opposition, after giving up all its essential demands, took office (in 1906 it repeatedly won the elections), though this coalition government of 1906–1910 fell into discredit. At the parliamentary elections of 1910 the coalition was defeated. The old government party, reorganized by István Tisza as the Party of Work came to power [B. V.].

15. For the modernization of the central administration: see Márher, op. cit. 172–184; a summary for the aspirations and results of the Bárczy-era, see *Fővárosi Almanach, Lexikon és útmutató 1913–1915* [Municipal almanach, encyclopedia, and guide 1913–1915], ed. Imre Guthi (Budapest), 13–107.

16. For the city economy, see Rácz, op. cit.

17. For summary of city administrative activities between 1914 and mid-1916: Ödön Wildner, "Budapest a világháborúban" [Budapest in the World War] in *Fővárosi Almanach, Lexikon és Útmutató 1916–1918* [Municipal almanach encyclopedia, and guide 1916–1918], ed. Imre Guthi (Budapest), III–X, and see 210–574.

18. In 1916 Mihály Károlyi and followers created the opposition Independence Party and Party of 1848 that was soon called the Károlyi Party. The party acknowledged the personal union, and demanded peace without annexation, universal suffrage, democratic social policy and land reforms. This pro-Entente party became popular during the war and was closely associated with other opposition forces [B. V.].

19. The Hungarian Social Democratic Party was founded in 1890 and envisioned socialism as its final goal. Although it did not get into Parliament until 1918, it played an increasingly important role in political life. It managed to mobilize hundreds of thousands of people to participate in its demonstrations

and rallies. During the war the party was in close contact with opposition parties [B. V.].

20. For trade see *Budapestfélévszázados fejlődése 1873–1923*, op. cit., 115–119; for credit institutes see corresponding chapters in Antal Alföldi, *A budapesti pénzintézetek története napjainkig* [The history of Budapest's financial institutions] (Budapest, 1928); for the manufacturing industry see Vilmos Sándor, *Nagyipari fejlődés Magyarországon 1867–1900* [The development of primary industry in Hungary, 1867–1900] (Budapest, 1954); Iván T. Berend and György Ránki, *Magyarország gyáripara az imperializmus első világháború előtti időszakában 1900–1914* [Hungarian manufacturing industry in the pre-World War I period of imperialism, 1900–1914] (Budapest, 1955); for retail trade see Lajos Bene, *Budapest székesfőváros kereskedői* [Merchants of Budapest, the capital city] (Budapest, 1929); for agriculture see Antal Bodor, *Budapest mezőgazdasága* [The agriculture of Budapest] (Budapest); for the war economy see Baron József Szterényi and Jenő Ladányi, *A magyar ipar a világháborúban* [The Hungarian industry in World War] (Budapest, 1933).

21. For town-planning see Árpád Schmelhegger, "Városépítés" [City planning] in *A negyvenéves Budapest*, op. cit., 378–419; corresponding parts of Gábor Preisich, *Budapest városépítésének története* [History of Budapest town-planning] (Budapest, 1964) vol. 2.

22. The Budapest cog-wheel railway was built between 1873 and 1890. It ran from Városmajor across Sváb-hegy (today Szabadság-hegy) to Széchenyi-hegy on a 3,433 méter long rail and was towed by a special engine [B. V.].

23. For the subway see Vörös, "A millennium kora" in op. cit., ed. Tóth, 224; for public utilities see Preisich, op. cit., 107–120; Schmelhegger, op cit., 421–428; for public health see Sándor Szabó, "A közegészégügy" [Public health] in *A negyvenéves Budapest*, op. cit., 484–499.

24. "Nyolcak" [Group of eight] was active between 1909 and 1912 and implemented modern aspirations. Károly Kernstok was its leading figure. The heritage of Paul Cézanne, fauvism, expressionism, cubism and the secession prevailed in their art. Its intellectual and esthetic aspirations are similar to those of *Nyugat* [B. V.].

25. *Ma* was an avantgarde literary and art magazine by Lajos Kassák and was published between 1916 and 1925. It comprised various artistic aspirations. [B. V.].

26. *Nyugat* was one of the most significant literary and review journal of Hungarian literary criticism between 1908 and 1941. It was the center of the turn-of-the-century intellectual renewal. Endre Ady, Mihály Babits, Zsigmond Móricz, Frigyes Karinthy, Gyula Krúdy were among the outstanding writers and poets who contributed [B. V.].

27. For the outlines of cultural development see Károly Vörös, "A művelődés és kulturális élet alakulása Budapesten 1873–1945" [Development of edu-

cation and culture in Budapest, 1871–1945], in *Tanulmányok Budapest múltjából* [Essays about the past of Budapest], ed. Miklós Horváth (Budapest, 1974), vol. 20, 97–106.

*Miklós Lackó*

# Budapest During the Interwar Years

## The Impact of War on the City's Demography

The post World War I period created new and more serious conditions both for the country and its capital. The dynamic development of the previous decades stymied by grave crises. There were significant positive effects of belonging to the Austro-Hungarian Monarchy, for after the Czech territories, Hungary was the main beneficiary of the connection. Hungary's rate of overtaking the economic level of Western European countries was greatest during the two decades around the turn of the century.

The peace treaty of Trianon in 1920 took away two thirds of Hungary's former territory and 58 per cent of its population. These caused severe national grievances and modified the social and economic structure of the country in many respects. Among these structural changes was the increasing importance of Budapest. Although several significant towns like Kolozsvár (Cluj), Pozsony (Bratislava), Kassa (Kosice), Nagyvárad (Oradea), Arad, and Újvidék (Novi Sad), and several smaller but socially and culturally not less important ones like Szabadka (Subotica), and some mining towns in former Northern Hungary were lost, the remaining territory was more developed economically than was historic Hungary. The strong agricultural character of the country somewhat diminished, and the new territory included the more industrial regions. Besides Budapest and its environs, however, hardly any mining and industrial districts remained, except for the newly developing bauxite mining as well as the oil drillings in Transdanubia and the southern part of the Great Hungarian Plains.

The ratio between the relatively modern agricultural large estates and peasant plots was higher on the remaining territory. The rate of the poor remained very high, they were hardly able to support themselves on their small plots received during the very meager land reform of the early 1920s. The poverty-stricken agrarian proletariat and the semi-proletarian masses were also significant. György Oláh, a political writer who later went over to the extreme right, justly called Hungary "the country of three million beggars". The development of the city slowed but did not stop even under the new circumstances. Here are a few statistical data to illustrate this situation:

### The Increase of Urban and Rural Population of Hungary between 1910 and 1941 (in per cent)[1]

| Type of settlement | 1910–30 | 1930–41 |
|---|---|---|
| Budapest administrative area | 7.1 | 15.7 |
| Six towns of county rank around Budapest* | 41.5 | 13.8 |
| Eleven villages with more than 10,000 inhabitants around Budapest | 51.8 | 48.0 |
| Twenty country towns (corporate towns) | 13.0 | 8.0 |
| Sixty-four regular towns | 6.1 | 7.2 |
| Villages with more than 10,000 inhabitants | 7.9 | 6.7 |
| Villages with less than 10,000 inhabitants | 4.6 | 4.6 |
| Total growth of the Hungarian population | 6.8 | 6.8 |

### Number of Inhabitants in Budapest

| | |
|---|---|
| 1910 | 880,000 |
| 1914 | 959,000 |
| 1920 | 929,000 |
| 1930 | 1,106,000 |
| 1941 | 1,165,000[2] |

---

* Towns of county rank (*megyei város*) stood higher in the hierarchy of administration than corporate towns (*rendezett tanácsú város*). They were headed by a mayor and his government. Self-government was excercised by the municipal council. From 1930 such towns were Budafok, Pesterzsébet, Rákospalota, and Újpest, from 1932 Kispest, from 1936 Pestszentlőrinc, and from 1949 Csepel.

The population increased even between 1941 and 1944, but this process inverted after the German occupation in March, 1944. The deportation and the attrocities committed against the Jewish population, the bombardments, and the military and civil losses during the siege of Budapest in 1944–45 were detrimental to the demographic conditions of the city.

The increased significance of Budapest after 1919 is illustrated also by the proportion of its inhabitants to the country as a whole. Prior to 1918, nearly 4.5 per cent of the country's population (20 million at that time) lived in Budapest. In 1920 this rate rose to near 12 per cent, in 1930 to 12.7 per cent of the 8,690,000 inhabitants, and in 1941 to 12.5 per cent of the 9,300,000 inhabitants. Including the belt of suburbs,[3] 17.9 per cent of the total population of the country lived in the capital in 1930, and 18.5 per cent in 1941. At the same time, the population of most other towns remaining in Trianon Hungary hardly increased. Only in certain industrial or mining areas (e.g., Miskolc and Veszprém) occurred significant growth. On the other hand, the population of several country towns on the Great Plains and along the new frontiers even decreased significantly. This was due to the loss of regions they had been the centers of.

Budapest had originally been the capital of a large multinational country. Under the new circumstances the question arose whether it was healthy to have such a large percentage of the total population in the capital. The percentage in other European capitals was much smaller: for example, 6.5 per cent in Berlin, 7 per cent in Paris, 4.4 per cent in Madrid, and 3.7 per cent Warsaw in 1930. The exception was Vienna, the home of more than a quarter of the inhabitants of Austria.

The Budapest population increased further in the interwar period. In the 1920s migration focused on the industrial belt, and in the 1930s on the inner parts of the city proper. So the capital absorbed nearly one third of the total population increase in the country. This, in turn, involved the growing weight of the city in the industrial, commercial, administrative, and cultural life of the country, and contributed to perpetuating the differences between the agrarian regions and the capital. At the same time, it also increased urbanization. The traditional leading classes proudly welcomed the development of the city in the late 19th century. They entertained a Liberal platform of the gentry but later became Conservative. During the era under discussion, they turned against Budapest. So did the new agrarian or right-wing elements, even though they never denied the significance of the metropolis. The writer Dezső Szabó believed in the myth of the peasantry as the vital force of the country. He criticized the predominance of Jewish bourgeoisie and intelligentsia in the city. László Németh advocated the idea of the "third road",[*] sharply criticizing the mass culture fostered by big cities in general, and spoke of domination by Budapest. Both of them wished to increase the Hungarian character of the city to replace its "Jewish" character. A person in Dezső Szabó's novel *Az elsodort falu* (The Swept-away Village, 1919) when looking down upon Budapest ponders on this problem: "... To conquer life entirely, to make these exploited, naive Hungarians the winners on all markets and at all contests. But not by force of fists and unjust laws, but by the inner impetus of instincts. To imbue this anachronistic crowd with democracy, and make them rush to become dealers, bankers, publicists, politicians, industrialists, soldiers, artists, or even usurpers and swindlers, if need be, but never to be cheated and exploited again."[4] In an article entitled *Budapest meghódítása* (The Conquest of Budapest), written in 1938, László Németh was pleased to acknowledge the great numbers of poor people coming to the capital from the countryside, representing a new wave of conquering Hungarians on the one hand, and the demographical decline of the Jewish population of the city on the other. As a result of this process the Budapest Jewry would disappear "upwards", and Budapest would become a fully Hungarian city in the following thirty years, or so he believed.[5]

Natural growth contributed to the population increase of the capital to an ever smaller degree, as in other big cities in Europe. Due to the decreasing but still very high mortality rates and the low birth rates, the natural growth of the population around 1930 was less than one per thousand. (As a contrast, there were 25.5 live births and 18.5 deaths per thousand inhabitants in 1910, but 16.3 live births and 15.5 deaths in 1940.)[6] Berlin and Vienna were the only cities in Europe that had a similarly low natural increase of the population.

The greater part of the population increase was thus due to immigration. In the first years after 1918 most people arrived from the territories annexed to the neighboring countries, mostly officials, teachers, and railwaymen. The majority of the newcomers in Budapest still came from the needy layers of the towns and villages. Formerly people came mostly from the vicinity of the city, from settlements in Pest or Fejér counties and the more developed counties in the western part of the country. Now they arrived primarily from the more backward counties in Northeastern Hungary and

---

[*] Editors' note: the first "road" was considered Western capitalist, the second the Soviet, the third was a particular Hungarian (East Central European) "road".

other territories east of the River Tisza. Skilled workers arrived mainly from Western and Northern Transdanubia, while unskilled workers from the region between the Rivers Danube and Tisza, and from the even more backward region east of the Tisza.[7] Migration also had another direction, namely from the inner parts of the capital toward the suburbs and the villages of the region not yet incorporated by Budapest. This suburban belt had 50,000 inhabitants who had been born in the city in 1920, and 82,000 in 1930, and their rate was gradually increasing.[8]

Already in the previous period some high-standard branches of industry like machine tools and the textile industries had settled in the suburbs or along the border line between the city and the suburbs. Although this belt increasingly became part of the city, it retained its rural character, so the living conditions for the poorer layers of the population (e.g., workers and pensioners) were favourable. Rents were lower, the environment was more like villages, plots were cheaper, houses were more available, and vegetable gardens supplied additional food. These advantages were, however, counterbalanced by the more backward housing conditions, the lower level of public utilities, the greater distance from institutions of higher education and urban culture, long commuting to one's place of work. Garden suburbs, another type of settlement, began to attract people in the 1920s, which intensified in the 1930s. The wealthier layers moved to the hilly parts of Buda, and the less well-to-do to the garden suburbs surrounding Pest or the southern parts of Buda.

The distribution of the population by place of birth illustrates this process. The stratification of a large town's population demonstrates two somewhat contrasting phenomena. On the one hand, the newer a city and the greater its attraction, the more of its inhabitants tend to be born elsewhere. On the other hand, older cities have a larger proportion of inhabitants native to that city. Budapest became a metropolis of a million inhabitants in just a few decades, and its attraction was still very strong in the period under discussion. Its layer of old dwellers committed to urban life was already strong, the rate of those born in Budapest being more than one third of the total population. According to census results, nearly 38 per cent of the population of Budapest proper had been born in the city, which rate was hardly below the comparable rates of Prague and Paris.[9] The remaining 62 per cent had, however, strong links with their rural past. Zsigmond Móricz, a realist writer of peasant and rural life, wrote several novels of Budapest in the 1930s illustrating these links. One of his characters, a young journalist just working his way into urban society says the following:

"Do you know what's interesting here?", he asked his wife. "Did you notice that the leaders, and not only in public life, come from the country-side? It's interesting that everyone in Pest has come from the country."[10]

It is sometimes hard for newcomers to adapt to the life-style of a big city. In his short novel *Az öreg tekintetes* (The Old Honourable), written prior to the First World War, the conservative writer Géza Gárdonyi described the tragedy of an old landowner who moved to Budapest. The old man was unable to adjust to the circumstances of the big city, although at first he found them interesting. Later he started to be indisposed and turned into despair. He felt at home only among the poor of *Józsefváros*, one of the most populous districts of the city, and in his solitude he ever more frequently went to the confines of the city just to see farmland. Finally he started to grow corn in cigar-boxes in his room. In the period under survey these problems ceased to be as acute as that, but the poor people arriving to the capital from the country had to endure severe hardships while accomodating themselves to the urban way of life.

The newcomers were attracted by the village-like suburbs of the city. Certain new circumstances also supported their accomodation. The war years removed the male population of the country from their original and restricted environment and mixed them with the urban population. The big city's demand for labor, which lagged far behind the last period of dualism, was substantial after the consolidation of the 1920s. Thereafter in the years following the great depression of the 1930s, and in the period between 1938 and 1943, owing to the war effort, demand for labor was once again considerable. Most of those who found work in the capital settled into better living conditions than what they left behind in the country, whether as agricultural laborers or handicraftsmen.

The religious distribution of the capital's population was different from the national average. On the territory remaining in Hungary after Trianon 63 per cent were Catholics in 1910 and 65 per cent in 1941. The rate of Calvinists amounted to one fifth of the country's population. The Lutherans constituted 6 per cent, the Jews 6.2 per cent in 1910, and 4.7 per cent in 1941.[11] The fall in the rate of the Jewish population was partly due to the territorial losses. (The regions of Northeastern Hungary with a massive Jewish population became parts of Czechoslovakia.) The decline was partly due to a declining rate of childbirth among middle-class Jews, and partly to an increasing emigration in the wake of the strengthening anti-

Semitic movements after 1919. About 25,000 Jewish people left the country in twenty years. Most of those who emigrated left from Budapest. Many of them belonged primarily to the highly qualified layers of the intelligentsia. The growing number of mixed marriages and conversions to Christianity also contributed to the decrease. The latter assumed larger proportions only after the state legislated anti-Jewish measures from 1938 on.

In Budapest the percentage of Calvinists was only 12 per cent, while that of the Lutherans was decreasing relatively (partly owing to the assimilation of the German nationality living in Budapest and its environment in large numbers). The ratio of Jews was exceptionally high, more than 20 per cent in 1920. This rate was, however, decreasing quickly and dropped to 15.8 by 1941.

The Jews represented a layer that was considered important not only from religious point of view, but also because they played significant roles in the development of the capital. Their social composition was unique, half of them living in towns, and 45 per cent in Budapest. More than 80 per cent of them settled down in certain districts, namely, in the inner city, *Terézváros, Erzsébetváros,* and *Józsefváros,* i.e., in districts V, VI, VII, and VIII. Their rate among those who had been born in Budapest was the highest of all ethnic groups, nearly 50 per cent.[12] Their overwhelming majority belonged to the lower middle class or worked in small-scale industry. But their rate among the middle and wealthier bourgeoisie, as well as the intelligentsia was also high. Most of them tried to assimilate as far as possible after the First World War and the post-war revolutions. The rate of Orthodox Jews was only 4–5 per cent in the capital. Tivadar Herzl, the Hungarian-born founder of Zionism, was right in saying that the Hungarian Jewry was "a withering branch on the tree of the Jewry". The majority of Hungarian Jewry could not be considered a separate nationality any longer. They represented an interesting color on the Budapest social palette with their religious and cultural traditions. This did not prevent the anti-Semitism of the Horthy regime, on the contrary, the assimilation process rather strengthened it. Anti-Semitism was not directed primarily against Jews preserving their separate national character, rather against the assimilated ones. Despite all obstacles in the way of assimilation, including the anti-Jewish laws and decrees passed between 1939 and 1942 which qualified approximately 100,000 Christian people racially Jewish in the entire country. In the early 1940s 62,000 of them lived in Budapest alongside with 184,000 Jews who remained faithful to their original religion.[13]

## Economy, Industry and Commerce

The social structure of Budapest was determined by the heritage of the dualist period, the trends of economic developments, and the effects of politics on society. As regards economy, the development of the city was inseparable from that of the whole country.[14] The years immediatelly following 1919 were times of regression, turmoil, and instability not only politically but also from economic point of view. The country and its capital had to tackle the aftermath of the war and the revolutions of 1918–1919, the difficulties arising from the fall of the Monarchy and the fact that the country was reduced to one third of its former territory, and many other detrimental events: the months of Romanian military occupation and the illegal expropriation of a significant part of the Hungarian means of production and transport by the Romanian army. The international economic relations of the country deteriorated. Former markets were lost owing partly to isolationist economic policy characteristic of the whole region, partly to the conditions in Austria and Germany, and partly to the hostile relationship with the neighboring countries. The economic setback was followed by a destructive inflation.

The leading circles in the Western countries considered Hungary a country of semi-feudal landlords and oppressors of nationalities. The West did not take into consideration the grave effects of the unjust Trianon peace treaty. As preconditions of their support and loans they demanded that Hungary should create political stability and suppress extreme right movements, particularly anti-Semitism. Political stabilization was led by the conservative politician, Prime Minister Count István Bethlen (1921–1930), who restored parliamentarism by the mid-1920s, even though the regime remained authoritarian. Only on this basis, with its concommitant economic policy, could the economic life of the country be restored. Four measures were introduced: inflation was utilized to increase internal capital and investment; protective tariffs were introduced to defend industry (mainly light industry); western machines and raw materials were imported; and economic life was stabilized through loans from abroad.

Budapest's economy utilized these opportunities very effectively. Although between 1919 and 1925 the development of manufacturing in the capital was slower than the national average, it accelerated from 1925–26. In 1929 the number of factories in Budapest and its industrial belt exceeded the 1913 level. One third of the machines, half of the production value, and more than half of the factory workers in Hungary were concentrated in Budapest and its environs. Development was mainly due to the growth of the formerly insignificant textile industry; other branches of mass production; electricity production, and the rise of chemical industry. In other spheres of industry, for example, in machine industry (at least in the most significant mammoths like Manfred Weiss Works of Csepel, the Hoffherr and Schranz Machine Factory, or the Ganz Works) modernization of facilities was the rule. Precision engineering and modern electrical engineering were introduced as new branches of industry in older factories. The pharmaceutical industry also flourished. Significant companies in the Budapest area were: *Magyar Optikai Művek* [Hungarian Optical Works], *Gamma, Egyesült Izzó, Lámpa és Villamossági Rt.* [United Electric Bulb, Lamp, and Electricity Co.], *Ganz Villamossági Gyár* [Ganz Electric Works], *Chinoin Gyógyszer- és Vegyészeti Termékek Gyára Rt.* [Chinoin Pharmaceutical and Chemical Factory Co.].

Other areas were, however, on the decline. Food industry lost its former importance mainly owning to the total setback of the formerly high-standard milling industry of Budapest. Some branches like meat-, tobacco-, and the canning-industry increased their production. There was a serious decline in construction industry and its branches. Production of building material amounted to only half of the pre-war level even as late as the late 1920s. Before the war, 10,000–11,000 rooms were built in Budapest a year, while between 1920 and 1929 hardly more than 5,000–6,000 (even in the years of economic boom in 1927–29). Between 1933 and 1938, however, construction picked up: 15,000–16,000 rooms were built each year in Budapest.[15]

Budapest was also the center of financial and commercial life. The old network of banks, quite developed throughout the country, lacked capital and the role of the big financial institutions solidified. At the end of the 1920s, 11 per cent of the banks of Hungary operated in Budapest, but they exercised control over two thirds of the country's economy. The influence of the two largest banks, the *Magyar Általános Hitelbank* [Hungarian General Credit Bank] and the *Pesti Magyar Kereskedelmi Bank* [Hungarian Commercial Bank of Pest], was the most notable. They controlled more than half of the Hungarian manufacturing industry, most of the mining industry, the largest iron works, the Manfred Weiss Works of Csepel, various factories of the Ganz Works, and a lot of factories connected with them. The international economic connections of Budapest and the rest of the country were ensured by these large banking institutions. Foreign (American, French, Austrian, and British) concerns held up to 20 to 30 per cent of the banks' capital. All these prove the significance, the international activity, and mobility of the big bourgeoisie in the capital. At the same time it also proves that, in spite of their mostly Jewish origin, the great capitalists of Budapest served Hungarian national economic rather than "cosmopolitan" economic interests in ways similar to the pre-war years. The steady development of Hungarian economy in the second half of the 1920s was seriously jarred by the Great Depression of 1929–33. Not only Budapest and Hungarian industry suffered but also the agricultural trades employing about half of the country's population. The new branches of light-, the textile-, and consumer goods industry satisfying internal demands could tide over the hardships easier. But the metal and machine industry involved in export were in a much more serious situation. Compared to its peak in 1929, the production of manufacturing dropped by 24 per cent in 1932, the worst year of the crisis. The number of industrial workers fell by 30 per cent, and 46 per cent of the handicraftsmen earned less than the tax-free minimum subsistence level. The industrial and agricultural crisis was combined with a grave financial and credit debacle as well.

In Budapest the industry started to recover from the shock of the depression only in 1934. The major recovery began only with the increasing preparations for war from 1938–39. The so-called "Győr Program" announced by the government in 1938 provided a public investment of one billion pengő to support war industries. Until the onset of the Second World War, the manufacturing industry of Budapest increased its production by 20 per cent compared to 1929, the number of workers increased by 22 per cent, and this upward trend continued also in the first years of the war. The political orientation of the masses was influenced very negatively by the fact that this short period of prosperity, a temporary rising living standard paralleled a strong pro-German orientation. Former parts of Hungary were recovered in those years with Italian and German support, and German influence became stronger in many fields.

The dynamic development of commerce also stopped in the years after the First World War. The commercial life of Budapest regained the level of 1913 by 1929 but surpassed it only very slowly after the Great Depression. The network of shops was extended  and modern networks appeared slowly, e.g. the Gyula Meinl Co. or the municipal bakery shops of the capital city. New department stores were also opened, among them the

Corvin in 1925. The purchasing power of the public was, however, poor and temporarily increased only in the more prosperous years during the preparations for and the first years of the war (1939–43), when the humble beginning of a consumers' society could be observed. The foreign trade of the capital was reestablished with extraordinary difficulties. Several factors contributed to the revival: the growing German demand for agricultural products, the discovery of new resources of raw materials (bauxite and oil), and the increased production of industries concentrated in the capital (tractor manufacturing and the modern pharmaceutical industry of Budapest).

Life in the capital was directly improved by changes in the infrastructure, electrification, and the development of new branches of communication, new means of transportation, and public utilities. The number of workers in public utility companies amounted to over 25,000 at the end of the period. Budapest also played a role in this development as a capitalist entrepreneur, and its income from the public utilities reached 68 per cent of the revenue.[16] Power production increased with the construction of new power stations. Gas-production in the capital practically stagnated between 1920 and 1929, but production of electricity increased threefold, the number of households with electricity grew by leaps and bounds. The consumption of the industry also tripled. These changes affected the public transportation also in the city. BESZKÁRT (the Transportation Company of the Capital City Budapest) incorporated the tramway companies formerly owned by foreign or Hungarian private investors, and the underground, the first on the Continent, the cog-wheel railway leading to the *Svábhegy* (Swabian Hill) of Buda, and the rail-lines of smaller companies around Budapest were united under one authority. New lines were built, and the rolling-stock of BESZKÁRT was modernized. The number of trams grew from 1300 in 1929 to 1760 in 1939. Road traffic (meaning cars and buses) also developed to a certain extent. In 1929 buses were responsible for only 5 per cent of all passenger traffic in the capital, which amounted to nearly 15 per cent by 1938. The Budapest car traffic remained insignificant compared with the western countries throughout the period. The construction of the Miklós Horthy Bridge (now Petőfi Bridge), completed in 1935, over the Danube greatly facilitated traffic and transport in Budapest. The construction of another one at the northern end of *Margitsziget* (Margaret Island) to be called Árpád Bridge was also in progress. The electrification of the railway lines also had a direct impact on the life of the capital. The first electric trains between Budapest and Hegyeshalom on the western border started running in the 1930s.

The sewer system of Budapest had hardly developed since the early years of the century, and especially the suburbs and villages were very backward in this respect even at the end of the period. The waterworks were significantly extended and modernized. Most steam-operated waterworks were motorized and new wells were dug north and south of the capital along the Danube. The postal service remained on its former level, but the telephone network was extended, although much slower than in Western Europe. Radio broadcasting started in 1925 as a new and revolutionary means of telecommunication and information. There were nearly 60,000 subscribers in Budapest in 1929 and more than 150,000 in the 1940s.[17]

The social heritage of the dualist period and the economic and cultural conditions between the two world wars left their mark on the social structure of Budapest. Census data from 1930 and 1941 offer the possibility of comparison, although the categories are not fully compatible. Only the most general demographic data of the 1941 census were processed before 1945. The occupational stratification of the population was analyzed in the Central Statistical Office in the 1970s by applying modern categories, such as "working in service". It can be established that the rate of self-employed decreased under the new circumstances and the rate of those earning wages and salaries (workers, employees and intellectuals) increased. The following table illustrates this point.

**Distribution of the Employed in Budapest by Type of Occupation, 1930–1941 (per cent)[18]**

| Type of occupation | Budapest | | Suburban belt | | Greater Budapest | |
|---|---|---|---|---|---|---|
| | 1930 | 1941 | 1930 | 1941 | 1930 | 1941 |
| Self-employed | 21 | 14 | 19 | 12 | 20 | 14 |
| Manual workers | 60 | 62 | 71 | 76 | 63 | 66 |
| Intellectuals and employees | 19 | 23 | 10 | 12 | 17 | 20 |

## Social Stratification

The population of the capital could be divided into four categories according to social status in this period: (1) leading elite (political and military cadres, leaders of administration, landowners living in the city, aristocrats, bank managers and financiers, and intellectuals belonging to the higher middle class), constituting 2 per cent of the population; (2) the well-to-do middle class (self-employed in industry and commerce, members of the professional intelligentsia in high positions, and other intellectuals making considerable money), constituting 8–9 per cent; (3) the lower middle class (handicraftsmen, small shopkeepers, clerks on lower posts, and the majority of the free-lance intellectuals), constituting about 25 per cent of the inhabitants; (4) workers (including unskilled workers, those employed in commerce, services, traffic and transport, those doing manual work in administration, and domestic servants), representing more than 60 per cent. In the suburbs the middle class constituted a narrower layer and the proletarians a much wider one (70–75 per cent).[19]

As far as settlements of various social classes are concerned, nearly all districts and suburbs had their own special character. Some of them, like the Castle, the inner parts of district XI formed mostly from parts of district I in the early 1930s, and the newly built villas of district XII were inhabited by the upper layers of the genteel classes. The inner city (district V), and the *Rózsadomb* (Rose Hill) of Buda were the homes of wealthy people, Jewish and non-Jewish alike. The proletariat was represented here mostly by domestic servants (country girls who usually went back to their villages to start a family after a few years of work in the city) and by people working in the services (janitors, servants, errand-boys, restaurant and tavern workers). Similar was the case of *Újlipótváros* (New Leopoldtown) or the area along Andrássy Street, built in from the late 1920s and inhabited mostly by wealthy Jewish people, members of the middle classes and the intelligentsia. The *haute bourgeoisie* of Jewish origin, however, tended to move to the green belt of Buda. The old inner districts of the city (district VI or *Terézváros*, district VII or *Erzsébetváros*, and district VIII or *Józsefváros*) were inhabited by the middle class and the petty bourgeoisie. They lived mixed with the proletariat in an ever increasing ratio by their distance from the inner city. The majority of the Jewish inhabitants of the city lived in these three districts, their rate in district VII was over 40 per cent. The greatest part of district XIII (*Angyalföld* or Angels' Land), formed in this period as a new administrative unit, remained a typical old workers' district even from architectural point of view. The inner parts of district IX (*Ferencváros*), bordered by the Great Boulevard, was mostly inhabited by non-Jewish intellecutals, officials and petty bourgeois elements, while the inhabitants of the outer parts of the district were mostly workers and other poor people. The majority of the newcomers settled in this part of the city and their rate in traditional workers' districts like *Angyalföld* and *Óbuda* (district III) or *Kőbánya* (then district X) on the Pest side that was an old residential area of workers and members of the petty bourgeoisie, was much smaller. New settlers were numerous also in the southern parts of Buda. Their links with their rural past were still strong, which left its mark on the outlook and atmosphere of the district and the rythm of life there. The settlements of the suburban belt also differed from each other socially. *Újpest* was nearly an independent town and the ratio of its Jewish population was similar to that of Budapest as a whole. All social classes and layers of the city were represented in the population, but the proletariat prevailed. On the other hand, *Pesterzsébet* in the southeastern part of the belt was a typical workers' settlement with only few self-employed handicraftsmen and a narrow layer of officials. Migration to the city after the turn of the century, very strong from the 1920s on, stopped there and a huge suburb was created in the formerly agricultural area. *Csepel* (district XXI today), also a traditional industrial and workers' center, expanded. The more modest suburbs or garden suburbs in the northeast like *Pestújhely* or *Rákosliget* sheltered mostly small pensioners and railway laborers.

The formerly very mixed ethnic composition of the city was over. The high rate of people speaking German as their mother tongue waned, although many descendants of former German citizens of *Óbuda* still spoke German. Next to the villas of wealthy members of the bourgeoisie or the aristocracy on the *Svábhegy* (Swabian Hill) or in their basements there lived several Germans. The majority of the inhabitants at *Soroksár*, a southeastern suburb on the Pest side, was also German. Some settlements of the belt on the Buda side were also predominantly German. The Jewish population concentrated in the large inner districts of Pest. *Óbuda*, the outer parts of district VIII and a separate area of district IX called *Dzsumbuj* sheltered many Gipsies.[20]

The middle classes were very heterogeneous. Its decisive masses belonged to the poor layers of the petty bourgeoisie and the intellegentsia throughout the country and in Budapest as well. Actually, they constituted one third of the capital's inhabitants. The well-to-do citizens of the middle class were far less numerous. Those layers of the middle class that took on bourgeois habits were still concentrated in Budapest. Among them the most stable sector of self-employed handicraftsmen, commercial and bank clerks, constituting nearly 35 per cent of the total of the country, more than 50 per cent of civil servants, 48 per cent of attorneys, 46 per cent of physicians, 40 per cent of teachers, and 66 per cent of private engineers. These middle layers were most affected also by the so-called Jewish question. The two extremes of the middle class were the wealthy Jewish businessmen of *Lipótváros* on the one hand and the civil servants belonging to the so-called genteel classes on the other. There were places where these different social types of the population were mixed, but the preponderance of the Jewish element was remarkable everywhere. More than 50 per cent of merchants, 32 per cent of handicraftsmen, 45 per cent of all employees of private offices, 51 per cent of attorneys, 42 per cent of physicians, and 26 per cent of engineers were of Jewish origin in the capital in 1930, while only 5 per cent of all public servants were Jewish. This rate even dropped to 1 per cent in the 1930s and 1940s in consequence of the anti-Jewish laws and the anti-Semitic public opinion.

These two layers of the middle classes were sharply separated also by their cultural traditions and their styles of living. The Jewish layer preferred the cafés New York and *Abbázia*, while the others the cafés *Pannónia* and *Philadelphia*, and the taverns of Buda. Their holiday resorts also differed. Those who visited Siófok, Balatonboglár or Balatonlelle at Lake Balaton would not have felt comfortable at the "Christian" Balatonfüred or Balatonföldvár. The taste of the former was more characterized by susceptibility to anything new and fashionable, and also by snobbery, while the latter by conservatism or disinterestedness.

Their organizations safeguarding their economic interest were also different. Both layers were present in the *Országos Magyar Kereskedők Egyesülete* (National Association of Hungarian Merchants), mostly led by liberals, and the more conservative *Iparegylet* (Industrial Association) of Budapest, but they visited different clubs. Some organizations of intellectuals resisted spreading anti-Semitism (e.g., the *Magyar Ügyvédek Szervezete* or Organization of Hungarian Lawyers), and some only to a smaller degree (e.g., the organization of physicians). From the late 1930s, however, the chambers of intellectual professions reorganized in the wake of the anti-Jewish laws aimed at elbowing out their Jewish members.

The other important class of urban society to be introduced in detail is the working class.[21] As all metropolises of the day, Budapest was a city of workers. 63 per cent of the employed population of the city called Greater Budapest from statistical point of view belonged to the working class in 1930 and over two thirds of them in 1941. Prior to the First World War one quarter of the industrial workers of the country lived in Greater Budapest, and in the period discussed the rate of the industrial proletariat was already 40 per cent, and that of the industrial workers 55 per cent. The ratio of the rest of the country increased only in the second half of the 1930s. In 1941 in Budapest the distribution of the working class taken in a broader sense of the word was as follows: half of them were industrial workers, 42 per cent worked in the services (in commerce, traffic, civil service, and in households), 4 per cent were casual day-laborers, and the rest were retired workers and one or two percent agricultural laborers in the suburban belt. (Until the 1930s pension was paid only for civil servants.) About 40 per cent of the industrial workers were employed in the fragmented handicraft industry. The distribution of industrial workers went through significant changes between the two wars.

### Distribution of Industrial Workers in Greater Budapest by Branches of Industry, 1910–1943 (per cent)

|                                     | 1910 | 1938 | 1943 |
|-------------------------------------|------|------|------|
| Iron, metal and machine industry    | 40.5 | 37.8 | 52.2 |
| Textile industry                    | 4.0  | 23.2 | 13.7 |
| Food industry                       | 12.6 | 8.8  | 7.9  |

### Number of Industrial Workers (person)

|         |         |         |
|---------|---------|---------|
| 129,000 | 176,000 | 231,000 |

The proportional changes, especially those taking place during the Second World War can be clearly understood from this chart. Also the distribution of the workers by the level of their qualification changed, the most significant change being the decreasing rate of skilled workers compared to the level of 1913. The decrease amounted to about 10 per cent in the machine industry. The developing textile and paper industry needed less skilled workers and the industrial growth during the war years was not so much due to technical innovations, but rather to the employment of unskilled workers in large numbers. The fact that the man-of-all-work, the skilled laborer doing mostly manual work was pushed to the background can be considered a kind of modernization after all, especially where it was coupled with technical development.

The living conditions of the workers did not change for the better as compared to the pre-war period. In fact, they did not reach the pre-war level until 1938 even in the best years. Real wages increased by 8 to 10 per cent only between 1939 and 1942, i.e., in the years of war economy. Housing conditions were very bad for the workers. According to a detailed survey from 1929, only 5–6 per cent of the workers in Budapest owned their apartments, and 87 per cent of those living in tenement-dwellings had only one room and a kitchen, or even less, i.e., an apartment consisting of a single room. More than half of the apartments had no water-supply, and nearly 80 per cent had no separate toilette of their own inside the apartment, and there were hardly any bathrooms. These circumstances changed a little in the 1930s, as the state, the capital, and some big firms started to build labor colonies or blocks of flats for workers. The workers of the Western European capitals also lived under inadequate housing conditions in that period. Large slums existed there, too. Such were in Budapest the *Mária-Valéria* and the *Auguszta* housing developments, and development at Lőrinc, the one called *Dühöngő* at Sashalom (a village belonging to the suburban belt), and the *Lenke* Street development in *Ferencváros*. If a newly-built development was considered too good for workers, it was soon turned into a civil servants' garden city. This is what happened to the *Wekerle* development, originally prepared for workers, that became a housing project for civil servants, accomodating 26,000 people. The municipal houses of Budatétény and Újpest also met the same fate. Miserable districts of the poor reminding one of South American metropolitan suburbs were also present in Budapest. Such were the *Ládaváros* (Box City) at Pestlőrinc, the *Hangya-telep* (Ant Colony) at Pesterzsébet, and the *Indiánfalu* (Indian Village) at *Lágymányos* (in the southern part of Buda). Some of them catered for several thousand people. In spite of all this, the life-style and living conditions of the workers underwent certain positive changes: electric lighting spread, cooking gas was gradually introduced, traffic was improving, the attendance of higher elementary schools became better, the radio, cinema, mass sports, and a greater devotion to sports contributed to a better life at least for better educated and younger workers. As a consequence of these changes these layers of the working class gradually became better integrated into the Hungarian society. It was, however, an interesting feature of these changes that they had not been triggered by the trade unions or the workers' movement, but rather by the impact of Nazi Germany and the right-wing radicalism strengthened by it. The number of organized workers significantly decreased in the 1930s and 1940s. The right-wing movements had an important mass party from 1938 onward led by Ferenc Szálasi, initially called *Magyar Nemzetiszocialista Párt* (Hungarian National Socialist Party), later *Nemzetiszocialista Magyar Párt—Hungarista Mozgalom* (National Socialist Hungarian Party—Hungarist Movement) or Magyar Nemzeti Szocialista Párt—Hungarista Mozgalom (Hungarian National Socialist Party—Hungarist Movement), and from March, 1939 *Nyilaskeresztes Párt* (Arrow Cross Party). In the spring of 1939, at the first general elections based on secret ballot, this party got into Parliament. It did not endanger the positions of the autoritarian and conservative government party which itself drifted toward the right. It, however, managed to push the Social Democrats to the background among the poor and also among the workers living in suburbs formerly called "red belt", and even got more votes than the government party at several places. This situation could not only be attributed to the bad, although improving living conditions of these layers, but also to other factors like the ever stronger pro-German attitude of the country. This attitude was a direct consequence not only of the spread of anti-Semitism and the partial recovery of the pre-Trianon borders through Italian and German aid, but also of the fact that even the skilled workers respected the high technological level and seemingly less hierarchical society of Germany. Nationalism of right-wing radicalism had its impact mostly on the lower layers of the working class. This type of nationalism better suited the dichotomous world view of the have-nots dividing the society into rich and poor or lords and servants than the one advocated by the genteel classes, and was a substitute for real social equality for them.

## City Government and Politics

The history of the leading bodies of a city and urban politics cannot be separated from the political life of the nation.[22]

The Horthy era inherited a high-standard and professional municipal administration and a basically open municipal policy gravitating toward liberalism. This period, hallmarked by Mayor István Bárczy, was over. The Social Democratic government in office for only a few weeks after the fall of the Béla Kun regime appointed Ferenc Harrer mayor of Budapest, a follower of the ideas of the October Revolution in Hungary. He was soon followed as acting mayor by Tivadar Bódy. However, he, too, was not good enough for the leaders of the restored regime. The act of self-government for the "guilty city", as Miklós Horthy called it, was passed by the parliament in the early summer of 1920. It was much more restricted than the earlier one. It stipulated that the municipal assembly should have sixty members elected by the electorate, two appointed *ex officio*, and twenty-four for each district, without regard to the number of their inhabitants. Municipal suffrage was also restricted. In September, 1920 the municipal elections took place and the result was surprising: 167 out of the 240 elected members belonged to different Christian-national parties. The Social Democrats boycotted the elections under the circumstances of the counter-revolutionary regime. The formerly very strong liberal and democratic parties won only 63 seat. The nationalist Christian factions soon founded the Christian Municipal Party (*Keresztény Községi Párt*) led by Károly Wolff until his death in 1936. His political attitude was much to the right from the government party of István Bethlen. It represented extreme versions of nationalist and Christian trends. The majority of the liberal and Social Democratic leaders of the city were replaced. New figures were put in positions at the various departments of the city administration and expert committees like the boards of public works and public education. However, the strongly conservative vocational intelligentsia of the city hall was not really pushed to the background.

The middle class and the workers were strongly unsympathetic with the city leadership of Wolff's party. Even Prime Minister István Bethlen urged a more moderate city politics. As a result, Ferenc Ripka, head manager of the gas works was elected mayor, who represented the intentions of the state government. "The city hall does not engage in politics, but works", he stated in his inaugural address. Socially conscious he was more concerned with the people and, being more public-spirited, he worked more for the betterment of the conditions of the poor. Ripka rallied also an urban party along Bethlen's lines, but it did not prove successful for a longer period.

Similar was the case in suburbs and villages belonging to Greater Budapest. Some of these settlements became towns of county rank just after 1919, and the Social Democratic or liberal tendencies were still stronger in them. At the 1922 municipal elections of Újpest 136 out of the 200 elected members belonged to the liberal bloc supported by the workers. The town assembly of Kispest, Pesterzsébet, Budafok had strong Social Democratic factions.

Both in the "red belt" and in Budapest proper there was a duality in the leadership: there were the numerous, and for a long time cooperating, Socialist and liberal factions on the one hand, and the similarly strong right wing among the members appointed *ex officio*, and especially among the office-holders.

This duality could be observed also after the municipal elections of 1925, when a strange equilibrium was created among the Socialist–liberal bloc (with 51 Social Democratic representatives within), Wolff's right wing (getting 36 per cent of the votes as opposed to the less extremist group supported by the prime minister, with 9 per cent), and the *ex officio* deputies.

Lord-Mayor (*főpolgármester*) Ferenc Ripka (1924–1932) and Mayor Jenő Sipőcz (1926–1932) and Lord-Mayor (1932–37), who represented a nobler trend of conservatism, helped the city reach considerable results based on the growing economic prosperity and urged by the Socialist–liberal bloc. The general meeting of the city assembly, the composition of which was more progressive than that of the Hungarian parliament, was the scene of sharp debates, and the bourgeois–Social Democratic faction was supported by the majority of the press organs of the capital. The debates centered around the taxes, the allocation of loans raised by the city, the development of public transportation, the determination of public utility costs and local taxes, cases of corruption, the extremely high salary of the leaders of the public utilities and the municipal offices, and many other similar problems. At the same time, small apartments were built for the poorer strata at several places, and steps were taken to eliminate slums. *Újlipótváros* was built up with modern houses, and streets were spreading also in the outer parts of *Erzsébetváros*. The newly established *Munkaügyi Bizottság* [Labor Committee] was very active in representing the interests mostly of the public utility workers. A social security system for the workers was organized under the name *Országos Társadalombiztosítási Intézet* [OTI, National Institute for Social Security], and one for clerks of private firms called *Magánalkalmazottak Biztosító Intézete* [MABI, Insurance Company of Private Employees]. Some new schools were also built, and a new children's hospital was added to the ten hospitals run by the city (its construction was completed in 1929). The newly established *Országos*

*Közegészségügyi Intézet* [National Institute of Public Health] and the *Fővárosi Bakteriológiai Intézet* [Budapest Institute of Bacteriology] were also set up in the capital and contributed to the fight against widespread diseases. Some new institutes for tuberculosis and venereal diseases were also established. The cause of public baths was also supported and several new baths were built in this period. In 1930 a modern indoor swimming pool on the Margaret Island, designed by the former Olympic champion swimmer, architect Alfréd Hajós, was inaugurated.

The suburban belt, where the Socialist and liberal movements were generally stronger than in other parts of the city, also witnessed positive changes in these years. At *Újpest* many small apartments were built, the sewer system was expanded, and the town was enriched by new institutions for social care. Improvements in gas and water supply took place at *Kispest, Pesterzsébet,* and *Pestlőrinc,* more money was invested into health care, and the very backward, unpaved network of roads was improved. This progress was interrupted by the Great Depression. The whole economy of the city declined and the resulting unemployment retarded development in nearly all spheres of life. In the worst phase of the depression in 1932 expenditure on public welfare was about 25 per cent higher than before, but the decrease of the salaries of the capital's employees was between 17 and 32 per cent. (Fortunately, commodity prices also declined in those days.) The sums spent on road construction and canalization dropped to half of the former expenditure, and 30 per cent less was spent on public education.

In 1930 the parliament passed a new law for the capital designed to increase the influence of the state government over the city to the detriment of the city's autonomy. At the municipal elections of 1930 Wolff's *Keresztény Közösségi Párt* got 46 seats, the *Egységes Községi Párt* [Unified Municipal Party] representing the state government got 22, other, right-wing groups 10, the Social Democrats 37, the liberals and the democrats got 30 seats. The results reflected the effects of the early depression and also the shift toward the right in the political life. This rightward drift was soon marked on national level. At the national elections of 1931 the government party won 200 out of the 240 seats in the parliament. From 1932 till his death in 1936 Gyula Gömbös, a supporter of the extreme right, was Prime Minister, carrying leadership in the capital to the right wing. In the background the largest mass demonstration of over one hundred thousand workers took place on September 1, 1930, protesting against the rightist trends.

The new municipal act of 1934 strengthened the direct influence of the state government on the capital. The national elections of 1935 sustained the spread of Gömbös' ideas and influenced also the municipal elections. The government party won 29, Wolff's party 36, the bourgeois opposition 18, and the Social Democratic Party won 21 seats in the municipal assembly. The democratic and left-wing forces suffered a serious setback. The followers of the government party and those of Wolff tending to support old racist ideas later united in the Budapest branch of the government party called *Magyar Élet Pártja* [Party of Hungarian Life] during the war years. The reform demagogy initiated by Gömbös on state level, an important element of which was anticapitalism directed against Jewish big capital, necessarily led to welfare measures like the regulation of working hours, paid holidays, a minimum of family allowance, better health care, and a minimal old age pension for agricultural laborers. However, no unemployment benefit was introduced. Paradoxically, these positive measures were mostly introduced under the impact of fascist welfare, contributing by this to a shift toward the right or toward political passivity among the workers.

In 1937, after the death of mayor Sipőcz representing a higher form of conservatism an insignificant right-wing politician, Jenő Karafiáth was appointed to his place by the Regent (1937–1942). This happened toward the end of the economic crisis and amidst the beginning of economic preparations for war, when the possibility of developing the city both economically and culturally was greater than before. Especially when the anti-German Minister of the Interior Ferenc Keresztes-Fischer helped the more moderate Károly Szendy into the position of mayor. However, these changes did not basically modify the impact of the spirit of the age on the leadership of the city, and self-government was declining further. It can be considered a relative success that the governments following the Gömbös cabinet managed to keep the growing fascist mass party, the Arrow Cross at a distance from the official leadership of the capital. The fact that no municipal elections were held in the second half of the 1930s or during the war years also served this purpose. Since at the national elections of 1939 the parties of the extreme right, especially the Arrow Cross made significant progress and won about 20 per cent of the votes, it seemed likely that the same would have happened at the municipal elections. The Arrow Cross made most progress mainly in the capital and its environs. At the national elections the government party got 10 out of the possible 27 votes in Budapest, the Arrow Cross Party and other parties of the extreme right won 9, the liberals 5, and the Social Democrats only 3. Out of the possible 6 votes in the formerly notorious "red belt" the Arrow Cross won 3. The majority of the suburbs and of the belt belonged to Pest County, its deputy head was László Endre, a supporter of aggressive racism and the extreme right from 1938 onward.[23]

The anti-Jewish laws passed in the years 1938–1941[24] exercised a serious effect on the life of the capital. The first act and the related decrees of 1938 caused serious financial problems and increased social exclusion for Jewish employees and those Jews who were professionally employed. The following acts and decrees stood increasingly on the basis of the German racial principles limiting economic activity for Jews. From 1941 the male Jewish population was compelled to do labor service, marriage between Jews and non-Jews was prohibited, and all sexual relations between Jews and non-Jews qualified as criminal miscegenation and disgrace to the Hungarian race. The economic activity of the Jewish citizens of Budapest playing such an outstanding role in creating a modern metropolis was curbed, and they were shut off from all possibilities of professional education. The press-law put into force from autumn 1938 and a row of decrees connected with it drastically limited the freedom of the press. Hundreds of opposition papers were prohibited. The non-Jewish middle classes also suffered from these restrictions, although less conspicuously and from different respects. The moderate layers of the middle class were pushed to the background and the groups interested in the forceful redistribution of wealth and positions came to the fore.

Hungary and its capital did not know the pains of war until 1941, and did not suffer from total war until 1943. On the contrary, it could reannex formerly lost territories in these years through Italian and German support, and there was a temporary economic prosperity due to war economy. Unemployment practically ceased, and various means of modern mass culture were available even for manual workers. This was probably the reason why resistance among the citizens was minimal in the face of quasi-fascist or definitely fascist aspirations, and the growing discrimination against Jewish citizens.

The drastic turn in the course of the war and the destruction of the Hungarian 2nd Army (1942–43) brought a change of attitute at last. Human losses, growing economic and political demands of Nazi Germany, effects of war economy on the broad masses in the form of rationing, military control of the factories binding workers to their work-places, immobilization of all political and trade union activities, radical decrease of trade union membership, and many other similar factors made it increasingly obvious that the war and the alliance with Nazi Germany were to have serious consequences.

The right-wing turn in the suburban belt took place abruptly because of economic factors. Not even right-wing demagoguery could hinder development there in the late 1930s and in the first years of the war. The territory's supply with public utilities was increasing, the big private corporations contributed to a better health care for their workers, better social conditions, and sporting facilities.

The German occupation of the country on March 19, 1944 was a serious blow. The Germans were justly alarmed that Hungary might withdraw from the war and the alliance. Hitler was surprised by the ease with which he occupied the country and the absence of resistance. The Hungarian army went over to the Germans immediately and parliament was equally cooperative.[25] When the developments of the war, D-day, and the protests of the Vatican urged the regent months later to say "no" to the ever increasing and ever more barbarian German demands, it was too late.

Hitler's Germany considered Hungary one of its most important outer protective zones. The country and its capital could not count on mercy from the Allies. The British and American bombardments began in early April, 1944. The main targets were the Budapest railway junctions and war factories. The civilian population also suffered great losses. In the meantime, the Nazis motivated by irrational hatred went on deporting and destroying the Hungarian Jewry. Even when they should have concentrated their forces on defending themselves from the approaching Soviets, they still went on sending thousands of Jews to ghettos on the enlarged Hungarian territories with considerable help from the Hungarian authorities. The Jews from the country, more than 400,000 people, were jammed into cattle-cars heading toward Germany in April and May, 1944. Besides passing decrees supporting the German war machine, the new Hungarian government and its leader, former Hungarian ambassador in Germany Döme Sztójay considered the persecution of the Jews its main task. At the end of April another anti-Jewish decree was added to the already existing ones on the compulsory wearing of the yellow star, on crowding the Jewish population into so-called Jewish houses designated by the authorities, and their exclusion from rationing. Most Jewish men, over 10,000 people in Budapest, were called up for labor service with the exception of very old people. Some of them soon landed in German concentration camps. The Jews of the suburban belt were deported in July, days after Horthy had refused deporting the Jews living in the capital under international pressure.

Not even the Szálasi regime coming to power on October 15, 1944 managed to deport all Jews from Budapest, though the Germans and the Arrow Cross regime incessantly forged plans to do it. Although they drove tens of thousands on foot from the capital to various German concentration camps or at least to the Hungarian border from the Budapest ghettos established in the autumn of 1944. There were nearly 75,000 people crowded in some streets of district VII and the deportation could not be executed fully owing to the changes in the war situation. Although over 5,000 people died in the ghetto, the losses of the Budapest Jewry were much smaller than those in the country, especially on the territories reannexed in the wake of the Vienna Awards. According to a survey done by a Jewish research group after the war, 58 per cent of the 200,000 Budapest Jews survived the disaster. The same rate for the country Jews was merely 30–31 per cent. Other sources put the Jewish losses higher. According to R. L. Braham, the losses of the Hungarian Jewry, increased by a population of 300,000 on the reannexed territories, were much higher in general, but those of the Budapest Jews in the central parts of the capital were considerably smaller. There are, however, countries (Poland, the Baltic states, Holland, and Greece) where the percentage of Jewish human losses was larger than those of the Hungarian Jewry in 1944. From among the neighboring countries Romania and the Bohemian–Moravian protectorate, occupied by the Germans, suffered slighter losses. The losses of the Slovakian Jewry were very high proportionally, much greater than the Hungarian ones.[26]

The war affected not only the lives of the Jewish population of the capital. The losses of the military and the civilian population were also great. According to the latest and very reliable estimations the army suffered 140,000–160,000 casualties, 230,000–280,000 people were lost as prisoners of war, and the human losses of the civilian population can be estimated to around 100,000. The losses among the deported Gypsies can be put to about 40,000.[27] The share of Budapest in the total loss of 800,000–900,000 lives cannot be estimated. It is, however, certain that the non-Jewish civilian population of the capital suffered more severe losses and damage in material goods and houses than the population of the country. (Prior to and during the siege 35,000 civilians are estimated to have lost their lives.) This can partly be attributed to the fact that the German general headquarters declared in November, 1944 that Budapest was a defensive fort and was to be defended from house to house. When the Soviet troops drove the German and Hungarian units out of the city in a two and a half months' siege (from November, 1944 to February 13, 1945), the capital looked like the ruined cities of Germany.[28]

## Architecture

The city changed very little in the inter-war years. Its character had been finalized by the early decades of the century.[29] A bird's-eye view would have noted few changes. A bridge and a half were added to the existing ones in this period (the Miklós Horthy Bridge, today's Petőfi Bridge, and the not completed Árpád Bridge). Buda now extended to the south including a new industrial and a residential district. The slopes of the hills were covered by more and more houses. The embankments of the Danube on both sides had been extended: on the Buda side to *Lágymányos,* while on the Pest side to *Újpest,* where the new district of *Újlipótváros* [New Leopoldtown] was added to the city. The empty plots between the city and the suburbs and villages around it were gradually disappearing, and the inner parts and the suburbs were growing together.

The expansion of the city is reflected also in the number of flats built in this period. Between 1920 and 1941 96,000 apartments were built, which was roughly proportional to the increase of the population. The number of flats in Buda was growing more rapidly than in Pest. However, the housing quality only slowly improved. The number of flats consisting of a single room doubled, and those with bathroom also increased, although it did not reach even half of the total number of flats in the capital in 1941. Most old slums still existed, and the modern flats were built mainly in the inner parts of the city or near it (in *Újlipótváros*), and in the garden suburbs of Buda. Housing conditions in the suburban belt were improving, but still were below western standards.

The demolition of the *Tabán* in Buda in the early 1930s drastically changed the townscape. This old and romantic district with its old houses, taverns, and small workshops of handicraftsmen had long been outdated, was insignificant from architectural point of view. It was soon converted into a park extending up to *Gellért* Hill, which the city badly needed. The architectural and cultural monuments of the district, the *Rác* (Serbian) bath and the church on *Szarvas* Square, were preserved. No significant changes took place in the inner parts of Buda in this period. Only the area around the Buda head of the future Árpád Bridge was modernized, and the northern parts of Buda were developed. The ruins of the old Roman military town of Aquincum were further excavated, and a municipal water sport beach called *Római part* or Roman embankment was built. The open-air baths of *Pünkösdfürdő* and *Csillaghegy* were built up on the medicinal spring-water of the area. On the Margaret Island a new indoor swimming pool was built, the *Nagyszálló* [Grand Hotel] was extended in 1933, the *Palatinus* Bath, and the open-air theater were created in 1936 and 1938, respectively.

The inner city hardly changed in the inter-war period. The plans for city embellishment were only partially realized. Significant new buildings were the skyscraper like center of the OTI [National Institute for Social Security] and the emergency hospital in the far end of *Józsefváros*. The modern row of buildings on *Kálmán Tisza* Square, the public housing for workers of *Magdolnaváros* (Magdalentown) in *Angyalföld*, as well as the development for the workers of the Hungarian State Railway (MÁV) in *Kőbánya*, and a miserly temporary public housing called *Auguszta* telep were built. Also the speedway leading to *Ferihegy* Airport was completed in this period. This civilian airport opened in 1926. Originally there were flights only between Vienna and Budapest but air traffic expanded rapidly. A new *Ferihegy* Airport was opened during the war years for military use.

The capital had only few historical monuments of architecture primarily due to the one and a half century Turkish occupation and the siege terminating it. Most of the old houses were Baroque, dating from the 18th century. The earlier centuries were represented only by a few buildings, parts of churches, or newly excavated monuments like the hunting villa of King Matthias in Buda.[30] In Pest neo-Classic buildings dominated dating from the first half of the 19th century. Many of them were pulled down during the inter-war period. This was unfortunate because that style represented the best traditions of Hungarian architecture until the turn of the century. In the second half of the 19th century, the quickly expanding city had been characterized by unassuming eclectic buildings and cheap materials. The better architects and art historians rightly called the city "mortar town".[31] The genuine Hungarian eclecticism or *Art Nouveau* reflected real ambition, although it produced only few buildings and did not change the appearance of the city. Its best architects such as Ödön Lechner, Béla Lajta, and Károly Koós created the unity of modern and Hungarian architecture in this style. After the First World War, however, eclecticism with neo-Baroque and neo-Gothic elements predominated, a style affected and non-functional.

The functional approach of contemporary Europe and the modern efforts of the day were slow to break into Hungarian architecture. In the 1930s these trends were represented in Budapest by the works of architects Farkas Molnár, Lajos Kozma, Bertalan Árkay, and Gyula Rimanóczy. Their work is to be seen in the church in *Városmajor*, the first modern church in the capital, the hospital in *Kútvölgyi* Street from 1941, and the buildings of the Post Office Headquarters [*Postavezérigazgatóság*] and the Central Corporation of Banking Companies [*Pénzintézeti Központ*].[32]

## Political Parties and the Press

The years after the First World War brought significant changes in public education, culture, and everyday life in the capital. Initially the counter-revolutionary regime proclaimed that it exalted rural values, i.e., Hungarian people identified with the country people, to counteract excessive liberalism and the Kun revolution. However, Budapest became the center of the counter-revolution and it remained the cultural and intellectual center of the country. Cultural and scholarly institutions concentrated in the capital. Cultural and educational opportunities were outstanding and the results shown in the cultural level of the inhabitants, and the high rate of intellectuals in the city. The majority of the intellectual elite concentrated in the capital.[33] Around the middle of this period 15.4 per cent of the country's population lived in Greater Budapest, but only 6.5 per cent of the illiterate, nearly half of the college graduates, and 51 per cent of the people with high school diplomas.

Budapest was the center of political life, and political trends were born there. Budapest was the birthplace of the "Christian—national" concept, the basic political principle of the new regime. The determining elements of this doctrine were: anti-liberalism, conservative reform, nationalism based on national grievances, and alternately mild and radical anti-Semitism. In the early 1920s the repesentatives of these ideas were radical and right-wing politicians of vision who later joined either Bethlen's conservative circles or fascist ones. One of the latter was Wolff's Municipal Christian Party with slogans like "developing commerce and industry through Christian morality" and contributing by this to "the foundation of a Christian and national society". Bethlen's conservative ideas concentrated in Budapest. His Christian and national approach suited well the demand for Hungary becoming part of western culture and civilization.

His approach also suited the monarchist ideals also present in the capital. The latter was embraced by the Jewish *haute bourgeoisie* and the approach became representative of liberalism among the aristocracy and the big bourgeoisie. The liberal and democratic trends were reduced to self-defence. Their Socialist–liberal coloration, along with the equally weakened bourgeois radicalism stood half-way between bourgeois liberalism and social democracy. The new parties of the opposition also had their headquarters in Budapest. Such were the *Független Kisgazda, Földműves és Polgári Párt* [Independent Smallholders', Farmlaborers' and Citizens' Party] becoming independent anew in 1930 as a democratic party of farmers and also intellectuals of the capital city. Here originated the movement of populist writers in the second half of the 1920s and became an important intellectual circle. Its party called *Nemzeti Parasztpárt* [National Peasant Party] was formally founded only in 1939. The movement remained an intellectual metapolitical trend throughout the period. Its "third road" ideology criticized cultural developments and aimed at improving the cultural and living standards of the peasantry. Social Democracy was a strong political movement in the years after 1919 with its strength based mostly on its relationship with the influential trade unións. It also offered a legal shelter for the weak illegal Communist movement exercising considerable influence on left-wing intellectuals.

When the Great Depression and the period of stabilization hallmarked by István Bethlen were over and Nazi Germany was increasing its influence on Hungary, these ideological and political trends underwent a thorough change. The Christian— national idea began to lose inner cohesion and ideologically broke into pieces. Its main forces tended to shift toward the extreme right. The conservative and liberal trend of its leading circles became stronger also. Social and national discontent found an outlet not only toward the extreme right, but also toward "third-road" populism, subsequently partly toward left-wing ideas, and humanism. At the same time, the fascist movements and trends (both the moderate ones like the Gömbös–Imrédy line and the radical populist ones like the openly fascist Arrow Cross Party) drew their strength from the fact that they were strongest and most influential in Budapest.

The most characteristic technical achievement of the inter-war period was the introduction of the radio as a new form of mass communication. At the same time, the old press organs were modernized. The radio was controlled by the government but it still was a propagator of high-standard culture as well. Its musical department was led by Ernő Dohnányi, its theatrical adviser was Antal Németh, the head of the literary department was László Németh (in 1934–35), and later László Cs. Szabó, a writer and essayist. The mass culture propagated by the radio was, however, in harmony with the spirit of the day as dictated by the regime: the musical programs were dominated by Gypsy music or, more precisely, substandard songs by contemporary composers imitating Hungarian folk music played by Gypsy bands, and other programs intended for the broad public (news and ecclesiastical programs) were characterised by revisionism and nationalism combined with a pious neo-Baroque approach.[34]

The versatile and advanced press of the late dualist period in Budapest got into a delicate situation, since the papers of the widest circulation were financed by capital considered to be of liberal leaning. Decrees limiting the freedom of the press were among the first to be passed by the new regime. On August 8, 1919 all press organs were temporarily banned with the exception of *Budapesti Közlöny* [Budapest Gazette] the official journal of the government. An act of 1921 "on the defence of the state and the social order" introduced sanctions against offences against of political nature committed by the press. The period of stabilization eased the tension a little, and only post-publication censorship was exercised. The majority of the papers of the extreme right published in the early 1920s did not endure. Publication of a regularly issued daily newspaper or periodical was strictly licensed. The Budapest press still remained versatile. In 1927 there were 715 papers, magazines, and periodicals appearing in the capital only, twenty of which were political dailies. In 1936 the previous number rose to 809. One in every 1,300 people bought a newspaper in Budapest, while one in every 50,000 in the villages.[35] The daily papers of the 1920s can be divided into three categories. The racist paper of the extreme right entitled *Magyarság* [Hungarians] was edited by the publicist István Milotay. The *Új Nemzedék* [New Generation] was influenced by the Catholic Church and could boast of authors like the historian Gyula Szekfű and several other members of the official scientific world. The original legitimist spirit of the paper later receded and it became the organ of István Bethlen's government. Both the *Magyar Távirati Iroda* [Hungarian News Service] supplying information for foreign countries and the *Magyar Országos Tudósító* [Hungarian National Information Service] represented more radical right-wing trends of the government. Bethlen soon made the *Budapesti Hírlap* [Budapest Journal], founded earlier, the official organ of the government. The semi-official daily of the government was the German-language *Pester Lloyd*. Bethlen's conservativism mixed with liberal elements made it possible for more liberal papers to survive. He defended them to a certain extent from extreme racist attacks. At the same time, this attitude secured the government the support of the *Budapesti Napilapok Szindikátusa* [Syndicate of the Budapest Dailies] led by wealthy bourgeois circles.

Besides the government journals, the liberal papers published by capitalist companies had the largest reading public and the greatest number of advertisers. The *Est* [The Evening] Company owned three dailies in the capital and the biggest publishing house of the country called *Atheneum*. Its three papers were the *Pesti Napló* [Pest Diary]; a high-standard tabloid paper appearing in the afternoon, called *Az Est* [The Evening] that could be considered the most characteristic newspaper of the city; and the *Magyarország* [Hungary] that had limited circulation. All of them supported the government's policies, especially its foreign policy, and, at the same time, they represented a liberal approach. The week-end issues also gave considerable publicity to high-standard literature. The *Pesti Hírlap* [Pest Mail], having great historical traditions, was a bit more conservative. The most widely read newspaper of the country was the *Friss Újság* [Recent News], a cheap paper for the masses not dealing with politics at all. The liberal and democratic ideas were represented in the *Újság* [Journal] and the *Esti Kurír* [Evening Courier], while bourgeois radicalism in the *Világ* [World] appearing before 1926, and later in the *Magyar Hírlap* [Hungarian Mail].

The press of the Social Democrats was also significant until its decline in the 1930s. Its daily, the *Népszava* [Word of the People] was widely read in the 1920s. Most larger trade unions issued weeklies. The left-wing press of the workers was much harrassed by the authorities even in its best period, the second half of the 1920s, and hundreds of libel suits were instituted against it. The shift to the right in the 1930s could be felt also in the press. The Gömbös regime brought about a new type of government press based mostly on political writing (*Függetlenség* or Independence and *Új Magyarság* or New Hungarians). In the late 1930s the mass organs of the Arrow Cross extreme right appeared in the streets of the capital (the *Magyarság* or Hungarians, the *Pesti Újság* or Pest News, and the *Virradat* or Dawn). Given the new situation, the *Est* concern and the other big capitalist firms were pressed to adjust to the government policy shifting toward the right without rendering services to either the German or the Hungarian fascists. The daily *Magyar Nemzet* [Hungarian Nation] was a novelty in the press of the capital when it was launched by Christian capitalist circles in 1938. Its editor was the conservative but boldly antifascist Sándor Pethő, and it became the most important organ of the anti-German wing of the government circles and the middle class. At the same time, the new press-law passed in the autumn of 1938 in the spirit of the first anti-Jewish law banned most liberal newspapers. 411 press organs were banned in the country in six months with *Az Est*, the *Újság*, and the *Esti Kurír* among them. Most of the banned papers had been published in Budapest. The German occupation totally standardized the remaining press organs.

## Science, Education, Belles-lettres

Central control of education had been made important for the administration by various causes. Among them were: the experiences of the revolutions of 1918 and 1919, the concommittant sharp social conflicts, the overall sense of crisis created by the Trianon peace treaty and manipulated according to the needs of a revisionist foreign policy. This new situation was recognized in the 1920s by Minister of Culture Kunó Klebelsberg. He launched a far-reaching program within the framework and in support of Bethlen's policy of stabilization. Elements of this program were: a special approach toward the cultural and scientific elite, financial support of the neglected elementary education in the country, modernizing secondary education, and shifting secondary education towards natural sciences. Klebelsberg's "neo-nationalism", proclaimed in the 1920s, had a double goal. Instead of stressing direct and, at that time, fully hopeless revisionist goals, he based his approach on the idea of Hungarian "cultural supremacy". On the other hand he promoted nationalism as an idea creating national coherence.[36] Beyond supporting the universities and the scientific institutions Klebelsberg's cultural policy did not pay much attention to public education in Budapest. The city hardly received its share from the ministry's comprehensive program of building schools and developing public education. The capital and the settlements around it had to realize this program on their own. Only few new schools were built in the capital, since the number of children was decreasing. Only networks of junior high and vocational schools were extended. Independent vocational schools were set up only in the 1930s.[37] There was a significant advancement in training elementary and secondary-school teachers. A highly important achievement was the introduction of medical officers into elementary and secondary schools in 1925. In the beginning the capital was divided into seven and at the end of the period into sixty districts of school medical services.[38]

In the second half of the 1930s, however, the high standards of Klebelsberg's educational policy gradually declined in the majority of public schools. The ecclesiastic schools maintained their original high standards. The idea of Hungarian cultural supremacy and neo-nationalism seemed already too conservative, and the chauvinist variety of nationalism prevailed. The principle of quality in education was coupled with slogans like the "education of the nation" and "knowledge of the nation", and the military training of the pupils. Toward the end of the period compulsory eight-grade elementary education was introduced, but it did not become widespread at that time. The practical change in elementary education was that while prior to 1918 most children of poor working parents attended only four grades of the elementary school, in the inter-war period six grades became common. Secondary education also underwent significant changes. During the First World War 16,000 pupils attended secondary schools in the capital, but by 1942–43 this figure doubled. The junior high school education significantly increased in the suburban belt also.

After-school education was not much financed by the capital. There was, however, a people's high school under the auspices of the Committee of Public Education [*Népművelési Bizottság*]. Cultural activities were carried on in 39 culture centers in the mid-1930s and this number significantly increased later with the big firms building their own cultural centers. The trade unions remained the main supporters of cultural life among the workers, and from the late 1930s they developed stronger links to the national culture as well. This could, however, not counterbalance their decline altogether.

Significant museums and libraries were also located in the capital. The following were connected to and directed by the municipal government. There were two such museums after 1919, the *Budapest Történeti Múzeuma* [Historical Museum of Budapest] and the *Aquincumi Múzeum* [Museum of Aquincum]. The former collected historical material concerning the capital, and the latter collected Roman relics. Besides these bigger museums, the *Károlyi* Mansion in the inner city housed the exhibitions of the *Székesfővárosi képtár* [Picture Galery of Budapest] and the *Zichy Jenő Múzeum* of old paintings from 1933. These two collections became later the basis of the old picture gallery of the *Szépművészeti Múzeum* [Museum of Fine Arts].

In the inter-war period several archaeological excavations enriched the collections of the museums of Budapest. In the early 1930s several valuable Roman works of art, Roman ruins and other objects were found in the inner city, on the territory of the ancient camp of the Romans. The hunting seat of King Matthias was excavated in *Óbuda* together with a Roman military cemetery, and valuable objects illustrating everyday life in the past were found when the *Tabán* was demolished.

An important institution of cultural life in the capital was the *Fővárosi Könyvtár* [City Library] that moved into the Wenckheim Palace in District VIII in 1927. The library owned nearly 500,000 items, half of which were allocated in the very popular branch libraries steadily growing in number. The central building of the library served mainly scholarly purposes. The *Pedagógiai Könyvtár* [Pedagogical Library] with its smaller stock was also in the hands of the capital and served the needs of experts. This library was the basis of teacher education in the framework of the *Fővárosi Pedagógiai Szeminárium* [Pedagogical Seminary of Budapest]. It also had a unique collection of periodicals, and half of the 300 titles were periodicals from abroad.[39] The libraries of the trade unions also played an important part in public education in the capital. Their stock in the 1930s reached 300,000 items. Although their stock was enriched also in the inter-war period, its composition did not satisfy the demands of the age. The literature of the turn of the centry dominated the stock including Anatole France's and Emile Zola's works. Their non-fiction material also represented the scholarly level of those decades.

The intellectual workshops and forums of the day can not fully be considered as characteristic of Budapest. The city as a capital of the country and the nation would cater for the institutions of science and art, and leading scientific personalities.[40] Besides Budapest only the university towns became regional cultural centers. Their importance was sometimes based on a single outstanding scholar's achievements depending on the field and scale of national immportance.

A scholar or scientist working in the country (or sent there in exile) could sometimes play a more important role in his field than his colleagues in Budapest. For example, the first periodical for the history of ideas entitled *Minerva* was founded and published at Pécs from 1921. The famous expert of ancient history and religion, Károly Kerényi also went there to teach in the second half of the 1930s, just like Lajos Fülep, who lectured on the history of art. Debrecen became a center of the populist writers' movement. Szeged became famous for natural and medical sciences (the

Nobel Prize winner biochemist Albert Szent-Györgyi (1937) worked there), sociography, and sociology. The most outstanding scholars worked in the capital. The greatest historians of the day, supported primarily by Klebelsberg, were Gyula Szekfű, István Hajnal, and Elemér Mályusz. Linguists like the internationally renowned Zoltán Gombócz and Dezső Pajzs or the modern linguist Gyula Laziczius also lectured at the Budapest university together with the greatest Hungarian literary historian of the day, János Horváth, the philosopher Ákos Pauler, who left positivism for neo-Thomism, and the philosopher of culture Lajos Prohászka. Ferenc Eckhart, who renewed legal history from a bourgeois point of view, and Gyula Moór, who courageously fought against fascist pseudo-science as a philosopher of law and a follower of neo-Kantianism lectured at the faculty of law. The medical faculty of the Péter Pázmány University offered high-level training for medical students comparable to other universities of Europe, for the great professors of the early 20th century were still lecturing there. The training of engineers at the Joseph Technical University was also on a high level with the exception of the lectures on the history of architecture. The leaders of the Hungarian Academy of Sciences preserved the old conservative mentality, but did not reject the 19th-century traditions of liberalism. The Academy, however, became a symbolic institution only and its attempts to control the various branches of science remained futile.

There are two factors influencing the Hungarian intellectual sphere that were connected with the modernization of the country and urban development and concentrated mostly at Budapest. The former distance between sciences and intellectual life (literature and art) decreased, which affected the development of sciences. This process can be illustrated by the contemporary debates around Ady. In the course of the debates the conservative circles and their periodicals rejecting Endre Ady's poetry before 1918 gradually gave up their ever more untenable anti-Ady attitude (the *Magyar Szemle* or Hungarian Review edited by Szekfű and following Bethlen's line, and the *Budapesti Szemle* or Budapest Review of the Academy). Prior to 1918, the literary periodical *Nyugat* [West], the forum of modern Hungarian literature, was forced to become an asylum of literary opposition, but its taste and concept of literature began to be accepted by the official circles by now. It stopped to arouse a scandal if an academic scholar wrote a contribution into it. Another aspect of the same process was the appearance of the modern Hungarian essay that wished to revive sciences from their dullness instead of knocking down the barriers between science and art, as some narrow-minded, though well-intentioned critics maintained.

Such an urban essayist, Gábor Halász wrote the best studies on the late 19th century and the neo-realist novel of the day, and another one, Antal Szerb, wrote the best history of Hungarian literature [*Magyar Irodalomtörténet*] and the best history of world literature [*A világirodalom története*] in that period.

The other significant change occurred in the cultivation of sciences. The debate centered around a strictly Hungarian and a universal method of cultivating the sciences. In the 1920s, the Academy turned away from the French and English world and tended to represent the narrow Hungarian view, accepting only the results of the very prolific German sciences. The situation changed in the 1930s, as German fascism met a growing resistance among Hungarian scientists. As a consequence, an increased interest turned towards scientific life in Western Europe. The official Christian—national approach of the post-1919 era was easing up. Especially among the younger generation scientific life became more colorful and open during the 1930s.

The science of statistics deserves to be mentioned separately. The Hungarian Statistical Office was up to the European standards. It prepared valuable demographic surveys, occupational statistics, and all kinds of social statistics, and it rallied the best statisticians of the country. The Statistical Office of Budapest [*Fővárosi Statisztikai Hivatal*] was especially important and followed all changes in the city and also in the suburban belt which from the 1930s belonged to "Greater Budapest". Volumes of the Stastical Review of Budapest [*Budapesti Statisztikai Közlemények*] and the surveys taken by Lajos I. Illyefalvi, Dezső Laki and others helped the leaders of the city in making decisions. The office collected invaluable historical source materials. For example the bulky volume from 1929 entitled *A munkások szociális és gazdasági viszonyai Budapesten* [Social and Economic Conditions of the Workers in Budapest]. That contains the data of 100,000 workers and several thousand apprentices of manufacturing and handicraft industry, including demographic conditions, wages, housing conditions, health, and cultural background. Other volumes described the living conditions of people by occupational distribution, based on census results, or the development of Budapest in the seventy years since the unification of the city in 1873. During the years of the Second World War a separate institute was set up for a distorted form of statistics serving racism.

Literary life also concentrated in Budapest. Most members of the first great generation of the *Nyugat* lived there. Their work climaxed in the

1920s and 1930s after a pre-1918 great beginning. Mihály Babits, Milán Füst, Dezső Kosztolányi, as well as Zsigmond Móricz, and Gyula Krúdy—these two belonged to an older generation and were not very close to the circles of the *Nyugat*—wrote their best works in that period.

In the first half of the 1920s the *Nyugat*, edited by Ernő Osváth and Mihály Babits, enjoyed its second heroic age. The official circles attacked it through their own periodical *Napkelet* [Orient] which was established to suppress *Nyugat*. Although it was quite high in quality, the majority of its literary essays were insignificant. The *Nyugat* courageously defended the real and self-proclaimed interests of literature, past and present. The periodical lost much of its glamour during the late 1920s. But it managed to safeguard its humanistic and European values in spite of the attacks from the avantgarde circles of Lajos Kassák, the younger bourgeois radical or "urbane" camp who were dissatisfied with the conservativism of Babits. The populist writers coming from the so-called second generation were also antagonists of *Nyugat*. Even in the 1930s, it maintained its high literary standards and remained a forum for writers of various orientations. In 1934 the populist writers (László Németh, Géza Féja, János Kodolányi, István Sinka, and others) founded a periodical under the title *Válasz* [Reply]. In 1936 the periodical *Szép Szó* [Fine Words] was launched by the urbanist group of writers [Attila József, Pál Ignotus, Ferenc Fejtő, Zoltán Gáspár]. The latter group confronted not only official Hungary but also the populists' attitude against bourgeois values and culture and their faith in the power of the peasantry to reform the nation.

The significance of the debate between the "populists" and the "urbane" writers went far beyond literature itself throughout the period.[41] The debate centered around the most important ideological problems of the country. The urbanists contrasted their neo-liberal and left-wing Socialist criticism of society with the populists' criticism of culture and romantic anticapitalism. The urbanists also criticized the distorted Communist pattern realized in the Soviet Union. They rejected the idea of renewing Hungarian culture exclusively through the revival of the already disappearing traditions of the peasantry. The populists' Hungarian and East European orientation was contrasted with the universal nature of European culture. The urbanists denied that Europe was on the decline. They stressed the rational concept of the political nation in contrast with the cultural nationalism of the populists bordering sometimes on racism. The most difficult point of the debate was the Jewish question, a subject sharply debated in the 1930s. The populists considered the prominent role of the Jews (or of persons of

Jewish background) in economic and cultural life as counter to the best interest of the Hungarian population. They related the so-called Jewish question to their critique of capitalism and bourgeois culture. The urbanists (the followers of many trends ranging from liberalism to left-wing ideas) saw in this a restriction of democracy and of militant humanism. From the late 1930s, the debate assumed a different character. Critique of populism was taken over from the urbanist intellectuals who found themselves hampered by the Jewish laws, and assumed by several members of Mihály Babits's circle, the students of Szekfű, who returned to liberalism in literary life, by Sándor Márai, and László Cs. Szabó. The debate also expressed the writers' attitude toward Budapest, most populists being obviously against the metropolis and its mass culture. Some of their criticism was just and well-founded, but was coupled with utopistic and conservative ideas (like favoring Debrecen as a Hungarian town vis-a-vis Budapest).

The third generation of writers appeared in the 1930s. Its most outstanding representatives were Géza Ottlik, Sándor Weöres, Zoltán Jékely, Andor Endre Gelléri, Miklós Radnóti, and István Vas. Some of them were still influenced by the populist trend, but followed it with less idealism, and with more urbanism than their predecessors and distanced themselves from the myth of the peasantry. From this generation came authentic students of country life, sociographers and sociologists seeking the ways of bourgeois development in rural communities. Among them were Ferenc Erdei, Zoltán Szabó, and Imre Kovács. The majority of scholars and writers of this generation were already less susceptible to the nationalist idea or other negative elements of the spirit of the age, no matter what trend they represented: historicism, neo-realism, or neo-classicism.

What was the attitude of Hungarian literature toward Budapest in the inter-war years? What inspiration did literature receive from the city environment, and what aspects were emphasized? It is generally true that the capital lost its unmitigated pride in all products of literature, including conservative writings prior to the turn of the century. It was not by chance that the first key work of the new period was Dezső Szabó's novel *Az elsodort falu* [The Swept-away Village] published in May 1919, in which the city is presented as one among those promoting the decline of the Hungarian race.

The writers of the day stopped being enthusiastic about Budapest. Even the liberal and left-wing authors had seen too much of the contradictions of life and culture in the big city, the life of the proletariat, of the clashes between the gentry and bourgeois attitudes to have a positive relationship with the city. After 1919 they had to see their city as not only the capital of progress and of revolutions but also that of counter-revolution. In the late writings of Gyula Krúdy one can find an ever stronger nostalgia for the Budapest of earlier times when it was still a town rather than a city. Dezső Kosztolányi in his novel *Édes Anna* [Anna You Sweet] describes in sharp contrasts the atmosphere of the city after the revolutions, and the antagonism between the gentry bourgeoisie and the urban and rural proletariats. Lajos Kassák in his autobiographical novel and his novel *Angyalföld*, described proletarian life in Budapest, the workers' movement, and the difficulties of a self-educated worker to establish himself in the literary life in the capital. The novels of Zsigmond Móricz illustrate the tension between the gentry and the Jewish bourgeoisie that can be resolved by love and an enforced happy ending (*Jobb mint otthon* - Better Than at Home, 1933). His *Az asszony beleszól* [The Woman Intervenes] speaks of the life of common people in a big city, while *A rab oroszlán* [Lion in Captivity] describes the waning of the gentry way of life. In the short stories written in his later years Móricz turned toward the life of the proletariat, which he described in a highly authentic manner.

Lajos Nagy spoke of Budapest as a sick organism and illustrated its troubles through grotesque caricatures, as well as in a sociographical diagnosis (*Budapest Nagykávéház* or Budapest Café). Tibor Déry left the surrealist world of *Budapesti felhőjáték* [Clouds Above Budapest] and adopted realism in the 1930s. In his bulky novel *Befejezetlen mondat* [Unfinished Sentence] he spoke of the uncertainty of the big bourgeoisie in *Lipótváros* contrasted with the distress of the proletariat of the city, and their determination to survive. The short stories and grotesque sketches of Frigyes Karinthy are inseparable from Budapest both in their setting and their attitude to life. Béla Zsolt's *Erzsébetváros* and other writings analyze the degeneration of the bourgeoisie and the lower middle class in the capital. Modern Hungarian drama is represented by "urbanist" playwrights like Ferenc Molnár, Dezső Szomory, and Milán Füst. From the late 1930s on some populist writers wrote dramas as well—*Földindulás* [Landslide] by János Kodolányi, and *Villámfénynél* [By the Light of Lightning] and *VII. Gergely* (Gregory VII) by László Németh. László Németh's novel *Bűn* [Sin] and his cyclic novel *Az utolsó kísérlet* [The Last Attempt] about the people and neighborhoods of the Castle, of the *Víziváros*, the *Tabán* and *Farkasrét* are published in the 1920s. Milán Füst's novel *A feleségem története* [The Story of My Wife], published toward the end of the period, was an outstanding example of contemporary literature even by West European standards. The short stories of Andor Endre Gelléri acquaint the readers with the life of the proletariat and the petty bourgeoisie of Pest and *Óbuda* in a naturalistic manner. István Vas's *Elveszett otthonok* [Lost Homes] is a lyric description of the inner city and *Lipótváros*. Many essayists dealt with the past of Budapest in the 1930s—Gábor Halász, László Cs. Szabó, and Antal Szerb among them. The background to Lőrincz Szabó's poetry is the capitalist city with its alienating and segregating effect. Attila József, Miklós Radnóti and the young poets growing up in the 1930s also chose the variegated world of Budapest and its suburbs as their recurring theme. Finally, the apocalyptic year of 1944 was reflected in the diaries of Lajos Nagy, Tibor Déry, and Miksa Fenyő sharing the experiences of the siege with the readers.

The country's largest publishing houses like the *Athenaeum*, the *Franklin*, the *Révai* Brothers, the Singer and Wolfner, the *Légrády* Brothers, and the *Szent István Társulat* [St Stephan Co.] were located in the capital along with the more prominent printing presses. Besides these, over a hundred smaller firms published books in the capital. Being capitalist enterprises, they were interested in profit, consequently in publishing popular light fiction; yet they published considerable numbers of true literary works as well. The majority of writers and poets lived miserably, and only a few famous writers had a regular, let alone significant source of income. Most had to pay for the publication of their own works or published them by canvassing for subscribers. Volumes of poetry sold a hundred or two hundred copies at best. Once the depression was over, the reading public became wider, partly due to the bookfairs organized each year from 1929 on, and supported by official circles. This upward trend coincided with the deterioration of the political situation in the 1930s, the negative impact of anti-Jewish laws, and the heavy-handed censorship. Still, independent publication was not really endangered before 1944. Books by middle-of-the-road writers continued to be published and new publishing houses, both of the extreme right and of the democratic circles, came into being: the *Turul* subventioned by the government and the *Magyar Élet* Publishing House specializing in the works of populist writers are examples of the former, and the *Cserépfalvi* and *Officina* of the latter.

Eighty per cent of all books were published in Budapest in the 1930s. The fact that the liberal and conservative capitalists played a significant part in this until the German occupation either openly or covertly was a positive feature of publishing in general. Given the Anglo-American orientation of certain leading circles during the war years, most works by significant Western authors were published in Budapest in those years. According to a German analysis based on wide sources Hungary was second after Britain in publishing books banned by the Nazis between 1933 and 1943. The writings of 76 banned and 11 undesirable, mostly exiled, German writers were published in Hungarian translation, while there were only seven translations of works recommended to the publishers' attention by the German authorities. Most publications represented modern German literature.[42]

## Music, Theater, and Creative Art

Music life in Budapest was upt to West European standards. The Opera experienced one of its greatest periods. Béla Bartók's operas and other pieces for the stage (with the exception of *A csodálatos mandarin*—the Miraculous Mandarin) that was banned in those years,[*] Zoltán Kodály's musical dramas based on Hungarian folk music, Wagner's operas restaged in the 1930s, and the first performance of Mussorgsky's *Hovanshina* reflected high standards of artistic activity. Some of the great performers of the era included conductors Sergio Failoni, Ernő Dohnányi, and János Ferencsik, singers Mária Basilides, Anna Báthy, Mihály Székely, and Endre Rösler, dancer Gyula Harangozó, director Kálmán Nádasdy, and stage manager Gusztáv Oláh.

Concerts were frequently held, though the audience was a relatively thin upper crust of society. Many turned to music or art in general to forget the harsh realities of the Horthy regime. Hungary gave many great artists to the world. Besides Bartók, Kodály and Dohnányi let us mention Ede Zathureczky, Annie Fischer, György Faragó, who died young, and the world-famous string-quartets of Waldbauer and Léner. This abundance of outstanding music was partly due to the outstanding work done at the Budapest Academy of Music and the activity of the great orchestras of Budapest (the ones of the Opera and the Philharmonic Society, the *Fővárosi Zenekar* or Orchestra of Budapest, and the *MÁV Szinfónikusok* or the Symphonic Orchestra of the Hungarian State Railways). The level of music life in the capital can be illustrated by an event relatively early in

---

[*]    Editors' note: it was banned not only in Hungary but in most West European countries as well. The most prominent person to forbid its performance was Konrad Adenauer, mayor of Cologne, later the first Chancellor of the Federal Republic of Germany.

the period under discussion, namely, the concert celebrating the fiftieth anniversary of the unification of the city in 1923. Bartók's *Táncszvit* [Dance Suite] and Kodály's *Psalmus Hungaricus* had their premieres on this occasion.

Musicology was also at a high level. Its institute dealt mainly with collecting and analyzing Hungarian folk music by complex methods and a comparative approach, and moved to the building of the Academy in the inter-war years. Besides the history of music, musical criticism was also flourishing at the hands of critics like Antal Molnár, Aladár Tóth, Sándor Jemnitz, and Bence Szabolcsi.

The theater had a much greater role in culture and society in those days than it has today in spite of the fact that financial difficulties made it extremely difficult to muster a large audience. Klebelsberg's cultural policies revived the National Theater from the 1920s, preserving its elegant national conservative traditions, through Sándor Hevesi, the outstanding theoretical expert and stage director. During his directorship artists like Gizi Bajor and Árpád Ódry reached the peak of their careers. The National Theater soon won over actors and actresses of the *Vígszínház* [Comic Theater] such as Anna Tőkés, Tivadar Uray, Sándor Pethes, and József Tímár. Although the theater preserved its high spirit, its repertoire became more varied, to include contemporary works as well. Hevesi's Shakespeare cycle was a great achievement of the period, yet his contract was not renewed in 1932, and he was soon replaced by Antal Németh. Németh did not have the stature of his predecessor and was greeted with suspicion by people both on the left and the right. (As a former avantgarde artist he was not welcomed by the right wing, either.) However, his contributions soon disproved the negative expectations, though his greatest concern was not so much with the author or with the acting as with directing and the spectacular stage-settings. An example of the latter was the modernized performance of the classic *Az ember tragédiája* [The Tragedy of all Humans] by Imre Madách. Németh's greatest merit was that he put the plays of the new generation of playwrights on stage from the late 1930s; thus the older plays of Zsigmond Móricz were followed by those of László Németh, János Kodolányi, Áron Tamási, and Sándor Márai.

The theater most beloved by the Budapest middle class was the *Vígszínház*, though it lost its former vigor and was often surpassed by the National Theater as regards artistic quality. Nevertheless, it remained the contemporary stage, its wide repertoire conforming to the exigencies of a not too demanding, broad middle-class audience. In the 1920s hardly a year passed without the premiere of a play by Ferenc Molnár, who represented a far higher level than the standard plawrights such as László Lakatos, László Bus Fekete, János Bókay and others. Besides classical Russian plays (like Maxim Gorki's *Night Shelter*) plays by George Bernard Shaw, Gerhart Hauptmann, Eugene O'Neill, Sommerset Maugham, and even Thorton Wilder were performed often. The series of Chekhov's plays was an outstanding achievement, as was the staging of some avantgarde plays like Bertolt Brecht's *Threepenny Opera* in 1930. Beside the great artists of the older generation (Gyula Csortos, Sándor Góth, and Artúr Somlay) new ones joined the theater in the 1930s (Margit Dajka, Mária Lázár, Mária Mezey, Andor Ajtay, Klári Tolnay, and others).

The *Magyar Színház* [Hungarian Theater] stood close to the spirit of the *Vígszínház*. Some plays of lasting value were staged there in those years, for example, several pieces by Ferenc Molnár, Dezső Szomori's *II. Lajos király* [King Louis II], and Jenő Heltai's *A néma levente* [The Speechless Cavalier] with Gizi Bajor and Jenő Törzs in the leading roles. It added considerably to the theater's prestige that Sándor Hevesi became the stage manager of the theater in the autumn of 1933.

Some other important theaters were the *Belvárosi Színház* [Inner City Theater], in the hands of the outstanding director Artúr Bárdos it was a highly sophisticated undertaking. It performed plays by August Strindberg, Franz Wedekind, Luigi Pirandello, Jean Giraudoux, and J. B. Priestley. One of its finest performances was George Bernard Shaw's *St. Joan*. The *Király Színház* [King Theater] and the *Népszínház* [People's Theater] had formerly been forums for plays about peasants or for operettas. It had excellent artists like Márton Rátkai, Sári Fedák, and Rózsi Bársony. In the 1920s they still had success with performances of musicals by Imre Kálmán, Ferenc Lehár, and Pál Ábrahám among others, but were soon overshadowed by the *Fővárosi Operett Színház* [Budapest Operetta Theater] with its more modern repertory.

The fine arts were represented in Budapest not so much through artists working there, but mainly through exhibitions and conferences of art associations. The *Képzőművészeti Főiskola* [College of Fine Arts] provided training in fine arts. Since the character of the country was still agrarian, the slowly changing cityscape of Budapest and the domination of impressionism and post-impressionism in painting, the capital was chosen by very few painters as their subject. They preferred to paint Buda with its historical atmosphere, in contrast to artists in Paris or New York. Most painters longed to get away from the city. This was how Szentendre, about 25 kilometers distant, became an artists' colony. Avantgarde art appeared in Hungary relatively late, and its most talented representatives (Lajos Kassák, László Moholy-Nagy, László Péry, Lajos Tihanyi, and others) went to exile after the fall of the revolutions of 1918 and 1919, joined the German *Bauhaus* movement or integrated into artistic life in Soviet Russia (Béla Uitz). Many outstanding avantgarde artists (for example, Aurél Bernáth and István Szőnyi) left radical modernism for a more moderate form of modern art. The excellent painter Gyula Derkovits, the internationally well-known artist of gobelin Noémi Ferenczy, and sculptor Béni Ferenczy living in exile in the Soviet Union until 1936 were strongly inspired by the city.

Architecture was not ready to accept all novelties of the modern era, and the restored regime raised the conservative and nationalist trends of neo-Gothic and neo-Baroque architecture to the rank of official art. The so-called Roman school, supported also by Minister of Culture Klebelsberg, was mainly under the influence of contemporary Italian art and rallied talented artists. It contributed to the revival of religious painting. On the whole, it was still a kind of pseudo-modernism.

The statues designed for public squares were characterized by nationalist historicism. When in 1937 a statistical survey of sculptures in Budapest was taken, it turned out that 132 of the 180 monuments or statues in the streets and squares of the capital portrayed historical personalities, and the rest religious subjects. Out of the 157 monuments to individuals 30 were dedicated to writers or scholars.

The long outdated academic art, the neo-Baroque decorations, the symbols and emblems present everywhere, and the affected national character of the pieces of fine workmanship reflected a world moving away from traditions, not yet at home in modern and practical technical culture. They maintained the low-brow culture of the masses as regards fine arts.

Modern urbanism and the spread of authentic folk culture, preferred especially by the city's intellectuals and the middle class, could not fully dominate this process. Folk music became better known through the work of Bartók and Kodály, and folk art through ever more intensive ethnographic research. As a consequence, folk songs became more and more popular even among the workers of the capital and played a part in the workers' movement.

Modern photography was far more interested in the city than the traditional branches of fine arts. Many of its most outstanding representatives, sooner or later in exile, became pioneers of the new art form of sociofoto.

## Urban Mass Culture

This leads us to the realm of urban mass culture. The present author does not share the extreme low regard for popular culture that still prevails in Hungary. It is not that the popular culture of Pest did not produce lots of kitsch. Nor do I believe that popular art was a stepping stone to "elite culture." The point is that popular art played a significant role in society: namely, it contributed to the process of assimilation to urban ways by the newcomers. This is why we view this much abused sphere of culture with greater tolerance. Urban popular culture was variegated and offered good films, good detective stories and good entertainment without pretending to be art. The products of this popular culture were "consumed" by society at large, to mention only Mihály Babits's taste for detective stories. A good crime story was better than a sentimental, light piece of reading, and good popular literature (e.g., the novels of Lili Bródy or the *Budapesti kaland*—An Adventure in Budapest, by Ferenc Körmendi—was better than the more pretentious lowbrow literature of the day like the so-called biographies of Zsolt Harsányi). There were even adventure stories, primarily those by Jenő Rejtő alias P. Howard, that described the ominous period of the 1930s and 1940s in a suggestive way and full of humor, disguised as stories about soldiers of the Foreign Legion.

Popular music was backward, if we leave the easily exportable operettas of Pest out of consideration. In the 1930s, however, some elements of jazz, popular tunes imitating folk music, and elements of the operettas were combined into a new style of popular music which, while losing its original charm and innocence, came to reflect the climate of political corruption.

The new mass medium of the century, the film, was also an expression of urban culture. Prior to and during the First World War the capital was the home of a considerable motion picture industry. The defeat in the war and the fall of the revolutions was a serious setback to the film industry. An upward trend began only with the spread of the sound picture, especially after the Great Depression. The audience got acquainted with Hollywood and the dark realism of the French film. The main achievement of the Hungarian cinema in the 1930s was that it managed to overcome the differences among the various srtrata of the middle class. Its most prominent genre was the comedy, and the best actors and actresses of the day contributed to its success. New stars were also discovered specially for the screen (like Gyula Kabos). In these comedies urban middle-class attitudes confronted gentry provincialism. With only a few exceptions like *Hippolit, a lakáj* [Hippolit, the Butler] and *Meseautó* [The Fabulous Car] almost all films of the period dealt with bourgeois careers naturally mixed with a love story, reflecting the important financial position of the middle classes. The threads of the story were usually interwoven with descriptions of declining country life and the life of the landowning aristocracy. For those choosing the bourgeois way of life the film offered an optimistic view of the future, so movies became a favorite pastime for members of the petty bourgeoisie and the middle class irrespective of their genteel or Jewish origins, and even for the better-to-do younger generation of the proletariat. As the war was approaching, and especially when it broke out, much of the Hungarian film industry fell increasingly in step with the deteriorating public life and the state intervened. Most of the excellent actors and actresses remained, but the topics changed radically. The films described the pseudo-democracy of fascism, the problems of the man-in-the-street, and the conflict between landlords and peasants were resolved by a sham moral sensitivity. At the same time, really valuable films were produced in this period by directors like László Ranódi and Géza Szőts (see *Emberek a havason*—People on the Snow-Capped Peaks).

There were three cinemas in Budapest seating more than a thousand people, and twelve seated over seven hundred. There were over a hundred movie theaters in the mid-1930s. The Hungarian capital was not so much a city of movie theaters as a city of cafés. There were about 200 of them in the city in this period. The cafés were at the same time cultural institutions (literary cafés like the *Centrál*, the *Japán*, and the *New York*), forums of business life (the *Simplon*, the *Baross*, and the *Emke*), places for newspaper reading, social life, recreation, and amusement. The cafés also suffered from the negative trends in public life and the war, and from the second half of the 1930s a new type of café started to spread in Budapest, the espresso or coffee-house. The small coffee-houses were designed for privacy and small talk and, unlike cafes, were unsuitable for an editorial office, for holding meetings, for writing fiction or poetry or for business talks. The papers could no longer be spread over the small tables of these espressos. These shrivelled substitutes for the cafés were for political gossip, and spreading jokes typical of Budapest (mostly ridiculing soft-headed aristocrats and the Jews) or rumors coming true. And they were the places where lovers could meet in secret.

# Notes

1. Based on data from *Magyar Statisztikai Szemle*, no. 7 (1942).
2. Official census data. See Alajos Kovács, *Magyarország népe és népesedésének kérdése* [Population and population growth in Hungary] (Budapest, 1941), 61ff; *Az 1941. évi népszámlálás* [The 1941 census], *Történeti Statisztikai Kötetek* [Historical statistics series] (Budapest, 1975), 87.
3. Called so informally from the 1930s. These satellite towns have been incorporated into the capital since then. Greater Budapest was a virtual concept until January 1, 1950 including the capital and the suburban belt around it. The idea of making it a single administrative unit emerged already before World War I. The results of the 1930 census were already published in this sense. In 1937 the authority of the Municipal Board of Public Works was extended also to the suburban belt. Finally, in December, 1949 Act XXVI was passed providing for the annexation of the seven suburbs and sixteen villages of the belt area to Budapest. The unification increased the number of the city's districts from fourteen to twenty-two. The territory of the city doubled and the number of its population grew by half.
4. Dezső Szabó, *Az elsodort falu* [The swept-away village], 2nd ed., (Budapest, 1919), vol. 2.
5. The article appeared in the Hungarian periodical *Kalangya* (June, 1938) in Yugoslavia.
6. For a detailed analysis see Tibor Bakács, *Budapest közegészségügye* [Public health in Budapest] (Budapest, 1948), 27ff. Between 1910 and 1940 infant mortality decreased from 14.7 to 9.1 per hundred live births, and death caused by tuberculosis from 35.5 to 16.8 per 10,000 inhabitants.
7. For more details see Miklós Lackó, *Ipari munkásságunk összetételének alakulása 1867–1948* [Changes in the distribution of our industrial workers, 1867–1948] (Budapest, 1961).
8. *Az 1930. évi népszámlálás* [The 1930 census], *Magyar Statisztikai Közlemények*, Új sorozat [new series], vol. 92 (Budapest, 1933), 37. The population of the suburban belt later belonging to Greater Budapest grew from 311,000 in 1920 to 450,000 in 1930, and to 560,000 by 1941.
9. See *Budapest Székesfőváros Statisztikai Évkönyvei* [Statistical yearbooks of capital city Budapest].
10. Zsigmond Móricz, *Az asszony beleszól* [The wife intervenes] (Budapest, 1934).
11. Census data. See notes 2 and 8.
12. *Budapest Székesfőváros Évkönyve* [Yearbook of capital city Budapest] (Budapest, 1933), 61.

13. For details on the Budapest Jewry see Hungarian Section of the World Jewish Congress, *Hungarian Jewry before and after the Persecution* (Budapest, 1949); Gyula Zeke, "Statisztikai táblák" [Statistical tables], in *Hét évtized a hazai zsidóság életében* [Seven decades in the life of the Hungarian Jewry] (Budapest, 1992), 187–192. These tables reveal that in 1930 34 per cent of Jewish wage-earners worked in the industry (mostly in small-scale industry), 42 per cent in commerce, and 8 per cent in intellectual occupations.

14. See József Szekeres, ed., *Budapest története a forradalmak korától a felszabadulásig* [The history of Budapest from the age of revolution to liberation], in ed. László Gerevich, Budapest története [History of Budapest] (Budapest, 1980), vol. 5; see also various writings on economic history by György Ránki.

15. Ibid., 124–127.

16. The concrete data in this and the following passages are from Szekeres, ed., op. cit.

17. For details see Tibor Frank, ed., *Tanulmányok a Magyar Rádió történetéből 1925–1945* [Studies on the history of the Hungarian Radio, 1925–45] (Budapest, 1975).

18. Census data from 1930 and 1941.

19. For the social structure and territorial distribution of the population in the capital see Miklós Lackó, "A főváros lakosságának osztályszerkezete" [Class structure of the capital's inhabitants], in Szekeres, ed., op. cit., 427–464.

20. Ibid., 437–451.

21. Ibid., 451–464; Miklós Lackó, *A magyar munkásosztály fejlődésének fő vonásai a tőkés korszakban* [The main features of the Hungarian working class in the capitalist era) (Budapest, 1967).

22. The best summary of urban politics in Budapest between the two wars has been written by Sándor Tarjányi in Szekeres, ed., op. cit., on the basis of all primary sources such as the minutes of the general meetings of the municipal authority, the documents of the office of the mayor, and the volumes of *Fővárosi Közlöny* [Capital city register]. My concise summary is based on his statements.

23. For the election results of the Arrow Cross Party in detail see Miklós Lackó, *Nyilasok, nemzetiszocialisták* [The Arrow Cross and the National Socialists] (Budapest, 1966), 166–176. The data in the book are from the National Archives and the Parliamentary Archives (K2, bundle 792, 1935–1939. Reports on the national elections).

24. For the anti-Jewish laws and their impact see Randolph Braham, *A magyar holocaust* [The Holocaust in Hungary] (Budapest, 1983), vol. 1; Lendvai, Sohár and Horváth, eds., vols. 1–2.

The anti-Jewish laws and major decrees are the following:

September, 1920: Act XXV of 1920 "On Immatriculation at the Universities of Sciences, the Technical University, the Faculty of Economics of the

University of Budapest and the Academies of Law" comes into force. The law stipulated that "the proportion of young people belonging to the various ethnic groups and national minorities [living in this country] among the students should possibly reach the national proportion of the particular ethnic group or nationality". This was the notorious *numerus clausus*. This stipulation of the act was superseded by Act XIV of 1928, so the rate of Jewish students improved a little.

May, 1938: Act XV of 1938 comes into force "On the Effective Balance of Social and Economic Life", it set the maximum number of Jews in the professions and in the civil service at twenty per cent. This was the so-called First Anti-Jewish Law.

Act IV of 1939 aimed to restrict the activity of the Jews in public life and the economy. Those people were defined as Jews who had at least one Jewish parent and two grandparents. State and public institutions were not allowed to employ Jews. They could represent no more than 6 per cent in chambers for the intellectual occupations. This was the so-called Second Anti-Jewish Law.

Act XV of 1941 (August 8, 1941) prohibited marriage between Jews and non-Jews, and qualified all sexual relations between Jews and non-Jews criminal miscegenation or a disgrace to the Hungarian race. This was the so-called Third Anti-Jewish Law.

Prime Ministerial Decree 21.870/1941. ME required Jews liable to military service to do labor service without rank.

Act VIII of 1942 excluded the Jewish faith from among the established religions and qualified it only as an acknowledged denomination. Consequently the Jewish schools and other Jewish institutions were excluded from any state or municipal support.

April, 1944: Prime Ministerial Decree 1600/1944. ME "On the Declaration of Jewish Wealth and Their Sequestration."

April 7, 1944: Decree 6163/1944. res. (confidential) of the Minister of the Interior established that all Jews should be taken to concentration camps regardless of sex and age.

April 26, 1944: Prime Ministerial Decree 1610/1944. ME "On Jewish apartments and homes, and on the determination of their dwelling place." All Jews were ordered to wear a yellow star to mark them off.

25. For the German occupation of Hungary and conditions in Budapest see György Ránki, *1944. március 19. Magyarország német megszállása* [March 19, 1944—The German occupation of Hungary], 2nd ed., rev. and enl. (Budapest, 1978).

26. Tamás Stark, "Hungary's Casualties in World War II," in *Hungarian Economy and Society during World War II*, ed. György Lengyel (New York, 1993), 194–195; Braham, op. cit., 141–145, 222–223; Braham, op. cit., vol.

2; Péter Sipos, *Adattár a második világháború történetéhez* [Statistics to the history of World War II] (Budapest, 1995), 87.

27. Ibid., 79–80.

28. According to statistics, only 14 per cent of the 34,000 houses in Budapest remained intact during the siege. 17 per cent was damaged severely, 64 per cent slightly, and 55 per cent (2,000 buildings) was completely destroyed. 20,000 of the 290,000 apartments were destroyed, and 60,000 very severely damaged. The Germans blew up all Danube bridges in the capital.

29. Pál Granasztói, *Budapest arculatai* [Views of Budapest] (Budapest, 1980); Virgil Bierbauer, *Budapest városépítési problémái* [Problems of urban construction in Budapest] (Budapest, 1933); Gábor Preisich, "Budapest és környékének helyrajza, műszaki fejlődése és építészete a két világháború között" [Topography, technical development and architecture of Budapest during the interwar era), in Szekeres, ed., op. cit., 123–127.

30. Sándor Garády, *Budapest Székesfőváros területén végzett középkori ásatások 1931–1941* [Excavations of medieval ruins in capital city Budapest, 1931–1941] (Budapest, n.d.).

31. This was what Lajos Fülep, the famous Hungarian historian and philosopher of art gave as a cause for his aversion to Budapest.

32. Ferenc Harrer, *A Fővárosi Közmunkák Tanácsa 1930–1940* [The Budapest Board of Public Work, 1930–1940] (Budapest, 1941); István Egyed, "Budapest önkormányzata" [Self-government in Budapest], *Statisztikai Közlemények* 78 (1935).

33. Dezső Elekes, "Budapest szerepe Magyarország szellemi életében" [The role of Budapest in the intellectual life of Hungary], *Statisztikai Közlemények* 85 (1938).

34. Frank, ed., op. cit., 85ff.

35. For details see László Márkus, ed., *A magyar sajtó története* [The history of the Hungarian press] (Budapest, 1977), and the chapter on the history of the press in György Ránki, ed., *Magyarország története 1919–1945* [History of Hungary, 1919–1945] (Budapest, 1976), 859–862.

36. See in detail Ferenc Glatz, "Konzervatív reform—kultúrpolitika" [Conservative reform and cultural policy], in Ferenc Glatz, ed., *Tudomány, kultúra, politika* [Science, culture, politics] (Budapest, 1990), 5–26.

37. "Adalékok a tanoncoktatás fejlődéséhez a Székesfővárosban" [Data on the development of vocational training in the capital], in *Statisztikai Közlemények* 75 (1934).

38. Bakács, op. cit., 102.

39. Árpád Halász, *Budapest húsz éve 1920–1939* [Twenty years in Budapest, 1920–1939] (Budapest, 1939), 29, 33.

40. For more details on scientific and literary life see Szekeres, ed., op. cit., 483–502; Miklós Lackó, *Szerep és mű* [Role and work] (Budapest, 1981),

298–340; *Korszellem és tudomány* [Science and the spirit of the age] (Budapest, 1988), 307–329.

41. See the periodical *Századvég*, no. 2 (1990) dedicated specially to this debate; Péter Sz. Nagy, comp. and ed., *A népi–urbánus vita dokumentumai 1932–1947* [Documents of the debate between populists and urbane writers, 1932–1947] (Budapest, 1993).

42. Dietrich Strothmann, *Nationalsozialistische Literaturpolitik* (Bonn, 1960), tables 8–9.

*László Varga*

# The Devastation of Budapest in War and Its Role in the Revolution, 1945–1956

## Dynamics of Demography

The population of the capital increased at an exceptional pace between 1941 and 1944 and in March, 1944 it reached 1.4 million. The losses in the last year of the war were, however, also exceptional. By March, 1945 the population had dropped to 64 per cent of its former size and amounted to less than 900,000. Although deaths among the civilian population were estimated to be "only" 12,000, the Jewish community of the city in itself lost approximately 100,000 people. By the end of 1945 many prisoners of war, deported Jews, and former refugees returned. People from the country towns and villages swelled the population, which surpassed one million once again. The pre-war level was reached only in 1951. Between 1950 and January 1, 1956 the number of inhabitants in Greater Budapest rose from 1.64 million to 1.9 million. Twenty-one per cent of the increase (55,279 persons) resulted from births, but the ovewhelming majority came from the country. The wave of emigration in 1956, especially at the end of that year, cut the population again. However, natural increase assumed unprecedented proportions mainly due to the radical limitations of abortion (following Cabinet Decision 1004/1953, II.8.) in the so-called Ratkó era (March, 1953–June, 1956 called so after Anna Ratkó, Minister of Public Health between 1950–53). By 1953 the increase was 2.2 times higher than in 1950. When these administrative measures were lifted, the number of induced abortions rose steeply again. (It is significant that there were 1,399 abortions in 1953, 12,270 in 1954, 24,577 in 1955, and 35,775 in 1956.)

The proportions of migration to the city (20,000 to 40,000 persons annually between 1950 and 1955) was to be expected. Statistics of population movement offer, however, a more precise picture. For example, in 1955 112,517 persons moved to the capital, 27,462 of whom as permanent and 85,055 as temporary residents. (The latter figure refers only to people above 16 years of age.) At the same time 73,870 people moved from Budapest to the country (21,096 permanent and 52,774 temporary residents), and 214,567 persons changed residence within the city. Every fourth citizen of Budapest was on the move in 1955.[1] As early as 1951 the government wished to restrict settlement in Budapest to those whose work-places were in the city. Those who contravened this ruling could theoretically be sentenced to one year in prison. However, this administrative measure was never put into practice.

In 1950, to counter-balance large-scale migration to the capital and the subsequently growing housing shortage, the *Népgazdasági Tanács* [Supreme Economic Council] decided to remove 200,000–220,000 old persons and pensioners to the countryside on a "voluntary" basis. The Executive Committee of the City Council discussed the project several times, but its realization was a complete failure.[2]

## Municipal Government and Politics

On January 21, 1945, the parties of the Hungarian National Independence Front (i.e., the Independent Smallholders', Farm Laborers', and Citizens' Party [FKgP], the Hungarian Communist Party [MKP], the Social Democratic Party of Hungary [SZDP], the National Peasant Party [NPP], and the Bourgeois Democratic Party [PDP] joining later) established the municipal body of self-government called *Budapesti Nemzeti Bizottság* [National Committee of Budapest]. The Committee elected János Csorba of the Smallholders' Party mayor of the city.

Power relations quickly shifted in the following months. On April 2, 1945 representatives of the capital joined the Provisional National Assembly meeting in Debrecen. The two worker parties and the trade unions appropriated two-thirds of the Budapest representatives. The Communist Party (identically with the Social Democrats) took 24 per cent of all representatives to the National Assembly. On May 16 the delegates of the above mentioned parties brought about the *Budapest Ideiglenes Törvényhatósági Bizottságának Közgyűlése* [General Assembly of the Provisional Municipal Committee of Budapest] that elected the Communist Zoltán Vas mayor of the capital.

The Provisional National Assembly met on September 5, 1945, for the first time in Budapest and passed Act VIII of 1945 on suffrage. Citizens over 20 years of age were franchised, but the age limit was lowered to 18 for former members of the armed anti-fascist resistance movement. Besides war criminals, practically the whole political elite of the inter-war period was denied voting rights.

The decree on local elections differed from the above only in minor details. The municipal elections were held on this basis in Budapest on October 7, 1945.

### Municipal elections in Budapest
### October 7, 1945

| | |
|---|---|
| All enfranchised voters | 644,410 |
| Actual voters | 587,629 |
| Valid votes | 584,044 |

| Parties | Votes | Seats |
|---|---|---|
| FkgP | 295,187 | 121 |
| MKP–SZDP | 249,711 | 103[3] |
| PDP | 22,292 | 9 |
| NPP | 11,741 | 5 |
| MRP[4] | 5,013 | 2[5] |

The Smallholders' Party won the absolute majority of the votes with 50.2 per cent. The worker parties on a single list received only 42.8 per cent. On December 14 the general assembly elected the Smallholder József Kővágó mayor of Budapest. At the national elections of November 4 the Smallholders' Party won 50.5 per cent of votes cast in the capital. This time the two workers' parties entered the elections separately. The Social Democrats won 23.7 per cent, and the Communists 19.6 per cent.

The election results of 1947 were significantly altered by the announcement of the political police that a "plot against the republic" had been revealed early that year. The Communist Party made use of the alleged plot to smash the Smallholders' Party. Béla Kovács, General Secretary of the Smallholders' Party, was arrested and carried off to the Soviet Union by Soviet military authorities, and in late May–early June they forced Prime Minister Ferenc Nagy and the Speaker of the Parliament Béla Varga of the Smallholders' Party to resign. On June 7 Mayor Kővágó also announced his resignation. His successor József Bognár was also a member of the Smallholders' Party, but a willing instrument of the Communists.

Having smashed the Smallholders' Party, the Communists called general elections for August 1, 1947. Even the election law of 1945 was amended and the categories of those deprived of their right to vote were significantly extended. Not only Smallholders but also Social Democrats were affected by this. The Communists resorted to open fraud when the election results lagged far behind their expectations. Yet they managed to become the strongest party both in Budapest and in the country at large. In the capital the Communist Party won 26.3 per cent of the votes, barely ahead of the *Magyar Függetlenségi Párt* [Hungarian Independence Party], the new party of the opposition established just before the elections, which won 25.8 per cent. The Social Democrats came in third with 20.5 per cent, and the Smallholders were the fourth with only 6.9.

The composition of the parliament and the municipal assembly of Budapest elected in 1945 changed significantly after the general elections of 1947. The Smallholders were reduced to the rank of an insignificant middle-size party. In the municipal assembly, however, they were still in relative majority with 102 seats. The largest party of the opposition, the Hungarian Independence Party founded on July 28, 1947 was dissolved by the government on request of the *Országos Nemzeti Bizottság* [Hungarian National Council] on November 30. This increased the number of Smallholder representatives in Budapest, because the most representatives of the dissolved party had formerly been Smallholders and obtained seats in the municipal assembly under that banner. In spite of all this the Communists gained hegemony with their 54 seats in the municipal assembly.

At the general elections of May 19, 1949 traditional democracy disappeared in Hungary. There was only a single list to vote for, that of the *Függetlenségi Népfront* [People's Independence Front]. 1,089,839 voters cast their "votes" of a total electorate of 1,134,676 in the country and 1,049,238 of them voted for the single list.[6] Nearly the same results were reached at the parliamentary elections of May 19, 1953. 98 per cent of the enfranchised voters of Budapest took part in the elections then (2 per cent more than in 1949). 98.7 per cent of them (the same rate as in 1949) cast their votes for the candidates of the Hungarian Independence Front, the existing single list.

The year 1950 witnessed a radical turn in the history of city government. On December 15, 1949 Parliament passed Act XXIX of 1949 on the territory of Budapest, and annexed seven towns and sixteen villages, thereby disregarding earlier plans for their independent development. The number of districts grew from 14 to 22, and the territory of the city almost doubled. Its population grew by nearly 60 per cent. The Communists were appearently alarmed when they failed at the 1947 parliamentary elections. They realized that they could have attained absolute majority had they included this larger territory.[7] Ironically, the difference came from votes cast by Social Democrats in the environs of Budapest, not by Communists.[8] However, by the time Greater Budapest became a reality, the Communist Party had already swallowed the Social Democrats.[9]

On June 15, 1950 the local municipal self-government was replaced by the City Council of Budapest, which put an end to the autonomy of the capital, already quite formal at that time. 99 per cent of the capital's population voted for the candidates of the Patriotic People's Front at the first council elections of October 22. The Communist Kálmán Pongrácz replaced József Bognár as mayor in 1949 and took the chair of the executive committee of the city council. The second council elections occurred much in the same way on November 28, 1954. 1,255,014 of a total of 1,289,216 voters turned up and 1,242,831 of them voted for the candidates of the Patriotic People's Front.

On November 1, 1956, i.e., in the days of the revolution the National Committee of Budapest was reorganized and József Kővágó was reelected as mayor of the city. However, neither the Committee, nor Kővágó had time to initiate meaningful activities.

## Siege of Budapest and Postwar Reconstruction

In early 1945 the population of Budapest received the Soviet troops with mixed feelings. They were afraid of the occupiers and their fears were not unfounded. Although the Arrow Cross propaganda presenting the Soviets as blood-thirsty conquerors[10] had been exaggerated, violence and rape became commonplace, and the number of Hungarians infected with venereal diseases increased. Plunder and theft mushroomed. On the other hand, Soviet victory meant the end of many years of war and several months of siege. Those who survived the siege had been starving for months. But the end of the war did not immediately improve food supplies. The city was on the verge of famine. Right after his appointment on February 15, 1945, Government Commissioner of Food Supply in Budapest Zoltán Vas organized food raids in the villages to supply the capital. In early March he ordered that all suitable plots, squares, and court-yards be utilized as gardens in the capital.[11] In late 1945 the daily ration of 200 grams of bread was reduced to 150 grams, and in the spring of 1947 it dropped to a mere 50 grams.

The devastations of the war had been terrible in the capital. All bridges had been blown up by the Germans. Public utilities were not functioning and the city lay in ruins. According to the census of 1941 there were 30,571 housing facilities in Budapest. Although their number increased a bit before 1945, the fact that 29,987 houses were listed as having been damaged meant that most of them had to undergo repair. Discounting minor damages like those done to roofs and window-frames, 74 per cent of the housing facilities were seriously damaged in the capital. This means that one quarter of the capital invested in real estate was lost. One quarter of the total number of rooms became unfit for use also.[12]

In his first decree the new Mayor János Csorba ordered that debris from all public places be removed at once. His second decree compelled the air-raid wardens of the houses to remove Arrow-Cross placards and inscriptions from the walls. Another decree was issued to ensure the burial of the dead[13] and animal cadavers.[14]

The siege was still in progress in Buda when the first trams were put to service in Pest on February 7. Two days later the first train arrived at the *Nyugati* [Western] Railway Station. On March 21 there were already two pontoon bridges on the Danube. Four days later the first train crossed the provisionally renovated southern railway bridge connecting the two parts of the city and also of the whole country. In January 1946 a temporary bridge designed by Elek Hilvert and Endre Mistéth[15] was opened south of the Parliament, called Kossuth Bridge.[16]

## Political Purges and the Establishment of the Political Police

Breaking with the past was just as important as the reconstruction of the city. Accordingly, the Budapest National Committee invalidated the anti-Jewish laws on January 21, 1945, the very day the Committee was formed.[17] On January 27 it decided to set up a People's Tribunal to call war criminals to account. The four political parties that founded the National Committee and the trade union delegated two lay members each to the five divisions of the tribunal. The presiding judges and the people's prosecutors were lawyers. The first sentence of the People's Tribunal—a death sentence—was pronounced on February 6.[18] During the period of 1945–46 all war-time prime ministers of Hungary with the exception of Miklós Kállay and Géza Lakatos (László Bárdossy, Béla Imrédy, Döme Sztójay, and Arrow-Cross leader Ferenc Szálasi) were sentenced to death and executed.

War crimes were investigated by the political department of the Budapest Police Headquarters led by Gábor Péter appointed by the Communists as early as January, 1945. Its activities were, however, much wider than war crime investigations almost from the very beginning. According to a report of the Budapest chief of police, the Political Department "registered 12,083 files, and arrested 5,908 persons in the course of actions of political cleansing, 592 of whom have been turned over to people's prosecution, 1,503 sent to internment camps, and 787 have been placed under police supervision" in the second half of 1945. The task of the political department was "to clear the capital of elements—produced by the past 25 years—who hinder democratic development," the chief of police established.[19]

The easiest way of cleansing the city was to relocate people without any legal procedure. Thirteen internment camps for 15,000 people were brought about in the capital and its environs in early 1945. The majority of the internees had actually been members of the Arrow Cross Party or the *Volksbund*, the organization of the German minority in Hungary. However, there were also people in these camps who had merely stood in the way of Communist aspirations for power. As early as February, 1945 Gábor Péter arrested Pál Demény, one of the leaders of the Hungarian Communists who had been in Hungary during the war, and thus was considered a dangerous rival by those Hungarian Communist leaders who had recently returned from Moscow. Later Demény was sentenced to imprisonment and was released only on October 15, 1956.

Besides the political police and the people's tribunal the so-called screening committees were intended to purge the work-places of all who had compromised themselves in the previous regime. The procedure implied loss of employment and could end in police investigation, internment or trial. The left-wing parties were, however, not satisfied with the purges. On February 14, 1946 the Budapest National Committee urged the government to reduce state administration radically, for "the National Committee establishes that all attempts at cleansing the staff of state and local offices failed in the past due to the unsuccessful activities of the screening committees."[20]

In early March a decree issued by the mayor cleared the way for mass dismissals in Budapest. By the end of that month his administration had given notice to three thousand officials and other employees.[21] Later this figure rose to 4,233, nearly one quarter of all civil servants in the city. Dismissals in the capital were winding down when, on May 1, 1946, the government called for a balanced appropriation.

Its aim was to dismiss "those employees whose activities do not actively contribute to the democratic reorganization of the country."[22] The number of those to remain in service was to be 90 percent of the staff employed during the fiscal year of 1937–38. This meant that the prescribed number of those to be dismissed in the capital (3,485 persons) had been significantly superceded by that time. This override gave rise to substantial difficulties both in central and local administration. The goverment therefore in an order issued on July 31, 1946, agreed to revise the case of 10 percent of employees already dismissed.

Indeed, some of those dismissed were rehired. The screening committees finished their activities, and more than 2,500 internees were released in Budapest alone after the examination of their cases.

The negative effect of the purges on the professional level of the administration was compensated to some degree by the fact that some Jewish intellectuals, who had been excluded from employment by anti-Semitic administrators of Jewish origin were employed in state and municipal administration who had formerly been excluded from such positions by the anti-Semitic administrators and by the anti-Jewish laws, were now hired by state and municipal administrations. It was especially the political police that attracted these people who became primary executors of the political purges, along with the freshly promoted "people's cadres." The relatively large Jewish presence in the organs of repression reinforced anti-Semitic sentiment.

Owing to the losses of Budapest's Jewry during the holocaust and the political mobility of some of the survivors, the capital lost its traditional middle-class character, represented primarily by the Jewish bourgeoisie. Before the war Jews constituted nearly one quarter of the city's population. In spite of their losses, the largest Jewish community in post-war Europe was that of Budapest. The final elimination of civil society in Hungary in the following years occurred without regard to religious affiliations and afflicted both Jews, Christians and non-believers alike.

The next attack on the bourgeoisie was the massive deportation of citizens from Budapest to the country in 1951. The "hostile fascist elements," as official terminology branded these victims of totalitarianism, were compelled to leave the capital within 24 hours and move to a predetermined place. According to available statistics, between May and July 1951, 13,670 persons were forced to leave their homes and move mostly to camps, hamlets and villages of the *Hortobágy* [part of the Great Hungarian Plain]. János Csorba, ex-Mayor of Budapest and a former member of the anti-fascist resistance was one of the victims.

## Economic Transformation and its Social Effects

Nationalization served the economic extinction of the bourgeoisie as a class. The first step in this direction was the nationalization of mines and power stations in late 1945 and early 1946.[23] From August, 1946 all electric plants and transmission lines were nationalized. In December they were followed by the three largest industrial firms of the country. In November, 1947 the banks, on March 25, 1948 the factories employing one hundred or more workers were nationalized. In October, 1949 wholesale trade, in December factories and workshops with ten or more workers, firms owned by foreigners, and theaters were taken over by the state. In 1950 the pharmacies were nationalized. The last step was the nationalization of apartment buildings. Over 36,000 buildings were on the list of properties to be nationalized, but the population was called upon to suggest even more. Even the budget of the capital was "nationalized" and incorporated into that of the state before the formation of the local councils.

The last phase of nationalization was directed against small businesses and trades. In October 1952 the city council launched a campaign against them. Retailers selling poultry at the markets were severely restricted and 262 licenses were revoked. By the end of the year there were only seven dealers selling poultry, fish, game, and eggs remained in the whole city. Grocery retailers were totally eliminated by the revocation of 580 licenses. 435 licenses were revoked from restaurant-owners. The nationalization of restaurants and inns was executed on the basis of a secret order issued by the Ministry of Internal Trade. On October 28, 1952, 206 privately owned bakeries were eliminated, resulting in a drastic decline in the quality of bread. Kálmán Pongrácz, Chairman of the Executive Committee of the Budapest City Council, even had to write a report to the Budapest Committee of the Hungarian Workers' Party (MDP) establishing that "both the color and the quality of the new bread are criticized by the population."

In three and a half months six thousand licenses were revoked from retailers, to be followed by another 1,200 later on. Besides the seven poultry-merchants only 647 greengrocers and 202 tobacconists weathered out the purges.[24]

Artisans met the same fate as retailers. The number of private iron and metal turners was reduced from 131 in 1950 to 31 in 1952. That of watchmakers and opticians dropped from 498 to 252 in the same period. In late 1950 there were 396 confectioners in the capital, and their number dropped to 3 in 1952. In early 1951 there were 797 butchers, 14 of whom were still allowed to trade once nationalization had been completed. While on January 25, 1951 27,412 artisans worked in the city, on February 1, 1953 only 11,396 of them were licensed, "exploiting" 2,621 employees. Half of them worked in four inner districts. This meant that districts like Kispest or Csepel, independent towns before 1949, were almost totally without artisans. Kispest had 217, and Csepel 80 licensed craftsmen in early 1953.[25]

Nationalization was coupled with the introduction of a planned economy in Hungary. State intervention into economic life during the war made transition easier in the years after it. The first Three-Year Plan was carried out between August 1947 and late 1949, and was successful in the reconstruction of wartime damage. However, after the period of reconstruction this strategy proved to be more of a burden from the point of view of economic growth and reproduction. Its only advantage was an unprecedented concentration of resources. The seeming economic growth involved an extreme waste of energy, raw materials, and labor force.

These contradictions came to the surface during the first Five-Year Plan beginning on January 1, 1950. The goals were set even higher than those of the previous plan, and they were doubled by the 2nd Congress of the Hungarian Workers' Party in early 1951 based on the successes in the period of reconstruction. War preparations made the development of heavy industry the priority. The goals specified a rate of development of 280 percent in five years. 94 percent of all industrial investments were earmarked for heavy industry.

An amended law in 1951 stipulated that the 1954 coal output was to cover all demands for fuel and result in significant reserves. Therefore the goal of increasing production to 18.5 million tons from 11.5 million in 1949 was further increased to 27.5 million tons in 1954.[26] According to the Central Statistical Office says, however, the base figure was already falsified: coal output in 1949 was only 9.9 million tons and in 1954 it remained below the original target of 18.5 million tons (it was less than 18 million tons actually).[27] Consequently the whole period under discussion was characterized by a chronic shortage of energy sources. In September 1956 the daily paper of the Communist Party announced that 600 trains would have to be suspended for three weeks the following month due to coal shortages.[28] The radio announced the same day that 500 buses and 1,000 trucks would meet the same fate for lack of fuel.

The largest investment in Budapest was to be the construction of a new subway line the first part of which was to be completed by 1954, and the whole line between the People's Stadium and the *Déli* [Southern] Railway Station by 1955. When the Ministry of Transport asked the government to suspend construction works in January, 1954, only one third of the line had been completed.[29] The underground construction was made difficult by the fact that it was supposed to meet military needs as well. Its primary military aim was to connect the Eastern and Southern Railway Stations.

The population of Budapest assumed an increasingly proletarian character in those years. The middle class disappeared, and the working class was levelling downwards. On the one hand, for political reasons, the Communists, controlling the country, presented a united front against the stratum of skilled workers who formed the traditional base of Social Democracy. On the other hand, collectivization of agriculture turned unskilled peasant labor into mass producers.

Fight against the enemy, whether personal or impersonal, became part of the daily routine. The primary aim of the campaign was to interpret conflicts and problems as sabotage. The party claimed that it was not shortage of raw materials or working tools, bad working conditions, forced industrialization that endangered production, the fulfillment of plans, and the increase of living standards, but disruption by the enemy.

Deteriorating labor discipline was handled as political crime and a new concept, "offence against planned economy" was born, branding those who left their jobs for another. In spite of all this, industrial production became practically uncontrollable. Laborers forced to leave the villages and work in the capital went home unannounced to do seasonal work in agriculture. Incidents of absence without leave almost tripled between the second and the fourth quarter of 1950 in metallurgical industry, nearly doubled in machine industry, and rose approximately to 50 per cent in heavy industry in general. In spite of all sanctions, absenteeism assumed ever greater proportions even apart from seasonal work in agriculture. At the huge Csepel works, renamed after the Communist leader Mátyás Rákosi, an average of "only" 688 workers were absent without leave each day in September, 1950. In February, 1951 this figure rose to 1,674. In 1951–52 sanctions resulted in a 50 percent decrease in absenteeism but, at the same time, legal forms of absenteeism were invented. In early 1952 the rate of absenteeism was between 11 and 14 percent in certain branches of industry. Seven to 9 percent of the total workforce was absent daily. Losses were made up by a regular raise of norms. This decrease in wages involved loss of quality, the majority of goods produced becoming unusable. The value of production did not even cover the cost of raw materials.

Working conditions in the factories also deteriorated to an enormous degree. Real wages dropped drastically (by 22.2 per cent in mid-1953 compared to the 1950 level) in the first half of the first Five-Year Plan. Even the falling wages lost their value due to the shortage of commodities—food, clothing, and articles of personal hygiene. Long lines outside stores became the norm. The regime, however, blamed the workers of nationalized businesses for the shortages calling it sabotage. Trials for sabotage became a common feature of the regime. Two leaders of the State Enterprise for Meat Supply were even sentenced to death and executed for hoarding.

Norms and prices were not "increased," only "adjusted", according to the terminology used; but the population was aware of the real meaning of the word. When rumors of Mátyás Rákosi's radio annoucement of the imminent "adjustment" of prices spread in the city, the population went on shopping sprees and turnover tripled in food and clothing stores overnight.

At that point the Hungarian planned economy, based on shortage and waste, collapsed. The unusual drought of 1952 revealed that the economy was no longer able to function. The real cause lay, however, in extremely inflexible planned economy. A strictly secret survey by the Central Statistical Office taken in the same year showed that a great portion of manufactured products were unmarketable, and unusable.

## The Post-Stalin Era: Imre Nagy's First Ministry

Despite the evident facts of the collapse, the demand for a change did not come from Budapest but from Moscow after Stalin's death. In June 1953 the principal political leaders of the country were summoned to appear in Moscow, where the Soviet leaders demanded the radical reorganization of economic life in Hungary. During these talks the Soviet leaders decided to remove Rákosi from his premiership and replace him by Imre Nagy, who had had differences with the official line in agricultural production already in the late 1940s.

A few days after the talks in Moscow the Central Committee of the Communist Party met and was informed by Mátyás Rákosi and Imre Nagy of Moscow's intentions. None of these reports or resolutions were ever published. General Secretary Rákosi's title was changed to First Secretary. Imre Nagy was elected to membership in the Political Committee, the narrow circle of leaders of the Communist Party, and he became the new Prime Minister.

Imre Nagy made his first appearance before the newly "elected" parliament on July 4. In his inaugural speech he resorted to traditional Stalinist terminology, but its content indicated the beginning of a radical turn in political life. The Prime Minister took the field against the forced development of heavy industry and in support of higher living standards. Nagy promised better perspectives for private farms, as well as the abolition of arbitrariness in all spheres of life, including internment and resettlement. He also promised amnesty to those condemned for political dissent.

While the rural population hailed the inaugural address of the Prime Minister, the population of the capital was still distrustful of the Communists and suspended judgment. Indeed, the turn called the "new course" brought changes mainly for the rural population. Large masses of peasants left the highly inefficient agricultural cooperatives. Attempts to achieve a sudden turn in industrial production were strongly opposed by the party cadres. Certain large-scale investments were cancelled especially in heavy industry, but anarchy increased and production continued to plummet.

Certain events, insignificant in themselves yet of symbolic value, heightened distrust. Government securities called "Peace Loans" were issued in order to withhold purchasing capacity. Subscription was practically compulsory. Although the governmental intentions were reflected in the fact that the total value of the securities issued was 35 percent lower than in the previous year, their nominal value still superseded the 1950 level. The construction of the subway system continued. The press reported success each day but made no mention of the delays. Stalin's final book, *Economic Problems of Socialism in the Soviet Union*, was published for the third time in 1953. This book fundamentally contradicted the targets of the Hungarian "new course".

Furthermore, the Prime Minister's platform raised doubts when the leader of the Party, Rákosi himself, attacked it. He hoped for a turn in Soviet attitudes. Consequently, Imre Nagy became ostracized by the Communist countries, and Western democracies were skeptical of his intention to implement change.

Yet positive changes could be observed in Budapest. Real wages were rising (due to the combination of a wage increase and the lowering of prices), the harvest was good, resulting in an improved food supply for the capital. Gábor Péter, the despised leader of the political police, was arrested and sentenced to life imprisonment. While the sentence was based on spurious accusations, as usual under a Stalinist regime, the outcome was applauded. In mid-1954 falsely condemned Communists, including János Kádár, the future party leader, were released from jail. The innocence of these people shocked that residue of the Budapest intelligentsia who had formerly trusted the regime and the party implicitly. Now they rallied behind Imre Nagy.

In October 1954 the Prime Minister seemed to be successful in defending his program. Under this "new course", however, industrial production was still in decline while the use of raw materials per unit had been rising. The problem was exacerbated by rising wages—especially among white-collar workers.

On Imre Nagy's initiative the Patriotic People's Front was formed to counter the tyranny of the Communist Party. His efforts were, however, thwarted by the Rákosi clique. Although Nagy managed to rally non-party intellectuals, the council elections in November showed that this organization was as important as the Independence Front of earlier years. The October offensive of Imre Nagy was, therefore, over by December. Once again, decisions came down from Kremlin functionaries. However successfully Nagy might have maneuvered amidst the "thaw" proclaimed by the Soviets and supported by the west, the freeze in the thaw of Soviet politics rendered his position ultimately hopeless.

## The Antecedents of the 1956 Revolution

On November 29, 1954, Rákosi returned from Moscow after a pro-longed visit. Two days later, with the consent of the Soviet leader, he sharply attacked Nagy at the meeting of the political committee with the consent of the Soviet leaders and ousted him from political life. Although Nagy was still Prime Minister, he appeared in public only once after this meeting (in Debrecen, on December 21, 1954). In 1955 the central committee sharply criticized him for his "right-wing views", and a month later he was relieved of his duties as Prime Minister. He was deprived of all his functions, even of his chair at the university. His earlier writings were banned, and late that year he was expelled from the party.

While Budapest was facing bleak days in early 1955, Vienna was jubilant, for Austria had just signed a state treaty that ensured its independence. It followed from the subsequent withdrawal of the Soviet troops from Austria that their stay in Hungary was no longer justified.[30] Prime Minister András Hegedűs, who succeeded Imre Nagy, signed the Warsaw Treaty the previous day (May 14, 1955), providing fresh justification for the presence of Soviet troops in Hungary.[31]

The Austrian state treaty had a profound impact upon Hungarian intellectuals. The idea of Hungary becoming a similarly neutral state spread rapidly and was a subject treated by Imre Nagy in an underground manuscript. These circles were similarly influenced by a speech of Khrushchev in Belgrade on May 26, 1955, in which the Soviet leader apologized for the hostile attitude of his country toward Yugoslavia in the recent past.

The Yugoslav question had always been a thorny issue in Hungary. From 1948 on Rákosi consistently denounced Tito. In 1949 the Communist László Rajk, in the greatest show trial of Hungarian history, was sentenced to death and executed as a Tito agent. Now Tito was proclaimed innocent by no less an authority than the Soviets themselves. Nagy's followers consequently demanded the settlement of Hungarian-Yugoslav relations immediately following Khrushchev's speech, and even raised the question of Rajk's rehabilitation, though still in a structured party-like manner. The party leaders threatened reprisals, but in vain. Discontent was spreading and even some of the dailies supported the dissidents. The replacement of the "guilty" editors-in-chief could not halt the process. In September 1955 there was a storm when the weekly of the Writers' Association, *Irodalmi*

*Újság* [Literary Magazine], was banned. All Communist members of the presidium of the Writers' Association resigned in protest. Fifty-nine leading Communist intellectuals wrote a memorandum against the manifestations of Stalinist cultural policy and the retaliatory measures of the present Hungarian leadership.

The Budapest Committee of the Communist Party organized a workers' meeting in which speakers demanded that the recalcitrant intellectuals be censured and brought to toe the line. The Party was only too pleased to fulfill this request. Some of those who had signed the memorandum revoked their signatures under pressure, while others were subjected to disciplinary action. There were arrests and trials. Even the Budapest correspondents of UPI and AP received prison terms.

On March 12, 1956, Mátyás Rákosi spoke at a meeting of the central committee about the Twentieth Party Congress of the Soviet Union, where Khrushchev's secret speech had been delivered. The Hungarian party leader tried to rationalize the new course in Moscow by maintaining that Stalinism had already been abolished in Hungary. The Twentieth Party Congress gave a new impetus to the intelligentsia that demanded the rehabilitation of Rajk and sometimes even openly objected to Rákosi. Two weeks after Rákosi's report before the central committee he was forced to admit publicly that Rajk's case had been based on provocation. He also announced the release from prison of several former Social Democrats. Not quite two months later, at a meeting in the Budapest Sports Hall, Rakosi confessed: "I have to tell you openly and frankly that I myself must share the guilt for the fact that serious illegalities might have been committed in the country. I am to blame as the person at the highest post in the party, but the party leadership of that epoch is also responsible to some degree."[32] With this admission Rákosi and the whole Communist movement lost their legitimacy.

The intellectuals' criticism of the regime emerged from its earlier ritual framework and was given voice in the Petőfi Circle formed about by the Budapest branch of the Communist Youth Organization. At the meetings non-party members could also express their dissenting opinions, addressing not just a narrow circle of party members but a wide general audience. At the most impressive meeting of the Petőfi Circle, held on June 27, 1956, which attracted a large crowd, journalists demanded freedom of the press and speeches were made about the future of the country in the event of Rákosi's fall from grace.

A unique demonstration took place at Imre Nagy's residence on June 2. A host of intellectuals gathered there to greet the former Prime Minister on his sixtieth birthday. Urged by the alarming news from Hungary, the Kremlin now sent Mikhail Suslov, its most experienced emissary, to Budapest to buttress Rákosi's position and to exercise pressure on Imre Nagy. Almost simultaneously, the Yugoslav President Tito went to Moscow demanding the immediate dismissal of Rákosi. However, Khrushchev declined to act, arguing that the Soviets were more concerned about Poland at the moment. Further, he explained that Hungary could be pacified by force, if necessary. The demonstration of Polish workers in Poznan a few days later confirmed Khrushchev's preoccupation with Poland.[33]

Encouraged by support from Moscow, Rákosi prepared for another showdown. The central committee banned the Petőfi Circle and there were rumors of a new wave of arrests in Budapest.[34] This, however, was more than enough even for the Kremlin. In a letter to Tito, written only four days earlier, Khrushchev had backed Rákosi, but on July 17 Anastas Mikoyan came to Budapest and announced his replacement at the meeting of the central committee on the following day. Unfortunately, he appointed the likewise Muscovite Ernő Gerő, the closest colleague of Rákosi, to replace the latter. The intellectuals within the party and, in fact, even some Communist leaders had expected the appointment of János Kádár. Many were convinced that only the Nagy and Kádár duo could save the party from falling apart. Tito, whose influence in Moscow had grown considerably in the previous year, contemplated a similar solution. Khrushchev and Tito spent the late summer and early autumn of 1956 together first in Yugoslavia, then in the Crimea. One of the highlights of these mutual visits was the meeting of Gerő and Tito arranged by Khrushchev unexpectedly on September 30 in the Crimea.

Tito invited Gerő to visit Yugoslavia, which was a kind of tacit diplomatic recognition. Gerő was also willing to please the Yugoslav leader in many ways prior to his visit. On the day of his visit (October 14) a communiqué was issued to announce the readmission of Imre Nagy into the party. (Nagy himself had not been willing to make concessions for that.) Four days later he regained his membership in the Academy of Sciences, and two days later his chair at the university. Even more important was Gerő's promise to have Rajk and the executed Communists reburied in a dignified manner. The Party leadership of Budapest had planned to do that anyway, but only in a private family ceremony.

Gerő was still in Moscow, and Kádár was attending the congress of the Chinese Communist Party when the Rajk funeral took place without their participation on October 6, 1956. The funeral drew a crowd estimated at 100,000. Although all speakers (with the only exception of Béla Szász) were loyal to the Communist ideals in their tributes, the ceremony was, in effect, a political demonstration suggesting a burial service for the Communist regime itself.

At the time of the funeral the Petőfi Circle was active again, but the debates were more moderate and focused upon professional problems. More and more high-school and university students indulged in harsh attacks against the regime after the summer holidays. The Communist Youth Organization planned to convene a "parliament for the youth" as a sign of its democratization. Secondary school and university students, and young workers met to prepare the parliament. At these meetings the demand for democracy formerly represented by intellectuals in and outside the Party was coupled with specific national demands.[35] The students of Szeged reestablished their independent youth organization, joined by high-school students from several other towns as well.

## Revolution in the Capital

At a meeting held at the University of Technology in Budapest on October 22, 1956, the students summarized their demands and outlined their revolutionary program. Their demands were as follows: withdrawal of the Soviet troops from Hungary; democracy within the party, i.e., democratic elections; convocation of a new party congress; election of new leading bodies for the party. They demanded, furthermore, the restructuring of the cabinet, the dismissal of Stalinist ministers, the appointment of Imre Nagy to the post of Prime Minister; general elections by secret ballot; the restoration of the multiparty system and political pluralism. The reconsideration of equal Hungarian-Soviet relations; the reorganization of economic life; the revision of working norms; the right to strike; freedom of opinion, speech, and of the press, and the removal of Stalin's statue were among the demands. Finally the students expressed their solidarity "with the Polish workers and the youth of Warsaw in their struggle for independence."[36] To support their claims, the students of the University of Technology called a demonstration for October 23 to lay a wreath at the feet of the statue of General Joseph Bem, a Polish general in the Hungarian

War of Independence of 1848–49 "to express sympathy with the Polish liberation movement."[37]

The students sent a delegation to the state radio office to have their demands broadcast before eight o'clock in the evening. When the delegation returned empty-handed,[38] the students began to type and reproduce their manifesto during the night. The professors of the university supported their students' claims but advised them to postpone the demonstration. If not, they "should remain reserved, refrain from any violent action, and march in an orderly way", so the professors warned.[39]

On October 23 the party and government delegation headed by Ernő Gerő returned from Yugoslavia after a ten-day visit. At the Western Railway Station Gerő declared he was very satisfied with the talks. Prime Minister András Hegedűs and János Kádár, second in rank in the Party since July, told the reporter of *Politika* from Belgrade that "events have taken a healthy course in Hungary."[40] The committee of welcome, however, included the person who had suggested that in case of a demonstration the police should be authorized to fire upon the dissidents.[41] Unawares, the students were distributing their manifesto and an invitation to a demonstration. They even visited several factories (e.g. the Csepel Iron and Metal Works among others) to win the workers over to their cause. The Petőfi Academy, which trained political commissars for the army, also issued a memorandum supporting "the just claims of the students". Imre Nagy, returning from Badacsony (a summer resort at Lake Balaton) the previous evening, discussed the situation with his friends, he opposed the demonstration.

The party delegation and the leaders receiving Gerő at the railway station drove right to the party headquarters where the political committee went into emergency session. They decided to forbid the demonstration. Accordingly, at 12:53 p.m. the radio announced that the Minister of the Interior had forbidden the demonstration of solidarity with Poland.[42] In the meantime, the representatives of other universities and colleges of Budapest and other towns gathered in the central building of the Loránd Eötvös University of Sciences and unanimously decided to go forward with the the demonstration. The Petőfi Circle and the Hungarian Writers' Association also demanded at the party headquarters that the demonstration be authorized. Both delegations were, of course, turned down. Sándor Kopácsi, police chief of Budapest, who was also a law student taking evening courses at the university, sent word to the law students that the police would not employ force against the students, should they stage the illegal demonstration.[43]

Not even the members of the political police backed the ban. They maintained that "neither the party, nor the government had taken suitable measures to stop the demonstration, should it be held despite the ban."[44]

Minister of Interior László Piros informed his colleagues of the prohibition. His deputies and Sándor Kopácsi told him, however, that neither the political police, nor the regular police force had the means to suppress the demonstration.[45] The Minister of the Interior immediately notified Gerő to that effect and, as a consequence, the political committee approved the demonstration. It even instructed the primary party organizations to send as many Communists to join the students in the streets as possible in order to "change the prevailing tone" there.[46] At 14:23 p.m. the radio announced that the Minister of the Interior had allowed the demonstration after all.[47]

At the Technological University the deputy Minister of the Interior told the students who were gathering there despite the prohibition that the Minister had changed his mind. Subsequently the students marched toward *Bem* Square close-ranked and in silence as they had promised their professors. They had specific plans for their route, and for laying wreaths. On the Pest side, one of the most famous actors, Imre Sinkovits, recited Sándor Petőfi's poem *Nemzeti dal* [Song of the Nation], evoking memories of the revolution of 1848. A large group of students arrived at *Kálvin* Square when the news of the Minister's consent reached them. Crowds were coming also from the direction of the Writers' Association. The students of the Petőfi Military Academy were allowed to participate only as individuals, yet they marched close-ranked, singing songs from previous revolutions. The youth of the other military academies joined those of the universities and endorsed their demands.

Péter Veres, President of the Writers' Association, read the writers' manifesto to the ever growing crowd. His voice could, however, hardly be heard. Some people intoned the *Himnusz* [National Anthem], and Ferenc Bessenyei, a celebrated actor, recited Ferenc Kölcsey's *Szózat* [Address to the Nation] written in the 19th century and denounced, like the national anthem, by the Communist regime for arousing patriotic sentiments. Soldiers in the windows of the barracks overlooking the square expressed their sympathy with the demonstrators and hoisted a flag with the Communist coat of arms cut out of the center. A call was heard urging the people on to the parliament, and the huge crowd marched across the two nearest bridges. The *Kossuth* Square in front of the parliament was soon jammed. Many more, mostly young workers, continued to arrive by trucks. The crowd waited in an orderly way for Imre Nagy, the former Prime Minister. He arrived at the Parliament around 9 o'clock and greeted the people in a short address, promising to continue the "new course", and asking the people to go home. His words could be heard only by those standing close to the building and they were disappointed. Nagy's advice was ignored, and smaller groups marched to the radio building, the editorial offices of the Communist daily *Szabad Nép* [Free People], and finally to Stalin's statue in accordance with the students' plan of the previous night.

A few hundred people gathered at the radio station around 5 p.m. They demanded that the students' manifesto be broadcast. In the meantime, units of the political police poured in. The guard at the radio fought against the crowd first with tear-gas and water-hoses, until they pretended to give in by offering the people a recording van and telling them to broadcast their manifesto themselves. The trick seemed successful for awhile, but the people living in the adjacent street placed their radios on the window-sills to enable the crowd to hear the manifesto. It turned out, however, that nothing was actually broadcast, so the crowd used the van to break the gates of the building. The leaders of the radio again pretended to agree with the crowd and let smaller groups into the building from time to time. As time went by, those outside realized that these groups must have been taken prisoner.

When the radio proclaimed that the prohibition had been withdrawn it also annouced that Ernő Gerő, First Secretary of the Party, would deliver a speech over the radio at 8 p.m. This announcement was repeated several times.[48] Those working at the radio station waited anxiously for the party leader's appearance, but he declared that he would speak from the safety of his own room. Gerő announced that the changes demanded by the crowd had already begun with Rákosi's replacement and his own appointment to the post of First Secretary in July. He promised, therefore, to continue the policy pursued since then and to correct possible errors. He went on to denounce the forces that wanted to turn the country against the "brotherly" Soviet Union. "We condemn those who strive to spread the poison of chauvinism among our youth and who have taken advantage of the democratic freedom ensured by our state to working people in order to carry out a nationalist demonstration."[49] Ernő Gerő's provocative radio speech drew more and more people to the radio building, hoping to view him in person. After Gerő's speech the radio announced that the political committee had called a meeting of the central committee for October 31.[50] Then the speaker corrected himself saying that the plenum was to take place in the very near future.[51] After 10 p.m. the radio announced that the central committee was going to meet promptly.[52]

In the meantime, a great host was converging toward Stalin's statue from the Parliament and other districts of the city. They demanded that the spotlights of the labor union headquarters opposite the statue be lit, which was done after some procrastination. Flyers demanding the demolition of the statue had been circulating in the city for days before. The crowd began to demolish the hated statue themselves, first hopelessly by hand, then by machinery. They tried to pull down the statue by tying it to a truck. When the wire snapped, workers from a nearby factory tried to cut it with a blowtorch. The statue tilted, the crowd cheered and began to sing the National Anthem. Suddenly the statue swung back and stood erect again. This scene repeated itself twice and only at the third attempt did the statue finally fall to the ground. It was hauled by the crowd to Blaha Lujza Square, where for days people removed small pieces as souvenirs, even during street fighting.

The soldiers defending the radio building managed to push the crowd back from Bródy Sándor Street. The people were, however, backed by two tanks and managed to push their way to the main entrance. The commander of the detachment withdrew his perplexed and demoralized men to the garden of the National Museum nearby. To strengthen their discipline and determination, he ordered them to shoot into the air. At that moment a unit of the political police arrived at the garden from another direction. Hearing the shots and seeing the flashes in the dark, they returned the fire. Those units of the political police inside the radio building assumed they were under attack, began shooting at the demonstrators.

Many soldiers sent to defend the building joined the crowd. In their search for weapons a group of dissidents entered the Lightbulb Factory at some distance from the radio station, for it was well-known that the factory actually produced fire-arms. Although it had stopped production during the summer, there were still many weapons in its stores. The demonstrators also went to police stations and other para-military organizations in order to seize weapons. Two hours after the outbreak of shooting at the radio station, the crowd started to return the fire. By midnight an armed conflict was in progress.

It soon became obvious that the army and the police were not only unable but even unwilling to suppress the insurrection. "Order" could only be restored by the Soviet occupation force, as Khrushchev had envisaged back in June during his talks with Tito. While a short while before, Hungarian Communist leaders were still observing the changes in the country with satisfaction, the Soviets had already taken concrete steps to suppress any dangerous rebellion. At this time there were few Soviet troops in Budapest, but those around the country had been alerted days before.

The students' demonstration was still peaceful when Soviet armored units were dispatched against the city from two directions. After his radio speech in the evening, Ernő Gerő turned to Soviet Ambassador Yury Andropov for advice. It was during this call that Andropov and Gerő agreed to intervene with Soviet troops.[53] The first units rolled into the city around midnight on October 23 and occupied its strategic points, such as the building of the Ministry of Defence. The troops arrived at the radio building, which was now occupied by insurgents. This occupation proved to be only a Pyrrhic victory, because the studio had been detached from the transmitter. Although in their official statements the Communist leaders spoke of a deliberately prepared counter-revolution, the insurrection resembled spontaneous revolutions of the nineteenth century. It was not prepared by western secret services. The demonstrators occupied the radio station, the editorial offices of the Communist daily *Szabad Nép*, and the international telephone central, but not the actual centers of political power like the parliament, the party headquarters or the headquarters of the political police.

By dawn, October 24, the first armed groups of insurgents had been formed in the capital. The Council of Ministers of the Hungarian People's Republic announced early in the morning that "reactionary, fascist elements have launched an armed attack against our public buildings and attacked our police squads." Public gatherings were banned by the government.[54] The party leadership decided to replace some of its members as a token of its willingness to make concessions. Imre Nagy and his adherents Ferenc Donáth and Géza Losonczy were recalled into the inner circle of leadership.[55] The Presidential Council exercising the functions of the head of state was instructed to appoint Imre Nagy Prime Minister.

At 8:45 p.m. it was already Imre Nagy who ordered the introduction of martial law, providing that "participation in the riot is punishable by death."[56] During the day Anastas Mikoyan and Mikhail Suslov arrived in Budapest and negotiated with the Hungarian leaders. They reinforced Ernő Gerő in his position and demanded the immediate repression of the revolution.

Early next morning the Soviet news agency TASS trumpeted abroad that the Budapest riots had been quelled. The Hungarian leaders were also deceived by this illusion. The curfew was lifted and the radio called upon the people of the capital to go to their workplaces in the morning.[57] Thousands of workers commuting to the capital from the neighboring settlements arrived by train in the morning and learnt only then about the events of the previous day. It was not that the Soviets and the Hungarian leaders underrated the armed insurrection. The occupation of Budapest was meant to intimidate the masses and defend the most important government buildings and traffic junctions. Calls for a general strike were sounded already on October 23, and the curfew contributed to its success.

The idea of another mass meeting outside the parliament was also raised on October 23. Consequently, students gathered at Hotel Astoria in the heart of the city on October 25 around 9 p.m. to march to the parliament together and hand over their demands to Prime Minister Imre Nagy. Six Soviet tanks were there "to keep order" and the students made friends with the soldiers. They had no problems in understanding each other, since Russian had been a compulsory subject in Hungarian schools. They even distributed flyers to the soldiers in Russian to persuade them. One of them quoted Marx as follows: "No nation can be free that oppresses other nations." As a result of fraternizing with the tank crews three of the tanks joined the demonstrators and rolled along with them to the parliament. As one of them broke down on *Szabadság* [Freedom] Square, not far from the American Embassy, the crowd was escorted by two Soviet tanks when they reached *Kossuth* Square, where other Soviet tanks were parked to defend the building. Fraternization continued, and a Soviet officer allowed a delegation of three to enter the building, though Imre Nagy was not there at the time.

Suddenly shots were fired from the top of the buildings opposite the parliament at the unarmed demonstrators. Hungarian soldiers and members of paramilitary units were shooting into a crowd of approximately 10,000. One of the Soviet tanks that had joined the demonstrators at Hotel Astoria returned the fire and chaotic firing began. The overwhelming majority of the victims were among the unarmed demonstrators. When shooting stopped, the crowd started to flee from the square. However, the temporary cease-fire did not mean the end of the fusillade. The building of the Communist Party headquarters was only two blocks from *Kossuth* Square and it was also defended by Soviet tanks, since the two Soviet emissaries, Mikoyan and Suslov, were inside. These tanks approached *Kossuth* Square and started an even more cruel bloodshed. The Hungarian frontier guard unit sent to defend the party headquarters saw the bloodshed and began firing at the political police squad defending the building. Even the room where Mikoyan and Suslov were negotiating with Hungarian politicians was hit by a salvo. The Soviet emissaries heaped reproaches on Gerő for the passivity of the Hungarian armed forces and urged his dismissal and the "election" of János Kádár as First Secretary. This decision came too late, for rumors of the massacre had turned the sympathy of the capital's population unanimously toward the insurgents.[58]

On the initiative of the leaders of the Communist Party and the Labor Union Alliance, workers' councils were set up in several large factories of Budapest on October 25.[59] On October 26 the leaders of the party promised the nation a new, national government, the withdrawal of the Soviet troops, and the restitution of Hungary's independence as soon as fighting stopped. The Presidential Council promised amnesty for all who ceased resistance. Although the armed conflict continued the following day, the Nagy government was reshuffled. Eleven new ministers were appointed. Two of them were Nagy's Communist followers, and two (Zoltán Tildy and Béla Kovács) were former Smallholder leaders.[60] On Soviet demand Ferenc Münnich became Minister of the Interior and Károly Janza Minister of Defence. The latter's first step was to order the Hungarian army units "to annihilate the centers of armed conflict and restore order."[61] In spite of certain conciliatory measures, the Military Committee established during the night of October 23 worked out a plan to blow up *Corvin köz* [Corvin Lane] defended by the largest group of armed insurgents. This plan was vetoed by the Prime Minister.

The Party leaders debated whether to end the movement by force or by political concessions. During the night of October 27 the political committee, attended also by Mikoyan and Suslov, chose the latter option. They discussed and accepted János Kádár's proposition to declare the "counter-revolution" a "popular insurrection." Furthermore they suggested the withdrawal of the Soviet troops from Hungary and the dissolution of the hated political police. The following morning *Szabad Nép* published an editorial with the consent of the political committee that informed the public about the interpretation of the armed insurrection. "We do not agree with those who qualify the events of the past few days as attempts of a counter-revolutionary fascist coup," the article said. It emphasized that the demonstration of the students which launched the insurrection reflected the demands of the whole population. On the basis of this demonstration "a great democratic, national movement evolved, uniting the whole nation, that had been repressed by the tyranny of the earlier years, but was ignited again by the first breeze of freedom." The article established that Gerő had not understood the real character of the demonstration and had not drawn lessons from it. It concluded, therefore, that "the workers, peasants, young intellectuals, students, and young working people constituting the majority of the insurgents cannot be considered enemies of the people's democratic regime."[62]

On October 28 the central committee of the Hungarian Workers' Party discontinued its activities and was replaced by a six-member presidium headed by Kádár. Imre Nagy was also among the members. At 1:20 p.m. he ordered suspension of hostilities,[63] and four hours later announced on radio that the government had conceded the main popular demands. Nagy called the events of the previous day one of the greatest shocks in Hungarian history. He established that his government "condemned the views according to which the present huge people's movement was a counterrevolution... In these actions a great national and democratic movement manifested itself with an overwhelming force." The Prime Minister promised to settle the lawful demands of the workers as regards wages, working conditions, minimum wage, minimum old-age pensions and family allowance. He promised support for the newly formed workers' councils and ordered suspension of hostilities. The armed forces were allowed to open fire only when attacked. Morevoer, Imre Nagy announced the formation of a new armed force including the police, the army, and the armed insurgents. In the meantime the withdrawal of the Soviet troops from the capital began. Nagy held out the prospect of negotiations with the Soviet Union in order to achieve the complete withdrawal of the Soviet forces and the restoration of Hungarian independence. In his radio speech the Prime Minister said that the government had dissolved the State Security Authority and granted full amnesty to the participants of the armed insurrection. The government accepted the Kossuth coat of arms, the symbol of the revolution and the demand that March 15 become again a national holiday.[64]

In keeping with Imre Nagy's platform, a *Forradalmi Karhatalmi Bizottság* [Revolutionary Committee for Public Safety] was formed at the Budapest police headquarters, headed by Béla Király. Although the Soviet troops were withdrawing from the capital, from time to time they still took part in armed conflicts. The political police was also dissolved, its members disarmed, some of them even arrested. Several of them took refuge among the Soviets.

The leaders of the Party asked Wladyslaw Gomulka and Josip Broz Tito, both enjoying great prestige in Budapest, to contribute public statements in support of the stabilization of the government and the restoration of order in the capital. The Yugoslav president subsequently wrote a letter to the Central Committee of the Hungarian Workers' Party. He spoke of the concern with which the people of Yugoslavia had followed the events in Hungary. At the same time he was aware that it was "the faulty and harmful policy" of the former leadership that had created this critical situation, he wrote. Tito called attention to the fact that the events in Hungary could not be considered as purely internal affairs and international consequences must be reckoned with. Tito hoped that the adherents of democratic Socialism would take the upper hand in Hungary and prevent "various reactionary elements from taking advantage of the events of today to achieve their own anti-Socialist goals." He hailed, therefore, the formation of the reconstituted Presidium of the Hungarian Party and the manifesto of the government dated on October 28. Furthermore he hoped that the Hungarian working class would be able to stop the senseless bloodshed.[65] Tito's letter was considered favorable both by the government and by the opposition, who were restive because of the government's delay in complying with their most important demands, especially the introduction of a multiparty system in Hungary.

On October 30 the Soviet government published a declaration in which it acknowledged the Socialist countries' equality of status and expressed its willingness to talk about the withdrawal of the Soviet troops from Hungary.[66] By the time the declaration was made public in Budapest on the next day, the Presidium of the Communist Party of the Soviet Union, headed by Nikita Sergeyevich Khrushchev, had instructed Minister of Defence Marshall Georgi Konstantinovich Zhukov to prepare the suppression of the Budapest revolt by force. Although the Western powers made it clear that they were against Soviet military intervention in Hungary, their attention was absorbed by the Suez crisis occurring at the same time.

The situation was ambiguous in Budapest in those days. Fighting in the streets subsided with the withdrawal of the Soviet army units, but did not stop altogether. The Military Committee, established on October 23 by Communist Party leaders, turned against the Presidium of the Party and the resolutions of the government, and worked out plans for a military dictatorship. Preparations for a military coup began at the Budapest Party headquarters on *Köztársaság* [Republic] Square. The Military Committee, however, did not dare to implement the plan without Imre Nagy's consent, and the Prime Minister strongly opposed the coup.

Even the Military Committee was divided upon the issue. Its more moderate members did not favor a coup. They thought it was enough to reinforce the newly created armed forces with reliable workers. The situation was aggravated by the fact that at the *Köztársaság* [Republic] Square the political police defending the party headquarters changed uniforms, wearing that of the ordinary police after their dissolution, could not remain hidden. A small group of armed insurgents made their way into the building early in the morning on October 30. They were promptly disarmed and arrested by the guard. When rumors of their arrest spread, armed groups in the nearby streets united their forces and launched an attack against the building, to wipe out the security police squad dressed in the uniform of the ordinary police. In the meantime the radio announced that the First Secretary of the Budapest Party Committee had been replaced and the party committee invited Communists to volunteer for the National Guard.[67]

However, this communiqué did not break off the attack upon the Party headquarters. The "siege" lasted several hours and the defenders' positions became hopeless. Their distress signals did not reach Imre Nagy, and the Russians refused to help, referring to the promise of withdrawal. Finally an army unit from the country sent a few tanks to relieve the defenders of the building, but most of them did not intervene. One of them even started to shoot at the building in support of the insurgents. The fate of the defenders was sealed. Even Imre Mező, Secretary of the Budapest Party Committee was killed when he left the building as a truce-bearer.[68]

The same day, having obtained the consent of Mikoyan and Suslov, Imre Nagy announced on the radio the restoration of the multiparty system early in the afternoon. An inner cabinet was set to include Imre Nagy, Ferenc Erdei, János Kádár, Béla Kovács, Géza Losonczy, and Zoltán Tildy.[69] One portfolio was reserved for the Social Democratic Party.[70]

On October 30, on order of the government, soldiers freed the Primate of Hungary, Cardinal József Mindszenty, who had been incarcerated for eight years. He arrived in Budapest early next morning. In his first speech he indicated that he wished to resume his work as a dignitary of the church. Many considered him a political alternative to Nagy and his reform Communist Party, but his speech gave no encouragement for such hopes. His address to the nation on November 3 revealed that he was not suitable for that role, because overlooking realities of the moment and the climate of opinion, he reclaimed the illegally nationalized institutions of his Church and called the coalition government formed on the same day "the heirs of the fallen regime." He dubbed the events of the previous days not a revolution but rather a fight for freedom.[71]

In a speech delivered on October 31 to a crowd in front of the parliament building Imre Nagy announced that Hungary was initiating negotiations to withdraw the country from the Warsaw Pact. He stressed the importance of the complete withdrawal of all Soviet troops from the country. At the same time the armed forces of the revolution began to organize into regular units. On orders issued on the previous day by Imre Nagy, Major General Béla Király announced at the *Kilián* Barracks, famous for legendary fights against the Soviets, that the Revolutionary Committee for Public Safety led by himself would take over supervision of the army, the police, and the National Guard formed by armed freedom fighters. On the same day the *Forradalmi Honvédelmi Bizottmány* [Revolutionary Council of the Hungarian Army], consisting of members of the military councils and young armed insurgents was organized at the Ministry of Defence. This Council was also headed by Béla Király. Most of its members were soldiers and policemen who had supported the insurgents from the very beginning: Colonel Sándor Kopácsi from the Police and Colonel Pál Maléter, head of the *Kilián* Barracks and deputy Minister, later Minister of Defence. The government appointed Major General Béla Király Military Commandant of Budapest.

While the situation in the capital was becoming more stable, partly as a result of the formation of a unified armed force, Soviet reinforcements were arriving in Hungary. By the evening hours of October 31 they were only 80 kilometers from the capital. The Soviet troops around Budapest seized control of the international airport and, on the following day, all airfields in the country, giving as their excuse that they needed to airlift their wounded comrades. Soviet army units continued to arrive from the direction of Záhony in Northeastern Hungary. Units withdrawn earlier from the capital entrenched themselves outside the city.

Under the influence of the Soviet invasion, the Nagy government announced Hungary's withdrawal from the Warsaw Pact and declared Hungarian neutrality. Minister of State Géza Losonczy told a press conference held on November 1 that the Hungarian government had turned to four great powers and the United Nations for guarantees of the country's neutral status. The following day the government designated Imre Nagy, Zoltán Tildy, Anna Kéthly, and Béla Kovács as members of a delegation going to the General Assembly of the UN. Discussing the Hungarian question, the Security Council of the United Nations decided to lay it before the General Assembly on November 4. The Hungarian government appointed a delegation to negotiate with the Soviets about their withdrawal from the country, and the negotiations began immediately. The government also appointed a delegation to be sent to Warsaw to negotiate the Hungarian withdrawal from the Pact.

Since the Communist Party had practically disintegrated, a new party was formed on November 1 in the spirit of the restored multiparty system, called *Magyar Szocialista Munkáspárt* [Hungarian Socialist Workers' Party]. Headed by János Kádár, the members of its Executive Committee were Ferenc Donáth, Sándor Kopácsi, Géza Losonczy, György Lukács, Imre Nagy, and Zoltán Szántó.

Before 10 p.m. Kádár delivered a speech on the radio condemning in harsh words "the blind and guilty policy of Rákosi and his clique ... reducing the pure ideals of Socialism to means of tyranny and national subjection." He called the revolution "the glorious insurrection of our nation" which had liberated the country from a reign of terror. He explained that the popular insurrection had come to a crucial point in those days, and its democratic development was threatened by an open counter-revolution. "Unless the insurrection ensures our people the fundamental achievements of democracy: the freedom of assembly and organization, personal freedom and security, law and order, freedom of the press, humanism, and honesty, we relapse into our former subjected state and fall into foreign servitude again." Finally Kádár announced the formation of the Hungarian Socialist Workers' Party consisting of Communists who had fought against the tyranny of Rákosi. The Party advocated "the Socialist goals of the working class".[72] However, by the time his speech was broadcast Kádár had already left both parliament and the government.

The greatest obstacle in the way of the stabilization of the government's position was the workers' strike on November 1 in Budapest and eventually in other towns as well. The labor unions, undergoing internal transformation to include Social Democrats, invited the workers' councils, recently founded in the days of the revolution, to two meetings. The representatives of the government clashed with those of the workers' councils in a fierce debate. The latter assured the Nagy government of their support, but objected to the participation of the guilty politicians of the former Communist regime. The workers were also alarmed by reports of Soviet reinforcements arriving in Hungary, since one of the stated goals of the strike was to obtain the withdrawal of the Soviets. Representatives of the government informed the workers of the negotiations with the Soviets and the declaration of neutrality. They tried to make the participants sign a declaration calling upon the workers of all factories in the country to resume work the next day. Finally they agreed to compromise and called upon the miners only.

Another meeting taking place parallel to the representatives of the workers' councils also refused to call off the strike. A delegation was dispatched to inform Imre Nagy of their concerns. The Prime Minister persuaded the delegates to return to work and to instruct the workers to do likewise. The only condition the workers laid down was that Pál Maléter, the "blameless soldier," would deliver a similar appeal to the nation. Both appeals were broadcast late in the evening.[73] The appeals and the measures taken by the government were successful: the workers' councils in the majority of the factories decided to return to work on Monday, November 5, and the preparations began already on Saturday.

Stabilization of the domestic situation, however, did not alter the decision taken in Moscow on October 31 to invade Hungary by a considerable military force. The Soviets considered the installation of a suitable puppet government a prerequisite for such a move. Several representatives of the previous Hungarian regime (former party chief Ernő Gerő, former Prime Minister András Hegedűs, former Minister of the Interior László Piros, among others) who were staying in Moscow at that time, were drawn into the discussions. Some high-ranking Hungarian army officers staying in the Soviet Union for various reasons were sent home to paralyze possible resistance.

Among the Hungarian politicians still holding office Ferenc Münnich seemed to be the most reliable from the Soviet point of view. Prior to 1945 Münnich lived in Moscow in exile, was ignored during the Rákosi regime and was, so to speak, rehabilitated when he was appointed Ambassador to Moscow in 1953. He was a personal friend of Khrushchev. On November 1 Soviet Ambassador Andropov warned him to leave the ministry and place himself under Soviet protection. Münnich took János Kádár with him, as instructed by the Soviet ambassador. It was early in the evening when they left for the Soviet Embassy where Kádár balked at getting into a waiting car, or so certain sources maintained. They were taken to the Soviet military headquarters at Tököl, near Budapest, and left the country by plane for Moscow the following day.[74]

At that time Khrushchev was already informing the leaders of the "brotherly countries" of the Soviet plans. In the evening of November 1 he talked to Polish leaders near the Soviet–Polish border. The next day he informed the Bulgarians, Czechoslovakians, and Romanians in Bucharest. It was there he heard the news of Kádár's and Münnich's flight to Moscow.

Late in the evening, on November 2, Khrushchev and Malenkov arrived secretly at Brioni, Yugoslavia. Their talks with Tito lasted till early next morning. On the Yugoslav initiative they decided to appoint Kádár Prime Minister instead of Münnich and met him in Moscow on November 3. The talks were attended by several members of the Presidium of the Soviet Communist Party, and also by former Hungarian Minister of Foreign Affairs Imre Horváth. At these talks Kádár no longer expressed reluctance to cooperate with the Soviets as long as he would be allowed to pursue an anti-Stalinist policy.

In the meantime, the Hungarian delegation negotiated with the Soviets at their headquarters, about their projected withdrawal from the country. General Serov, head of the Soviet State Security Commission (KGB), appeared in the conference-room in person with an armed escort and arrested the Hungarian delegation including the legally appointed Ministers Erdey and Maléter.

These details were unknown in Budapest, but news that the delegation had disappeared caused alarm. The next day Imre Nagy ordered Maléter and the other members of the delegation by radio to return to the capital immediately. Signs of a military intervention became apparent, and it actually began at daybreak, November 4. The Hungarian Prime Minister announced on the radio after 5 a.m. that Soviet troops "attacked our capital with the obvious intention of overthrowing the legal Hungarian democratic government."[75] The forces of the revolution were in combat, he said. Apart from smaller army units, units of the National Guard were the only ones in position to offer resistance.

## The Dawn of the Kádár Era

Almost simultaneously, in a radio speech broadcast by the Soviets, Kádár announced the formation of the Revolutionary Worker–Peasant Government. He appointed himself Prime Minister and Münnich, Minister of Armed Forces and Public Security, his deputy.

Violent street-fighting began. Resistance was especially lively in Districts VIII and IX, in Csepel and Kőbánya. The Soviet army was far more merciless than on October 24 and thereafter. It shelled nearly all buildings where they were encountered resistance. Freedom fighters in *Corvin köz* and the Kilián Barracks held their ground till November 7 despite extremely violent Soviet attacks. The casualties exceeded the number in the earlier days of the revolution by far. On November 9 the Soviets started to shell Csepel, which had been successfully defended by armed workers. These workers even shot down an airplane. Béla Király, Commander in Chief of the National Guard, withdrew his troops from the capital and was joined by other military, with whose support he fought a last encounter with the Soviets at the village of Nagykovácsi on November 10–11. Apart from sporadic firing, this was the end of armed resistance in the capital. The Soviet leaders had given their army three days to subdue the revolution, but it took them many more days to do so.

Although Imre Nagy announced in his radio speech of November 4 that "the government was at its post", he himself soon sought refuge in the Embassy of Yugoslavia. In the spirit of the agreement concluded at Brioni the previous night, the Yugoslavs called upon the Prime Minister and several leading Communist politicians after the radio speech to place themselves under Yugoslav protection, in view of the country's interests. During the night of November 2 to 3 Tito promised Khrushchev that he would try to "exclude" the Nagy government so that the Prime Minister would not be able to call upon the nation to offer resistance and take the lead. This was why Ambassador Soldatic asked Imre Nagy to go to the Embassy with a view to his own and his government's interests. As soon as he arrived, he was given the message of President Tito in which he summoned him to resign. Apart from Kádár and Kopácsi, the latter had already been arrested by the Soviets, the whole leadership of the Hungarian Socialist Workers' Party, i.e., its executive committee remained at the Yugoslav Embassy.

This group of Hungarian Party leaders decided, on Zoltán Szántó's and György Lukács's initiative, that Imre Nagy should not resign. The Yugoslavs told Nagy that he was free to go to Yugoslavia even without a letter of resignation. However, the Soviets and Kádár envisaged a different future for Imre Nagy. By not being quick enough to "exclude" and prevent him from delivering his radio speech the Yugoslavs violated the secret agreement, according to the Soviets. Under the circumstances they saw no point in making Nagy resign and did not consent to his going to Yugoslavia.

Kádár, however, wished to reinforce his own position by Nagy's resignation and wanted him to recognize his own government as lawful.

The Soviet leaders agreed with the Romanians to transfer Imre Nagy and his group to Romania. The Yugoslavs, however, resisted and referred to the right of political asylum. They discussed the matter with Kádár, who finally agreed to a "safe conduct" to their homes and immunity from arrest. When Nagy and his fellow politicians left the Embassy on November 22, they were hijacked to Romania despite Kádár's promise.

When in the morning of November 4 Imre Nagy left the parliament, the only member of the government to remain in the building was István Bibó. According to Soviet plans the Parliament building was to be occupied by a unit coming from Tököl that included a number of former members of the Hungarian political police in order to forestall charges that the symbol of Hungarian state authority was occupied by foreign troops. They carried with them Pál Maléter as a prisoner. On their way to the parliament they were fiercely attacked by a unit of the Hungarian Army that had not been disarmed. Maléter's armored car was hit, but the minister was not hurt. One of the two Soviet soldiers guarding him died, the other was seriously wounded. The unexpected resistance forced the mixed unit of Soviets and Hungarians to make a considerable detour and to delay the occupation of the parliament.

István Bibó took advantage of this delay to draft a manifesto on behalf of the government as its last official action. In it he proclaimed that the government did not wish to pursue an anti-Soviet policy. At the same time he warned the nation not to recognize the occupying power and its puppet government. Bibo had just finished writing the manifesto when the Soviet troops encircling the parliament were ordered to occupy the building without waiting for the unit from Tököl. As no resistance was offered, the soldiers walked into the building and ordered Bibó to leave. He did so, but on his way home he stopped at several embassies to deliver the manifesto in person. His arrival at the American Embassy caused a great stir. Cardinal Mindszenty had preceded Bibo there. The officials of the embassy phoned to Washington to ask if they should also grant political asylum to the minister standing outside their building. They were relieved to learn that he only wished to hand over his memorandum.

The streets of the Hungarian capital still echoed with the sound of gunfire when Bibo drafted a project on "a compromise for the solution of the Hungarian question." His starting point was that democracy could be created in Hungary only by taking the interests of the Soviet Union as a superpower into consideration. The Soviets did not find this proposal convincing enough, and the western democracies did not consider it their duty to force them to accept a compromise. Bibó's ideas influenced only the Hungarian workers offering unarmed resistance.

On November 14, at the United Electric Plant at Újpest, the northernmost district on the Pest side (where the first workers' council of the city was formed on October 24) 500 delegates of all workers' councils of Budapest[76] founded the Central Workers' Council of Greater Budapest. Bibó's plan for a compromise were read out to the delegates and influenced the struggle and goals of the workers' councils to a considerable degree. The resolution adopted by the meeting expressed distrust of the Kádár government and demanded that Imre Nagy be returned to the post of Prime Minister. It advocated a multiparty system and Hungary's neutral status. A delegation of nineteen was sent to János Kádár that same evening. Kádár declined all demands of the workers or at least made them dependent on conditions that could not be fulfilled.

Because Kádár was visited by several delegations of workers from different factories, he realized that their demands and tactics were not concerted. His principal objective was to end the strike in Budapest. On November 14 the Workers' Council of Budapest was set up. At its meeting in the inner city at the Budapest Municipal Electric Streetcar Company discussion centered around the withdrawal of the Soviet troops and the question of resuming work. Lenin's example in 1917 led some workers to advocate the formation of a national workers' council and establish the rule of the working classes. But Kádár feared a Bolshevik-type dual power. When he met the leaders of the Budapest Workers' Council again in the evening, he expressed his indignation saying "what the delegates of the Budapest Workers' Council suggest is unprecedented in the world and there is no need to set up a national organization like that [i.e., a national workers' council] in a people's democracy."[77]

To prove its legitimacy and support on the part of the workers the Budapest Workers' Council decided to call off the general strike begun on November 4.[78] At the same time it convened a meeting of all workers' councils of the country to set up the National Workers' Council. Accordingly, the Council called upon the workers to return to work on Saturday, November 17. "We solemnly declare, however, that our present decision does not mean any concession as regards the fundamental goals and achievements of our national insurrection."[79] On Monday, November 19, the delegates of all workers' councils of the country were convened to

meet on November 21 to form the National Workers' Council despite Kádár's emphatic objections. However, the Soviets interfered again and surrounded the Sports Hall with their tanks. Some delegates still met in the
building of the Budapest Workers' Council and demanded that Kádár
should recognize the National Workers' Council. Another strike was announced for the next 48 hours as a protest against military action.

The workers' resistance and the new strike did not prevent the puppet
government, backed by the Soviets, from "restoring order" in the capital
by large-scale arrests. While the strike was still in progress the Budapest
Workers' Council suggested that the government discuss the matter anew.
The government's representative conveyed that the talks could not begin
that day (November 22) because "Kádár is having important and long-
drawn conversations at the Romanian Embassy."[80] The government liaison
did not mention that Romanian Secretary-General Dej and Prime Minister
Stoica were staying in Budapest and they were discussing the transfer of
Imre Nagy and his group to Romania on the following day. Kádár still
met the delegates of the workers' councils but in an atmosphere of mutual
distrust. The latter told Kádár that they had no confidence in him or in his
government. They were still willing to give up the idea of setting up a
national workers' council in return for Kádár's recognition of the one in
Budapest.

The next day, one month after the outbreak of the revolution, resistance
assumed a passive character. For an hour in the afternoon traffic stopped
in the capital and people vacated the streets in commemoration of the
events a month earlier. Even the daily paper of the Party, the *Népszabadság*, wished to join this more moderate form of resistance and published
an article to express their views in the ever wider polemics on the kidnapping of Imre Nagy in the Soviet and Yugoslav papers. When the leaders
of the Party prohibited the publication of an article arguing with the Soviet
daily *Pravda*, the staff of *Népszabadság* went on strike. The Party responded by dismissing the editor-in-chief.

On December 4 a memorial demonstration was held by women in Budapest to commemorate those who had lost their lives during the revolution
and the second Soviet military aggression. The armed forces and the Soviets dispersed the demonstration and another wave of arrests followed,
directed primarily against the workers' councils. On December 6 the Central Workers' Council of Greater Budapest declared in a memorandum that
in spite of abstaining from any disturbance and armed resistance, their
talks with Kádár had ended in failure. "The Hungarian people have lost

any hope of a way out."[81] Despite this they demanded that the talks resume, though the workers in the capital were disillusioned by the eagerness of the Budapest Workers' Council to grant concessions. Strikes broke out spontaneously. Kádár did not welcome the attitude of the Budapest Workers' Council and the talks of December 7 were doomed to failure.

When their memorandum was rejected, the Central Workers' Council of Greater Budapest assessed the situation at a dramatic meeting of December 8.[82] Representatives of several workers' councils from the country were present. In the meantime news arrived that in Salgótarján armed forces fired at protesting workers. Consequently the delegates called for a two-day general strike in protest. The government reacted by banning workers' councils organized on a territorial basis (in districts, counties, and towns), including Central Workers' Council of Greater Budapest. The Presidential Council proclaimed that because "counterrevolutionary elements, common criminals, irresponsible trouble-makers" were in possession of firearms, they must declare martial law. Kádár called Sándor Bali and Sándor Rácz, leaders of the Central Workers' Council of Greater Budapest, to resume talks in the parliament building and used the meeting to arrest them.

At this stage of resistance various organizations among the intelligentsia s et up during and after the suppression of the revolution (one of them was the Revolutionary Council of Intellectuals headed by the world-famous composer Zoltán Kodály) drafted their own demands, recognizing the leading role of the Budapest Workers' Council in the continued resistance. When the workers' councils were banned, the Hungarian Writers' Association met on December 28 and expressed its loyalty to the goals of the revolution, as well as its solidarity with the arrested writers. This was one of the last events of revolutionary resistance. The Writers' Association was subsequently banned. In early January workers still demonstrated in two working-class districts, Csepel and Kőbánya, but they were easily put down by the armed forces.

# Notes

1. Központi Statisztikai Hivatal Budapest Városi Igazgatósága, *Budapest Statisztikai Zsebkönyve* [The Statistical Handbooks of Budapest] (Budapest, 1956 and 1957).
2. Ferenc Gáspár and Klára Szabó, eds., *Források Budapest múltjából* [Sources from Budapest's past] (Budapest, 1985), vol. 5A, 18.

3. Out of these 103 seats the Communists got fifty-two and the Social Democrats fifty-one.
4. *Magyar Radikális Párt* [Hungarian Radical Party].
5. The Local Board filled up its own ranks with 10 invited members. The FKgP, the MKP, and the SZDP gave two members each, the others were nonparty members.
6. Data are available only for the constituency of Greater Budapest that did not coincide with the administrative districts of the day.
7. Gáspár, ed., op. cit., vol. 4. (Budapest, 1973), 383–386.
8. The Social Democratic Party proved to be the most successful in the towns and villages annexed to the capital at the time of the 1947 elections.
9. The "fusion" of the two parties took place on June 12, 1948. The "new" party was called *Magyar Dolgozók Pártja* [Hungarian Working People's Party].
10. It was not by chance that General V. I. Chernishov, the Soviet Military Commander of Budapest, gave orders on January 22, 1945 that church services were allowed to be held. See *Szabadság*, January 22, 1945. (The first issue of *Szabadság* appeared on January 19.)
11. Gáspár, ed., op. cit., 58–60.
12. Report of the Statistical Office of capital city Budapest May 2, 1946, in ibid., 248–262.
13. Soviet soldiers could be buried only with the permission of the Soviet military command. Their graves were to be marked with the five-pointed star of the Soviets.
14. *Fővárosi Közlöny*, no. 1 (1945).
15. Mistéth soon became one of the principal defendants in the *Magyar Közösség* [Hungarian Community] case, one of the "plots against the republic" based on false accusations and trumped-up charges.
16. The demolition of the Kossuth Bridge began in 1960.
17. *Szabadság*, January 21, 1945.
18. Brigadier General Alajos Haynal was sentenced to death *in contumatiam*. The death sentences of the other two defendants, Company Sergeant Major Péter Rotyis and Lance Sergeant Sándor Szívós were hanged in public on a square called Octogon in Pest the next day.
19. *Fővárosi Közlöny*, no. 7 (1946). The political police was even more active in the first part of the year. By April 2 it had arrested 8206 persons, 1869 of whom were interned, 1607 were placed under police supervision, and 809 were turned over to People's Prosecution.
20. Gáspár, ed., op. cit., 237.
21. *Szabad Nép*, March 6, 1946.
22. National Archives, *Governmental decree* no. 5,000/1946. M. E.
23. In Czechoslovakia and Poland nationalization was much more radical at that time. In Czechoslovakia factories employing five hundred or more workers,

banks, insurrance companies, mines, and foundries were nationalized, and in Poland all factories with fifty or more workers.

24. Gáspár and Szabó, eds., op. cit., 220–222.
25. *Budapest Statisztikai Zsebkönyve*, 1956.
26. Central Trade Union Archives, SZOT Eln. 1951/10.
27. *Statisztikai Havi Közlemények*, no. 9 (1957), 16.
28. *Szabad Nép*, September 26, 1956.
29. The first section of the underground line between *Örs vezér tér* [Square] and *Deák tér* [Square] was finally inaugurated in 1970. The whole line with the Southern Railway Station as its hub was completed two years later.
30. The Paris Peace Treaty of 1947 stipulated that the Russian occupation of Hungary was over. However, the Soviets were allowed to station troops in Hungary as reserves for their units in Austria.
31. Interestingly enough, the Treaty did not authorize the Soviets to do so and no secret clause is known to have been added to this effect.
32. *Szabad Nép*, May 19, 1956.
33. Over 10,000 workers demonstrated in Poznań on June 28, demanding free elections. The political police dispersed the demonstrators by gunfire. Several workers died and even more arrested.
34. Certain Communist leaders who no longer supported Rákosi said that there was a list containing four hundred names of people to be arrested. There are, however, no documents to support this information.
35. The youth demanded, for example, the declaration of March 15, the day of the 1848 Revolution, national holiday, the replacement of the Stalinist coat of arms of the country with the Kossuth coat of arms evoking memories of that revolution, and the replacement of the Soviet-type uniform of the soldiers.
36. In Warsaw the Polish Communist party, called United Workers' Party of Poland, elected Władysław Gomułka, fresh from prison, First Secretary for the second time despite emphatic Soviet protest. Defying open threats of Soviet military intervention, the Polish people forced the Soviet leaders to retreat when their delegation, headed by Khrushchev, hastily travelled to Warsaw.
37. *A Jövő Mérnöke*, October 23, 1956.
38. The Radio was willing to broadcast only half of the students' demands, but they did not agree.
39. Gosztonyi Archivs, Bern, *Original-Dokumente von den Ereignissen an der Technischen Hochschule in Budapest am 22/23. Oktober 1956* (Zürich, 1981).
40. *Komárommegyei Dolgozók Lapja*, October 24, 1956.
41. Gyula Kállai, "A kétfrontos harc" [Two-front struggle], in *Visszaemlékezések 1956* [Recollections: 1956], ed. János Berecz (Budapest, 1986), 71.

42. János Kenedi, ed., *A forradalom hangja. Magyarországi rádióadások 1956. október 23.–november 4.* [The Voice of the revolution. Radio broadcasts in Hungary, October 23–November 4, 1956] (Budapest, 1989), 18.

43. Recollections of László Révész in Péter Gosztonyi, ed., *Histoire du soulevement hongrois 1956* (Saint-Just-La-Peudue, 1966).

44. Archives of the Institute for the History of Politics of the Hungarian Socialist Party (hereafter IHP) 867. f. 1/s-186.

45. Sándor Kopácsi, *Életfogytiglan* [Sentenced for life] (Budapest, 1989), 97–98.

46. IHP 867.f. 1/r-131.

47. Kenedi, ed., op. cit., 18.

48. Ibid., 19.

49. Ibid., 23–26.

50. The political committee of the party really decided to do so at its meeting in the morning.

51. Kenedi, ed., op. cit., 26.

52. Ibid., 27.

53. The following day the Russians wanted to obtain the newly appointed Prime Minister Imre Nagy's signature on a document to the effect that it was him who had called in the Russians. The signature was denied. However, the documents was signed subsequently by previous Prime Minister András Hegedűs.

54. Kenedi, ed., op. cit., 29.

55. However, Donáth and Losonczy did not wish to cooperate at that time, because they refused to accept the official evaluation of the demonstration.

56. Kenedi, ed., op. cit., 30.

57. Ibid., 63.

58. Several estimates have been published about the number of the victims. Official reports spoke of twenty to twenty-five casualties, other—mainly foreign—sources of over two thousand. The actual figure was at least two hundred. See László Varga, "A harmadik napon 1956. október 25." [On the third day, October 25, 1956], in László Varga, *Az elhagyott tömeg 1950–1956* [The forlorn crowd, 1950-56] (Budapest, 1994), 99–126.

59. The creation of workers' councils went back to Yugoslav traditions of self-government to workers rather than to Hungarian revolutionary traditions. Workers' councils had been formed in certain large factories even prior to this date both in Budapest and in the country.

60. This was really more than a simple political gesture, since the other two Smallholder leaders of 1945–46, Ferenc Nagy and Béla Varga, were in exile, and Béla Kovács returned from Soviet captivity only the previous year.

61. Kenedi. ed., op. cit., 103.

62. "Híven az igazsághoz" [Telling things truthfully] *Szabad Nép*, October 28, 1956.

63. Kenedi, ed., op. cit., 126.

64. Ibid., 131.
65. *Népszava*, October 30, 1956.
66. *Magyar Nemzet*, October 31, 1956.
67. Kenedi, ed., op. cit., 223.
68. The besiegers and the unarmed people around them watching the events were infuriated at seeing that the defenders fired aimed shots at the ambulance-men on the square. The ruthless showdown and Mező's death caused general consternation and exerted a decisive influence also on János Kádár.
69. Nagy, Kádár, and Losonczy were Communists, Kovács and Tildy were Smallholders. Erdei belonged to the Peasant Party, but was generally held crypto-Communist, and not without justification.
70. The coalition government formed on November 3 was also headed by Imre Nagy. Apart from the above mentioned politicians of the Smallholders' Party it included among others Anna Kéthly of the Social Democrats, and István Bibó of the Peasant Party. The Communist Party was represented by Imre Nagy, János Kádár, and Géza Losonczy.
71. Kenedi, ed., op. cit., 461–463.
72. Ibid., 370–371.
73. Ibid., 375–376.
74. It was obscure for decades where Kádár spent these crucial days. Some years later he seemingly gave himself away suggesting that he had not gone further than Uzhgorod near the Hungarian border. This view was maintained by western historians for a considerable time. However, some historians held his visit to Moscow was more probable, mostly on the basis of the published diary of Mićunovic, then Yugoslav Ambassador in Moscow. The problem was finally solved by the hand-written notes of Hungarian Minister of Foreign Affairs Imre Horváth from November 3, prepared at the talks in Moscow and made public a few years ago, when the Hungarian archives were opened before historians. Soviet sources have also corroborated this version since then.
75. Kenedi, ed., op. cit., 487.
76. The meeting was originally convoked to November 13, but the townhall of Újpest, the announced scene of the meeting, was surrounded by Soviet army units.
77. *Népszabadság*, November 16, 1956.
78. The workers' councils wished to end the strike begun on October 24 as early as November 1, but the Soviet military invasion of November 4 prevented them from doing so. After November 4 they proclaimed a new general strike.
79. *Népszabadság*, November 17, 1956.
80. IHP 290.f. 58. ő.e., 33–35.
81. István Kemény and Bill Lomax, eds., *Magyar munkástanácsok 1956-ban* [Hungarian Workers' Councils in 1956] (Paris—Highland Lakes, 1986), 100–102.

82. The government sent word in the morning that it considered the meeting illegal. Accordingly, many participants were arrested right after the meeting.

*János M. Rainer*

# The City: Center of Post-Revolutionary Crisis, 1957–63

Resistance in Budapest was crushed in a few days by a large-scale Soviet attack, beginning on November 4, 1956.[1] To prevent having to face the whole Hungarian army, the Soviets arrested Minister of Defence Pál Maléter and his staff at Tököl on November 3. The armed resistance of national guard and army units in Budapest and in the country met with severe Soviet riposte. Ultimately the Hungarian army was disarmed, and insurgents, seeing that further armed struggle was senseless, either disappeared in the city or fled to the West.

In this way the Hungarian revolution lost its armed forces and, concurrently, its most radical reactive force and its political center. The Imre Nagy government, supported by a majority of Hungarians collapsed. Since November 1, it had already been restricted almost exclusively to political bargaining, because there had been no normative administration since October 23. Nagy and his closest colleagues, leaders of the former opposition, took refuge at the Yugoslav Embassy of Budapest. The leaders of the non-Communist parties were watching the developments more or less passively except for István Bibó, Minister of State of the Petőfi Party, who tried to maintain the integrity of the revolutionary government in parliament until November 6. When he was forced to vacate the building, he tried to continue political conciliation and drafted a political platform for the situation after November 4.[2]

Despite serious losses, the majority of Hungarian society, which had rallied behind the fundamental goals of the revolution, did not believe that all had been lost. November 4 put an end to the political diversity of the previous days. Although the Soviet intervention vitiated the various political programs of the dissident political parties, nevertheless the fervor of the previous days, the experience of freedom, the willingness to sacrifice, and the devastated city strengthened the belief that this rising had not been in vain. The illusory hope for help from the west decreased significantly

233

after November 4 but did not cease altogether. It was even reinforced by the debate in the United Nations on the "Hungarian question" for a while.[3] This strange mentality of a population that was not willing to submit to defeat was based on a deceptively solid foundation. Certain organizations of the revolutions were not crushed right after November 4. Some local revolutionary committees still existed for weeks, though they were deprived of their former authority by one of the first decrees of the Kádár government on November 7. The workers' councils formed in the factories during the days of the revolution were, however, recognized by the government, and assumed overall importance in the following weeks. The workers' councils, which based themselves on direct democracy, even reelected at most places in November leaders and members who had distinguished themselves during the days of the revolution and identified themselves with its goals. Workers' councils were organized for districts in the capital and for the counties, and even the Central Workers' Council of Greater Budapest was established on November 14 despite the government's counter-measures. Two days later its new leadership — even more radical than the previous one — was elected including Sándor Rácz, Sándor Bali, György Kalocsay, and Ferenc Tőke. Since the establishment of the National Workers' Council planned for November 21 was prevented by Hungarian and Soviet armed forces, the Central Workers' Council of Greater Budapest functioned as a national organization. Due to the chaotic state of affairs, working places became the only workable basic units of life in the country, and they were controlled by the workers' councils. They had a formidable weapon even after November 4, namely they were able to direct the spontaneous political strikes going on practically since October 23, which not even the Nagy government could countermand. The Central Workers' Council called upon the workers to take up work on November 17 and they gradually did so. The 48-hour strike launched because of the incident of November 21 was, however, almost general.[4]

It was not easy for the government to get rid of the workers' councils, because in one respect they strongly resembled the pre-1956 opposition within the party. It was difficult to prove them to be "alien to the regime". They had had nothing to do with the extremities of late October, were not influenced by political parties (they stood up against "partizan behaviour" and even prohibited the organization of party cells in working places), and had no connection whatever with armed groups. On the contrary, they considered themselves the true Socialists in the original sense of that word.

This meant that most of their leaders fully identified themselves with the cause of the revolution.

After heated debates with the party presidium of Moscow on November 2 and 3 János Kádár undertook to be the leader of the country. As the available fragmentary records testify,[5] he did not intend to restore Stalinism to Hungary. He must even have thought that the soviet leadership, particularly Nikita Khrushchev, was troubled by the obvious weakness of the revolutionary government and its seemingly unpredictable efforts to achieve independence. He wished to return from Moscow quickly and was prepared for political bargaining that might entail compromise. He must have hoped that the Hungarian society would realize how they had gone too far in opposing the Soviet empire and would accept the compromise dictated by the Soviets: a drastic curtailment of independence and democratic policies in exchange for assurance that the leading figures and methods of the Rákosi regime would never return. However, he became very much disappointed at the beginning in virtually all his expectations. Imre Nagy, on whose support he counted as a politician second in rank in the country, rejected the offer even before it had been fully formulated and chose rather his tragic road, personifying the fate of the revolution.[6] Kádár could not get rid of Soviet control for the Communist Party of the Soviet Union sent three emissaries—Georgi Malenkov, Mikhail Suslov, and Averki Aristov—to supervise his negotiation and also left Ivan Serov, head of the State Security Committee (the notorious KGB), and Ambassador Juri Andropov in Hungary. Three confidential employees of various Soviet organs remained in Kádár's quarters at the Parliament building. This squad followed Kádár everywhere and the Soviet cadre controlled the first post-Stalin "normalization" until the middle of December. The Kremlin's detachment left its mark on everything from the kidnapping of Imre Nagy and Kádár's ever more rigorous negotiations with the workers' councils, to the first arrests and trials, as well as the first repressive measures taken between December 9 and 14, 1956 (the introduction of martial law, internment, banning of the local workers' councils and the Central Workers' Council, and other oppressive measures). They also took pains to discuss with Kádár sentence by sentence the famous decision of the Central Committee of the Hungarian Socialist Workers' Party made at its plenary session in December, which became the ideological foundation for evaluating the 1956 revolution.[7]

All this does not explain, however, the switch from seeking compromise in early November to imposing strong-arm policies one month later.

Should Kádár actually have wanted to oppose the Soviets, he could have done so even under these circumstances. He managed, for example, to stop the deportation of captured freedom fighters and civilians to the Soviet Union.[8] He was chastened by the large-scale resistance of Hungarian society. Notes taken in Moscow reveal that Kádár expected to negotiate with party leaders and leaders of the former opposition, hoping to rely on his experiences of the post-1945 period. Instead he was confronted with young leaders of the workers who represented overall resistance. The party opposition, who were at the Yugoslav Embassy, did the same: they shared the intransigence of Imre Nagy. The others supported the Central Workers' Council by lining behind it the organizations of intellectuals such as the Writers' Association, the Journalists' Association, and the Revolutionary Council of Hungarian Intellectuals. The only sphere Kádár could feel at home was the slowly organizing leadership of the Hungarian Socialist Workers' Party. Even there the tune was called until early December by those who sympathized with the "moderate opposition within the party" including such politicians as György Aczél, Lajos Fehér, Antal Gyenes, József Köböl, and László Orbán.[9] The partners Kádár envisaged either turned out to represent no viable political force or else withdrew from the public forum. Some of them had even gone over to the opposition.

Besides the Soviet Union and so-called allies like the Romanian party leader Gheorghe Gheorghiu-Dej openly urging for retaliation, Kádár could rely only on former Stalinists sneaking back to upper and middle layers of party leadership. Toward the end of the year he decided to cooperate with them. Resisting the forces of restoration would have meant his losing power and being replaced if not by Rákosi himself then by a self-appointed successor. At the same time, Kádár seemed to set aside his former doubts and to be willing to interpret the continuity of the October events and the resistance following them no longer as social and political developments but as the outcome of anti-Communist plots. And in his book plots could only be dealt with by a policy of the strong hand.

Paralelly with the measures introduced in early December, the newly organized armed forces put an end to the last wave of mass demonstrations by firing volleys at unarmed crowds at several places all over the country. The most tragic of these events was the salvo at Salgótarján killing dozens of people.[10] On December 16 the first execution under martial law took place to be followed by one or two for each week following.[11] In early January the definition of martial law was extended to include fomenting a strike. As a consequence, the Central Workers' Council of Csepel, which had largely taken over the coordinating role of the Central Workers' Council of Greater Budapest, dissolved itself. The suspension of the Writers' Association on January 18 and that of the Journalists' Association two days later deprived the resistance of the intellectuals of its legal framework. Its former revolutionary leaders were forced to leave the students' organization called *Magyar Egyetemisták és Főiskolások Egységes Szervezete* or *MEFESZ* [Unified Organization of Hungarian University and College Students]. In mid-February a large-scale show trial began at the Budapest Municipal Court. A group of resistance fighters active after November 4 was put to trial in the case of Ilona Tóth and fellow defendants including conceptual elements and a formidable murder story. Articles on "counter-revolutionary terror" appeared in the press in conjunction with the campaign and the publication of White Books commenced. With similar contents in Hungarian and in four world languages these interpreted the "counter-revolution" on the basis of examples taken out of their contexts. A workers' guard and party militia formed on February 19 held several joint demonstrations in support of the party in the streets of Budapest in the following weeks, e.g., on March 15.[12]

By spring 1957 Kádár attained significant political successes. He had managed to forge the unity of party leadership and win the support of the Soviet presidium during his visit to Moscow in late March. He agreed with the Soviets also about the future trial of Imre Nagy, which had become increasingly important for him personally. That might demonstrate the existence of a plot on the highest levels, thus the collapse of the regime in October and the resistance against him in November would be explained. Equally important, Mátyás Rákosi and his group were to remain outside Hungary in the future.[13] While Kádár was negotiating in Moscow, György Marosán organized the first Communist mass meetings in the capital on March 29. On May Day, just preceding the session of parliament and the national conference of the party, the two of them were waving to a crowd of about a hundred thousand at the *Hősök tere* [Heroes' Square].

Large-scale resistance had ceased already in January, 1957. The kidnapping of Imre Nagy on November 23, 1956 and the arrest of the leaders of the Central Workers' Council in early December deprived the resistance of its symbolic leaders. Reprisals were accelerated (arrests, martial law afflicting average persons, statements issued by the regime, e.g., the December decision of the provisional central committee of the party and the government's statement of January 6).[14] All these made it increasingly obvious that no compromise was to be expected. Not only had the leaders been lost, but the number of groups and personalities which revealed divergent political ideas had also decreased significantly. Many of these people had left the country, the wave of emigration having reached its peak in late November and early December.[15] Those who stayed at home were persecuted in various ways. What seemed for Kádár rigidity on the part of the still existing revolutionary organizations was seen as a maximum of concessions from the others' point of view. The Central Workers' Council ultimately sat down at the conference table and *de facto* endorsed the Communist leaders. Although it was unfeasible wholly to abandon the program of the revolution, it was, nevertheless, practicable to make compromises in attitudes and in behaviour.

In early 1957 a wave of acceptance marked the collective psyche of Hungary when great masses poured into the streets on May Day. This could not be achieved by the artillery barrage of November 4. It was as if the people now recognized that the cause of the revolution had been lost and the present situation was fastened firmly in place. All resources had been exhausted—strikes, conference tables, heated speeches, and mass meetings all had failed. It seemed to be impossible to go further. Overall frustration contributed to political apathy with the reigning cliché "nearly everything was an illusion". The desire grew for a "normal" everyday life, even if it meant returning to the *status quo*. At the same time, the measures that could be traced back to October (e.g., the abolition of collecting surplus agricultural produce and livestock, measures improving living standards, or the absence of mass purges in all walks of life) were highly appreciated. ("We have still achieved something... this much could only be achieved"). These could even be put to the credit of the new government. Once life returned to its former patterns, it seemed wiser to follow old customs.

On May 1, 1957 at the Heroes' Square of Budapest the beneficiaries of the pre-1956 regime gathered. Contrary to general opinion today, there were quite a lot of them there. In October they had felt terrorized, in November humiliated or conscience stricken. They might even have come to conflict with themselves. This motley crew equally celebrated a kind of liberation and victory, some of them harboring the hope of revenge, but it was not only they who filled the square.

Hungarian society had learned the lessons of 1956, but its changing attitude did not urge the representatives of the regime to draw similar conclusions under the new circumstances. They had ceased to feel terror but still felt stress and fear, and decided to counterattack in the form of terrorizing specific sections as they adjusted to new techniques of control. The Kádár regime drew the conclusions of the revolution only after it had made the society draw them first.

The concepts of consolidation entertained by this *soi disant* "new" regime can be clearly traced in the minutes of 1956–57 meetings within the Hungarian Socialist Workers Party.[16] It is clear that in the first flush of his victory Kádár tried to return to what he considered the "golden age" of the Rákosi regime in the years 1948–49, to the period between the fusion of the two workers' parties[17] and the trial of László Rajk.[18] This had been the epoch of nearly total party control, but general conditions had not deteriorated yet. At that time the core of party leadership had already "left the road of Marxism–Leninism" at least from late 1948, but had not deviated from the narrow golden path yet. That is what the resolution of the Central Committee of the Hungarian Socialist Workers' Party indicated at Kádár's instigation in December, 1956. In 1948–49 certain institutions even enjoyed a certain degree of autonomy as long as it suited the demands of power. They informed the party leaders of their activities, but were not yet controlled directly from above through telephone calls and direct orders. Kádár did not want to base legislation actually on representation in the spring of 1957, just like Rákosi did not want it in 1948 or 1949. He admitted that the fusion with the Social Democrats must have been a "political shock" for many, but he did not want to hear of Social Democrats within the Hungarian Socialist Workers' Party, referring to the "sacred unity" of the working class. He was willing to accept fellow travellers like Ferenc Erdei, József Bognár, László Nánási, and even Béla Kovács who was really independent and seemingly impressionable due to his illness. Just as the State Security Authority (*ÁVH*)[19] prosecuted a great number of "enemies of the people's democracy" and "reactionary elements" on the basis of Act VII of 1946,[20] so Kádár also blamed "Horthyite army officers, gendarmes and the like" for 1956, whose cases "do not actually have to be tried", but who "are to be brought to justice, sentenced to death and hanged in a procession."[21] After 1948 economic life developed as intended by the party leadership, but there were no plans like the ones that created tension later on.

In 1948–49 mass enrollment into the party began, but did not induct such numbers that would have made the new membership uncontrollable. In early 1957 Kádár wished to restore this size and state of the party where the executive committee could exercise control easily from above and even the local party organizations were articulate, making it easy for the leaders to intervene should any deviation from the party line occur. This would have been an ideal situation with the party holding in hand all elements of exercising power (trade unions, women's movements, the youth, the government, the economic special committees, the parliament, the councils, among others), but not being forced to deal with everything from the five-year plans[22] to harvest campaigns. So the first stage of the Kádár regime envisioned a return to the Rákosi era but without its tyrannical abuse of power.

It would have been more logical to return to the years 1953–54, i.e., to the period of Imre Nagy's reforms. The year 1948 (the creation of the single party system) led to 1949 (the purges beginning with the trial of László Rajk) after all, and then to 1951 when Kádár himself was put to prison on the basis of trumped up charges. Turning to 1953 as a starting point would have enabled Kádár to draw a line between Rákosi and himself, which he failed to do. The evaluation of the "new course"[23] of 1953 remained ambiguous throughout the Kádár era, although there were remarkable similarities. Even Imre Nagy's attempts at a political reform by creating the Patriotic People's Front in 1954 resembled ideas about extending the government and a new "policy of alliances" outlined in December, 1956. It was, however, not easy to find the way back to 1954. The rift of 1956 and the person of Imre Nagy created a serious obstacle. Yet his reform policies of 1953–54 were connected by a narrow, but not fully impassable path with the goals of the Prime Minister of 1956. In October 1956 even Kádár himself took this path and learned that it was too dangerous for him. For Kádár the Imre Nagy case was a challenge and an antithesis of his new regime by personifying one of its opposites, the revolution of 1956.

The "responsibility of Nagy and others in the events in Hungary and their legal consequences" were first raised at the summit talks of five East and East Central European Communist parties (the Soviet, the Hungarian, the Romanian, the Czechoslovak, and the Bulgarian) in Budapest between January 1–3, 1957. Interestingly, the protocols of the leading bodies of the Hungarian Socialist Workers' Party hardly mention these talks. The only document on this event, the short note of the Czechoslovak delegation does not name the party that raised the idea.[24] If a decision had been made, Kádár would probably have informed the Provisional Executive Committee about it. In January, 1957 he sent Gyula Kállai to Bucharest to foster division among Nagy' group and to make them all exercize self-criticism. The person of the former Prime Minister was no longer important for him, but his possible statement of self-criticism and his acknowledgement of political responsibility could have brought political advantages. Imre Nagy remained, however, unshaken and true to his decisions in October and November. It was before the provisional executive committee on January 29, 1957 that Kállai first used the word "judicial court" when informing the committee of the failure of his mission: "In connection with Imre Nagy and [Ferenc] Jánosi, who both played an important role in organizing, leading and intellectual direction of the counterrevolution, it is necessary that a trial should be considered."[25] Kállai also said that in Bucharest he had consulted Romanian and Soviet leaders and "all positions were assumed as suggested by me." The idea of a trial is unlikely to have come from Kállai himself. Rather it seems to have come from Kádár or a narrow circle of party leaders on a Hungarian initiative. The executive committee decided to "collect information on the activities of Nagy's group in October and November."[26] This was confirmed by the Provisional Central Committee in February[27] and the material was produced in the first (and for the time being not circulated) White Book on Imre Nagy's crimes entitled "From Right-Wing Ideas to Class Betrayal" tracing the events back to 1948.[28]

In early March, 1957, again in Bucharest, Kállai informed Boris Nikolayevich Ponomariev, head of the department in charge of foreign relations within the Communist Party of the Soviet Union, that "the majority of the members of the Executive Committee (comrades Kádár, Marosán, Münnich, and Kállai) had agreed upon organizing the judicial procedure for Nagy and his group." In his report Ponomariev mentions an "earlier plan" of calling these people to account, obviously referring to Kállai's mission in January.[29] The approval of the highest levels had to be obtained. At the Soviet-Hungarian summit in Moscow in late March, 1957 "the question of Imre Nagy and his group came up also. It was our delegation that raised it. The comrades approved of calling them to account with satisfactory severity," Kádár remembered.[30] The idea was endorsed by the executive committee and also by the central committee on April 5. On April 9, 1957 Kádár made the executive committee adopt a decision "on the arrest of certain elements [Kádár generally did not mention the name of Imre Nagy when important decisions were made] on the recommendation of the Ministry of the Interior, and on launching a legal procedure against them."[31] This same session devised the concept of the investigation and the trial with a report later on published under Gyula Kállai's name entitled "The Events of October and November in Hungary in the Light of Marxism-Leninism".[32] The phrases it used (especially the ones stating that Imre Nagy and his organized group prepared the revolt consciously and "in cooperation with the imperialists" were often repeated word by word in questions put by the investigators, their reports, the indictment, and the verdict alike. So the construction and the scheme of the trial was completed already before the arrest of the main character in the play. It only had to evolve to the logical climax.

Lieutenant-colonel Sándor Rajnai from the Hungarian police (a former member of the political police) was sent with his special unit to arrest Imre Nagy and his group in Romania in late March, 1957. Imre Nagy was arrested in Snagov on April 14 and was taken to Budapest. Interrogations began already in Romania. The Ministry of the Interior wished to comply with Kádár's instructions and "draw the poison-fang" in no time without waiting 8 to 10 months or for years. However, it took a year and a half before the verdicts were passed.

The problem was that the political decision about the trial upset the schedule of the Department of Political Investigation at the Ministry of the Interior for calling to account the "principal criminals of the counter-revolution". It took months to define the circle of these principal criminals. It finally included also Pál Maléter and Sándor Kopácsi, arrested on November 4 and originally planned to be tried separately, and Miklós Gimes, a leading figure of resistance after the revolution. The way of making the trial and perhaps the whole procedure public was not clear at that stage. For this reason the case of General Béla Király, the emigrated Commander in Chief of the National Guard, was separated from the main trial, because it would have been senseless to condemn him *in absentia* through a secret proceeding. The Ministry of the Interior wanted Zoltán Tildy to be arrested in early April, yet he was arrested only in late May, 1957 for political reasons. Investigation proceeded slowly also because most defendants pleaded not guilty, and torture was avoided in order to preserve the legal proprieties.

Imre Nagy and his companions were accused of having organized a plot from 1955 on "to overthrow the people's democratic regime" and "to seize power", and in October, 1956 they merely followed their clandestine schemes. Imre Nagy and Pál Maléter were accused also of high treason. With a few exceptions, the charges were based on the actual activities of the defendants (oppositionist activities, governmental functions during the revolutions, decisions, public statements, diplomatic initiatives), which were presented as criminal as defined by the indictment. The defendants were isolated from one another and kept in solitary confinement. They reacted to the serious charges and the psychological pressure differently. Most of them ultimately admitted their responsibility without accepting the interpretation of the facts. József Szilágyi, secretary of Imre Nagy during the days of the revolution, refused to cooperate with the authorities altogether. Imre Nagy tried to do the same at first and did not answer a single question until late May, 1957. Then he realized that the investigation was proceeding rather quickly, so he found it better to try to establish at least the facts, his own decisions, and the actual circumstances under which they had been made. However, together with Pál Maléter he refuted the charges. Géza Losonczy, who had been accused among a second-level cadre, collapsed first psychologically, then due to his hunger strike also physically. In his delirium he confessed to nefarious deeds not even raised by the prosecution. The defendants did not agree on several points. Imre Nagy, for example, tried to mitigate the role of the opposition within the party to avoid being accused of conspiracy. The investigators tried to increase these differences and not without result. It was still the behaviour of the primary defendants, especially that of Imre Nagy, which made it impossible to make the procedure public. The show trial took place *in camera* from its first moment to the very last.[33]

At the meeting of the central committee on June 22, 1957 preparing the next party conference Kádár remarked that "investigation was going on with difficulty and was making little progress."[34] He enumerated several causes but omitted the most important one, the international implications. Due to the international significance of the trial, the Soviets followed it watchfully, though no documents have been found to prove their direct participation in it. Prior to the above-mentioned meeting of the Central Committee Kádár and Minister of the Interior Béla Biszku smoked off to Moscow in secret to inform the Kremlin of the preparations for the party congress, as well as of the investigation. He took three documents along: a report on the present stage of the investigation including the behaviour of the defendants, the list of the exhibits, and a note on the relations of Imre Nagy and his co-defendants with Yugoslavia.[35] The Soviet leaders must have been most interested in this latter. By early August, 1957 the Ministry of the Interior had prepared the indictment that was taken to Moscow by Biszku alone. He informed the Soviets that although the projected sentences had yet not been defined by the leaders of the Hungarian Socialist Workers' Party, "opinions were voiced during the discussions that ...the heaviest punishment should be inflicted upon Imre Nagy,

Losonczy, Donáth, Gimes, Maléter, and Béla Király." The indictment was "basically acceptable but was to be improved further", especially as regarded the relationship of "the treacherous group of Imre Nagy and the imperialists."[36] The trial was scheduled to take place after the special session of the UNO in September, but on Soviet request it was postponed until the Communist summit in Moscow in November, 1957.[37] On December 21, 1957 the secret sitting of the Central Committee of the Hungarian Socialist Workers' Party, the minutes of which were kept in Kádár's safe until his death, decided to "let the legal procedure take its course."[38] The indictment was prepared rapidly, and the trial began on February 5, 1958. At the same time, the Soviets requested postponement for a second time due to the planned summit with the western powers. Kádár reflected nervous impatience because of the delay. "Retaliation would have been the most understandable on November 4–5 last year, but we were the weakest just at that time," he said in December, 1957 at a closed meeting of the central committee. "The problem is that the greater the delay, the more complicated the whole case becomes....At the time when we could have settled the case, we had not the strength to do so," he said on February 14, 1958 when the second Soviet request was discussed. He proudly stated that "discretion was also maintained, which is very good".[39] This statement soon filtered out to the west and the *Irodalmi Ujság* of London quoted it in the following distorted form: "When this trial was topical, we had no strength to institute it. Now that we are strong, it is no longer topical."[40] It was never established whether the Soviet request suggested the possibility of a lighter sentence than death, at least not in Kádár's filtered report. The central committee finally accepted the proposal of the First Secretary and postponed the trial instead of influencing its course in this direction, although the "peace offensive" of the Soviets in early 1958 and the imminent visit of Khrushchev to Budapest would have justified a political amnesty. After the December decision Khrushchev showed interest in such a solution through the Soviet Ambassador in Budapest. Kádár informed his Communist cohorts about this in the following manner: "Comrade Khrushchev said he approved of our efforts to get to the bottom of this matter. He asked how we were going to do it. He was probably interested in what we were going to do: to send them to prison, reprimand them or what? He approves of finishing the matter."[41] Kádár disagreed. "Should we grant amnesty now, it would include the principal criminals, which would weaken the people's democratic order", Kádár explained in December,

1957, and nearly all leaders of the party agreed. However, the debate over postponement in February divided them. Márton Valkó said that the death sentence, a term overscupulously avoided until then, should be followed by an immediate pardon. "This is not feasible," Kádár indignantly replied. When on March 24, 1958, John Gollan, General Secretary of the British Communist Party asked Kádár if the Hungarian leaders were mindful of the interests of the other Communist parties, he answered roughly as follows: "Had we not taken the interests of the international Communist movement into consideration, we would have done away with the gang of Imre Nagy long ago."[42]

By the spring of 1958 the position of Kádár was entrenched enough to effect what he wanted. "If you compare climates of public opinion now with that of a year and a half ago, the political success really seems unexpected," he said after Khrushchev's visit in April 1958.[43] At the same time, Kádár was very cautious. The political committee ordered that a plenary meeting of the central committee be convened in late April to deal with the Imre Nagy trial, among other topics. However, Kádár postponed the meeting to early June. In the meantime he went to Moscow once again to collect information on the recently deteriorating Soviet-Yugoslav relations and the negative western reception of Soviet initiatives to hold a summit. On May 27, 1958, the political committee, and on June 6 the central committee held secret meetings and resolved that "the court procedure against the special counter-revolutionary group guilty of intending to overthrow the legal order of the people's democracy should take its course".[44]

The trial was resumed between June 9 and 15 in closed chambers. Imre Nagy denied the charges throughout the trail and refused to acknowledge the competence of the court. When sentenced to death, he did not sue for mercy, but declared that the final verdict on this case would be delivered by the Hungarian people and the international working class. Nagy, Maléter, and Gimes were executed on June 16. (József Szilágyi, whose case had been separated from the Nagy case, had been executed in April.) The facts of the trial and the sentences were announced on June 17, when the death sentences had already been carried out.

The fate of Imre Nagy's group epitomized the mood of reprisal that characterized the late 1950s. During his already mentioned visit to Moscow in March 1957 Kádár agreed with the Soviet leaders about accelerating reprisals and trying the cases in closed chambers. This was probably necessary because of the world-wide protests. In those days resistance was practically over in Hungary, since by that time the party organizations formed in the workplace had replaced the legally constituted workers' councils.

Mass reprisals lasted from April 1957 to the spring of 1959. The people's courts instituted in April 1957 tried not only those who resisted after November 4, but also great masses of those who had taken part in the revolution and in its preparations (i.e., members of the opposition parties). Following April 1957 the police arrested large numbers of citizens. Summary jurisdiction continued until the autumn of 1957. There were cases that dragged on for months or even a year. The prosecutor's office and the people's courts could not cope with the mammoth task. More than 20,000 persons were tried for political offences in 1957 alone, of whom more than 6,000 were committed to terms in prison or some other punishments, in the same year.

By early spring 1959 conditions began to imrpove. A partial amnesty was granted. There was no evidence of civil unrest, international relations had improved, the collectivization of agriculture preoccupied the authorities, and an overzealous police made even the country's leaders nervous. All these factors resulted in a relaxation of terror, but not all means of coercion were abandoned. It was at the time of this "minor" amnesty of 1959 that a significant group of intellectuals who çontinued to resist after the defeat of the revolution was tried and condemned. Moreover, political trials continued sporadically even after that date.

From the spring of 1959 to 1963 the number of political sentences for offences in 1956 decreased, except for several important political charges against Catholic priests and their parishioners. The special legal institutions created in the spring of 1957 also disappeared (internment in April 1960, and the people's courts in April, 1961). In the years 1961 and 1962 most officers of the state security police were discharged. Although this latter decision was made in connection with cases prior to 1953 against Communist leaders, those who participated in them were not called to account for their activities in those years or after 1956. Kádár and his colleagues considered the police personnel dangerous because "destalinization" gathered momentum again in the early 1960s. They saw in it the potential for resumption of power by the followers of Rákosi. This was why they gave high priority to purging the police.

There was also an international brake applied to Kádár's reprisals. The United States had kept the "Hungarian question" on the agenda of the U.N. since late 1956 despite the fact that arrests had stopped and amnesty was granted to those committed to short jail terms in 1959 and 1960. After secret negotiations the U.N. removed the Hungarian question from the agenda in the autumn of 1962. In March 1963 a general amnesty was declared, involving the release of most victims of the reprisals of 1956. Neither foreign public opinion, nor Hungarians in general cared for those who had been convicted of "murder" and were ineligible for amnesty. Former prisoners were to suffer all kinds of disadvantages for decades to come (e.g., they were not issued passports, were watched by the police, were not allowed to work in their profession, and did not recover their confiscated apartments and personal belongings).

From late 1956 to 1959 at least 35,000 people were investigated for suspected political "crimes". 26,000 people were brought to trial and about 22,000 sentences were handed down. Most of these were condemned for acts allegedly committed during or after the revolution. Some of the "political" cases concerned unauthorized crossing of the borders. Between 1957 and 1960 approximately 13,000 people were sent to internment camps at Tököl and Kistarcsa. Tens of thousands were banned from their homes, dismissed from jobs (e.g., over one thousand teachers, mostly outside Budapest), or placed under police supervision. Oppression affected more than 100,000 people and their families. Death sentences and imprisonment were only the tip of the iceberg.

Beside being a mass phenomenon, reprisal was also very cruel. Between December 1956 and the summer of 1961, when the last death sentence was carried out for offences in 1956, 341 people were hanged, as many as in the darkest years of the Rákosi regime. Of this number 229 were sentenced to death because of their role in the revolution.[45] Most were workers or soldiers in their twenties who had taken part in street fighting. Prison terms were severe: almost half of those brought to trial were sentenced to terms of more than five years.

Reprisal after the revolution differed from the reign of terror in the Rákosi era in one important respect. Rákosi was at war with the whole Hungarian society from "class enemies" to the highest-ranking party leaders. After the revolution, reprisals were aimed at groups which could be defined. These groups show rather uniform features as far as age and occupation are concerned (people in their twenties and thirties). The determining factor, however, was their participation in the revolution and their presumed attitude toward the Kádár regime. Three such groups can be distinguished clearly.

The first group includes mostly unskilled workers and apprentices between 18 and 25 who either participated in the fights or were connected to the armed insurgents in one way or another. They represented the smaller proportion of the cases, but it was this group that was convicted under martial law. They were sentenced in people's courts and received the most severe punishment, including a great number of death sentences. The majority of those denied amnesty also belonged to this group. They had chosen the most radical form of fighting against Stalinism, so they were suspected of being the most bitter opponents of the regime. The largest number of those fleeing to the west fell into this category. They were the most determined, and the most naïve.

The most numerous group of those condemned consisted of members of workers' councils and local revolutionary or other committees. They were mostly workers between 28 and 35 years of age, foremen in direct control of production, peasants, and also intellectuals (teachers), influential members of their communities. They constituted the local vanguard of the revolution. These workers were usually tried by ordinary courts and the sentences were less severe. The majority of the judgments and other kinds of repressive measures affected them. They were suspected of promoting democracy for the future, hence were considered dangerous.

Less numerous but more prominent were members of the opposition party prior to 1956 and left-wing fellow-traveling intellectuals, most of whom identified with the democratic and national goals of the revolution. Many became active in the resistance after November 4. They had acquired experience in opposition activities under the dictatorship prior to the revolution or even prior to 1945. One of the main goals of Kádár's regime was to eliminate this kind of political activity, so members of this group received heavy sentences.

Much as Budapest was the center of events in the days of the revolution, it also became the center of reprisals. A quarter of the sentences for revolutionary activity were passed there. If one takes only the most severe cases (those of cabinet members, armed insurgents, military leaders, leaders of workers' councils, writers, among others) into consideration, the concentration of reprisals in the capital is still more obvious. Most of their cases were tried in Budapest and the most severe judgments were passed there, including the majority of the death sentences, almost three quarters of which were carried out in the "transit prison" [*Gyűjtőfogház*] in district X.[46] The whole machinery of reprisal was concentrated in Budapest, including the records of the Department of Investigation at the Ministry of the Interior, the prosecution, the courts, and the law enforcement agencies.

Beyond the deterrence factor and the factor of revenge for their own fears during the revolution, the reign of terror of the Kádár regime served long-range goals. It had to find an explanation for the revolution and the collapse of the old regime in October 1956. Kádár and the élite of the new regime had personal experiences of the spontaneous and mass character of the revolution. Many had even shared some of its democratic, anti-Stalinist goals and aspirations for independence. However, they preferred to interpret them as the result of a plot by a consciously anti-Communist, reactionary cadre. For this reason the investigators and the courts did not need to fabricate tales of horror as in the early 1950s, though such accusations did crop up in later cases. The main idea was to give an interpretation of the events that would qualify them as crimes. Thus critical opposition attitudes were interpreted as "a plot to overthrow the people's democratic regime", and members of the revolutionary committees came to be called "participants in a movement against state order". Armed resistance to occupying forces became "murder and wrecking state property". On the basis of their ancestors or without any basis defendants were termed "old reactionaries and clericalists". Workers and peasants who had been convicted on trumped up charges of sabotage directed against the realization of economic plans in the early 1950s were described as "jailbirds, ragamuffins, and kulaks" if they participated in the revolution. It is not clear for whose benefit was this terminology invented, but it became part of the official ideology of the regime toward the outside world, the allies, and the Soviet Union. This was the explanation the regime offered to its supporters at home. The regime did not consider it important to convince the public or even to make the people share this interpretation.

Despite some initial hesitations and local initiatives, reprisal did not become a general campaign penetrating all segments of society. The press reported on the sentences very briefly, if at all. The "show trials" took place behind closed doors. The flow of publications unmasking the "heinous crimes of the counter-revolution" both at the local and national levels (local and national White Books[47]) was soon exhausted, and the books were not discussed in seminars around the country. Those who did anything during the days of the revolution could safely count on reprisal of some kind, but those who remained silent were let alone. And this was the main lesson of reprisal: it paid to remain silent. The aim was to break the morale of the most active groups of society and render their resurgence impossible whether as groups or as individuals, and this aim was fully achieved.

Already at the June 1957 congress of the Hungarian Socialist Workers' Party Kadar stated that people are not interested in grand political matters, but rather in their own material well-being. The Hungarians shaken by the suppression of their revolution were really glad to see even minor signs of freedom and opportunities, a growing range of goods in the shops, visas for tourists and the possibility of buying seventy dollars' worth of foreign currency, and the cancellation of the category "social background" from university admission procedures. State intervention into private life became less obtrusive or disappeared altogether. There were no compulsory political seminars at the working places, the party daily was not read out and discussed with the workers every morning, and no longer was there synchronized and collective applause. There was no need to demonstrate one's support for the regime. The behavior of those who had not taken part in the most turbulent events of the revolution or had not been involved in political life at all became the standard. The lesson to be drawn from their career was that it was safer to remain personally subordinated to the reigning political regime. Kádár's regime had always been predictable in the period of repression, much more than that of Rákosi, and was to remain so in the coming years. The demand for predictability was underlined by the fact that the dominant groups of society after 1956 accepted the prospect and called it Socialism.

However, everything had to be paid for, and a "nationwide suppression" of feelings and memories—as described by Ferenc Mérei—followed. Discussion of the revolution and its supression was taboo and no one dared to speak about those in jail or released from jail. "Peace" achieved in this way opened up vistas of personal comfort but destroyed social solidarity, precisely the kind of solidarity which had manifested itself so clearly in the days of the revolution. It was a tragic consequence of this period, primarily of the reprisals, that democratic activity became impossible for almost two decades, until the appearance of a new generation.

# Notes

1. For the general history of the Hungarian revolution see György Litván, János M. Bak and Lyman H. Legters, eds., *The Hungarian Revolution of 1956. Reform, Revolt and Repression 1953–1963* (New York, 1996); on Soviet maneuvres after November 4, 1956, see Jenő Györkei and Miklós Horváth, eds., *Szovjet katonai intervenció 1956* [Soviet military intervention, 1956] (Budapest, 1996); for a general overview see Bela K. Kiraly, Barbara Lotze and Nándor Dreisziger, eds., *The First War between Socialist States: The Hungarian Revolution and Its Impact* (New York, 1984).

2. For Bibó's proclamation of November 4 see István Bibó, *Democracy, Revolution, Self-Determination. Selected Writings*, ed. Károly Nagy (New York, 1991), 325–327. The essence of his solution was to preserve the main targets of the revolution (such as national independence, a multi-party system, workers' councils, democratic liberties), and to give guarantees to the Soviet Union (a treaty with the Soviets after the withdrawal of their forces, guarantees against the persecution of Communists in Hungary, the inclusion of certain elements of Socialism into the constitution, etc.). Seę István Bibó, *Összegyűjtött munkái* [Collected works], ed. István Kemény and Mátyás Sárközi (Bern, 1993), vol. 3, 881–885.

3. The first stage of the debate came to an end when a committee of five was set up that was, however, not allowed to enter Hungary by the Kádár government. So it prepared its report on the basis of testimonies and data avaliable abroad. See United Nations, *Report of the Special Committee on the Problem of Hungary*, General Assembly, Official Records: Eleventh Session Supplement, 18 (A/3592) (New York, 1957).

4. For the workers' councils and the resistance led by the Central Workers' Council see László Varga, "Munkástanácsok 1956" [Workers' councils, 1956], in László Varga, *Az elhagyott tömeg 1950–1956* [The foresaken crowd, 1950–1956] (Budapest, 1994), 199–237. For documents of the Central Workers' Council see László Varga, "A Nagybudapesti Központi Munkástanács irataiból", *Társadalmi Szemle*, nos. 8–9 (1991), 142–155; no. 11 (1991), 79–93. For recollections of leaders of workers' councils see Gyula Kozák, Adrienn Molnár, eds., *"Szuronyok hegyén nem lehet dolgozni!" Válogatás 1956-os munkástanácsvezetők visszaemlékezéseiből* [You cannot work poked with bayonetts. Recollections of Workers' Council leaders from 1956] (Budapest, 1993). The recollections of Miklós Sebestyén and Ferenc Tőke can be found in Gyula Kozák, ed., Szemle. *Válogatás a brüsszeli Nagy Imre Intézet folyóiratából* [Review. Selected writings from the periodical of the Imre Nagy Institute in Brussels] (Budapest, 1992), 50–69. See also Bill Lomax, ed., *Hungarian Workers' Councils in 1956* (New York, 1990); István

Kemény and Bill Lomax. eds., *Magyar Munkástanácsok 1956-ban* [Hungarian Workers' Councils in 1956] (Paris, 1986).

5. Viacheslav Sereda and János Rainer, eds., *Döntés a Kremlben 1956. A szovjet pártelnökség vitái Magyarországról* [Decision in the Kremlin in 1956. Debates of Soviet Party leaders on Hungary] (Budapest, 1996), 75–95, 145–151. Published also in Russian: Viacheslav Sereda, "Kak reshalis 'voprosi Vengrii'", *Istoricheskii Arhiv*, no. 2 (1966): 73–105 and no. 3 (1996): 87–122; in English: János M. Rainer, ed., "The Road to Budapest, 1956. New Documentation on the Kremlin's Decision to Intervene," *The Hungarian Quarterly*, no. 142 (summer 1996), 24–41 and no. 143 (autumn 1996), 16–31.

6. For Imre Nagy's behavior after November 4, 1956 see János M. Rainer, "A Parlamenttől a Fő utcáig. Nagy Imre gondolati útja 1956. november 4.–1957. április 14.", in Az 1956-os Magyar Forradalom Dokumentációs és Kutató Intézete: *Évkönyv I.* [Yearbook] (Budapest, 1992), vol. 1, 113–146.

7. For the documents about the activities of Soviet leaders in Budapest in November–December, 1956 see Viacheslav Sereda and Alexandr Stikalin, eds., *Hiányzó lapok 1956 történetéből. Dokumentumok a volt SZKP KB levéltárából* [Missing pages from the history of 1956. Documents from the Archives of the Central Committee of the Communist Party of the Soviet Union] (Budapest, 1993), 135–191, 223–239; in Russian: "Vengria, oktiabr–noiabr 1956 goda", *Istoricheski Arhiv*, no. 5 (1993), 132–161.

8. Éva Gál, et al., eds., *A "Jelcin-dosszié". Szovjet dokumentumok 1956-ról* [The Jeltsin file. Soviet documents on 1956] (Budapest, 1993), 132–133.

9. *"A KB nov. 11-ki ülésének jegyzőkönyve"* [Minutes of the meeting of the Central Committee, on November 11], in Sándor Balogh, ed., *A Magyar Szocialista Munkáspárt ideiglenes vezető testületeinek jegyzőkönyvei* [Minutes of the provisional leading bodies of the Hungarian Socialist Workers' Party], vol. 1, *1956. nov. 11–1957. jan. 14*, ed. Karola Vágyi Némethné and Levente Sipos (Budapest, 1993).

10. János Dávid, Sándor Geskó, and Pál Schiffer, *Forradalom, sortűz, megtorlás* [Revolution, volleys, and reprisal] (Budapest, 1990).

11. For martial law and retaliation in general see János M. Rainer, "Adatok az 1956-os forradalmat követő megtorláshoz" [Further data on reprisal after the Revolution of 1956], *Beszélő*, no. 19 (1987), 43–63. (Under pseudonim Elek Fényes). Republished in Fanny Havas, ed., *Beszélő összkiadás* [Beszélő, reprint] (Budapest, 1992), vol. 2, 649–663; See also János M. Rainer, "The Reprisals", *New Hungarian Quarterly*, 33, no. 127 (autumn 1992), 118–127.

12. For this process see János Kis, "Az 1956–57-es restauráció" [Restoration of Power in 1956–57], in András B. Hegedüs, ed., *Ötvenhatról nyolcvanhatban* [About 1956 in 1986] (Budapest, 1992), 217–249.

13. For Kádár's report on his visit to Moscow see Balogh, ed., op. cit., vol. 2, *1957. jan. 25–1957. ápr. 2.* ed. Karola Vágyi Némethné and Károly Urbán (Budapest, 1995), 339–358.

14. Balogh, ed., op. cit., vol. 1, 238–249, 281–300; *Népszabadság*, January 7, 1957.

15. Between November 1956 and February 1957 approximately 200,000 people escaped from Hungary mostly to Austria, and to Yugoslavia to a lesser extent. Some 10,000 soon returned, but most refugees settled either in Western Europe or North America. See a top secret report of the Central Statistical Office from 1957: "KSH-jelentés az 1956-os disszidálásról" [Central Statistical Office report on defection in 1956], *Regio*, no. 4 (1991), 174–211.

16. Vágyi Némethné and Sipos, eds., op. cit.; Vágyi Némethné and Urban, eds., op. cit., Balogh, ed., op. cit., vol. 3 *1957. április 5–1957. május 17.*, ed. Magdolna Baráth, István Feitl (Budapest, 1995); Balogh, ed., op. cit. vol. 4, *1957. máj. 21–1957. jún. 24.*, ed. Magdolna Baráth and Zoltán Ripp (Budapest, 1994).

17. The Hungarian Communist Party and the Social Democratic Party merged in June, 1948 under the name *Magyar Dolgozók Pártja* (Hungarian Workers' Party). Those Social Democrats who were against the fusion (in fact, the majority of the leaders and party members) were expelled from the Social Democratic Party already in the first half of 1948.

18. Former Minister of the Interior and Minister of Foreign Affairs László Rajk was arrested on trumped up charges in late May, 1949. After a show trial he was executed in September. This was the first in the row of Stalinist purge trials in Hungary.

19. This was the name of the political police in Hungary between 1948 and 1956.

20. Originally meant to defend democratic state order, the law came to be applied against all supposed and real enemies of the regime after the Communist takeover.

21. Kádár's report at the meeting of the Provisional Executive Committee of the Hungarian Socialist Workers' Party on April 2, 1957, in Vágyi Némethné and Urbán, eds., op. cit., 357.

22. Planned economy began in Hungary with the first Three-Year Plan of 1947–49. It was followed by the first Five-Year Plan in 1950–55. The targets of a second one were discussed in the spring of 1956, but the plan was never realized.

23. "New course" was the name of the policy followed after Imre Nagy assumed power as prime minister on July 4, 1953. As ordered by the Soviets, Nagy slowed down industrialization, put an end to forceful collectivization, raised the living standard of the population, and eased the political pressure on society to a significant degree. When in 1954 Imre Nagy tried to put these

goals into action, the orthodox Stalinist under Rákosi removed him from his post and expelled him from Party leadership in April, 1955.

24. It was presumably the Czechslovakian Prime Minister Viliam Siroky who took short notes on the agenda of the talks that were later found by Tibor Hajdu in the archives of the former Communist Party of Czechoslovakia in Prague. I express my special thanks for his calling my attention to this document.

25. Vágyi Némethné and Urbán, eds., 79.

26. Ibid., 75.

27. Ibid., 157–237.

28. With no author indicated, the numbered copies of the book appeared at the party's own publishing house bearing the name of Kossuth.

29. Sereda and Stikalin, eds., op. cit., 260–264.

30. Vágyi Némethné and Urbán, eds., op. cit., 348.

31. Vágyi Némethné and Feitl, eds., op. cit., 69.

32. Gyula Kállai, "A magyarországi ellenforradalom a marxizmus-leninizmus fényében" [The Hungarian counterrevolution in the light of Marxism-Leninism], *Társadalmi Szemle*, no. 1 (1957), 12–39.

33. The documents of the trial were carefully guarded in the archives of the Ministry of the Interior until 1989. Today they can be found at the National Archives (*XX-5-h. Legfelsőbb Bíróság Népbírósági Tanácsa iratai V-150.000 sz. Nagy Imre és társai pere*).

34. Baráth and Ripp, eds., op. cit., 192–193.

35. For Kádár's and Biszku's preparations for their visit to Moscow see Éva Gál, et. al., eds., op. cit., 193–199. The Politburo of the Central Committee of the Communist Party of the Soviet Union dealt with the documents they presented at its meeting on June 19, 1957. To be found at *Centr Hranenia Sovremennoi Dokumentacii* (Moscow), f. 89. op. 2. d. 5, 35–137.

36. Biszku must have visited Moscow with the indictment prior to August 26, 1957. See ibid., 199–201.

37. See Andropov's report from August 29, 1957 in ibid., 202–204. At that time Andropov was already head of the department of international party relations of the Central Committee of the Communist Party of the Soviet Union.

38. Zoltán Ripp, ed., "Döntés a Nagy Imre-csoport ügyében. A Központi Bizottság zárt ülése 1957. dec. 21-én" [Decision on the case of the Imre Nagy group. Closed session of the Central Committee on December 21, 1957], *Múltunk*, no. 4 (1990), 159–178. Kádár kept three copies of the document in his safe until his death.

39. József Kiss and Zoltán Ripp, "'Mi inkább az elnapolás mellett vagyunk, minthogy enyhe ítéletet hozzunk most.' Három dokumentum a Nagy Imre-per 1958. februári elhalasztásáról" ["We prefer postponing the trial to passing a light sentence right now." Three documents on the postponement of the Nagy Imre trial in February, 1958], *Társadalmi Szemle*, no. 4 (1993), 82–95.

40. "Budapesti jelentés" [Report from Budapest], *Irodalmi Újság* (London), May 1, 1958.
41. MOL MDP–MSZMP iratok osztálya [Hungarian National Archives, Department for the Documents of the Hungarian Working People's Party and Hungarian Socialist Workers' Party], 288/5/59. ö.e. A PB ülése 1957. dec. 28. [Political Committee Meeting on December 28, 1957].
42. Viaceslav Sereda, "V. Sz. Bajkov naplójából" [From the diary of V. S. Baikov], *Tekintet*, nos. 5–6 (1995), 201.
43. MOL MDP–MSZMP ir., 288/5/75. ö.e. A PB ülése 1958. ápr. 15 [Meeting of the Political Committee on April 15, 1958], 34.
44. MOL MDP–MSZMP ir., 288/4/17. ö.e. A KB ülése 1958. jún. 6. [Meeting of the Central Committee on June 6, 1958], 1.
45. The rest were sentenced to death for committing common crimes, mostly murders, and for war crimes committed during World War II. See Attila Szakolczai, "A forradalmat követő megtorlás során kivégzettekről" [On people executed during the reprisal after the revolution), in *Évkönyv* (Budapest, 1994), 237–257. The figures pertaining to the reprisal are still not final and are based on estimates published by the author in an article in 1986 (see note 11).
46. See note 11.
47. Information Bureau of the Council of Ministers, *The Counter-Revolutionary Forces in the October Events in Hungary* (Budapest, 1957), vols. 1-4. The documents were published also in German, French, and Russian, as well as in the language of most Socialist countries. The White Books published in the individual counties in 1957–58 summarized local counter-revolutionary events.

*Judit Kósa*

# Budapest During the Kádár Era, 1957–1988

Budapest has undergone unprecedented changes over the past century and a half. Its administration and structure adjusted to the demands of unification twice, and the boundaries of its extended territory changed several times. The two-storied neo-Classical Pest-Buda of the Reform Era was enriched by four-storied eclectic buildings in the years around the millennium. Its street pattern changed, and several opportunities for development appeared possible. Similarly large-scale changes occurred in the second half of the 20th century. While the city was still bearing the marks of World War II and the street-fighting of 1956, its suburbs were gradually absorbed by the city, and new town centers were built to relieve the growing housing shortage. The single-story houses on the outskirts of Pest, built on the plains, were turned into high-rise estates by the 1970s.

## Demography and Employment

The number of inhabitants in the capital grew rapidly. The drop in 1956–57 resulting from the flight of masses from the country was followed by steady growth. In the late 1950s 20,000–25,000 people moved into the city from the country each year, bringing the population to over 1.8 million by 1960. In the 1960s this influx continued owing to the demands of industrial growth. Mortality rates exceeded the birthrate already in those years, hence the decrease could only be compensated by newcomers from the countryside.[1] The rate of population growth slowed down in the 1970s, in fact, dropping to a quarter of its former level. The population of the capital grew from 2,001,083 in 1970 to only 2,059,347 in 1980, and even this figure was steadily decreasing in the 1980s. In the mid-1990s the population dropped below 2 million once again.

The population distribution within Budapest also underwent change. At the time of the unification in 1873 dictrict VIII was the most heavily populated, but when the first large housing estates were built in the 1950s and

1960s the population of districts XI and XIV increased significantly. In the 1970s districts III, XV, and X developed rapidly. In the 1980s fewer housing estates were built, consequently only the population of districts IV, XVII, and XVIII increased. By the end of the period under consideration only districts with large-scale housing developments experienced population increase, but the most densely populated areas were still in the older parts of the inner city.

Women have traditionally outnumbered men in Budapest. Not only was their mortality rate lower but also a higher percentage of women arrived from the countryside to bolster the workforce in the post-war decades. The age distribution of the population was also unbalanced. The proportion of elderly people grew steadily between 1949 and 1990. In certain inner districts with no large housing developments, such as the Castle district and the downtown area, the problem became especially serious. This phenomenon was particularly unfavorable to the labor requirements of industry. The number of working age people was decreasing, especially women. At the same time, the growing ratio of the dependent elderly was not balanced by adequate number of children.

The number and ratio of children were flucntuating in this period. Due to lifting the restrictions on abortion in the 1960s, the birthrate decreased. In the 1970s, however, when the "Ratkó generation" born in consequence of the restrictions became parents around 1974–78 and childrearing was encouraged by various subventions, such as the childcare benefit, the number of children increased suddenly and rapidly. Yet another wave of decrease commenced in the early 1980s. As far as the marital status of the inhabitants is concerned, there was a definite tendency for an increase in single people. The divorce rate increased, while the number of marriages has decreased since the 1980s.

Although the primary aim of the masses migrating from the country to the capital was to obtain employment, the post-war decades were marked by labor shortages. Long lists hung on the factory gates soliciting employees. Even unskilled and semi-skilled workers were in short supply. The lack of manual workers was due to the fact that the educational level of the population in the capital (especially the ratio of those with higher education) steadily rose after the 1950s. This fact and the state policy of full employment resulted in the disproportionate growth of intellectual occupations in the city. Overemployment in white collar occupations assumed unprecedented proportions: clerks hiding behind piles of papers doing nothing, drinking coffee and making private calls all day long became the cliché for contemporary comics and comedians. In the first half of the 1970s the number of manual workers decreased by 90,000, while that of service employees increased by more than one fifth. Because factories could not employ additional clerks, the city council in 1976 was forced to find jobs for people finishing secondary school. However, the tendency remained. While in 1960 47 per cent of all manual workers in the country lived in Budapest[2], in the first half of the 1980s this ratio dropped to 18 per cent[3], partly because of the development of industry in the countryside. At the same time, 40 per cent of all professionals lived in the capital. The process seemed irreversible. The ratio of manual workers in Budapest decreased by another 13 per cent between 1980 and 1985.

Since the campaign to move industry from the capital to the country in the 1960s and 1970s did not prove successful, the state attempted to achieve full employment for all manual workers in the capital. It followed from the ideology of the Kádár regime that the intelligentsia should never earn more than physical workers, at least officially, while the latter enjoyed several privileges: they were given priority in acquiring apartments, and their children had priority in admission to elite schools. There were still branches of industry that suffered from chronic labor shortage, so the so-called "migratory birds" who changed jobs frequently were given higher wages at each new job in the hope of keeping them there. In the 1970s the state was forced to introduce measures to stop this intra-city migration. From 1971 the unemployed had to apply for jobs at employment agencies that limited their choices among vacancies. The efficiency of these measures was, however, reduced by the fact that the most notoriously "migrant" branches like the construction industry were exempt from these rules. It followed from the very nature of the regime that there could be no viable solution.

## Municipal government

Administration of the significantly extended territory of the capital hardly changed in this period. It was based on the system introduced in 1950 and remained essentially unchanged, even though the Council Act of 1970 implemented new elements into the election of the city council. Henceforth members of the city council were not elected directly by the inhabitants, but by district councils, the members of which were elected by the population. The district councils were entitled to send one representative for every 10,000 inhabitants to the city council. This representative could be anyone with the right to vote, but the majority of the representatives were expected to be members of the local councils. The same law provided that parliamentary and local elections were to be held every other year from 1971 on.

Although the structure of the councils hardly changed in this period, their significance and influence in the economic life of the city grew significantly. In 1950 Budapest had only thirty plants owned by the municipal government, employing 49,000 workers, while in the early 1970s the number had augmented to 125, employing 205,000.[4]

With such control over individual citizens the powers of the councils began to change. When standardized printed forms were introduced in 1973, the *Népszabadság*[5] found it worthy of mention that "from July 1 the tone of printed forms will also change: clients will not be "summoned" but "notified." The real estate registry was also standardized in the same year. Ten years later census and professional registers were processed already by computers. Given the system of personal code numbers, all data pertaining to an individual could be tracked.

## City Development

By the time the first General urban planning program of Budapest was adopted in 1960, the major ravages of the war had been repaired. The first new housing blocks were built in *Csepel*, along *Kerepesi* Road, and *Nagy Lajos király* Road. It was obvious, however, that no further development was possible without a comprehensive town-planning program. The population of the city was growing rapidly, while 87 per cent of the housing were still single-story, and the health of the population was at risk because of the mixing of residential and industrial areas. The comprehensive town plan tried to increase the number of apartments without extending the built-in areas significantly, i.e., by multi-story buildings.[6] The plan tried to increase the rate of areas with high-rise buildings by 42 per cent. The open spaces of *Lágymányos* and *Kelenföld* seemed suitable for that purpose. The overpopulated inner districts with their outdated apartment-houses were in need of modern housing complexes (*Ferencváros*, *Józsefváros*, *Óbuda*). Smaller blocks were planned for *Zugló* and *Újlipótváros*, vacant lots were to be built up all over Budapest, while family housing and cooperative apartment sections were also planned. The Program emphasized that the number of flats pulled down in 15–20 years was to be no greater than 25 per cent of the flats built during the same period. The targets were 58,000 demolished homes versus 250,000 new ones. Ten years later, when the program was revised, it became obvious that only new city centers in the former outskirts with cultural institutions, shopping centers and services could meet the needs of people living in large housing blocks to relieve overpopulation in the inner city. The comprehensive plan envisaged the creation of bedroom communities around Budapest, whence people could reach the city and their job-sites by mass transportation in 25–30 minutes. The program also covered park planning, and transportation. Maintenance and widening of roads, building of multi-level crossings were meant to facilitate ever-increasing traffic. The extension of the subway system was considered of utmost importance for mass transportation.

Apartment construction was given the highest priority in the plan. Tens of thousands of new apartment units changed the appearance of the city. Their number grew by 74 per cent between 1949 and the mid-1990s, or approximately 350,000 new apartments in absolute numbers. As a consequence homes became less crowded in Budapest. In the decade between 1970 and 1980 alone 100,000 apartment units were built.[7]

Despite these efforts, the housing shortage was barely eased in the capital, because the decrease in population was partly due to the decreasing number of people living in workers' hostels and other communal dwellings. On the other hand, the decrease was much smaller among those living in flats. At the same time, aging along with the growing ratio of single households (by 87 per cent between 1970 and 1980) increased the demands for flats. The efficiency apartments in the modern prefabricated buildings were unsuitable to the cohabitation of several generations.

The state tried to relieve the tension caused by the housing shortage. One of the measures intended to improve the climate of public opinion was that there were no more allotments for sublets after 1957. At the same time, flats turned into offices earlier were gradually transformed into homes again. The high cost of construction of modern housing blocks did not leave enough funds for the renovation of housing in the inner districts. These buildings, built around the turn of the century, were in poor condition, often lacking modern conveniences. Consequently the people living in them applied for new homes or at least for swaps. Applications had to be renewed at least once in every decade, so there were approximately 100,000 applicants in the 1960s and 1970s. When state investment into building homes stopped, the number of those waiting for living space rose again from 51,000 in 1985 to 71,000 in 1990.

In the meantime life in council flats was inexpensive.* The rents collected by the councils did not cover even the costs of maintenance, so the conditions of these council buildings were deteriorating without possibility of renovation. To compensate for this shortcoming, after 1961 families with less than two persons per room had to pay an excess floorspace tax in Budapest. The collected extra tax was not enough to balance the budget, but it gave impetus to swaps and to subletting. Ten years later rents were drastically raised, but the majority of the tenants received rent allowances from their work-places or, in the case of retired people, directly from the state. (Rents collected by the state exceeded the sums invested into maintenance for the first time in 1990) Housing regulations issued in 1971 reflected significant changes in the attitude of the state toward the housing problem. The regulations gradually broke with the former notion of tenancy as a civil right and made it clear that the individual had to contribute financially to home construction.

The circle of those entitled to apply for tenancy was restricted in the 1970s. Those who had any private property or real property in the family or whose income was high were not allowed to apply. Young married couples, manual workers or foremen directly controlling production were given preference. Work-places were also involved in these allotments, and the category of tenements owned by the employer appeared. The state, however, was unable to build the necessary amount of apartment units on its own. From the mid-1970s people were urged to build their own homes either in blocks of cooperative homes in the suburbs or buy them in privately owned housing blocks. These people were given state and company loans at a low rate of interest to be repaid over a period of several decades. They also received the so-called "social political discount" in a direct ratio to the number of children. Young couples who agreed to bear two children were able to purchase an apartment almost without a down-payment.

By the late 1970s, however, it became apparent that the construction industry was unable to keep up with the plan. Homes were built very slowly, and by the 1980s it became obvious that the state could no longer

---

* Editors' note: the massive building of homes as well as the irrationally low rents were parts of the notorious "Kádár gulyás communism": life standards above available means. The deficit was covered by foreign loans which is to be repaid with interest by the generation of the post-Communist era.

finance large-scale apartment building projects. The sixth Five-Year Plan for the first half of the 1980s still contained provisions for the construction of 90,000 new homes and the renovation of all state-owned houses built before 1950. However, due to the general investment freeze, only a small fraction of the goal was realized.

Viewed from the air, the city seemed to have been buried in concrete. Blocks built of grey precast units dominated the cityscape. The quality of housing built in different periods was not uniform. In the late 1950s, for example, tiny efficiency apartments were built by the thousands. Being small, a recess had to be added to the kitchen in lieu of a bathroom. By the early 1960s most tenants living in such flats applied for an exchange. The city council of Budapest decided to construct an experimental housing development at Óbuda, in an area between *Vörösvári* and *Bécsi* Streets. Several designs were considered, including ones which were appropriate for mass production. The development included kindergartens, schools, shops, and cultural institutions. It never became more than an experiment, since by the time it was occupied by tenants, the first Soviet-type factory producing ferro-concrete panels had been put into operation on the northern rim of Buda in 1965.

Panel (prefabricated element) technology had been used in Budapest as early as the first half of the 1960s. The first ten-story or taller buildings were built in *Lágymányos*, the outer parts of *Ferencváros*, and around the Pest end of the *Árpád* Bridge. Soviet-type panels speeded up construction significantly. The first Hungarian prefrabricated housing factory built units for both Southern and Northern Buda, *Kelenföld*, and the Óbuda end of *Árpád* Bridge within a few years. In 1967 a new prefabricated housing plant was opened in *Ferencváros*, on the south side of Pest, using Danish technology, and in the early 1970s another one in northern Pest, near Dunakeszi. They were soon followed by a plant for prefabricated housing in Budafok, Southern Buda. The latter two were more modern versions of the Soviet type. In the 1970s single-family homes were replaced by large prefab buildings in *Kőbánya*, in the central areas of *Józsefváros, Zugló, Óbuda, Újpalota, Örmező, Újpest,* and *Angyalföld*. On the outskirts the new housing blocks either replaced the small villages surrounding the capital or occupied large vacant lots. This is how the housing developments of *Békásmegyer, Kőbánya-Újhegy,* and *Káposztásmegyer* were built.

The Inner City as a traditional administrative and commercial center of the capital could no longer cope with the needs of so many households, so the new housing developments needed centers of their own with mass

transportation infrastructure, shopping and service centers, and local administration offices. Since funds were never enough, and apartment construction was an utmost priority, these complementary investments were
often omitted. In Óbuda, for example, the area designated for a future
administrative center still serves as a park for dogs. Forced simplicity even
became an explicit principle: the Council of Ministers declared in January
1974 that expensive structures serving only decorative purposes should be
omitted when planning the new city centers.[8]

The suburbs and the settlements unified with the capital were transformed to a great degree. All of them received at least some new housing
blocks around modern town centers (as in the case of *Kispest* and *Pestlőrinc*). The former townscapes evoking an old-time atmosphere were reduced to a few blocks not unlike open-air museums (as in *Óbuda* and
*Kőbánya*). The word "reconstruction" assumed a new meaning: instead of
improving old buildings it meant demolishing them and replacing them
from bottom up. The old one-story single-family homes with courtyards
and the smaller tenement houses of the suburbs disappeared and were replaced by more commodious blocks of flats. This involved an exchange
of population, since people were often moved from the demolished homes
to new blocks at the other end of the city.

In the meantime, equally significant changes occurred in the traditional
old tenement houses of the inner districts, though they did not affect the
appearance of the city. Toward the late 1960s, when janitors ceased to
have additional "administrative" duties such as spying on tenants, the state
found it difficult to pay them. The old caretakers retired, few young people
were willing to do this round-the-clock job, all the less so since most
former janitors remained in their official quarters even after their retire-
ment. Hence there was no one left to make minor repairs, call the professional services when greater problems occurred, and keep the houses clean
and tidy. When the tenants were given keys to elevators and gates in 1965,
the doors tended to remain open all night, the elevators broke down more
often and the staircases became exceedingly dirty. Block janitors replacing
the former caretakers had time only for administration. Minor problems
often degenerated into major damage, and the old buildings deteriorated.
The communal management enterprises in charge of several hundreds of
apartments could not cope with their task.

The city was also transformed by the growing traffic. Traffic jams,
hitherto known only from the movies, became common from the 1960s,
and rush hours also became longer. Traffic lights had to be installed, and

it became imperative to ease traffic by building underground pedestrian crossings at the busiest intersections. Partly as a result of subway construction, the first underground crossings were built at Hotel Astoria, then under *Blaha Lujza* Square, *Ferenc* Boulevard, *Deák* Square, and *Liberation* [now *Ferenciek*] Square. They also served as entrances to the subway stations. The reconstruction of *Erzsébet* Bridge—blown up during the war—became urgent, since traffic was growing and the *Kossuth* Bridge, serving only as a foot-bridge in its last years, was demolished in 1961. The reconstructed bridge and the streets leading to it were inaugurated in late 1964. Twenty years later the inauguration of the extended *Árpád* Bridge was an equally important step in the development of traffic and transport in the city.

The 1960s and 1970s brought significant changes in the Castle district as well. The former residence of the regent, the royal palace on Castle Hill had been in ruins since the war. In the early 1960s the government decided to turn it into a museum and library. The restoration of the dome was finished by 1963. Between 1967 and 1985 the following institutions moved into the castle: the Budapest Historical Museum, the Museum of the History of the Working Class Movement, the Hungarian National Galery, the Castle Theater, and the National Széchényi Library.

Finding a suitable site for the annual international fair of Budapest [*Budapesti Nemzetközi Vásár*] attracting large masses to the capital was crucial. By the 1960s the fair could no longer be accomodated in the City Park [*Városliget*]. It was relocated by governmental decree to *Lágymányos* along the Danube in 1963. The area was cleared (mainly by volunteer work), but ten years later a more suitable place was found in *Kőbánya*, where the agricultural fair used to be. Such hesitation was characteristic of major ventures in townplanning during those years. The same can be said about the fate of the National Theater. Its former building on *Blaha Lujza* Square had to be pulled down in 1965 because of static problems arising from the subway construction below the building. Plans were prepared for a huge, multi-function theater building to be built in *Dózsa György* Street, but the financial backing for its construction could not be found. In 1983 the government and some social organizations launched a fund-raising campaign. Several hundred million forints have been collected. Until recently, the construction of a National Theater has, however, remained on the drawing board. Now it is decided that it should be built by 2000 on *Erzsébet* Square. The Pest Concert Hall [*Vigadó*] was more fortunate, though it had been almost totally ruined during the war. It opened its gates only as late as 1980, but was reconstructed in its original form.

In 1957 it narrowly escaped being pulled down to be replaced by a glass palace.

## Tourism, Mass Transportation, and Utilities

The so-called "conference tourism" of the 1970s and 1980s contributed to the prosperity in Budapest. The city had been famous for its medicinal baths, beautiful panoramas and for being the capital of "the jolliest barracks" in the Eastern Bloc. Yet, despite its potentials, it could not offer much to the tourists coming in large numbers. Most hotels had deteriorated during and after the war, and many tourists had to be placed with families as paying guests. Although there were some exceptions like Hotel Budapest Intercontinental built earlier, major construction of hotels began only in the late 1970s. Hotels like the Thermal, Fórum, Hyatt, Novotel, and Ramada followed in quick succession to accomodate foreigners coming to conferences or sporting events. A conference center was soon built in Buda followed by the Budapest Sports Hall in Pest, in the vicinity of the People's Stadium.

Mass transit, unbearably overburdened in the 1950s, began to improve from the 1960s. The introduction of the system of seated ticket vendors and controllers on the vehicles made rides much easier for the passengers in 1958. The stock of vehicles was modernized and, in the early 1960s, articulated buses appeared in the streets of Budapest. Later articulated trolley-buses and streetcars were joined the fleet. There was, however, a growing labor shortage in mass transport in the 1960s, so even the seated ticket vendors disappeared. The complicated system of tariffs was simplified in July 1966. Ticket prices were very low and did not change for almost twenty years. School-children, students and pensioners had special passes. From July 1969 ticket vendors and collectors disappeared from the vehicles. From January 1968 the streetcar and bus companies merged into a single company called *Budapesti Közlekedési Vállalat* [Budapest Transport Company].

Because the above outlined measures did not improve transport significantly, in 1964 the government decided to complete the construction of the subway system suspended ten years earlier. The first section between *Örs vezér* Square and *Deák* Square was completed by April 2, 1970. Two and a half years later the whole line was completed with *Moszkva* (Moscow) Square as its northern terminal point. Another government decree ordered the construction of the line between *Kőbánya-Kispest* in the south and the *Árpád* Bridge in the north. The line was built between 1976 and 1984. In the early 1970s the millennial subway was extended and the cogwheel railway renovated to commemorate the hundredth anniversary of the unification of the city.

At the same time the number of cars on the roads and in the streets of Budapest also rose tremendously. In 1972 approximately 100,000 private cars were registered in the capital, while in 1981 their number was estimated to be a quarter of a million. Roads had to be widened, and traffic limited within the area encircled by the Grand Boulevard. Parking along thoroughfares was gradually prohibited. In 1972 the first parking meter appeared in the capital, indicating that parking had become a major problem.

Finding a taxi had always been a problem. Taxi stands were set up even in the suburbs, but there had never been enough of the traditional "checkered" cabs. The shortage was eased somewhat when a second taxi company was chartered in 1969. The problem was not really eased until 1982 when a government decree allowed private taxi drivers to be licensed in the city.

Public utilities in Greater Budapest could not meet the increased demands. In the late 1950s a water shortage occurred every summer in the city. The lacking amount of water was estimated around 15 per cent[9] that had to be supplied at considerable additional cost. The construction of waterworks was of special importance. Wells were bored on *Csepel* and *Szentendrei* Islands the water of which was filtered by river-gravel. As the River Danube became increasingly polluted and acquired too much iron and manganese, the *Csepel* Island water had to be purified from the 1980s on. In the first twenty years from 1950 watermains were extended 2.2 times their original length, while the number of consumers rose threefold. Today running water is available all over the city, but the sewage system has not been similarly extended. Between 1950 and 1980 it grew only by 65 per cent. In the 1980s, however, it became one and a half times as long as it had been before. The network is still insufficient in some suburbs and in the hills of Buda, which endangers the karstic waters and medicinal springs in the famous caves of these hills.

In 1959 substantial gas fields were found in Hungary. The gas was transported to Budapest from the 1960s, making gas heating available in homes, a development which significantly reduced air pollution. Demand for gas was growing, since city factories began to use natural gas. The gas pipes and gas appliances in the whole city were adapted for natural gas between 1971 and 1988. While in 1965 1.5 per cent of all homes in Budapest used gas for heating, this figure rose to 57 per cent in 1993.

The modernization of electric power became urgent in the late 1950s. In particular, single-phase and direct current had to be replaced. It was now possible to supply areas hitherto overlooked. The number of consumers grew by approximately 100,000 every ten years after 1950, and the overall household consumption was nearly ten times higher in the early 1990s compared to forty years earlier. Street-lighting also developed extensively in the period after the 1950s. Gas was replaced by electricity, and the number of street lamps grew from 65,000 to 92,000 in the 1960s. In the 1990s this figure rose to over 135,000. Modernization was continuous in the inner districts, while in the suburbs the same old street lamps were glimmering for decades. Street-lighting in the outer districts was modernized only in the 1980s.

One of the greatest problems facing the population of Budapest was the scarcity of telephones. Although three main telephone exchanges were put into operation during the early 1960s and the remainder was modernized, they could not meet the growing demand. With the construction of large housing developments whole districts applied for telephones. The system of party lines was also unpopular. Some technical innovations like special subcenters eased the tension for awhile. From 1974 on direct long distance dialing became possible and at the same time rates were charged according to the actual duration of calls. The problem was solved only during the free market innovations of the 1990s when several new telephone companies were chartered.

## Environmental protection

Growing industrial activity and population increase brought environmental hazards to the capital. Traffic noise and air pollution in the inner districts had reached intolerable levels already in the 1960s. The Budapest city council issued an ordinance on June 29, 1962, regarding air pollution. It ordered plants using especially dangerous technology to be removed from the capital, and factory chimneys had to be topped with filters. Changes were, however, slow and the situation improved significantly only when natural gas was introduced for heating. From the 1970s on air pollution became serious again with the ever growing number of cars and the replacement of many streetcars by buses. At the same time, the overall park area in the city decreased. The construction fever of 1970–1974 uprooted 12,000 trees. Although they were replaced by 66,000 pollution resistant bushes, green spots continued to disappear in the city. Ironically, the prospects improved with the growing economic difficulties of the country, forcing suspension of large-scale construction. The extraordinary amount of garbage also posed a great problem already by the 1980s. On April 30, 1982, the Rákospalota garbage disposal works were completed. The problem of its waste gas was resolved only in 1995 with the help of a Japanese loan.

## Mass Dwellings and the Standard of Living

The only solution to housing shortage was a massive construction program in which quality and esthetics were secondary to quantity.

Apartments in such housing blocks were not designed as comfortable homes for both day and night; they were primarily shelters for the night. Consequently, in the 1950s and 1960s no separate bedrooms were planned. Pressure of space forced people to enclose balconies and squeeze cupboards into staircases. Those whose middle-class homes had been pulled down and who had been forced to move to a new housing development brought their unwieldy furniture with them. They were supposed to get accustomed to a new lifestyle under new circumstances. In the 1960s the expectation was that home life would be restructured according to party congress directives. Restaurant meals or eating fast food was to replace cooking. Yet tradition prevailed, but cooking in apartments with tiny kitchens and no pantries proved extremely difficult.

The typical lifestyle of housing estate residents has been thoroughly analyzed. Architects dreamt of huge buildings, almost towns in themselves, offering a communal way of life for thousands. Such was, for example, a plan prepared by Elemér Zalotay in the early 1960s.[10] He envisaged a three kilometer long 40-story building with 20,000 apartments for 70,000–80,000 tenants to be built along the Danube. It was supposed to have a central kitchen with dinner lifts to all floors, sports facilities, and kitchen gardens imitating a real town, the scene of both private and social life. The plan and its creator were both swept away in 1965. Ten years later it became obvious, however, that even housing projects of much smaller proportions presented major problems. A study published in the periodical *Budapest*[11] concluded that despite the large number of apartments built recently, high-quality habitats were sadly lacking. The article suggested turning these bed-room communities into towns with modern services making life more comfortable and efficient. The idea was to do housework collectively, with collectively owned household appliances. At a time, however, when washing machines and refrigerators, spin-driers, vacuum-cleaners and the like were already common in the households, such an idea could not be successful. These appliances had become widespread in the previous decade, a period of spectacular development in this respect. Supermarkets and community services were planned to accompany the housing projects. Small retail stores and private services also spread on the groundfloor of the buildings filling the spaces between the concrete pillars. Storage rooms and garages metamorphosed into small private shops and workshops.

Supplying the population with consumer goods remained a problem throughout the whole period. Purchasing power increased significantly in the 1960s and 1970s, and there were always certain products in short supply. State controlled trade with unmotivated store clerks did not work well. As early as 1968, the executive committee of the city council passed a resolution in favor of small private retailers, but the new housing developments remained without them for years to come. A survey taken in 1975 revealed that 250,000 square meters of shops, i.e., the equivalent of approximately 17 department stores, were missing in the capital.[12] In 1976 the first cooperative, i.e., not state-owned store, the *Skála*, was opened in Budapest to be followed by several new shopping centers in the outskirts. In 1981 the city council was forced to lease shops, restaurants, and workshops to private persons, and they soon proved very successful.

Modernizaton in the city demanded victims. Old lampposts, wrought-iron railings, wooden gates, quaint old shop-fronts disappeared to be replaced by uniform aluminum or smooth, undecorated modern surfaces. Valuable reminders of art from the past, sculptures, street fixtures, old shelters at streetcar-stops dating from the turn of the century were uprooted. A single enthusiast, art historian Mihály Ráday, a cameraman at the Hungarian TV, aroused the people and created a movement in a surprisingly short time making the recreation of the former appearance of the city and the defence of the still remaining values a public issue. With his TV-program "Our grandchildren will not see this any more..." called attention to the preservation of what is valuable in the city under the circumstances of the irrational planned economy, and this without any overt political theme.

The City Embellishment Association of Budapest was founded on May 5, 1983. The members of the movement took photos and notes of every building in the inner districts. They organized exhibitions and initiated preservation or restoration of existing items of value. The Podmaniczky medal, the award they founded, was given primarily to people who managed to prevent thoughtless destruction of irreplaceable artistic values of the past.

## Cultural Life

Budapest is not only the capital of the country, but its disproportionate head also. All state and social organizations are centered there. Budapest is the seat of legislation, the goverment, the Supreme Court, and of the Chief Prosecutor's Office, to mention only the most august institutions. Obviously, Budapest is also the cultural center of the country, housing national collections, the most important museums, the State Archives, the National Széchényi Library, two opera theaters, the Hungarian Radio and Television Company, film and recording studios, the majority of cinemas and theaters. There are important universities and colleges in the city. All newspapers distributed throughout the country were published there for decades after 1956. Most of the publishing houses work in the capital.

Budapest has been the cultural center of the nation for over a century. The socialist state aimed to increase the educational level of the population. The rate of those who finished the eight-grade primary school grew from 54 per cent in 1960 to 87 per cent in 1990. The rate of those completing secondary school rose from 20 to 45 per cent in the same period. University graduates were below 7 per cent of the population in 1960, but this figure rose above 19 per cent in 1990. From the 1960s evening and correspondence courses made it possible for people who were gainfully employed to study. In order to acquaint secondary-school studnents with factory work they received training one day a week in a trade in the 1960s. Albeit interesting conclusions could be drawn from this experiment, it failed by the 1970s.

Tickets to theaters, cinemas, and concert halls, along with books remained inexpensive. In return the state retained the right of censorship of the press and performing arts. The "three Ts", the initials of the Hungarian for prohibition [*tiltás*], toleration [*tűrés*], and support [*támogatás*] affected cultural life throughout the country. The capital was, however, in a favored position. There was an autumn music festival from the late 1950s on and a spring festival of art from 1981 on, still organized each year. The *József Attila* Theater opened in 1956, and the *Madách* Theater in 1961. There was an open-air theater on *Margitsziget*, and a new one by *Feneketlen-tó* [Bottomless Lake], named after Béla Bartók. Summer stock theaters opened also in *Kőbánya*, *Városmajor*, and *Városliget*. Several cinemas were built, too. All major housing projects included a monumental movie theater, though television was relegating them into the background from the late 1960s on.

The most typical cultural institutions of the day were the cultural centers or houses of culture harboring study circles, music bands, folk groups, lecture series, debating societies, and the like. Their number rose from 21 in 1955 to 39 in 1963. Labor unions, which supported them, also backed libraries as their contribution to the dissemination of culture. There were libraries in schools and factories, and the *Ervin Szabó* Library of Budapest had over one hundred branches all over the city.

Besides "official" or "subventioned" culture there were trends and movements falling into the "tolerated" category. There were some remnants of the legendary café culture of earlier times, and there was the famous *Fészek klub* ["nest"] where actors, writers, and other prominent figures of cultural life could gather. The youth clubs of the 1960s were famous for their rock bands. The Illés group performed in the *Bosch* club, Omega fans visited a club in *Kinizsi* Street, and the Metro played at the Metro club. In summer there were rock concerts at the Ybl-bazaar built around the turn of the century, now called the Youth Park of Buda. The *Fiatal Művészek Klubja* [Club of Young Artists], opened in 1965, was a favorite meeting place for young art lovers. Besides the theatrical performances and debate sessions held in private homes this club became the scene of political activism from the 1970s on.

# Notes

1. Hedvig Pletscher Novotnyné, *A főváros 120 éve, 1873–1993* [120 years in the history of the capital, 1873–1993] (Budapest, 1995), 67–78.
2. Ferenc Lovászi, *Fővárosunk jelene és jövője. Budapest Általános Rendezési Terve* [The present and future of our capital. The general town planning program of Budapest] (Budapest, 1964).

3. "Budapest krónikája" [Chronicle of Budapest] (manuscript).
4. Sándor Fekete, Zoltán Halász, and Béla Esti, *Mit kell tudni Budapestről?* [What do we have to know about Budapest?] (Budapest, 1973), 64.
5. *Népszabadság*, May 26, 1973.
6. *Fővárosunk jelene és jövője...*
7. *A főváros 120 éve...*, 88.
8. "Budapest krónikája".
9. *A főváros 120 éve...*, 97–115.
10. Gábor Miklós, "Szalagháztól toronyházig" [From row houses to apartment towers], *Népszabadság*, May 8, 1993.
11. János Szinai, "Korszerű lakásforma—korszerű életforma" [Modern flats—modern lifestyles], *Budapest* (March, 1976).
12. "Budapest krónikája".

*László Baán*

# Budapest at the Dawn of Democracy 1989–96

The breakdown of communism and the construction of democratic political institutions during 1989–90 involved legal procedures. The processes might be called a "lawful revolution",[1] the most important element of which was the total restructuring of the communist constitution. The original 1949 constitution and its gradually altered versions during the following forty years were formally modified by the last Parliament of the communist era, based on an agreement with the democratic opposition. This modification encompassed every essential article of the constitution and the constitutional setup that legitimized the free parliamentary elections of 1990 and resulted in a democratically structured social life. As a *bon mot* of the day says, there was only one sentence left untouched from the communist constitution after the modification: The capital of Hungary is Budapest.

Budapest was the center of major changes in 1989–90, just as it had been ever since the 1848 revolution. At times during the course of history the political events of the capital sometimes had been violent and out of balance. On an everyday level the checks and balances from the dynamics of accumulated intellectual and financial resources promote advances and continuity in Budapest.

## Change of Regime and the First Years of the Democratic Local Governments

In Budapest as in the whole country the 1989–90 change of regime brought about a spectacular transformation in the political and public lives. Since the beginning of the 19th century every significant political change had been initiated in Pest, or in Budapest after the unification of 1873. It was no different in 1989–90, when all the important events took place in Budapest. The media also focused on the significant role of the city. The cliché that anything that is important takes place in Budapest has always been so much a part of popular thinking that it created reality. Budapest as a focal point of the national media enhanced its leading position by the end of this century. The media indicated that Budapest, in addition to being a place of highest significance, was also a center that synthesizes prevailing political thought, political currents and ideas of the moment for rural Hungary.

Budapest played a leading role during the change of regime, both symbolically and practically. Political demonstrations,negotiations and agreements to secure a peaceful transition all took place in Budapest. Although the Hungarian regime change was constitutional and followed similar changes in the Soviet Union, there were mass demonstrations indicating that people entering the road to democracy did not wish to turn back. Initially the demonstrations centered around issues of general interest such as the project for the construction of a Danube Dam and forced destructions of villages in Transylvania rather than political transformation. Thus the foundations of open public opposition toward the regime were paved by environmental and ethnic issues, usually taboo under communism.

The most significant political watershed, however, was the re-evaluation of the 1956 revolution and its martyred prime minister, Imre Nagy.[2] The accelerating transformation was marked by two events: a demonstration to commemorate Imre Nagy in the summer of 1988 violently broken up by the police and, less than a year later, in the reburial ceremonies of Imre Nagy and his martyred companions on *Hősök tere* [Heroes Square], with the participation of hundreds of thousands including the reform-communist government and the democratic opposition parties.

The most exciting breakthrough of the transition, however, happened in the media. Several taboos were overcome, beginning with the resurgence of a free press which helped destroy political barriers and open up the world information market to the Hungarian public.

Strenghthened by the free press, Budapest became the center of civic pride and courage among the opposition parties and the Opposition Roundtable. Budapest was also the site where the last communist government and the democratic opposition signed the agreement about the legal transition and the new constitution. The agreement specified that the Republic of Hungary would be officially declared in Budapest in front of the parliament on October 23, 1989, the 33rd anniversary of the 1956 October Revolution.

In the Spring of 1990 Budapest became the center for parliamentary election campaigns marking the end of the communist system. It was common knowledge that the party winning the elections in Budapest would win the national election. The Hungarian Democratic Forum (MDF) established in September 1987 and first totally ignored by the communist government, obtained a landslide victory in Budapest and in Hungary in 1990.[3]

The conservative coalition government (Hungarian Democratic Forum, Independent Smallholders Party, Christian-Democratic People's Party) as well as its liberal parliamentary opposition (the Alliance of Free Democrats, the Federation of Young Democrats) considered the local implementation of change essential; thus the Soviet-type council system was replaced by democratic local governments. The new parliament adopted its first bill on the local governing institutions. This was the first of the "two-third acts", reflecting the power structure in parliament since the conservative government coalition had to rely on the votes of the liberal opposition.[4]

Urged by the government coalition, the President of the Republic considered holding local elections as early as in September 1990, placing all parliamentary parties under pressure. If they did not wish to launch the activities of the new freely elected local governing bodies under the old council system, new legislation had to be created during the summer. With the consensus of the six parliamentary parties, but not without compromise, a new bill was adopted in August 1990. It assured free, independent local governing bodies even by European standards.

The new local governing system differs from the Soviet-type council system in the following ways: each settlement in the country is entitled to a self-governing local government, the local government is not subordinated to any other local government or to any state oganization, its activities are regulated only by provisions of law, it receives a substantial share of the state properties, and its income comes without discrimination from the central state budget.

The most significant achievement of the transition period both locally and nationally was to allow the electors to choose openly between the competing political views of parties and individual candidates by eliminating the monolithic, centrally and hierarchically operated political system. This gave way to a controlled, democratic, self-regulating political market.

A chapter of the Local Government Act deals with Budapest. It declares that a separate act should be drawn up about the local governing bodies of the capital. It is to be noted, that a paragraph ensures the dominance of the municipal body over the district bodies, as advocated by the conservative government coalition in line with previous expectations and historical tradition. The opposing Free Democrats, however, fearing a conservative victory even at the municipal level, insisted on regulations favoring the districts. This provision was to turn against the Free Democrats, since they won the municipal elections, and the framework devised by them raised difficulties in everyday issues.[5]

## The 1990 Local Elections

Following the adoption of the Local Government Act it was evident that the Budapest Municipal Act (which could have been created by simple majority, without the liberal opposition) was to be devised according to the election results. Fearing the government's victory would be replicated at the local levels, the two liberal parties (SZDSZ—Alliance of Free Democrats and the FIDESZ—Federation of Young Democrats) formed an alliance which resulted in an unexpected landslide victory both in the provincial towns and in Budapest. The election rules which are clear for the electors, although complex in computation, regulate parliamentary elections through individual and party lists for the 22 district local governing bodies, while only a party list exists for the municipal governing body.[6] Altogether 414 individual and 392 party list mandates were available for the local governing bodies of the 22 districts. From among the individual mandates 138 went to the SZDSZ-FIDESZ common candidates, as well as 119 to SZDSZ, and 76 to FIDESZ candidates. There were 333 liberals encompassing 80 per cent of the individual mandates. The parties of the conservative government coalition (MDF, KDNP, FKgP) received 68 mandates. (The Hungarian Socialist Party, the successor of the Communist Party received 10 per cent of the party list mandates and not a single one at the individual level.) SZDSZ received 118 and FIDESZ received 95 of the 392 district party list mandates. The parties of the conservative coalition won 138 party list mandates, while the Hungarian Socialist Party 31, and the Hungarian Socialist Workers' Party (the party with a communist program) 7. The overwhelming majority of district representatives were liberal: 19 districts elected SZDSZ mayors and two districts FIDESZ mayors out of a total of 22. The conservative coalition gained a majority only in the first (Castle) district where the mayor became an MDF member.[7]

In the Municipal Assembly, the body of representatives in the municipal government, 66 members were elected through the party list and 22 were delegated by the district governments. The end result of the party list election, including only the ones with a minimum of 4 per cent votes, was the following: SZDSZ 34.68 per cent (25 mandates), MDF 27.35 per cent (20 mandates), FIDESZ 18.16 per cent (13 mandates), MSZP 7.25 per cent (5 mandates), and KDNP 4.95 per cent (3 mandates). The 22 district governments, according to the agreement between the two liberal parties that opened the way for Gábor Demszky's election as mayor of Budapest, sent 10 SZDSZ, 10 FIDESZ, and two MDF delegates to the Municipal Assembly. 58 seates went to the liberal parties, 22 to MDF, five to MSZP, and three to KDNP in the 88 member Assembly.

## The Critical Days of the Young Democracy

The "taxi blockade" on October 26, 1990, is still considered to be the greatest crisis of the new democracy. This happened after the local elections but before the statutory meeting of the Municipal Assembly. Following the unexpected increase in gas prices, taxis occupied the vital strategic points of the transportation network all over the country, including Budapest. All Budapest bridges except one were blocked, and only ambulances and fire engines were allowed to cross. The Budapest surface traffic was paralyzed, although the subway continued to function. People had to walk or stay at home. Fear of a clash and its consequences was growing. But democracy acquitted itself well. Extremism did not prevail and negotiations between the government and the blockade leaders were successful on the third day. By the evening of October 28 the blockade, which evoked painful memories especially among the older generations, was lifted in Budapest and the whole country.

## Local Governments after 1990

Both the Mayor of Budapest, Gábor Demszky, elected at the statutory meeting of the Municipal Assembly on October 31, 1990, and the district mayors inherited difficult problems from their predecessors. Although the local councils—unlike the state government—did not leave a debt behind, they did leave problems unsolved. The relative backwardness and shabbiness of the Budapest infrastructure, the deteriorating social situation, environmental pollution, and the growing problems of public security had to be confronted and solved within a couple of electoral cycles by an almost completely new list of local officials.[8]

The cooperation among municipal and local governments after the liberal victory could have been ideal, but the possibility of a united front soon dissipated. The "time bomb" built into the Local Government Act was that 23 equal local governments (22 district governments and the municipal government) were supposed to cooperate voluntarily without daily conflicts between the two levels.

Once election results became known, the conservative coalition abandoned its own stand about the dominance of the municipal level and enacted a municipal act based on extensive decentralization. The essence of the Act was that there would be a unique two-tiered local governing system in the capital with an elected body of representatives in each district and in the municipal government. According to the Act there would be 23 local governments in Budapest: 22 district and a municipal government functioning on the same territory. The district and municipal governments are equal. With respect to their tasks, activities, institutions, and properties, the district governments are independent, even when placed in international context. Primary education and certain secondary schools are supervised by district governments. All the apartment buildings in a district, other properties in the area, and real estate that used to belong to the local councils would now belong to the district governments. Moreover, authorizing detailed growth plans for the city is a significant part of their activities.

According to the Act the municipal level is a government with a wide range of responsibilities, but a limited sphere of authority. Its responsibilities include mass transportation, public sanitation, maintenance of main thoroughfares, water, gas, and district heating, townplanning, sewage, flood and internal water control, and public cemeteries. The municipal government also runs hospitals, social, cultural, and educational institutions including secondary schools.

The sphere of activity of the municipal government has been especially limited in the area of town-planning, drafting the budget, and passing ordinances. According to this Act a general town-planning project is to be endorsed by the municipal level and a detailed town-planning project by the district governments. The municipal government allotted the proper share of the national budget to the local governments, but with the consent of the district governments' majority. Since there is no hierarchical relationship between the municipal and district ordinances, there remains uncertainty in areas not regulated by exact rules.

The decision that the Alliance of Free Democrats (SZDSZ) and the Federation of Young Democrats (FIDESZ) not to become a government coalition further complicated the ambiguous situation of the municipal government. The FIDESZ strategy of the day stressed differences with the SZDSZ. City Hall was the site of everyday negotiations between the two parties, although SZDSZ governed as a minority in Budapest. In practice, the two parties governed the city up to the end of 1994 in a dispute-ridden coalition.

The basic philosophy of the municipal government was acceptance of responsibility for satisfying the needs of the public, that was to define strategies and methods, and the negotiations about them. The results of the negotiations gained practical meaning in the figures of the local budget. Internationally compared, the Hungarian local governments' share of the GDP is outstanding with its 15 per cent.[9] The economic importance of the towns and specifically Budapest is significant. The municipal government stands out with its expenses that surpass 125 billion forints in 1996.[10] The Budapest local governments, including the municipal and district governments, had a budget of 250 billion forints[11] in 1995.

The Local Government Act provides high responsibility for the local governments contributing as well to the transition from the centrally planned economies to a market economy, as real freedom at the local levels has enhanced the mobilization of resources.

However, the new system has generated its own problems, too. One is, that the monetary and fiscal policy of the central government obviously influences the resources and consequently the development strategies of the local governments.

Central governments in the region of the transitional countries recognized that it is easier to influence local governments through financial regulation than through legal-administrative means. Central governments try to shift the economic deficit at least partially onto the local governments.

Local government revenues can be described by the following categories: local own-source taxes and revenues, shared taxes and central grants.
In Hungary, average own-source funds account for 25 per cent of all revenues and shered taxes for less than 10 per cent, while central transfers
account for almost two-third of revenues. The financial system changes
year by year, and it can be illustrated by the personal income tax (PIT)
transfer. The annual Budget Acts determine the share of the total PIT revenue that is transferred to the local level, on the basis of derivation. This
was 100 per cent in 1991, 50 per cent in 1992, 30 per cent in 1993–94,
and 35 per cent in 1995.

The major items in the local budget that the municipality can directly
influence are those included in "own revenues": local taxes and proceeds
from the sale of assets. After lengthy negotiations between the districts and
the Municipality of Budapest the potentially most important local taxes
were "shared" between the two levels of administration: the property tax
became district revenue while turnover tax was allocated mainly to the
municipality.

The latter, property tax, is a significant revenue source for the municipality, accounting for approximately 17 per cent of its revenues (excluding
social security transfers). The sale of assets is also a potentially substantial
revenue source, however, is very volatile: in 1996 and 1997 it should
exceed the amount of turnover tax but later it is expected to fall back to
a much lower level.

Regular revenues from taxes and grants have not kept pace with inflation—with the local governments' regular expenditure, with the operating
costs of their institutions. In such a situation there is always a great temp-
tation to use non-regular resources (revenues from selling assets) for financing regular tasks, in the long run using up assets.

The refusal of this approach is a key element in the budget strategy of
the Municipality of Budapest. In its philosophy operational costs can be
financed only from regular resources.

However, the 7-year forecast of municipality revenues and expenditures clearly show the problems on the revenue side: regular revenues
cannot be expected to match inflation up to 2000.

At the same time, keeping up the level of urban services demand a
certain amount of investments, about 20 per cent of the annual budget.
Regular income cannot finance the whole of the necessary investments,
while one-time resources (selling assets, privatization) will essentially dry
up in two-three years.

The financial leadership of the municipality treats this relatively short period a chance. The aim is to reach 20 per cent surplus (operational surplus) in the balance of regular incomes and operational costs. This surplus is to cover the financing of the necessary investments at a time when one-time resources exhaust.

In the next few years the municipality plans to apply restrictions on operational costs on the one hand. On the other hand investments should be concentrated first of all to encourage innovations in the operation of institutions, which leads to lower operating costs. To achieve this aim, investment funds have been created to increase the efficiency of the institutions. The savings in operating costs of the institutions are expected to be high and to lead to a more balanced budget in the long run.

The structure of expenditures diverge at the municipal and district levels. The district governments spend primarily on operational maintenance while the municipal government appears also as a main investor in the infrastructure and communal investment market. The table below shows the total expenses and the investment totals between 1990 and 1995.

| Expenses | 1990 | 1991 | 1992 | 1993 | 1994 | 1995 |
|---|---|---|---|---|---|---|
| | In billion forints | | | | | |
| **Municipal Government** | | | | | | |
| Total Expenses | 49.1071 | 54.8507 | 65.4306 | 74.1468 | 92.0456 | 115.4019 |
| Development, Investments | 8.7069 | 6.9585 | 10.6346 | 14.2513 | 21.7816 | 24.7588 |
| Ratio of developmental to total expenses (%) | 17.7 | 12.7 | 16.2 | 20.8 | 23.7 | 21.5 |
| **District Governments** | | | | | | |
| Total Expenses | 39.3659 | 48.9328 | 62.9302 | 97.7327 | 133.7596 | 140.2358 |
| Development, Investments | 4.5281 | 3.2247 | 7.6467 | 9.6880 | 12.4379 | 7.2064 |
| Ratio of developmental to total expenses (%) | 9.22 | 5.87 | 11.7 | 13.1 | 13.5 | 6.71 |

The above figures, reveal the politically cyclical nature of these investments as is the more moderate developmental rates. The investment rate increases both at the municipal and district levels in 1993–94, induced by the coming elections at the end of 1994.

The shift in investment strategy was significant beyond politics even in the election year of 1994 namely development consciousness gained priority in the management of the city, even at the expense of drastic cuts in operational expenses and the increase of bank loans.[12] The most important communal developments financed by public funds were managed as municipal government investments.[13]

The municipal investments often received significant state funds, despite the ongoing conflict between the liberal metropolitan and the conservative state governments between 1990–94. This controversy was manifested in the EXPO issue. EXPO, a category B world fair, originally planned in conjunction with Vienna and, after the latter's withdrawal, solely by Budapest, had generated sharp political debates. The conservative government coalition was pro-EXPO, while the liberal majority in the municipal government opposed the world fair.[14] After lengthy polemics and secret negotiations, an inevitable compromise was concluded. By this agreement the government secured funding for several major municipal projects—inevitable for the future of the city—in return for the "yes" vote of the municipal government. The compromise, however, became inoperative after the 1994 government change. The social-liberal government and the parliament cancelled the world fair.

Significant municipal government developments—also in connection with EXPO—have been implemented since 1993–94. The leadership of the municipal council changed its basic concepts and launched new development projects instead of applying the concept of operational preservation. The construction of the *Lágymányosi* Bridge in South-Budapest,[15] the first new Budapest bridge since World War II, was such a project. The bridge and the full length of the connecting *Hungária* Boulevard, envisioned already in the first half of the century, were inaugurated in 1995. With World Bank and EBRD (European Bank for Reconstruction and Development) loans the metropolitan bus fleet was modernized, streetcars, rail lines renovated on a large scale, and the full reconstruction of the old subway line (constructed in 1896 as first on the European continent) implemented. The latter involved the complete reconstruction of *Andrássy* Street, the most elegant avenue in Budapest. The reconstruction of *Vígszínház* [Comic Theater], originally built for the first millennial celebration of the arrival of the Hungarians in the Carpathian Basin, was completed along with the reconstruction of the Central Market Hall, the largest traditional market hall in Central Europe, also dating from a hundred years ago.

Less spectacular but equally important and expensive infrastructural investments were completed in this period: the sewage systems, wastewater purifiers, and the dumps. Smaller but pleasing projects for the inhabitants of the capital were also launched: the playground and park refurbishing program, alley and avenue reconstruction, transformation of the southern segment of *Váci* street, the best-known shopping street, into a pedestrian zone, and the modernization of street and flood-lights. One comes across new construction sites on a daily basis which, apart from the momentary irritation, are promising sights.

A continuous publicity campaign accompanied the projects; consequently the mayor has become very popular. Gábor Demszky became one of the bestknown politicians nationally. In 1996 a new slogan appeared on the information boards of the construction sites, reflecting the general atmosphere: "The city gained momentum."

This momentum was gained not only by local government investments, the rate of which is not too high: 5–10 per cent for all public and private projects. The strongest impetus came from foreign capital. Half of the total capital invested in ex-communist countries (not including the GDR) came to Hungary and more than 60 per cent of that was utilized in Budapest. Between 1990 and 1995 one third of the total 24 billion dollar foreign investment in Eastern Europe, that is about 8 billion dollars landed in Budapest. (More than 70 per cent of this capital was contributed by four countries: Germany, Austria, the United States and Holland.)

Besides the impact investment had on industrial production, there was also a spectacular change in the supply of consumer goods. There was a sudden quantitative and qualitative increase in privatized stores. The number of stores grew from 20,000 in 1991 to over 31,000 by 1994, while the number of catering industry units increased to over 9,200 from 6,500—an overall expansion of 50 per cent within three years. Obviously, it is not only the number of the stores that increased. Significant amounts were invested in the renovation, modernization of existing units, too.

The development of the telephone system, an archaic remnant from the communist era, was also connected to privatization. The number of private lines increased from 330,000 to 490,000 by 1994, and the public phones from 120,000 to 160,000. Development during these four years outpaced that of any previous decade.

As a result of one-time foreign investments many facets of the town-scape changed: a multitude of office buildings, shopping centers were created either as new investments or as complete reconstructions of old, deteriorated buildings. Banks and insurance companies built or renovated appealing, impressive headquarters. By 1996 there were 53 different banks and financial institutions and 20 insurance companies in Budapest. Thus Budapest has an opportunity to become the financial center of the East-Central European region.

The years following the change of regime did not breed solely success and progress. There are many losers in the deep social structural changes and certain areas deteriorated immensely following 1989–90. The deterioration affected several spheres the population Budapest is most sensitive about: public safety, employment, home construction, public hygiene, and mass transportation.

## The 1994 Local Elections

At the local elections held in December 1994 the city population voted about the accomplishment of the city development policies and their directions, both at the municipal and district levels. Voting for parties[16] rather than personalities was a decisive political experience for the young democracy.

The parliamentary elections in the spring of 1994 brought a landslide victory for the Hungarian Socialist Party, the successor of the Communist Party. This victory matched the general trend in East-Central Europe. In 28 of the 32 individual electoral districts in Budapest the socialist candidate won the seat while the Hungarian Democratic Forum, the governing conservative party won only four. The Hungarian Socialist Party gained a 54 per cent absolute majority in parliament and formed a coalition government with the Alliance of Free Democrats. Thus social-liberal government coalition gained 72 per cent of the seats in parliament, exceeding the 67 per cent majority, required for passing laws in "qualified" special cases.

Since the government coalition supported by the media did not lose popularity following its formation, another victory was expected at the local elections. This expectation and the change of legislative rules covering local elections compelled three parliamentary opposition parties

(Federation of Young Democrats, Christian Democratic People's Party, and the Hungarian Democratic Forum) to establish a national coalition called the Civil Alliance. The Hungarian Socialist Party, trusting its own power, did not bother to form an alliance with its own coalition partner. Three significant forces competed for the mandates in the local elections in the winter of 1994: the Hungarian Socialist Party; the liberal Alliance of Free Democrats; and the conservative alliance (the latter often in alliance with the Independent Smallholders, who were also in opposition and pursued an independent national policy). The confidence of the Hungarian Socialist Party was not justified: none of the three blocs competing for seats was able to gather a majority—which translated into a moral victory for the oppositon alliance according to the political climate of the day.

As a result of modifications of regulation in 1994 the mayor of every settlement was elected directly (as opposed to the earlier practice when a body of representatives elected the mayor in case of settlements of over 10,000 people). The local campaigns became more personal with the candidates often reflecting personal ties to their constituents. This election favored the incumbents; two thirds of them were reelected nation-wide.

A different lesson of the two elections in 1994 was that people expressed their party preference at the parliamentary elections but voted for political personalities at the local ones. Since the party list election system was operative in municipal election, a divergence in the number of ballots for mayoral candidates and the parties they represented can be observed. The chief beneficiary of this divergence at Budapest was the Free Democrat Gábor Demszky while the real loser was Etele Baráth, the Socialist candidate. The votes cast at the Budapest party lists was the following: MSZP won 30.03 per cent, FIDESZ-KDNP-MDF 27.03 per cent, SZDSZ 26.83 per cent and FKgP-MIÉP 10.28 per cent. The government coalition parties, MSZP and SZDSZ, entered into coalition in the municipal assembly as well, thus gained a secure 60 per cent majority of votes.

A substantial number of the constituents divided their votes. The mayoral candidates of the different qualifying parties received votes in the following proportion: Gábor Demszky (Alliance of Free Democrats) 36.28 per cent, János Latorczai (Federation of Young Democrats—Christian Democratic People's Party—Hungarian Democratic Forum) 28.42 per cent, Etele Baráth (Hungarian Socialist Party) 26.17 per cent, and János Szabó (Independent Smallholders/ MIÉP) 5.66 per cent. Gábor Demszky's personal triumph is evident, since the rate of votes given to him personally surpasses the rate of votes given to his party by nearly 50 per cent. His success is even more significant if the district election results are examined, since he most probably helped the Free Democrats' municipal party list results also. The party distribution of the district election seats, which due to the change of the local government law can be considered vote proportionate, evolved along the following lines among the three main political forces: Hungarian Socialist Party 35.28 per cent, FIDESZ-KDNP-MDF 33.48 per cent, and SZDSZ 16.29 per cent. Twelve of the directly elected district mayors won as candidates of the conservative Civil Alliance. Three out of these twelve were also supported by the SZDSZ. This fact indicates the success of the center right election coalition. Independently the MSZP got four mayors elected, the SZDSZ three, and three mayors won as common MSZP–SZDSZ candidates. In one district an independent candidate, the mayor under the previous cycle, won.

The political palette in December 1994 became more colorful than after the 1990 liberal victory in the local elections. In the previous cycle when the municipal and district governments enjoyed practically the same legal status, so many "colors" would have led to serious political disfunction in the capital. In the summer of 1994, after the parliamentary elections, but before the local governmental elections, the Local Government Act was modified to the advantage of the municipal level. This modification slightly moved the structure of local governments in the capital towards the model that prevails in Europe. The most important change was that the municipal government has got the final word on the distribution of regular central grants financing the services provided by the municipal and the district governments. However, every year the municipality launches a process of bargaining, through which it gains the approval of the majority of the districts for the reallocation of these resources. Beyond the effort for a justifiable reallocation, bargaining is a must too, because it is not in the interest of the municipality to confront with the districts that have remained strong enough even after the amendment of the Local Government Act. With increased authority the municipal government was able to avoid the political trench warfare of the past, despite the heterogenous election results.

## Day-to-day Silent Revolution

Multitudes of changes occurred in the everyday lives of the inhabitants as a result of the change of regime and by the substitution of the last "soft" dictatorship of the communist era with the political and social institutions of a democratic society. For the seventh time in the 20th century the Hungarian people experienced radical political change. The 1989–90 change can be compared to the 1948–49 communist takeover in significance. In 1948 a 40-year-long experiment in tyranny impacted upon the social fabric of the country and diverted Hungary from the European model. Although from the 1960s the government gave its citizens relatively the most freedom among the communist countries, nontheless 40 years inflicted deep injuries upon society. Because of the limited rights of the citizens and the lack of free market, generations grew up without experiencing the methods, values, advantages and shortcomings of western societies.

From the 1980s, as the communist regime softened, economic opportunities for various enterprises increased with a flow of goods and information between East and West. Hence, the accelerated social and political processes of the 1989–90 transition did not create either a shock or euphoria, while the quantity, quality, and the speed of change entailed mayor modifications in everyday lives.

The liberation of market powers was the most crucial point. Suddenly items formerly unobtainable became available.[17] The novelty of this opening was an explosive growth of supply; everything and everybody had a price. State subsidies ceased and inflation surged.[18] The market economy influenced the rate of employment also; some fared well while many were squeezed out of the labor market, or faced a gradually deteriorating financial situation.

The most spectacular breakthrough brought about by the regime change was the free flow of information. The triumph of freedom of opinion and of the press, the free access to authors and publications banned earlier, brought a boom in the media: a multitude of magazines were published, the number of copies of published books achieved records, cable television and satellite channels became available. The written and electric media style diverged. The altered linguistic paradigm impacted thinking. The rich information supply previously unavailable to many citizens mostly conveyed the images of western lifestyle that quickly reshaped behavioral patterns, consumption attitudes, and ideas about the world.

# Demography

Demographic trends are indicative of the lifestyle of a community. In this respect Budapest has shown little change over the years. The number of marriages has decreased. The average during the 1970s was almost 20,000 weddings annually; through a continuous downward trend, the number decreased to 9,500. The birthrate has declined also, with an average of 27,000 in the 1970s to 17,000 by 1994, while the number of deaths was 30,000 annually over the past 25 years. As a result, the population of the capital showed a regular decrease of 10,000 a year between 1980 and 1994. Yet the total population number did not significantly decrease because of migration into Budapest. Altogether the population of the capital decreased by little more than 60,000 people between 1980 and 1993. Due to the drop by the end of 1993 less than 2 million people remained in the capital, dropping to the level of 25 years earlier. The population tends to age in the 1990s. By the end of 1995 more than half a million pensioners lived in Budapest, that is 28 per cent of the total population of the capital compared with 26 per cent in 1990. Based on these tendencies the General Organizational Plan of the capital projects 1.7 million inhabitants in Budapest by 2015.

# Housing Development

Housing conditions—contrary to common opinion—have slowly improved. The relation of population to available dwellings attest to it: the gradual increase in the number of dwellings in the capital, coupled with the decrease of the population result in a lower ratio of people per apartment: in 1980 2.83, in 1990 2.54, and in 1995 2.38 people per dwelling. The relative improvement in the 1990s is due to the population decrease since the rate of home constructions decreased radically after the change of regime.

The decreasing tendency is not new. From the mid-1980s on, along with the deteriorationg financial situation of the country, the state and the local councils gradually withdrew from constructions and after 1990 apartment building construction financed by public resources were discontinued. By way of illustration, in 1995 only one per cent of the total number of newly constructed dwellings in Budapest (total of 3,354) was financed by state or local government. The private sector was unable to take over the growing financial burdens of housing construction, since not only were the state investments discontinued, but the state subventions for private constructions dwindled. By 1995 the number of housing constructions plunged to 20 per cent of the rate registered in 1980, sinking under the lowpoint of Great Depression in the 1930s.

The post-1990 vigorous privatization of properties owned by the local governments is another characteristic of the period. The natural human desire for ownership accelerated this process coinciding with the intention of the district governments to rid themselves of burdensome maintenance obligations, once state subsidies disappeared. According to new regulations those renting government housing could purchase them at a favorable price. The price was well under the market value which was motivation enough to disregard future maintenance expenses. Compared with the 50 per cent rate before the change of regime, by 1995 the rate of housing owned by local governments dropped under 20 per cent in the capital.

Besides the drop in housing units owned by local government, a market for renting private homes has developed. The rents, however, are so high that this option is available only to a small fraction of the population. The monthly rent for a typical two-room apartment, not including utilities, reaches the level of the average monthly net salary. Housing is still the most significant problem for hundreds of thousands in the capital.

Housing privatization had a gratifying socio-psychological effects: the notion of ownership, de-emphasized by forty years of communism, now returned. Even the conditions of the former state owned apartment buildings improved after privatization. Private sources, however meager, were more efficiently utilized for maintenance and repair than state distributed subsidies used to be. At the same time the poor state of repair[19] of the apartment buildings in the capital, because renovation projects were repeatedly cancelled during the four decades, reached a critical level. Because hundreds of billions of forints are needed for massive housing renovations, a real "apartment bomb" is ticking away in Budapest.

## Public Security

One of the most sensitive issues is the nation-wide deterioration of public security in the period following the change of regime. It is a complex issue combined with the deteriorating social status for vast layers of society, a growing gap in living standards, an underfinanced police force, the slowness of the courts, and new opportunities offered by increased freedom. The deterioration of public security affects the whole country, yet the most afflicted site, with a growing metropolitan crime rate, is Budapest.

In 1990 the number of recorded crimes exceeded 100,000 (versus 50,000 per year in the mid-1980s. This figure grew another 30 per cent in 1991, then, after a slight decline, it settled to about 130,000 by 1994. 100,000 of these are crimes against property. The inhabitants have to adjust to a higher criminal hazard against property and less personal safety. The situation is the same in most metropolitan areas of the world, yet the deterioration of public security has become a major liability in the life in Budapest. According to public surveys, improvement in public security is the greatest concern of the citizens of Budapest.

## City Transportation

Experts and tourists entertain high regards for public transportation of Budapest. Although the inhabitants of the capital are never fully satisfied with the level of a public utilities, public transportation has been considered convenient. This is a significant result when the rate of people using public and private transportation was 80 per cent in the early 1980s. Ten years later, this rate was still 70 per cent, indicating a very high ration of people relying on public services.

The shift in ratios is due to the sudden increase in the number of private cars. While in 1985 360,000 cars were registered in Budapest, in 1994 there were 200,000 more. The number of cars per 1,000 is almost 300. This is short of other Western European city rates, but the difference is insignificant. For example there were 360 cars per 1,000 inhabitants in Vienna in the early 1990s.

In addition to the larger number of cars in circulation and the expanding circle of owners own different makes of cars from before. Eastern-bloc makes have been relegated to the background and Western-European, American, and Japanese models took over. This spectacular shift was due mostly to the influx of used cars,[20] but luxury cars have also found a good market.[21] From the early 1990s the vehicular traffic in the city started to resemble the scene in West-European cities both in intensity and makes.

Maintaining public transportation, through subsidizing the Budapest Transportation Company, is one of the largest expenses of the municipal government. The subsidy amounted to nearly 10 billion forints in 1995, which is more than the total annual budget of a Hungarian town of 100,000. Due to accelerated inflation even this vast subsidy began losing its value. The Company had to resort to gradual price hikes, to spacing vehicle routes, and even to cancelling certain lines.[22]

## Cultural Life

Budapest is the second largest city (Berlin being number one) of Central Europe. It has been offering a wide range of cultural events. The change of regime meant liberation of cultural activities from political supervision, narrow-minded taboos, limitations, censors at different levels. Unpublished, unplayed, prohibited works of art became suddenly available. The liberation, however, brought about a serious problem: government subsidies of cultural products has diminished. The decrease in the real value of cultural subsidy resulted in a significant price increase and consequently a major setback in demand in most cultural areas.[23]

Although the demand for cultural products decreased in Budapest also, the more concentrated demand of the population of the capital, coupled with state and local support, made preservation of important cultural values, even their expansion possible. Smaller cultural enterprises needing lower investment have multiplied. Video stores, small art galleries, alternative theater companies, dance and theater studios, pubs with live music have multiplied. Even so patrons have not abandoned traditional institutions in critical numbers. Based on comparative data it can be established that cultural consumption in Hungary, and especially in Budapest, does not lag behind the Western European level.[24]

Budapest with its cultural offerings has become one of the most exciting European cities by the early 1990s; witness its theater life. In Budapest 139 plays were presented in one week in the spring of 1995 as opposed to 150 plays featured in London, with its 8 million inhabitants.

Art films are also outstanding; Budapest is third in Europe, after Paris and London, in this respect. The company owned by the municipal government runs an "art cinema" network that supplies films for 800,000 spectators a year. Budapest is also the center of the world famous Hungarian music culture and pedagogy, as well as of other branches of the fine arts, including establishments for teaching, shows, and professional publications.

In spite of the economic difficulties the cultural life of the capital is thriving. Its cultural atmosphere is enhanced by the presence of cultural institutions, programs, natural[25] and architectural potentials. Historical remains with Celtic and Roman ruins serve as backdrops for modern culture; Turkish baths are still active today; the city boasts of baroque and classical buildings of the Castle district, and turn of the century eclectic city blocs.

As with every spirited city, the attractions of Budapest have been sung in the first seven decades of the century. Generations have sung and will sing them. "Budapest, Budapest, you wonder...", "My Paris is Pest, I always dream about it ...", "My heart is yours, Budapest". The residents do not simply live in this city but have a relationship with it that might be loving, impulsive, devoted or argumentative. Budapest this versatile, whimsical and lively town has a secure future as long as it can captivate people.

# Notes

1. Editors' note: No 84 in our series deals with this epoch in Béla K. Király and András Bozóki (eds) *Lawful Revolution in Hungary*, 1989–94 (1995).
2. One of the pillars and taboos of the Kádár regime was that the 1956 Revolution had to be referred to as a counter-revolution.
3. The strong contender for the Budapest election, the liberal Alliance of Free Democrats, SZDSZ managed to obtain only nine of the 32 mandates, while the Hungarian Democratic Forum obtained 23.
4. The successor of the communist party, the Hungarian Socialist Party, received 10 per cent of the votes and became a parliamentary party but it was under "political quarantine" in the first parliamentary period, its opinion was not considered.
5. The daily negotiations with the 22 districts (20 Free Democrats) turned out to be the most arduous task of the City Mayor, the Free Democrat Gábor Demszky elected in the Fall of 1990.
6. In 1990 in Budapest the mayors were elected by bodies of representatives rather than directly by citizens, reenforcing the "weak mayor strong council" model that was often applied during the communist era to counterbalance totalitarian rule.
7. The territorial distribution was not even. It was evident that certain electoral districts had party preferences. This was particularly true of the more affluent

I, II, XI, and XII districts where the conservative parties fared well all the elections between 1990 and 1994.

8. The dimensions of personnel changes and the total replacement of the political elite are illustrated by the fact that there was only one member in the 88-member General Assembly who had served in the previous Municipal Council of the communist era.

9. In Western Europe only Denmark approaches this rate, while in Holland and Italy it is around 1 per cent.

10. 6 per cent of the Hungarian national budget.

11. About 2 billion dollars (in 1995 forints).

12. In 1992 the municipal government obtained one billion forints in loan and almost 12 billion forints in 1995.

13. The district governments are responsible for building maintenance and local, smaller investments.

14. The EXPO debate had an individual history side with Etelka Pataky Barsiné being the 1990 rival of Gábor Demszky for the office of city mayor. She also became the leader of the opposition Hungarian Democratic Forum faction in the Municipal Assembly and was EXPO government commissioner. The 1994 socialist rival, Etele Baráth was an EXPO government commissioner on behalf of the last reform-communist goverment prior to Etelka Pataky Barsiné.

15. In 1944 during the siege of Budapest the Germans blew up all eight of the Budapest bridges. Their reconstruction was completed by the mid-1960s. Prior to Lágymányosi Bridge, a new, temporary bridge had already been constructed in Budapest, the Kossuth Bridge at the Parliament which served the capital between 1945 and 1961.

16. Prior to December 1994 there was no relevant experience at the local level since the 1990 local elections were without antecedents. The 1990 landslide liberal victory was a similar experience since people tended to vote for parties rather than persons, at least in large towns.

17. A significant mass demonstration of the late 1980s, a symbolic criticism of the regime, took place on April 4, 1989, a national holiday hailing the Soviet Union, when 150,000 people crossed the Hungarian-Austrian border on a shopping spree, causing immense traffic jams.

18. The average annual rate of inflation was 20–30 per cent between 1990 and 1995.

19. In the downtown area 50 per cent of the apartments were built before the turn of the century.

20. In 1994 the average registered car was ten years old in Budapest.

21. In early 1995 speaking in Parliament the Minister of Finance alluded to the much richer Austria that did not have so many S 600 Mercedes as Hungary.

22. 50 per cent of the 1.5 billion passengers using public transportation travel by bus. Hence the 15 per cent decrease, between 1992 and 1995 from 181 to 152 lines was significant.

23. While the general price level increased twofold between 1990 and 1993, the price of theater and museum tickets tripled, the books cost 3 or 4 times more, and movie tickets four or five times more.

24. Paradoxically, the relative decrease of consumers means real value, since the present demand is based on real consumers' preference as opposed to the organized nature of culture during the communist era.

25. Beyond its magnificent location, Budapest is a unique metropolis with its many spas.

# Name Index

# Biographies of Key Personalities

Aczél, György (1917–91), Communist party official. Highest cultural executive of Hungary from the late 1950s to the late 1980s.

Adorján, Bishop of Transylvania between 1190 and 1201, head of the royal chancellery as Provost of Buda in 1186.

Ady, Endre (1877–1919), poet and journalist, the greatest figure of literary and intellectual revival in the early 20th century.

Ajtay, Andor (1903–75), actor.

Albrecht Kasimir (1738–1822), Prince of Saxony and Teschen, Governor of Hungary between 1765 and 1780.

Albrecht of Habsburg (1817–95), Austrian archduke, Duke of Teschen, civil and military governor of Hungary between 1851 and 1860.

Alexander Leopold of Habsburg (1772–95), Palatine of Hungary.

Andersen, Hans Christian (1805–75), Danish writer, author of fairy-tales, visited Pest-Buda.

Andrássy, Count Gyula, Sr. (1823–90), Prime Minister between 1867 and 1871, Minister of Foreign Affairs of the Austro-Hungarian Monarchy until 1879.

Andropov, Yuri Vladimirovich (1914–84), Soviet Ambassador to Hungary in 1954–57, later chairman of the *KGB* or State Security Committee, Chairman of the Presidium of the Supreme Soviet in 1983–84.

Anjou dynasty—a reigning family of French origin. At the death in 1301 of Andrew III, the last ruler of the Arpad dynasty, Charles Robert, a member of the Anjou dynasty became King of Hungary.

Anonymus, notary of King Béla III (1172–96). In his chronicle *Gesta Hungarorum* he recorded the history of the Hungarian people from the earliest days.

Aristov, Averki Borisovich (1903–73), Secretary of the Central Committee of the Communist Party of the Soviet Union between 1955 and 1960.

Árkay, Bertalan (1901–71), architect.

Árpád (d. ca. 907), Prince bearing the title *gyula*, founding father of the Árpád dynasty.

Babits, Mihály (1883–1941), Catholic poet and novelist, translator of literary works.

Bajoŕ, Gizi (1893–1951), actress.

Bajza, József (1804–58), poet, critic, journalist, stage manager.

Bali, Sándor (1923–82), toolmaker, during the Revolution of 1956 a leader of the Central Workers' Council of Greater Budapest.

Barabás, Miklós (1810–98), portrait-artist in the Romantic and Biedermeier styles.

Baráth, Etele (1942–), engineer and politician. Member of Parliament for the Hungarian Socialist Party, government commissioner of the projected world exhibition of 1990–92.

Bárczy, István (1866–1943), lawyer, liberal politician. Mayor of Budapest between 1906 and 1918, Chief Mayor in 1918–19.

Bárdos, Artúr ((1882–1974), theater-manager, director, playwright.

Barkóczy, Ferenc (1710–65), Bishop of Eger, later Archbishop of Esztergom.

Barsiné Pataky, Etelka (1941–), engineer and politician. Member of Parliament. Member of the Budapest General Assembly in 1990–94. High Commissioner of the projected world exhibition (EXPO) in 1992–94.

Bársony, Rózsi (1909–77), actress, operetta singer.

Bartók, Béla (1881–1945), composer, pianist, musicologist, a prominent composer of modern music who created a universally valid musical language expressing the contemporary world.

Basilides, Mária (1886–1946), opera singer. The best interpreter of Bartók and Kodály.

Báthy, Anna (1901–62), opera singer.

Batu (ca. 1206–55), first Khan of the Golden Horde between 1227 and 1255. Grandson of Genghis Khan. He conquered the Russian principalities and led campaigns against Poland, Bohemia, and Hungary.

Beatrice of Aragon (1457–1508), Queen of Hungary, daughter of Ferdinand I of Aragon, King of Naples, second wife of Matthias Corvinus, King of Hungary between 1476 and 1490.

Béla III (1148–96), of the Árpád dynasty, King of Hungary from 1172 to his death.

Béla IV (1206–70), of the Árpád dynasty, King of Hungary from 1235 to his death. Rebuilt the country after the Mongol invasion of 1241–42.

Bem, József (Josef) (1794–1850), Polish army officer, fought in the Hungarian Revolution and war of independence of 1848–49 as a general.

Bernáth, Aurél (1895–1982), painter.

Bessenyei, Ferenc (1919–), actor, member of the *Nemzeti Színház* [National Theater] and *Madách Színház* [Madách Theater].

Bethlen, István, Count (1874–1947), Prime Minister between 1921 and 1931. Opposed one-sided pro-German attitudes, becoming a leading politician of Anglo-American orientation.

Bibó, István (1911–79), lawyer, political philosopher, university professor. Leading member of the Petőfi Party from October 31, 1956, minister without portfolio in Imre Nagy's cabinet in November that year.

Biszku, Béla (1921–), Communist party functionary, Minister of the Interior between 1957 and 1961.

Bódy, Tivadar (1868–1934), lawyer, politician. Deputy mayor of Budapest between 1913 and 1918, then mayor until 1920.

Bognár, József (1917–96), politician of the Smallholders' Party. Minister of Trade between 1949 and 1956.

Bókay, János (1892–1961), writer and playwright.

Bonfini, Antonio (b. between 1427 and 1434, d. in 1502), Italian humanist historian. Lived at the Buda court of King Matthias Corvinus from the autumn of 1486.

Borostyáni, Nándor (1848–1902), journalist and writer. Editor of *Pesti Hírlap* between 1881 and 1885.

Brecht, Bertolt (1898–1956), German poet, playwright, and esthetician.

Brein, Ferenc (mid-19th century), architect, member of a distinguished dynasty of architects. Designed several Romantic buildings in Pest, the Pekáry House among them.

Bródy, Lili (1906–62), writer and journalist.

Bús-Fekete, László (1896–1971), playwright and script-writer.

Caracalla, Marcus Aurelius Antonius (186–217), Roman emperor from A.D. 211 to his death. He annexed the legionnaire camp *Brigetio* to Lower Pannonia.

Casimir III, the Great (1310–70), the last Polish king of the Piast dynasty between 1333 and 1370. Upon his death the Polish nobility elected the Hungarian King Louis I to rule Poland.

Cézanne, Paul (1839–1906), French painter, representative of post-impressionism.

Charles Louis John of Habsburg (1771–1847), Austrian archduke, Duke of Teschen. Minister of War from 1806, Commander-in-chief of the imperial army.

Charles of Habsburg (1887–1922), Emperor of Austria as Charles I, King of Hungary as Charles IV (1916–18).

Clark, Adam (1811–66), British engineer, building engineer of the *Lánchíd* (Chain Bridge), designer and engineer of the *Alagút* (Tunnel).

Clark, William Tierney (1783–1852), British designer of bridges, designed the *Lánchíd*. Visited Pest several times and wrote a book about *Lánchíd*.

Cs. Szabó, László (1905–84), writer, essayist, and critic.

Csorba, János (1897–1986), attorney, vice-chairman of the Liberation Committee of the Hungarian National Uprising in 1944.

Czuczor, Gergely (1800–66), Benedictine monk, teacher, poet, and linguist. Editor of the great dictionary issued by the Academy. Dramaturgist of the National Theater.

Dajka, Margit (1907–86), actress, primarily at the *Vígszínház* in Budapest.

Dayka, Gábor (1769–96), Catholic priest, teacher, and poet, faithful disciple of the Enlightenment.

Demény, Pál (1901–91), engineer, member of the Hungarian Communist Party from 1919. Arrested by the Communists in 1945, released from prison only in 1956. Member of Parliament from 1990 to his death.

Derkovits, Gyula (1894–1934), painter, representative of Hungarian art in the interwar years.

Déry, Tibor (1894–1977), writer. One of the leading figures of the literary opposition from 1955.

Dohnányi, Ernő (1877–1960), composer, pianist, and conductor. Professor, later director of the Music Academy of Budapest.

Donáth, Ferenc (1913–86), agricultural economist, Communist politician, member of the party opposition around Imre Nagy. Member of the provisional leadership of the Hungarian Socialist Workers' Party during the Revolution of 1956. From 1960 worked as a researcher and became a leading member of the democratic opposition in Hungary afterwards.

Döbrentei, Gábor (1785–1851), writer, translator, stage manager and editor.

Eckhart, Ferenc (1885–1957), historian, specializing in the history of law.

Elizabeth Amalia Eugenia of Wittelsbach (1837–98), daughter of Maximilian, Prince of Bavaria. Empress of Austria from 1854, Queen of Hungary from 1867.

Endre, László (1895–1946), politician of the extreme right. Played a prominent role in deporting Jews from Hungary.

Erdei, Ferenc (1910–71), politician, writer, sociologist, and agrarian economist. One of the founders of National Peasant Party in 1939. Minister without portfolio in the Imre Nagy cabinet during the Revolution of 1956.

Eugene of Savoy (1663–1736), imperial general, chairman of the Austrian War Council.

Failioni, Sergio (1890–1948), Italian conductor. Worked in Budapest between 1928 and 1945. Ardent advocate of the music of Bartók and Kodály.

Faragó, György (1913–44), pianist, professor at the Musical Academy of Budapest.

Fedák, Sári (1879–1955), actress.

Fehér, Lajos (1917–81), Communist party functionary, responsible for agricultural policies.

Féja, Géza (1900–78), writer, journalist, a significant figure of the Hungarian populist writers' movement.

Fejér, György (1766–1851), historian, university professor. Director of the University Library from 1824.

Fejérváry, Géza (1833–1914), army officer, Minister of Defence between 1884 and 1903. Commander of the Hungarian Royal Guardsmen (1904–5 and 1906–12), Prime Minister in 1905–1906.

Fejtő, Ferenc (1909–), writer, historian, and critic. A founder of the urbanist periodical *Szép Szó* in 1936, and its first editor.

Fenyő, Miksa (1877–1972), critic, editor, and liberal politician. A founder of the periodical *Nyugat* and executive director of the Hungarian National Manufacturers' Association for many years.

Ferdinand I of Habsburg (1503–64), King of Bohemia and Hungary between 1526 and 1564. Holy Roman Emperor between 1556 and 1564.

Ferdinand V of Habsburg (1793–1875), Emperor of Austria and King of Hungary between 1835 and 1848.

Ferenczy, Béni (1890–1967), sculptor.

Ferenczy, Noémi (1890–1957), painter and tapestry-weaver.

Ferencsik, János (1907–84), conductor.

Feszl, Frigyes (1821–84), architect, outstanding representative of Romanticism in Hungary. Designer of the *Vigadó* (Music Hall) built between 1859 and 1864.

Fischer, Annie (1914–95), pianist.

France, Anatole (1844–1924), French writer.

Francis I (1768–1835), Holy Roman Emperor from 1792, Emperor of Austria from 1804, King of Hungary and Bohemia between 1792 and 1835.

Francis Joseph I of Habsburg (1830–1916), Emperor of Austria from 1848, King of Hungary (1867–1916).

Francis Stephen of Lorraine (1708–65), Grand Duke of Tuscany (1737–65), Holy Roman Emperor (1745–65), husband of Maria Theresa.

Frederick I (1123–90), Barbarossa, Holy Roman Emperor. Returning from the third crusade in 1189, he was received in Buda by King Béla III and his wife Margaret Capet.

Fülep, Lajos (1885–1970), philosopher of esthetics and art historian. University professor in Budapest (1946–61).

Füst, Milán (1888–1967), writer, playwright, poet, and esthetician.

Galeotto, Marzio (1427–97), Italian humanist writer and scholar, professor at the universities of Bologna and Padua. Stayed at the court of King Matthias Corvinus (1465–71, 1471–72, and 1478–79).

Gárdonyi, Géza (1863–1922), author of novels and short stories.

Gáspár, Zoltán (1901–45), journalist, editor of the periodical *Szép Szó* between 1937 and 1939.

Gelléri, Andor Endre (1906–45), writer.

Gellért, St., Gerardus (around 980–1046), Bishop of Csanád, author of the first book on theology produced in Hungary, entitled *Deliberatio*. Died a martyr in 1046.

Geringer, Karl Baron (1806–89), Austrian government official. Provisional Governor of Hungary in 1851.

Gerő, Ernő (1898–1980), Member of the narrowest circle of communist leaders from 1944, after his return form the Soviet Union. First Secretary of the Hungarian Working People's Party [MDP] between July and October 1956.

Géza (940–97), Prince of Hungary from 972. He spread Christianity in Hungary and started to integrate the country into the community of Western Christian countries.

Gheorghiu-Dej, Gheorghe (1901–65), Romanian Communist politician, Secretary-general of the Communist Party from 1945, head of state from 1961.

Gimes, Miklós (1917–58), journalist, an opposition leader before and during the Revolution of 1956.

Giraudoux, Jean (1882–1944), French playwright.

Giselle (around 985–1065), Bavarian princess, daughter of Bavarian Prince Henry II, younger sister of Holy Roman Emperor St. Henry II, Queen of Hungary, married to King Stephen I in 995 or 996. Imre was the only one of her five children to reach maturity.

Gollan, John (1911–77), Secretary-general of the Communist Party of Great Britain after 1956.

Gombócz, Zoltán (1877–1935), linguist, university professor, director of the Eötvös *Kollégium* from 1927.

Gomulka, Władysław (1905–1982), Polish Communist politician. First Secretary of the Central Committee of the United Workers' Party of Poland from October 1956.

Gorki, Maxim (1868–1936), Russian writer.

Góth, Sándor (1869–1946), actor, one of those who introduced modern bourgeois drama in Hungary.

Gömbös, Gyula (1886–1936), Minister of Defence (1929–36). Prime Minister (1932–36).

Görgey, Artúr (1818–1916), Hungarian general, Supreme Commander of the Hungarian army in 1849. The first Minister of War in the Szemere government.

Grassalkovich, Antal (1771–1841), patron of the National Museum and other cultural institutions.

Gül Baba (?–1541), *dervish* of the *Baktashi* order, who died during a thanksgiving service held by the Turks in the Matthias Church in Buda. He was considered a miracle-worker, and his tomb on *Rózsadomb* [Rose Hill] has been a Moslem place of pilgrimage.

Gyenes, Antal (1920–96), Communist party functionary, Minister for Collecting Surplus Produce and Livestock during the Revolution of 1956.

Hadrian, Publius Aelius (76–138), Roman emperor. Born in Spain, he was adopted by his relative, the emperor Trajan, whom he succeeded.

Hajnal, István (1892–1956), historian, professor at the Budapest university (1930–50).

Hajnóczy, József (1750–95), lawyer, politician, a leader of the Hungarian Jacobin movement.

Hajós, Alfréd (1878–1955), architect, Olympic champion in swimming in 1896.

Halász, Gábor (1901–45), critic, literary historian, and essayist.

Haller, József (?–1812), member of the Administrative Council, a leading politician in the 1790s.

Harangozó, Gyula (1908–74), dancer, choreographer, interpreter of Bartók's ballets.

Harrer, Ferenc (1874–1969), liberal politician. Deputy Mayor of Budapest in 1918.

Harsányi, Zsolt (1887–1943), writer, journalist, author of best-sellers.

Hauptmann, Gerhard (1862–1946), German playwright.

Haynau, Julius Jacob Baron (1786–1853), illegitimate son of the Prince-elector of Hessen. General, Commander-in-chief of the Austrian imperial forces occupying Hungary in 1849–50.

Hegedüs, András (1922–), member of the Communist Party from 1942, Prime Minister (1955–56).

Hentzi, Heinrich (1785–1849), Austrian general, commander of Buda Castle from January 1849. Fatally wounded on May 21, 1849.

Hermina of Habsburg (1817–42), Austrian archduchess, daughter of Palatine Joseph.

Herzl, Tivadar (1860–1904), writer, founder of modern Zionism.

Hevesi, Sándor (1873–1939), stage director, theoretician of drama.

Hild, János (1761 or 1766–1811), architect, father of the town-planning program in Pest.

Hild, József (1789–1867), architect, master of neo-Classical architecture. One hundred of his nearly nine hundred buildings still exist, most at Budapest.

Hilvert, Elek (1895–1977), architect. Designed the Kossuth bridge together with Endre Mistéth. Designer of the Budapest subway system and its first building engineer.

Hofmannsegg, J. C. (1766–1849), Saxon traveller, natural scientist.

Horváth, Imre (1901–58), Communist politician. Minister of Foreign Affairs from 1956 till his death.

Horváth, János (1878–1961), literary historian professor at Pázmány Péter University of Sciences in Budapest.

Ignotus, Pál (1901–78), writer, liberal journalist, editor of the periodical Szép Szó (1936–39).

Illyefalvy, I. Lajos (1881–1944), statistician, Director of the Statistical Office of Budapest from 1926.

Imre [Emeric] (1174–1204), of the Árpád dynasty, King of Hungary from 1196 to his death.

Imre [Emeric], prince (1000 or 1007–31), son of King Stephen I.

Imrédy, Béla (1891–1946), politician of the extreme right. Prime Minister in 1938–39.

Ioannes VIII (Palaeologos) (1392–1448), Byzantine emperor (1425–48). Spent eight weeks in Buda in the summer of 1424.

István, Saint (ca. 970–1038), Reigning Prince from 997 to 1000, then King of Hungary till his death. Son and successor of Prince Géza. Originally called Vajk. Founder of the Christian Hungarian state.

Jánosi, Ferenc (1916–68), Calvinist minister, later Communist politician, son-in-law of Imre Nagy.

Janza, Károly (1914–), Communist politician, Minister of Defence in October 26–31, 1956.

Jékely, Zoltán (1913–82), poet, writer, translator.

Jemnitz, Sándor (1890–1963), composer and music critic.

John of Luxembourg (1296–1346), King of Bohemia (1310–46).

Joseph Anthony John of Habsburg (1776–1847), archduke, Palatine of Hungary from 1796 until his death.

Joseph August of Habsburg (1872–1962), archduke, army officer, *Homo regius* in 1918, Regent of Hungary in 1919.

Joseph II of Habsburg (1741–90), Holy Roman Emperor from 1765, King of Hungary (though not crowned as such) from 1780. An enlightened despot.

Joseph of Habsburg (1776–1847), Austrian archduke. Palatine of Hungary from 1796 till his death. Advocated town-planning and development in Pest-Buda.

József, Attila (1905–37), poet in the interwar years.

Kabos, Gyula (1887–1941), actor, popular comedian and screen actor.

Kádár, János (1912–89), Communist Party functionary, First Secretary of the Hungarian Working People's Party [MDP] and Minister without portfolio in the Nagy cabinet during the Revolution of 1956. First Secretary of the Central Committee of the Hungarian Socialist Workers' Party between 1957 and 1988, President of the Party in 1988–89.

Kállai, Gyula (1910–96), Communist party functionary. Member of the Political Committee of the Hungarian Socialist Workers' Party (1956–75).

Kállay, Miklós (1887–1967), conservative politician. Prime Minister of Hungary (March 9, 1942–March 19, 1944).

Kálmán, Imre (1882–1953), composer of operettas.

Kalocsay, György (.....), member of the Workers' Council of Greater Budapest.

Kamermayer, Károly (1829–97), civil servant, first Mayor of Budapest (1873–96).

Karafiáth, Jenő (1883–1952), lawyer, right-wing politician. Mayor of Budapest (1937–42).

Karinthy, Frigyes (1887–1938), writer and humorist.

Károlyi, Antal (1732–91), Lord Lieutenant of Szatmár County for life, member of the Seven-member Court of Appeal.

Károlyi, Mihály (1875–1955), Chairman of the Hungarian National Council in 1918, Prime Minister (1918–19), President of the Republic (1919).

Kassák, Lajos (1887–1967), writer, poet, and painter, the most important figure and organizer of the Hungarian avantgarde.

Kazinczy, Ferenc (1759–1831), writer, leader of a movement for the revival of the Hungarian language.

Kerényi, Károly (1897–1973), historian of antiquity and religion.

Keresztes-Fischer, Ferenc (1881–1948), Minister of the Interior (1933–35 and 1938–44). An exponent of the Anglo-American orientation in politics.

Kernstok, Károly (1873–1940), painter.

Kéthly, Anna (1889–1976), Social Democratic politician, minister without portfolio in the Imre Nagy government. Emigrée politician after 1956.

Khrushchev, Nikita Sergeyevich (1894–1971), Secretary of the Central Committe of the Communist Party of the Soviet Union (1949–53), First Secretary from 1953 to his fall in 1964. Premier (1958–64).

Király, Béla (1912–), founding commander of the Zrínyi Miklós Military Academy. Commander-in-chief of the National Guard of Hungary and Military Commander of Budapest during the Revolution of 1956. Member of Parliament (1990–94).

Kisfaludy, Károly (1788–1830), writer, poet, painter. The first leader of the Romantic generation of writers.

Kisfaludy, Sándor (1772–1844), poet, army officer, patron of the theater, master of neo-Classical poetry based on Hungarian traditions.

Kisfaludy, Sándor (1788–1830), writer, poet, painter, organizer of literary life in Pest.

Klebelsberg, Kunó, Count (1875–1932), Minister of the Interior (1921–22), Minister of Education (1922–31), reformer of Hungarian cultural life.

Kodály, Zoltán (1882–1967), composer, researcher of folk music, colleague of Béla Bartók.

Kodolányi, János (1899–1969), writer, member of the movement of populist writers.

Kopácsi, Sándor (1922–), Head of the Budapest Police, Deputy Commander-in-chief of the National Guard in 1956.

Kossuth, Lajos (1802–94), editor, an outstanding Hungarian statesman. Minister of Finance in 1848, later President of the National Defence Commission, Governor-president of Hungary in 1849. Exiled politician.

Kotzebue, August (1761–1819), German playwright and poet.

Kovács, Béla (1908–59), Smallholders' Party's Secretary General (1945–47). Minister of Agriculture and minister without portfolio in the Imre Nagy government.

Kovács, Imre (1913–80), writer and journalist. Secretary-general of the National Peasant Party (1939–46).

Kozma, Lajos (1884–1948), architect, industrial designer and graphic artist.

Köböl, József (1909–), Communist party functionary. Member of the Political Committee of the Workers Party during the Revolution, member of the Central Committee of the Hungarian Socialist Workers' Party (October, 1956–57).

Kölcsey, Ferenc (1790–1838), poet and critic. Liberal deputy of Szatmár County in the diet and leader of the reform opposition in the Lower House. Author of *Himnusz*, the Hungarian national anthem set to music by Ferenc Erkel in 1844.

Körmendi, Ferenc (1900–72), writer. Worked for the Hungarian Department of the British Broadcasting Corporation and for the Voice of America.

Kővágó, József (1913–96), Deputy Mayor of Budapest (May–December, 1945), Mayor of Budapest (1945–47 and November 1956).

Krúdy, Gyula (1878–1933), writer, journalist, representative of modern Hungarian prose. Recorded life in Budapest.

Kurszán (?–904), paramount religious chief of the Hungarians at the time of the conquest, bearing the title of *kende*. A descendant of a dynasty of Khazar origin.

Laczkovics, János (1754–95), army officer, a leader of the Hungarian Jacobin movement.

Ladislas, St. (1040–95), of the Árpád dynasty, Hungarian king between 1077 and 1095.

Lajta, Béla (1873–1920), architect.

Lakatos, László (1882–1944), playwright, journalist.

Lakits, György Zsigmond (1739–1814), author of books on canon and public law, university professor.

Laky, Dezső (1887–1962), statistician and university professor.

Lángh, Ignác (1812–64), defence attorney, reporter for the *Pesti Hírlap*. Captain-general of Pest in 1848.

Latorcai, János (1944–), Member of Parliament for the Christian Democratic People's Party. Minister of Industry and Commerce in 1993–94.

Lázár, Mária (1895–1983), actress, primarily at the *Vígszínház*.

Laziczius, Gyula (1896–1957), linguist and literary historian.

Lechner, Ödön (1845–1914), architect, representative of *Art Nouveau*. Created the Hungarian version of eclectic design.

Léner, Jenő (1894–1948), violinist. Established his celebrated string quartet in 1919.

Liszt, Ferenc (1811–86), pianist and composer, president of the Academy of Music in Budapest (1875–86).

Losonczy, Géza (1917–57), journalist, Communist politician, one of the leaders of the opposition within the Party. Minister without portfolio in the Imre Nagy government during the Revolution of 1956.

Louis the Great (1326–82), of the Anjou dynasty, King of Hungary (1342–82). His courts at Visegrád and Diósgyőr were important centers of Gothic and pre-Renaissance art.

Lukács, György (1885–1971), philosopher, leading ideologist of the Hungarian Communist Party. University professor. Joined Imre Nagy's group in 1956.

Madách, Imre (1823–64), writer and playwright. His principal drama is *Az ember tragédiája* [Tragedy of Men].

Malenkov, Georgi Maximilianovich (1902–88), Premier of the Soviet Union (1953–55), acting Premier (1955–57).

Maléter, Pál (1917–58), Commander of a labor corps (1955–56). One of the military leaders of the Revolution of 1956 with the rank of Major General. Minister of Defence in the Imre Nagy government.

Mályusz, Elemér (1898–1989), historian, university professor at Szeged, then in Budapest between 1930 and 1945.

Márai, Sándor (1900–89), novelist.

Marastoni, Jacob (1804–60), painter of Italian descent. Worked in Pest from 1836 in Biedermeier style. Founder of the first private school of painting in Hungary.

Marczibányi, István (1752–1810), Deputy head of Csanád County, aulic councillor. A literary maecenas who left his collection of antiquities and other treasures to the National Museum.

Margaret, French princess of the Capet family (ca. 1158–98), daughter of the French King Louis VII. Married Hungarian King Béla III in 1186. Upon the death of her husband in 1197, she went to the Holy Land and died there.

Maria Christine (1742–98), archduchess, wife of Albrecht, Prince of Saxony and Teschen.

Maria Theresa (1717–80), Empress of Austria and Queen of Hungary and Bohemia between 1740 and 1780.

Marosán, György (1908–92), Social Democratic, later Communist party functionary, member of the Political Committee of the Hungarian Socialist Workers' Party (1957–62).

Martinovics, Ignác (1755–95), leader of the Hungarian Jacobin movement.

Martinuzzi, György (1482–1551), of Dalmatian Croat origin, nicknamed Friar George, King János Szapolyai's confidential advisor. Also known as Utiesenich. Bishop of Várad, cardinal, and Governor of the Eastern region of the Hungarian Kingdom after 1541.

Matthias I. Hunyadi (1443–90), known by his humanist name as Corvinus. King of Hungary (1458–90). Patron of Renaissance culture and art.

Maugham, William Somerset (1874–1965), English novelist.

Mérei, Ferenc (1909–86), psychologist, one of the leaders of the revolutionary committee of students in 1956.

Metternich-Winneburg, Klemens Lothar Wenzel Prince (1773–1859), Austrian diplomat. Minister of Foreign Affairs from 1809, President of the Council of Ministers and minister of the imperial court (1826–48).

Mezey, Mária (1909–83), actress.

Mező, Imre (1905–56), Communist politician. Died of his wounds after the siege of the party headquarters on *Köztársaság* Square on October 30, 1956.

Mikoyan, Anastas Ivanovich (1895–1978), Soviet Communist politician, First Deputy-chairman of the Council of Ministers in 1956.

Mindszenty, József (1892–1975), Archbishop of Esztergom from 1945, Cardinal from 1946. Arrested in 1948, released in 1956. Took shelter at the Embassy of the United States in Budapest on November 4, 1956.

Mistéth, Endre (1912–), architect, politician of the Smallholders' Party. Co-designer of Kossuth Bridge.

Moholy-Nagy, László (1895–1946), painter and photographer. Professor at Bauhaus (1923–28).

Molnár, Antal (1890–1983), viola-player, esthetician of music, composer.

Molnár, Farkas (1897–1945), architect, graphic artist, one of the leading representatives of functional architecture in Hungary.

Molnár, Ferenc (1878–1952), writer, playwright, journalist, author of middle-class Hungarian drama in the first half of the 20th century. In 1930 he moved to Switzerland, subsequently to the United States.

Moór, Gyula (1888–1950), philosopher of law, professor at Budapest university from 1929.

Móricz, Zsigmond (1879–1942), writer, author of realistic prose illustrating peasant life in Hungary.

Munkácsy, Mihály (1844–1900), noted Hungarian painter. Most successful in Paris where he was rewarded with the golden medal of the World Exhibition for his painting of Milton and his daughters.

Münnich, Ferenc (1886–1967), Communist party functionary, police chief of Budapest (1946–49). Minister of the Interior in the Kádár government from November 1956. President of the Council of Ministers (1958–61).

Nádasdy, Kálmán (1904–80), director at the Budapest Opera from 1922.

Nagy, Ferenc (1903–79), politician of the Smallholders' Party, President of the Hungarian Peasant Alliance (1941–43) for the second time in 1945, then President of the Independent Smallholders' Party, member of the Provisional National Assembly. Prime Minister in 1946–47.

Nagy, Imre (1896–1958), Communist politician, Prime Minister (1953–55 and in October–November 1956). Leader of the 1956 revolution. Upon the suppression of the revolution he took shelter at the Yugoslav Embassy, but was lured out and transported to Romania.

Nánási, László (1906–85), politician of the National Peasant Party, labor union leader from 1949.

Napoleon I (1769–1821), Emperor of the French between 1804 and 1815.

Németh, Antal (1903–68), stage director and drama specialist. Director of the National Theater (1935–44).

Németh, László (1901–75), writer, essayist, and critic, a significant figure of Hungarian literature in the interwar years.

O'Neill, Eugene (1888–1953), American playwright.

Ódry, Árpád (1876–1937), actor, stage director, professor at the Academy of Dramatic Art.

Oláh, Gusztáv (1901–56), director and set-designer at the Budapest Opera from 1921, later stage manager.

Orbán, László (1912–78), Communist party functionary, member of the Central Committee of the Hungarian Socialist Workers' Party from 1957, head of the Scientific and Cultural Department of the Party Center.

Osvát, Ernő (1876–1929), editor and critic. Founder and editor of the periodical *Nyugat* from 1908 to his death.

Ottlik, Géza (1912–90), writer. Author of the novel *Iskola a határon* [School on the border] (1959).

Pais, Dezső (1886–1973), linguist, university professor in Budapest (1937–59).

Pauler, Ákos (1876–1933), philosopher, university professor in Budapest from 1915.

Pázmány, Péter (1570–1637), Cardinal, Archbishop of Esztergom (1616–37). Leader of the Counter-Reformation in Hungary, an outstanding representative of Baroque literature, founder of the present University of Budapest.

Péri, László (1889–1967), painter, graphic artist, and architect.

Péter (1011–46), of the Árpád dynasty, King of Hungary in 1038–41 and 1044–46.

Péter, Gábor (1906–93), head of the political police (*ÁVO* and *ÁVH*) (1945–53).

Pethes, Imre (1864–1924), actor.

Pethő, Sándor (1885–1940), journalist and historian. Founder and editor of the anti-fascist daily *Magyar Nemzet* in 1938.

Petschnig, Johann (1821–97), Austrian architect from Styria.

Philip II (Philip Augustus) (1165–1223), King of France (1180–1223).

Pirandello, Luigi (1867–1936), Italian writer and playwright.

Piros, László (1917–), head of the political police (*ÁVH*) from 1953, Minister of the Interior in 1954–56.

Pollack, Mihály (1773–1855), architect, exponent of neo-Classical architecture in Hungary, designed the building of the National Museum.

Pongrácz, Kálmán (1898–1980), Mayor of Budapest from 1949, President of the City Council of Budapest between (1950–58).

Ponomarev, Boris Nikolayevich (1905–), Soviet party official, head of the International Department of the Communist Party of the Soviet Union (1955–57), member of the Central Committee (1956–86).

Pray, György (1723–1801), Jesuit friar, professor and historian, director of the University Library.

Priestley, John Boynton (1894–1984), English writer and critic.

Prohászka, Lajos (1897–1963), philosopher, professor of pedagogy at the Pázmány Péter University of Sciences in Budapest from the mid-thirties.

Pyrker, János László (1772–1847), Archbishop of Eger, poet writing in German, founder of schools, patron of literature and art. Financed the construction of the cathedral in Eger.

Rácz, Sándor (1933–), President of the Central Workers' Council of Greater Budapest in 1956.

Ráday, Mihály (1942–), cameraman, reporter. Initiator of a movement for preserving architectural values and city-scapes in Budapest. President of the City Beautification Association. Commissioner for Preserving the City-scape from 1995.

Radnóti, Miklós (1909–44), poet and translator of poetry.

Raguzai (Ragusanus), Felix (?–?), head of King Matthias' nearly thirty, mainly Italian, copyists of codices at their Buda workshop.

Rajk, László (1909–49), Minister of the Interior (1946–48).

Rajnai, Sándor (1922–94), officer of the political police (*ÁVH*) before 1956, deputy head of the Political Investigation Department of the Ministry of the Interior after 1956.

Rákosi, Mátyás (1892–1971), Leader of the communist group which returned in 1944–45 from the Soviet Union and ruled Hungary until 1956. Secretary-general of the Hungarian Communist Party and the Hungarian Working People's Party (1945–53), First Secretary from 1953. President of the Council of Ministers (1952–53). Removed from the post of First Secretary in July, 1956.

Ranódy, László (1919–83), director of motion pictures.

Ransano, Pietro (1428–92), humanist scholar and diplomat, author of the first humanist summary of Hungarian history, *Epithoma rerum Hungarorum* [A short summary of the history of the Hungarians).

Ráth, Károly (1821–97), defence attorney, civil servant, the first Mayor of Budapest (1873–97).

Rátkai, Márton (1881–1951), actor, a popular operetta singer.

Regiomontanus, Johannes (1436–76), German astronomer, worked for a short time at the Buda court of King Matthias in charge of the king's Greek manuscripts. Professor at the university King Matthias established in Pozsony under the name *Academia Istropolitan.* Called to Rome by Pope Sixtus IV in 1474 to help with the reform of the calendar.

Reischl, Gáspár (?–?), master carpenter.

Rejtő, Jenő (1905–43), writer of absurd adventure stories.

Rimanóczy, Gyula (1903–58), architect.

Ripka, Ferenc (1871–1944), lawyer and politician. Chief-Mayor [*főpolgármester*] of Budapest (1925–32).

Rippl-Rónai, József (1861–1927), painter, graphic artist, industrial designer, a major artist of the post-Impressionist period in Hungary.

Rottenbiller, Lipót (1806–70), first deputy mayor of Pest, Mayor (1848, 1861 and 1865–67).

Rösler, Endre (1904–63), opera singer.

Rumbach, Sebestyén (1764–1844), medical officer of health in Pest. Founder of the first medicinal bath in Pest.

Schönwisner, István (1738–1818), Jesuit friar, archaeologist, university professor.

Schwartner, Márton György (1759–1823), statistician, historian, and university professor.

Serov, Ivan Alexandrovich (1905–91), Soviet general, Director of the KGB between 1954 and 1958. In charge of suppressing the revolution in Budapest in 1956.

Severus, Lucius Septimius (146–211), Roman emperor (193–211). Raised Aquincum and Carnuntum to the rank of coloniae.

Shaw, George Bernard (1856–1950), British playwright.

Sigismund of Luxembourg (1368–1437), son of Emperor Charles IV. King of Hungary from 1387, Roman King from 1410, Holy Roman Emperor from 1433.

Sigray, Jakab, Count (1750–95), associate judge at the District Court of Appeals at Kőszeg, a leader of the Hungarian Jacobin movement.

Simontsits, János (1783–1856), second deputy head of Pest County administration, stage manager of the National Theater (1841–43 and 1849–52).

Sina, Georg Baron (1782–1856), banker, landowner. Consul-general of Greece in Vienna. In cooperation with István Széchenyi he financed several enterprises of the reform era, including the construction of the Chain Bridge (*Lánchíd*).

Sinkovits, Imre (1928–), actor.

Sipőcz, Jenő (1878–1937), defence attorney, politician. Mayor of Budapest (1926–32) and Chief-Mayor (1932–37).

Soldatić, Dalibor (1909–?), Ambassador of Yugoslavia in Budapest from November 1953, protocol chief at the Yugoslav Ministry of Foreign Affairs from January 1957.

Somlay, Artúr (1883–1951), actor, mostly at *Vígszínház*.

Stalin, Iosif Visaryonovich (1879–1953), Secretary-general of the Communist Party of the Soviet Union from 1922 to his death, Prime Minister from 1941.

Stoica, Chivu (1908–75), Romanian Communist politician. Prime Minister (1955–61).

Strindberg, Johan August (1849–1912), Swedish playwright.

Suleyman I (1494–1566), the Magnificent, Ottoman sultan whose reign represented the golden age of the Ottoman Empire. His troops annihilated the army of the Hungarian kingdom at the Battle of Mohács in 1526 and occupied Buda in 1541. Died at the siege of Szigetvár in Hungary.

Suslov, Mikhail Andreyevich (1902–82), Secretary of the Central Committee of the Communist Party of the Soviet Union (1947–82). Member of the Presidium of the Central Committee from 1955.

Szabó, Dezső (1879–1945), writer, an important figure of Hungarian literature in the interwar years. He influenced the populist movement to a great extent.

Szabó, János (1941–), Member of the Independent Smallholders', Agricultural Laborers' and Citizens' Party. Member of the Budapest General Assembly and leader of the Smallholders' facton following the local elections of 1994.

Szabó, Lőrinc (1900–57), poet and translator.

Szabó, Zoltán (1912–84), an outstanding representative of the "village explorers."

Szabolcsi, Bence (1899–1973), Member of several scientific societies abroad, the Royal Asiatic Society of London among them.

Szálasi, Ferenc (1897–1946), leader of a radical fascist movement in Hungary. Came to power with German aid on October 15, 1944.

Szántó, Zoltán (1893–1977), member of the Executive Committee of the Hungarian Socialist Workers' Party from November 1, 1956.

Szapolyai, János (1487–1540), King of Hungary (1526–40). He was able to maintain his rule against Ferdinand I of Habsburg in one part of the country by placing himself under the protection of the Ottoman sultan, Suleyman the Magnificent.

Széchényi, Ferenc Count (1754–1820), Lord Chamberlain, Deputy Lord Chief Justice. His collections bequeathed to the nation in 1802 formed the basis of the National Library and the National Museum.

Széchenyi, István Count (1791–1860), liberal politician, an advocate of reform. An outstanding Hungarian statesman. Author of political essays. Minister of Transport and Public Works in 1848.

Széchenyi, Ödön Count (1839–1922), The younger son of István Széchenyi. Turkish general from 1874. Founder and first commander of the military fire-brigade in Constantinople.

Szécsényi, György (1592–1695), Archbishop of Esztergom (1685–95), patron of culture.

Székely, Mihály (1901–63), opera singer.

Szekfű, Gyula (1883–1955), historian, journalist, university professor in Budapest.

Szemere, Bertalan (1812–69), Minister of the Interior in 1848, Government Commissioner in Upper Hungary, Prime Minister in 1849.

Szemere, Pál (1785–1861), writer, esthetician and supporter of Kazinczy's movement for language reform. Editor of the periodical *Élet és Irodalom* [Life and literature] from 1826, and of *Muzarion* from 1833.

Szendy, Károly (1885–1953), Deputy Mayor from 1934, Mayor of Budapest from late 1934 to the German occupation in March 1944. Editor of *Budapest története* [History of Budapest], 3 vols. (Budapest, 1942–44).

Szent-Györgyi, Albert (1893–1986), biochemist, university professor first at Szeged, then in Budapest. Nobel-prize winner in medicine in 1937.

Szentkirályi, Mór (1807–82), deputy head of Pest County and deputy for the County in the diet, later physician. Mayor of Pest (1867–68).

Szentmarjay, Ferenc (1767–95), a leader of the Hungarian Jacobin movement.

Szilágyi, József (1917–58), Imre Nagy's secretary during the Revolution.

Szomory, Dezső (1869–1944), writer and playwright.

Szőnyi, István (1894–1960), painter, professor at the School of Fine Arts (1938–60).

Szőts, István (1912–), director of motion pictures.

Taksony (931–72), Reigning Prince of Hungary (955–72).

Tamási, Áron (1897–1966), writer. Described life in the *Székely* villages of Transylvania.

Teleki, József Count (1790–1855), the first president of the Hungarian Academy of Sciences and founder of its library. Governor of Transylvania in 1842.

Thaisz, Elek (1820–92), head of the Pest police in 1861 and between 1867 and 1885.

Tihanyi, Lajos (1885–1938), painter.

Tildy, Zoltán (1889–1961), Calvinist minister, politician of the Smallholders' Party. Prime Minister (1945–46), President of the Republic (1946–48). Minister without portfolio in the Imre Nagy government during the Revolution.

Tímár, József (1902–60), actor.

Tisza, István (1861–1918), Prime Minister (1903–05 and 1913–17). Speaker of the House of Representatives (1912–13).

Tito, Josip Broz (1892–1980), President of the People's Federal Republic of Yugoslavia (1953–80).

Toldy, Ferenc (1805–75), physician, literary historian, critic, university professor, director of the University Library. A major organizer of literary life in Hungary from the 1830s.

Tolnay, Klári (1914–), actress.

Tóth, Aladár (1898–1968), musicologist and music critic. Ardent supporter of Béla Bartók and Zoltán Kodály, director of the Budapest Opera (1946–56).

Tóth, Ilona (1932–57), medical student. Took part in resistance after the revolution.

Tóth, István (1861–1934), sculptor, mainly of monuments with religious subjects. Winner of the Wolfner Award in 1921 and two major state awards.

Tőke, Ferenc (1930–), member of the Central Workers' Council of Greater Budapest in 1956.

Tőkés, Anna (1903–66), actress of Transylvanian origin.

Tököli-Popovics, Sabbas (Száva) (1761–1842), Serb politician, landowner, patron of Serb cultural and educational institutions in Hungary.

Törzs, Jenő (1887–1946), actor, supported modern drama.

Trajan, Marcus Ulpius (A.D. 53–117), Roman emperor (98–117). Born in Seville.

Trattner, János Tamás (1789–1824), printer and bookseller, patron of Hungarian literature. His enterprise was further developed by his brother-in-law, István Trattner-Károlyi.

Ugoletto, Taddeo (?–?), humanist scholar born in Parma. Director of King Matthias' famous library, tutor to János Corvin, the king's son.

Uitz, Béla (1887–1972), painter.

Uray, Tivadar (1895–1962), actor.

Valkó, Márton (1911–), Communist party functionary.

Varga, Béla (1903–95), Roman Catholic priest, founding member of the Independent Smallholders' Party. Chairman of the National Assembly (1946–47). Leading exile politician from 1947.

Vas, István (1910–91), poet, writer and translator.

Vas, Zoltán (1903–83), government commissioner of food supply and Mayor of Budapest in 1945.

Vázsonyi, Vilmos (1868–1926), defence attorney and democratic politician. Minister of Justice (1917–18).

Veres, Péter (1897–1970), writer. Minister of Housing and Public Construction, Minister of Defence, and President of the National Peasant Party from 1947. President of the Writers' Association (1954–56).

Vörösmarty, Mihály (1800–55), the greatest romantic poet of Hungary, writer, editor, and playwright.

Waldbauer–Kerpely Quartet, founded in 1909 by violinist Imre Waldbauer (1892–1953), violincellist Jenő Kerpely (1885–1954), violinist János Temesváry (1891–1964), and viola-player Antal Molnár (1890–1983).

Wedekind, Franz (1864–1918), German poet and playwright.

Weöres, Sándor (1913–89), poet and translator.

Wesselényi, Miklós Baron (1796–1850), liberal politician supporting reform. Author of works on politics, the first national leader of the reform opposition struggling for bourgeois transformation.

Wieser, Ferenc (1812–69), architect, representative of Romantic style in architecture. Designed and built the neo-Baroque steeple of the Franciscan church of Pest between 1858 and 1863.

Wilder, Thornton (1897–1975), American writer and playwright.

Wolff, Károly (1874–1936), lawyer and politician.

Wortley, Mary (Lady Montagu) (1689–1762), British writer and traveller.

Ybl, Miklós (1814–91), architect, a major figure of neo-Renaissance architecture in Hungary. His crowning achievement was the Budapest Opera.

Zathureczky, Ede (1903–59), violinist.

Zhukov, Georgi Konstantinovich (1896–1974), Marshal of the Soviet Union, Chief of General Staff during the Second World War. Minister of Defence (1955–57).

Zichy, Jenő, Count (1837–1906), explorer in Asia.

Zichy, Károly (1753–1826), Lord Chief Justice, leading political figure in the 1790s.

Zola, Émile (1840–1902), French novelist.

Zrínyi, Miklós (1620–64), count, poet, general, and politician. Ban (governor) of Croatia from 1647. Led his most successful campaign agaist the Turks in 1663–64. His masterpiece in literature is the heroic epic *Szigeti veszedelem* [The disaster at Szigetvár].

Zsolt, Béla (1895–1949), writer and journalist.

# Contributors

Ágoston, Gábor Assistant Professor, Eötvös Lóránd University of Budapest, Department of Medieval and Early Modern History of Hungary.

Baán, László Comissioner for Cultural Affairs, the City Council of Budapest.

Csorba, László Associate Professor of History, Eötvös Lóránd University of Budapest, Department of Cultural History.

Gerő, András Professor and Chairperson Department of Social and Economic History, Eötvös Lóránd University of Budapest.

Kósa, Judit Journalist of the daily *Népszabadság*.

Lackó, Miklós Scientific Advisor, Hungarian Academy of Sciences, Institute of History.

Poór, János Associate Professor of History, Department of Medieval and Early Modern History of Hungary.

Rainer, M. János Research Fellow and Deputy Director, Institute for Documentation and Research on the Hungarian Revolution of 1956.

Varga, László Head Director, Archives of the Capital City of Budapest.

The late Vörös, Károly Professor Emeritus, Department of History, Eötvös Lóránd University of Budapest.

# Index to Streets and Other Locations of Budapest

## (Map is to be found at the end of the volume)

**Notes:**

Roman numerals I–XXIII designate districts of Budapest
*U.* or *utca*: Street
*fasor*: row of trees
*liget*: grove
*sétány*: promenade
*kőrút*: boulevard
*tér*: square
*lépcső*: stair

*út*: avenue
*mélykút*: deep well
*körtér*: circus
*híd*: bridge
*park*: park
*bástya*: bastion
*köz*: passage
*rakpart*: quay
*lejtő*: slope

# Volumes Published in
# "Atlantic Studies on Society in Change"

## A Series distributed by Columbia University Press

No. 1     *Tolerance and Movements of Religious Dissent in Eastern Europe.* Edited by Béla K. Király. 1977.

No. 2     *The Habsburg Empire in World War I.* Edited by R. A. Kann. 1978

No. 3     *The Mutual Effects of the Islamic and Judeo-Christian Worlds: The East European Pattern.* Edited by A. Ascher, T. Halasi-Kun, B. K. Király. 1979.

No. 4     *Before Watergate: Problems of Corruption in American Society.* Edited by A. S. Eisenstadt, A. Hoogenboom, H. L. Trefousse. 1979.

No. 5     *East Central European Perceptions of Early America.* Edited by B. K. Király and G. Bárány. 1977.

No. 6     *The Hungarian Revolution of 1956 in Retrospect.* Edited by B. K. Király and Paul Jónás. 1978.

No. 7     *Brooklyn U.S.A.: Fourth Largest City in America.* Edited by Rita S. Miller. 1979.

No. 8     *Prime Minister Gyula Andrássy's Influence on Habsburg Foreign Policy.* János Decsy. 1979.

No. 9     *The Great Impeacher: A Political Biography of James M. Ashley.* Robert F. Horowitz. 1979.

No. 10   *Special Topics and Generalizations on the Eighteenth and*
Vol. I*    *Nineteenth Century.* Edited by Béla K. Király and Gunther E. Rothenberg. 1979.

---

*   Volumes Nos. I through XXXVI refer to the series *War and Society in East Central Europe.*

No. 11      *East Central European Society and War in the*
Vol. II     *Pre-Revolutionary 18th-Century.* Edited by Gunther E.
            Rothenberg, Béla K. Király, and Peter F. Sugar. 1982.

No. 12      *From Hunyadi to Rákóczi: War and Society in Late*
Vol. III    *Medieval and Early Modern Hungary.* Edited by János M.
            Bak and Béla K. Király. 1982.

No. 13      *East Central European Society and War in the Era of*
Vol. IV     *Revolutions: 1775-1856.* Edited by B. K. Király. 1984.

No. 14      *Essays on World War I: Origins and Prisoners of War.*
Vol. V      Edited by Samuel R. Williamson, Jr. and Peter Pastor.
            1983.

No. 15      *Essays on World War I: Total War and Peacemaking, A*
Vol. VI     *Case Study on Trianon.* Edited by B. K. Király, Peter
            Pastor, and Ivan Sanders. 1982.

No. 16      *Army, Aristocracy, Monarchy: War, Society and*
Vol. VII    *Government in Austria, 1618-1780.* Edited by Thomas M.
            Barker. 1982.

No. 17      *The First Serbian Uprising 1804-1813.* Edited by Wayne
Vol. VIII   S. Vucinich. 1982.

No. 18      *Czechoslovak Policy and the Hungarian Minority*
Vol. IX     *1945-1948.* Kálmán Janics. Edited by Stephen Borsody.
            1982.

No. 19      *At the Brink of War and Peace: The Tito-Stalin Split in*
Vol. X      *a Historic Perspective.* Edited by Wayne S. Vucinich.
            1982.

No. 20      *Inflation Through the Ages: Economic, Social,*
            *Psychological and Historical Aspects.* Edited by Edward
            Marcus and Nathan Schmuckler. 1981.

No. 21      *Germany and America: Essays on Problems of*
            *International Relations and Immigration.* Edited by Hans
            L. Trefousse. 1980.

No. 22      *Brooklyn College: The First Half Century.* Murray M.
            Horowitz. 1981.

No. 23      *A New Deal for the World: Eleanor Roosevelt and*
            *American Foreign Policy.* Jason Berger. 1981.

No. 24    *The Legacy of Jewish Migration: 1881 and Its Impact.*
Edited by David Berger. 1982.

No. 25    *The Road to Bellapais: Cypriot Exodus to Northern
Cyprus.* Pierre Oberling. 1982.

No. 26    *New Hungarian Peasants: An East Central European
Experience with Collectivization.* Edited by Marida Hollos
and Béla C. Maday. 1983.

No. 27    *Germans in America: Aspects of German-American
Relations in the Nineteenth Century.* Edited by Allen
McCormick. 1983.

No. 28    *A Question of Empire: Leopold I and the War of Spanish
Succession, 1701-1705.* Linda and Marsha Frey. 1983.

No. 29    *The Beginning of Cyrillic Printing — Cracow, 1491. From
the Orthodox Past in Poland.* Szczepan K. Zimmer. Edited
by Ludwik Krzyzanowski and Irene Nagurski. 1983.

No. 29a    *A Grand Ecole for the Grand Corps: The Recruitment and
Training of the French Administration.* Thomas R.
Osborne. 1983.

No. 30    *The First War between Socialist States: The Hungarian*
Vol. XI    *Revolution of 1956 and Its Impact.* Edited by Béla K.
Király, Barbara Lotze, Nandor Dreisziger. 1984.

No. 31    *The Effects of World War I, The Uprooted: Hungarian*
Vol. XII    *Refugees and Their Impact on Hungary's Domestic
Politics.* István Mócsy. 1983.

No. 32    *The Effects of World War I: The Class War after the Great*
Vol. XIII    *War: The Rise Of Communist Parties in East Central
Europe, 1918-1921.* Edited by Ivo Banac. 1983.

No. 33    *The Crucial Decade: East Central European Society and*
Vol. XIV    *National Defense, 1859-1870.* Edited by Béla K. Király.
1984.

No. 35    *Effects of World War I: War Communism in Hungary,*
Vol. XVI    *1919.* György Péteri. 1984.

No. 36    *Insurrections, Wars, and the Eastern Crisis in the 1870s.*
Vol. XVII    Edited by B. K. Király and Gale Stokes. 1985.

| No. 37<br>Vol. XVIII | *East Central European Society and the Balkan Wars, 1912-1913.* Edited by B. K. Király and Dimitrije Djordjevic. 1986. |
|---|---|
| No. 38<br>Vol. XIX | *East Central European Society in World War I.* Edited by B. K. Király and N. F. Dreisziger, Assistant Editor Albert A. Nofi. 1985. |
| No. 39<br>Vol. XX | *Revolutions and Interventions in Hungary and Its Neighbor States, 1918-1919.* Edited by Peter Pastor. 1988. |
| No. 40<br>Vol. XXI | *East Central European Society and War, 1750-1920. Bibliography and Historiography.* Complied and edited by László Alföldi. Pending. |
| No. 41<br>Vol. XXII | *Essays on East Central European Society and War, 1740-1920.* Edited by Stephen Fischer-Galati and Béla K. Király. 1988. |
| No. 42<br>Vol. XXIII | *East Central European Maritime Commerce and Naval Policies, 1789-1913.* Edited by Apostolos E. Vacalopoulos, Constantinos D. Svolopoulos, and Béla K. Király. 1988. |
| No. 43<br>Vol. XXIV | *Selections, Social Origins, Education and Training of East Central European Officers Corps.* Edited by Béla K. Király and Walter Scott Dillard. 1988. |
| No. 44<br>Vol. XXV | *East Central European War Leaders: Civilian and Military.* Edited by Béla K. Király and Albert Nofi. 1988. |
| No. 46 | *Germany's International Monetary Policy and the European Monetary System.* Hugo Kaufmann. 1985. |
| No. 47 | *Iran Since the Revolution — Internal Dynamics, Regional Conflicts and the Superpowers.* Edited by Barry M. Rosen. 1985. |
| No. 48<br>Vol. XXVII | *The Press During the Hungarian Revolution of 1848-1849.* Domokos Kosáry. 1986. |
| No. 49 | *The Spanish Inquisition and the Inquisitional Mind.* Edited by Angel Alcala. 1987. |
| No. 50 | *Catholics, the State and the European Radical Right, 1919-1945.* Edited by Richard Wolff and Jorg K. Hoensch. 1987. |

| | |
|---|---|
| No. 51<br>Vol. XXVIII | *The Boer War and Military Reforms.* Jay Stone and Erwin A. Schmidl. 1987. |
| No. 52 | *Baron Joseph Eötvös, A Literary Biography.* Steven B. Várdy. 1987. |
| No. 53 | *Towards the Renaissance of Puerto Rican Studies: Ethnic and Area Studies in University Education.* Maria Sanchez and Antonio M. Stevens. 1987. |
| No. 54 | *The Brazilian Diamonds in Contracts, Contraband and Capital.* Harry Bernstein. 1987. |
| No. 55 | *Christians, Jews and Other Worlds: Patterns of Conflict and Accommodation.* Edited by Phillip F. Gallagher. 1988. |
| No. 56<br>Vol. XXVI | *The Fall of the Medieval Kingdom of Hungary: Mohács, 1526, Buda, 1541.* Géza Perjés. 1989. |
| No. 57 | *The Lord Mayor of Lisbon: The Portuguese Tribune of the People and His 24 Guilds.* Harry Bernstein. 1989. |
| No. 58 | *Hungarian Statesmen of Destiny: 1860-1960.* Edited by Paul Böndy. 1989. |
| No. 59 | *For China: The Memoirs of T. G. Li, former Major General in the Chinese Nationist Army.* T. G. Li. Written in collaboration with Roman Rome. 1989. |
| No. 60 | *Politics in Hungary: For A Democratic Alternative.* János Kis, with an Introduction by Timothy Garton Ash. 1989. |
| No. 61 | *Hungarian Worker's Councils in 1956.* Edited by Bill Lomax. 1990. |
| No. 62 | *Essays on the Structure and Reform of Centrally Planned Economic Systems.* Paul Jonas. A joint publication with Corvina Kiadó, Budapest. 1990. |
| No. 63 | *Kossuth as a Journalist in England.* Éva H. Haraszti. A joint publication with Akadémiai Kiadó, Budapest. 1990. |
| No. 64 | *From Padua to the Trianon, 1918-1920.* Mária Ormos. A joint publication with Akadémiai Kiadó, Budapest. 1990. |
| No. 65 | *Towns in Medieval Hungary.* Edited by László Gerevich. A joint publication with Akadémiai Kiadó, Budapest. 1990. |

No. 66        *The Nationalities Problem in Transylvania, 1867-1940.*
              Sándor Bíró. 1992.

No. 67        *Hungarian Exiles and the Romanian National Movement,*
              *1849-1867.* Béla Borsi-Kálmán. 1991.

No. 68        *The Hungarian Minority's Situation in Ceausescu's*
              *Romania.* Edited by Rudolf Joó and Andrew Ludanyi.
              1994.

No. 69        *Democracy, Revolution, Self-Determination. Selected*
              *Writings.* István Bibó. Edited by Károly Nagy. 1991.

No. 70        *Trianon and the Protection of Minorities.* József Galántai.
              A joint publication with Corvina Kiadó, Budapest. 1991.

No. 71        *King Saint Stephen of Hungary.* György Györffy. 1994.

No. 72        *Dynasty, Politics and Culture. Selected Essays.* Robert A.
              Kann. Edited by Stanley B. Winters. 1991.

No. 73        *Jadwiga of Anjou and the Rise of East Central Europe.*
              Oscar Halecki. Edited by Thaddeus V. Gromada. A joint
              publication with the Polish Institute of Arts and Sciences
              of America, New York. 1991.

No. 74        *Hungarian Economy and Society During World War Two.*
Vol. XXIX     Edited by György Lengyel. 1993.

No. 75        *The Life of a Communist Revolutionary, Béla Kun.* György
              Borsányi. 1993.

No. 76        *Yugoslavia: The Process of Disintegration.* Laslo Sekelj.
              1993.

No. 77        *Wartime American Plans for a New Hungary. Documents*
Vol. XXX      *from the U.S. Department of State, 1942-1944.* Edited by
              Ignác Romsics. 1992.

No.78         *Planning for War against Russia and Serbia.*
Vol. XXXI     *Austro-Hungarian and German Military Strategies,*
              *1871-1914.* Graydon A. Tunstall, Jr. 1993.

No. 79        *American Effects on Hungarian Imagination and Political*
              *Thought, 1559-1848.* Géza Závodszky. 1995.

No. 80        *Trianon and East Central Europe: Antecedents and*
Vol. XXXII    *Repercussions.* Edited by Béla K. Király and László
              Veszprémy. 1995.

| No. 81 | *Hungarians and Their Neighbors in Modern Times, 1867-1950.* Edited by Ferenc Glatz. 1995. |
|---|---|
| No. 82 | *István Bethlen: A Great Conservative Statesman of Hungary, 1874-1946.* Ignác Romsics. 1995. |
| No. 83 Vol. XXXIII | *20th Century Hungary and the Great Powers.* Edited by Ignác Romsics. 1995. |
| No. 84 | *Lawful Revolution in Hungary, 1989-1994.* Edited by Béla K. Király and András Bozóki. 1995. |
| No. 85 | *The Demography of Contemporary Hungarian Society.* Edited by Pál Péter Tóth and Emil Valkovich. 1996. |
| No. 86 | *Budapest, A History from its Beginnings to 1996.* Edited by András Gerő and János Poór. 1996. |
| No. 87 | *"The Dominant Ideas of the Nineteenth Century and their Impact on the State."* Volume 1. *Diagnosis.* József Eötvös. Translated, edited, annotated and indexed with an introductory essay by D. Mervyn Jones. 1996. |
| No. 88 | *"The Dominant Ideas of the Nineteenth Century and their Impact on the State."* Volume 2. *Remedy.* József Eötvös. Translated, edited, annotated and indexed with an introductory essay by D. Mervyn Jones. 1997. |
| No. 89 | *The Social History of the Hungarian Intelligentsia's in the "Long Nineteenth Century," 1825-1914.* János Mazsu. 1996. |
| No. 90 Vol. XXXIV | *Pax Britannica: Wartime Foreign Office Documents Regarding Plans for a Post Bellum East Central Europe.* Edited by András D. Bán. 1997. |
| No. 91 | *National Identity in Contemporary Hungary.* György Csepeli. 1996. |
| No. 92 | *The Hungarian Parliament, 1867-1918: A Mirage of Power.* András Gerő. 1997. |
| No. 93 Vol. XXXV | *The Hungarian Revolution and War for Independence, 1848-1849.* A Military History. Edited by Gábor Bona. 1997. |
| No. 94 | *The End of Assimilation: "The Jewish Question" in Hungary.* Tamás Ungvári. 1997. |

No. 95          *Academia and State Socialism: Essays on the Political History of Academic Life in Post-1945 Hungary and East Central Europe.* György Péteri. 1997.

No. 96          *Through the Prism of the Habsburg Monarchy: Hungary*
Vol. XXXVI    *in American Diplomacy and Public Opinion during World War I.* Tibor Glant. 1997.